THE BUSINESS OF WAR

The
Business of War

THE WAR NARRATIVE OF
Major-General Sir John Kennedy
G.S.M.G., K.C.V.O., K.B.E., C.B., M.C.

Edited and with a Preface by
BERNARD FERGUSSON

Introduction by
WALTER MILLIS

WILLIAM MORROW AND COMPANY
New York • 1958

TO
CATHERINE

INTRODUCTION

by Walter Millis

THE processes of high command during the Second World War offer a study not only endless in its fascinations of character and clashing personality, but pregnant in its significance for our current problems of democracy and freedom in a still militant and militarized age. In many ways the Second World War was unlike any previous major struggle. It is true that the probabilities introduced by the development of nuclear and electronic warfare are against the repetition of another long-drawn war of peoples of this kind; but whether the next major war is over in three weeks or never comes at all, the problems of 'cold war' policy and strategy, of the adjustment of military means to political purposes, of the management of free, individualistic peoples to achieve the unavoidably regimented ends of modern military and economic organization, remain very similar to the problems with which the democratic statesmen and staff officers struggled—lashed by a terrible responsibility in the face of imminent disaster—in the years between 1939 and 1945.

In a degree not true of any earlier great war, the Second War, above the field level, was not fought; it was administered. It was directed not by great military geniuses but by political leaders and staff planners; and the fact that the intricate staff systems elaborated for the purpose have been increasingly imitated, in recent years, in democratic civil administration reflects the extent to which the problems of civil government are coming to resemble those thrown into high relief in the Second War era. And it indicates the relevance of the history of the wartime high commands to the issues which our soldiers, our statesmen and our people face today.

Sir John Kennedy's contribution to that history is, even after all that has been written about it, singularly useful, ·lively and illuminating. Sir John is a Scottish professional soldier. Like so many other of the great military figures of the second conflict—Eisenhower, Marshall and many more—he learned his trade as a young officer in the First World War, thereafter rising through the routine obscurities of the peace years to attain the threshholds of high command just as the Second War was impending. In September, 1939, he was deputy director of Military Operations on the British army staff; for a time he then held a field command, but with the catastrophe of the fall of France in June, 1940, he was recalled as director. Until exhaustion and illness forced his retirement in in late 1944, with the war already virtually won, he served under the successive chiefs and vice chiefs of staff as the next highest, most responsible, director of Britain's armies in the field. His post, throughout, corresponded to that which Eisenhower held at the time he was appointed to the European command.

He was thus at the center of British plans and policies. He was at the same time shielded by one remove from the terrible Churchillian energies. It permitted him to achieve a certain detached frankness as to that towering figure, and to report aspects of Britain's war leadership which do not appear so clearly, or with such a soberly human touch, in other narratives. The First War is famous for its battles between the 'frocks' and the 'brass hats'; the Second has been regarded as a notable example of their comparative absence. General Kennedy makes it plain that the battles were there; it was only Churchill's personality and prestige which prevented their breaking out in open and disastrous results. There is an illuminating report of how Ironside, appointed C.I.G.S. (the equivalent of our Army Chief of Staff) on the outbreak of war, addressed his civilian superior, the War Minister, on assuming his post:

'Now, Mr. Belisha, I have formed a better opinion of you during the last few weeks. You have behaved extremely well, and I have changed my mind about you. But understand this—I never asked to become C.I.G.S., and I accept it only on condition that you are perfectly frank with me, that you never go behind my back or speak contrary to or without my advice on any military matter. If I find you doing that, I will have you out or I will go.' There spoke the old 1914 military spirit. But it was not to survive either the changed conditions or the Churchill power.

It was not that Churchill's chiefs of staff submitted meekly to his civilian direction of the war. One of Kennedy's tributes to Dill (C.I.G.S. during much of the period) is that 'it was he who bore the brunt of Churchill's fury when the latter's multitudinous ideas and projects were opposed by the chiefs of staff. On one occasion, after a long argument about some especially unsound suggestion, Churchill accused him to his face of being "the dead hand of inanition." On another, the Prime Minister, watching the chiefs

of staff as they filed out of his room after a midnight sitting, remarked to one of his entourage, "I have to wage modern war with
ancient weapons." ' Alanbrooke, who succeeded Dill, once crossed
out nine-tenths of a minute for the Prime Minister with the remark,
'The more you tell that man about the war, the more you hinder the
winning of it.' Churchill actually suffered a loss of prestige in the
dark days of early 1942; and Kennedy recalls the atmosphere (at
any rate, among the soldiers) by quoting a note he made as late as
July of that year: 'In spite of what one may feel about Winston's
methods and his judgment, I do believe that, on balance, it is best
that he should continue as Prime Minister.' But earlier Kennedy
himself had recognized that 'all other politicians are pigmies compared with him, and that his hold on the country and his place in
the eyes of our allies are such that a change in leadership at this
time is unthinkable.'

The soldiers' difficulty was never with Churchill's broad leadership or his assertion of civilian supremacy. It was with what they
considered his ill-advised meddling in strictly military or strategic
issues which they felt he did not understand. Kennedy puts it well
in speaking of a 'directive' handed down in April, 1941, by Churchill
without consultation with his chiefs of staff:

'Many years have passed since I first saw the original directive
in the War Office, but my feelings about it remain now as they
did at the time. It was cast almost in the form of an operation order
by a commander-in-chief; and it included unsound and impracticable
propositions which could only be dismissed after hours and days
of unprofitable work by busy and responsible men who would have
been better employed by getting on with their jobs. But it breathed
a splendid spirit of courage, defiance and initiative. It appeared in
our "In Trays" at a moment when our fortunes had suffered grievous
setbacks, and, even as we grumbled at the work it caused us, we
could not but delight in its sentiments.' The contrast between a
'galloper' flinging himself from a frothing horse with despatches
for a Wellington, and the sudden appearance of courage and
initiative in the bureaucratic 'in tray' speaks volumes for the nature
both of modern war and modern government.

It illuminates also the practical fact that modern strategy has
become too important for the strategists. Political considerations
have to be melded with 'purely military' calculations; and if courage
and initiative cannot be distilled from the military slide rules and
logistic tables, they must be infused by political direction. Kennedy
believes most of Churchill's inspirations were profoundly imprac-

tical and wrongheaded. His criticism of at least one major policy —the emphasis on independent air power, which Churchill powerfully backed—is peculiarly relevant today, when our own civilian secretaries are having their powers still further enlarged in order that they may dictate solutions for this same sort of interservice difference.

With the British, even more than with ourselves, the Air Force was virtually a law unto itself, beyond effective control through the chiefs of staff committee (the equivalent of our joint chiefs). In 1942 Kennedy was concluding that 'the only well-grounded criticism of our central war direction lies in the use we are making of our Air Force . . . I should like to take 50 per cent of the bomber effort off Germany even at this late hour and distribute it in the Atlantic and in the Middle East and Indian theaters. The price we pay at sea and on land for our present bombing policy is high indeed.' In 1944 the Air Force made up its own plan for the support of the Normandy landing without consulting the Army general staff which was directly responsible.

'It seems,' he noted at the time, 'incredible . . . But such is the case. Eisenhower was quite unaware (until I told him) that we had not been consulted. He also seemed quite unaware of how vast the task would be of damaging railway communications to such an extent that *military* movement would be hampered . . . Eisenhower's comments at the meeting showed at once his weakness and his strength—his weakness in lack of real knowledge of his plans and over-delegation to subordinates, and his strength in avoidance of friction. He repeated several times that all he wanted was the best [air] support he could get and that the United States and the British Empire could not afford a failure.'

In retrospect, Kennedy was 'more than ever convinced that we were never able to harness our air power to the war effort in the most effective way' due to the unresolved divergencies between the Air Staff and the General Staff. He thought the preinvasion air 'interdiction' plan, about which so much was heard then and has been heard later, was completely useless; while the Air Force concentration on bombing had left the invasion 'saddled with a force which was sadly deficient of types of aircraft suitable for close cooperation . . . We had to do the best with what we had, but the waste was colossal in many directions.'

That was, of course, true of the whole war. They had to do the best with what they had; they had to reconcile, somehow, widely divergent concepts and interests, political and military; and they had to do it with insufficient understanding of their instruments and without the knowledge and data on which surely to predict the consequences of their logically reasoned plans. They had to do it in the war; today, to an appalling degree, we have to do the same thing in peace. Staff planning combined with political leadership seems the only available recipe for even approximately successful results. Kennedy's reflections on the outcome in the war are instructive. Often the Prime Minister was obstinately wrong; at times he was brilliantly right in the face of his staff advice. The British reluctance to invade Western Europe was, he thinks, justified by everything they knew at the time; but he is glad of the American pressure which finally brought about the invasion just in time to save Britain from possible destruction by the German flying bombs and rockets.

The Second World War was administered. The intricate and often amusing play of personality; the diversity of considerations to be weighed; the complex interweaving of military, political and inter-allied relations involved in this process are here seen sharply drawn against the terrible and urgent background of a great war. But these things are not just a part of war. They are a part of the administration of the modern free society under the conditions in which we are condemned to live today.

CONTENTS

MAPS

PREFACE

WHEN Dr. Johnson in his *Lives of the Poets* reached the period of his own contemporaries, he wrote: 'I begin to feel myself coming to the time of which it will be proper rather to say nothing that is false, than all that is true.' This should be the maxim of all those who have witnessed or shared in great events, when the time comes to tell their tale. And about biography Johnson wrote: 'It is surely better that caprice, obstinacy, frolick and folly should be silently forgotten, than that a pang should be given to a widow, a daughter, a brother or a friend.'

The chronicler of his own time whose memories include public secrets and private confidences is in a dilemma. His object may be merely to entertain, in which case he must tread carefully if he is not to offend against Johnson's maxim. But his object may be also to instruct, to derive what are known in the Army as 'Lessons Learnt'; and in this case he has a positive as well as a negative duty. When Sir John Kennedy offered me the privilege of editing these reminiscences of the war, he laid down two strict conditions: the book was not to be a write-up of himself, 'which would just be silly'; and nothing was to be included that 'would hurt people's feelings'. It seemed to me on reading them that they contained a good deal that was not yet known; a good deal that threw new light on what was known already; and a good deal that was interesting *per se*. It struck me also that here was an account of the war from a privileged but unfamiliar angle, written by somebody with no conceivable personal axe to grind.

As warfare has grown more complicated and more technical, so has the art of Planning. Its very existence and status as an art was hardly recognized before the First World War; it was at best an *ad hoc* business, and at one time in our history consisted largely of saying: 'Send a gun-boat'. (Queen Victoria is said to have ordered the Fleet to bombard La Paz, being ignorant of the fact that it was two hundred miles from the sea, and twelve thousand feet up.) The near-disaster of Mesopotamia and the fiasco of the Dardanelles in the First World War were due as much to want of planning as to any other factor. There is a good deal more to it than what Southey called 'the art babbleative and scribbleative'. There is, first and foremost, the need to recognize that the militarily desirable is rarely the same as the administratively possible, a point admirably brought out in Professor Butler's volume on *Grand Strategy* in the Official History. But although in every war throughout our history we have learned afresh that we must cut our coat according to our cloth, there is still very little in the literature of planning; and much of what there is is repellently dry.

It would be foolish to suggest that you can have or devise a blue-print for planning. A planning organization may vary according to a dozen factors, of which personalities are not the least important. Planning covers every facet of military endeavour: the abstract as well as the concrete, personalities as well as resources. It is no sort of substitute for the cardinal military virtues; it would have been little comfort at Thermopylae for Leonidas to assure his Three Hundred, as they combed their hair on the sea-wet rock, that the Planning Staff of Sparta was the best in the world. Planners must be something more than dedicated troglodytes; more imaginative and positive than Bagehot's description of professional soldiers of his day: 'quiet, grave men, busied in charts, exact in sums, occupied in trivial detail'. No fewer than three senior British planners lost their lives in the course of hazardous journeys during the war: Vivian Dykes, D. G. Stewart and Frank Vogel.

The art of Planning is best practised by the best officers, and not entirely by academics with slide-rules, though these, too, must be the best of their kind. Even so, planners are not magicians; plans take time to mature. Early in the war the Chiefs of Staff were told that it would be the responsibility of Ministers to warn them when Singapore must be reinforced; the Chiefs of Staff had to point out that it would take three months after the word was given for reinforcements to reach the island.

A project planned for one purpose sometimes turns out to have its greatest value for another. When, for instance, the Prime Minister insisted on mounting an expedition against Madagascar, in the face of much Service advice, the Service advisers were glad in the end to have been overborne, because of the effect of the expedition's arrival in the Indian Ocean on the relative strengths of the British and Japanese fleets. There were other occasions when Service advice was rejected by the War Cabinet, and the event proved the War Cabinet right. One such decision—and a very bold one— which was fully justified by events, was the repeated reinforcement of the Middle East in terms of armour, at times when it was by no means certain that the threat of invasion was over.

Just as the militarily desirable may not be administratively possible, so also do military and political needs often diverge. At the very beginning of the book, we find Sir Archibald Montgomery-Massingberd struggling in vain to convince the Government that its conception of what was politically acceptable as the Army's strength was far below what was militarily safe. Not until the late Lord Hore-Belisha became Secretary of State for War was much progress made; and it is notable that his political methods of persuading the Cabinet succeeded where military persuasion had failed. That was almost on the eve of war; and General Kennedy derives paradoxical comfort from our failure to build up our forces earlier. He suggests that if we had done so, we should have committed and lost far more man-power in Flanders in 1940 than we did. He suggests on the other hand that the setbacks suffered by the Army in the earlier years of the war were due at least in part to an insufficiency of trained junior leaders. Our expansion had been so rapid that there was simply not enough butter to cover so much bread.

Over and over again throughout the war we see military appreciations being distorted by political considerations. In some ways this was bound to be so. But Sir John Kennedy deplores the fact, for instance, that no strictly *military* appreciation was ever received from Lord Wavell on the question of intervention in Greece. Whether or not that intervention was *politically* essential, he infers, is quite another matter, and irrelevant to the military problem as such. Every soldier fully recognizes that political considerations must often override military, and may necessitate a gamble, as in Greece. But Sir John holds that a soldier in a situation such as Wavell's should clearly distinguish between the two, regardless of the statesmen who are breathing down his neck.

I happened at that time to be a junior officer on Wavell's General Staff, and was involved, at what one might call the servants' hall level, in the discussions and staff work that went on in Cairo and Ankara during those early months of 1941. When the decision was taken to go into Greece, I remember saying to a colleague that it would probably be a perennial subject of argument in the staff colleges, comparable to the great controversy between Easterners and Westerners in the First War. I was wrong: for it is, in fact, generally held to have been an error of judgment, and likely to have failed even if Papagos had carried out his original undertaking to withdraw to the Aliakmon Line. Yet, as General de Guingand (whom I clearly recall as the most uncompromising opponent of the venture in G.H.Q.) has recorded in his book,

Wavell wrote in his familiar handwriting across the top of an appreciation submitted by his intelligence staff:

' "War is an option of difficulties"—*Wolfe*'.

I suggested *An Option of Difficulties* to Sir John Kennedy as a possible title for this book.

Perhaps I should say at this point that General Kennedy was disposed to think that there is too much about the Greek affair in this book. If so, the responsibility is mine. The whole episode is an epitome of the difficulties that arise in war; some of the cross-currents are still obscure; and it seems to me that the degrees of pressure from various quarters, and the ramifications which resulted, are of interest both intrinsically and as a matter of history.

General Carton de Wiart has written that politics and soldiering are like port and champagne—they don't mix. But unfortunately they impinge. The soldiers are the instruments of the statesmen. It is no good expressing a pious hope that

> *Noble statesmen do not itch*
> *To interfere in matters which*
> *They do not understand.*

The understanding must be mutual; and it is tragic as well as amusing to read of General Marshall coming over to Britain armed with a copy of Sir William Robertson's *Soldiers and Statesmen*, on his guard against (one supposes) 'caprice, obstinacy, frolick and folly' on the part of the 'frocks'. Despite the improved communications of the 1940's (so much to be regretted in many ways), which enabled the Prime Minister to hurl his thunderbolts like Jove from Downing Street or Chequers at commanders in the field, the relations between the British soldiers and statesmen were infinitely better in the last war than in the war before, and have remained so since.

It was apparently a shock to many to read in *The Turn of the Tide*, Sir Arthur Bryant's book based on Lord Alanbrooke's Diaries, of the clashes of opinion between the Prime Minister on the one hand, and the Chiefs of Staff (and in particular, two successive Chiefs of the Imperial General Staff) on the other. Sir John Kennedy's account, written from one echelon lower in the hierarchy, confirms Sir Arthur Bryant's; and the Official Histories, as they appear, confirm both. There was something of an outcry in certain quarters when *The Turn of the Tide* appeared, but it was quite unjustified: there was nothing against Dr. Johnson's canons. If we are to be debarred from reading history, we shall be debarred from profiting by its lessons. There are lessons to be learned in plenty. One of them is that, for the successful defence of our realms and territories, and those of our allies, we want the best quality of leaders and counsellors that we can get, whether in uniform or plain clothes—or zip-suits. We should never have escaped the full penalty of our unpreparedness for war if we had not had a national leader whose imagination and zest were matched by his aggressiveness, and Chiefs of Staff who were not afraid to stand up to him. It was our great good fortune that their opposite numbers in Germany lacked that essential characteristic.

The powers of the Chiefs of Staff Committee had certain curious limitations. In two respects the Royal Air Force was independent of it, and held an unwritten charter direct from the War Cabinet. The Chiefs of Staff, as such, had little say in the bombing policy, or in the matter of deciding what types of aircraft should be built. The Royal Air Force had had a precarious youth. Although now of age, and highly robust at that, it still had a tendency to look on the Royal Navy and the Army as wicked uncles who, although ostensibly reformed, might once again revert to predatory instincts. Who could say what might happen if the two older Services should taste blood, in the shape of selecting targets, or in the form of aircraft specially designed for the close support of the Army and Navy? (I remember as late as 1943 an Air Chief Marshal telling me in Cairo that he regarded every transport aircraft built at the expense of a bomber as a major tactical defeat.)

Yet for all these reservations the Chiefs of Staff were a band of brothers; and although at times in these pages we see a varying line-up over different problems, the conception of their organization proved brilliantly workable. There was no better trium-virate—and triumvirates are tricky things—in history. Cunningham replaced Pound, Brooke Dill, and Portal Newall; but the machine continued to run superbly. It was fortunate in its unique brand of lubrication—General Ismay.

The hours kept, and especially the night work, must have been dismal. Only the institution of one day off in the week could have kept the staffs from insanity. The Prime Minister's eager determination to examine every scintilla of possible offensive action bore hard on officers at every level. Perhaps he felt like Democritus, in the *Anatomy of Melancholy*: 'Who cannot give counsel? 'Tis cheap, it costs them nothing.' It did in fact cost them many a night's sleep, and many an hour both of daylight and darkness which might have been better spent on other plans more likely to be applied. Yet it is pretty obvious that every encounter with the Prime Minister, whatever his mood, was exhilarating.

Even when he is off-stage, Sir Winston dominates the book. We have the feeling that at any moment we may be summoned, to be harangued, scolded or exhorted. But if it was a strain to be in close personal touch with the Prime Minister, it was hardly less so to be in touch with him by signal. When Sir Robert Cassels, commanding an Indian cavalry brigade in Mesopotamia in 1918, became aware that his hot pursuit of the routed Turks was likely to be halted by an armistice, he took a sledgehammer to his one and only wireless set. No such congenial course was open to Lord Wavell. Although every effort was made in the War Office and by the Chiefs of Staff to avert or minimize the flow, there was hardly an hour in G.H.Q., Middle East, when some signal or other from the Prime Minister was not being deciphered, and an answer to its immediate predecessor being prepared.

General Kennedy suggests that Wavell was too acquiescent, in consenting to adventures urged, or even ordered, from home against his better judgment. General Kennedy is himself a warm admirer of Wavell, and his criticisms may be well founded; Wavell's predicament, and his reactions in it, must have been agonizing to watch from London. For those in high positions at critical times, whether those positions be military or civil, the decision about whether or when to resign or to refuse directives can be the most burdensome responsibility of all. It is very far from being a private or personal matter. If such a decision is taken, whether over policy or on grounds of conscience, the shock to the cause and to the machine is bound to be grievous. Wavell did not ask to be relieved, although he let it be known, through the most restricted channel of communication available to him, that he was prepared to go if confidence in him had been lost at home. The news of his super-session reached him early one morning, while he was shaving in his house on Gezira Island in Cairo. The signal was read out to him by his devoted Chief of Staff, Sir Arthur Smith. All Wavell said was: 'I think the Prime Minister is quite right: this theatre wants a new eye and a new hand'; and he went on shaving. A few days later I accompanied him as private secretary to his new appointment in India; and he was in the best of good heart, reading and declaiming Flecker's *Hassan*, and going for a swim at Baghdad.

I found of extreme interest Sir John Dill's letter of advice to Sir Claude Auchinleck on his assumption of Wavell's former appointment as Commander-in-Chief in the Middle East (p. 134). The question at once arose in my mind: was Sir Claude following it, consciously or subconsciously, when he refused to be stampeded by the Prime Minister's signals into what he considered to be premature action? Was he deliberately applying the lessons so painfully learned by Wavell? Had he in mind the events of May and June 1941, when Wavell allowed himself to be dragooned into undertaking three simultaneous campaigns—in Syria, Iraq and the Western Desert—with resources which he thought sufficient for two at most?

Another point which may strike the reader is the wide variety of personalities among the military *dramatis personae*. Those Generals in the book who bore the supreme responsibility of high command are very far from being cast in a single military mould, as if they were tin soldiers out of the same box. There could be no greater contrast, for instance, than between General Kennedy's several successive chiefs—Gort, Ironside, Dill and Alanbrooke. It is difficult to convey to those who never met him the aura of integrity which wrapped Dill like a mantle; few generals have inspired such deep affection. Wavell, Alanbrooke and he were intimate friends; the nation was fortunate to have such a trio in such an hour. To my generation, the personalities of the Army Commanders of the First War, except for Plumer and Allenby, are indistinguishable the one from the other. Not so those of the second. Apart from the fact that they are contemporary, their fortunes and experiences varied more widely than those of their predecessors; and there was more scope for an individual General to win or lose in the Second War than in the strictly linear development of the First.

It may well have been a stroke of luck that the American conception of strategy prevailed over the British, in the matter of the invasion of Normandy. It is well known that the British were anxious to exploit the favourable situation which had developed in Italy in 1943 and 1944, at the expense of 'Overlord'. Viewed from fifteen years later, the British conception still seems the sounder in the light of our then knowledge; but the Americans would have none of it. It was just as well: for had the landings in Normandy been abandoned or postponed, the rocket-launching sites in the Pas de Calais would not have been overrun in time to prevent incalculable damage to London and southern England.

Sir John Kennedy did not keep a continuous diary throughout the war. From time to time he wrote notes on contemporary events, which he threw haphazard into a steel box, along with copies of memoranda and appreciations. In 1946, he was appointed Governor of Southern Rhodesia; and there, in his leisure moments, he compiled a continuous narrative based on the contents of the steel box. It is this narrative, reduced to a little more than half its length, which comprises the present book.

My part has been limited to selection, in close consultation with General Kennedy. My own view of the war was from a very different angle to his. It is not always easy for an editor to remain aloof and detached concerning assessments and controversies about which he may have strong views of his own; but I have tried to be objective throughout, and to preserve the contemporary judgments which give the book its freshness and its sense of living in momentous times. The history of any episode, and particularly of a war, is not produced by a sort of electronic computer, in which every factor is automatically given its due weight; but if there were such a machine at work on the history of the last war, its calculations would not be complete, in my view, without this account. And I have sought to adhere strictly throughout to Sir John's mandate and Dr. Johnson's maxims.

Auchairne, Ballantrae

ACKNOWLEDGMENTS

I wish to acknowledge my indebtedness to friends for their kindness in allowing me to quote private letters, and to the War Office for passing the typescript and official letters, papers and telegrams for publication.

I would also acknowledge the readiness with which friends have allowed me to publish certain of the conversations recorded in this book.

My thanks are due for permission to print extracts from the following:

The Crown of Wild Olive, by John Ruskin (St. Martin's Press, Inc., and Macmillan & Company, Ltd.)

Letter from Grosvenor Square, by John G. Winant (Houghton Mifflin Company)

Operation Victory, by Sir Francis de Guingand (Charles Scribner's Sons)

Death in the Afternoon, by Ernest Hemingway (Charles Scribner's Sons, copyright 1932 by Charles Scribner's Sons)

The Turn of the Tide, by Sir Arthur Bryant (Doubleday and Company, Inc.)

Grand Strategy, Volume II, by Professor J.R.M. Butler (H. M. Stationery Office)

I owe a special debt of gratitude to Mrs. Burke, Miss R. Taylor and Mr. Charles Green who generously devoted much of their spare time to typing and retyping the script so patiently and so efficiently.

I am also deeply grateful to my friends who read the typescript for their wise and helpful criticism.

Above all I specially want to thank my editor, and I hope he has enjoyed our collaboration as much as I have.

Temple Sowerby

JOHN KENNEDY

I

UNEASY PEACE

1934–6

SIR JOHN DILL was a completely dedicated man. Soldiering to him was more than a profession; it was a vocation. The Army came before everything else. On himself he imposed a spartan self-discipline; to everybody else he displayed great courtesy and a most endearing warmth of heart. I never met anybody of more obvious sincerity; and like everyone who ever served with him, I loved him.

I had met him in France in the First World War. I was a regimental officer; he was on the staff. A less 'gilded' staff officer one could hardly imagine; his heart was in the trenches, and so was he more often than most of his colleagues. In the early 1930's, he was Commandant of the Staff College at Camberley, and I was one of his instructors. He was looked on as one of the coming men, and his reputation was growing every year. It was no surprise when in 1934 he was appointed Director of Military Operations at the War Office.

Less than a year later he sent for me to join him, and I was both flattered and delighted. I found myself in charge of that section of the General Staff which devilled strategy and war plans for him; and although I realized that the job would be full of frustration, its interest and the fact that I would be working with him fully compensated me. This was the first time I had ever been concerned with plans for a possible war against Germany.

The C.I.G.S. was Field Marshal Sir Archibald Montgomery-Massingberd; and he was having an uphill fight. He was striving to persuade the Government to put the Army into a reasonable state of preparedness for war. He maintained that the very least we could accept was a field force of four or five divisions in the United Kingdom which could take the field at once. Otherwise we should have nothing to contribute to the common cause if France were attacked by Germany; and there was a real danger that the Germans might occupy the Low Countries in the early stages of a war, which would give her air and submarine bases from which to attack Britain.

Montgomery-Massingberd fully realized that in the prevailing political climate we had no prospect of raising enough forces in peace-time to redress the balance of numbers as between France and Germany. The most he could hope to achieve was enough to send a token contingent to France, like the original B.E.F. in 1914, on the outbreak of war. A dictum of Foch's was still widely believed: that the tactics of each war began where those of the last left off; and it was deduced from this that we might expect an initial period of trench warfare in which to build up bigger British forces.

The controversy between Ministers and the General Staff dragged on wearily, confused by many red herrings and false prophets. Thus the Maginot Line was pronounced impregnable; the attack in modern warfare could not possibly prevail over the defence; air forces alone would suffice to stop the advance. Those years were the heyday for cheapjack purveyors of bogus military nostrums.

But the greatest impediment to vigorous military preparations was the belief, sincerely held by our political leaders, that it would be possible to achieve a settlement without a war. They failed, and the word 'appeasement' became for ever debased and derogatory; but their repeated and patient attempts to reach a settlement did achieve one thing: we had proved to the world that fighting was unavoidable, and we went into the war a completely united nation.

It is always tempting to speculate on what might have happened if things had been done differently. For instance, if the British and French had adopted a tougher policy in the years before the war, the Germans might have turned towards the East. Probably nothing could have prevented Germany from re-arming in course of time. If they had then conducted their policy in such a way as to engage Russia in single combat, they would very probably have beaten her; and the West might have been faced by a far more formidable combination than Hitler's axis of 1940.

Again, if a tougher policy had brought about the fall of Hitler, over some such issue as the reoccupation of the Rhineland, we might eventually have had to deal with the Germans under some other leader. It is difficult to believe that any other would have played into our hands as Hitler did, by committing so many major strategic blunders.

Yet again, if we in the General Staff had had our way before the war, we should probably have had sixteen or seventeen divisions committed in France before the end of 1939, and perhaps double that number in 1940. Knowing what we now know of the fighting quality of the French, it is more than likely that a British army even of this strength could not have prevented a German breakthrough; and the despatch of an expeditionary force of such a size might have led to its loss, for want of shipping to take it off the beaches.

All these are what President Roosevelt once called 'iffy questions'; so many 'ifs' are involved that perhaps such speculation is fruitless. But in some ways the weakness of our policy in those years may have brought us benefits.

We had two other major problems during this spell of mine in the War Office. The first was a possible war with Japan. We put it to the Government that, with our resources, there could be no question of waging simultaneous war with Germany and Japan with any hope of success. We were told not to concern ourselves with this contingency. The defence of Singapore was therefore based on the provision of a strong British fleet and air force, which could be sent to the Far East only if we were not at war in Europe.

The second problem was the Abyssinian affair. We gave it as the view of the General Staff that sanctions in themselves would be ineffective against Italy unless the Government was prepared in the last resort to apply the final sanction of war. This opinion did not find favour. I remember well that, when it had been decided that we should stand aside while the Italians had their own way with Abyssinia, Dill said to me, 'I wonder if we are right to allow this thing to happen. I have a feeling that *morally* we are wrong, and that we shall suffer for it.'

In the autumn of 1936 I left the War Office for a year's regimental duty in Egypt. I acquired a knowledge of the Libyan Desert which was a great help to me when the war came; and I spent many delightful days learning about the birds of the desert, and exploring Palestine, and the Red Sea, and some of the oases. In January 1938 I was sent as a student to the Imperial Defence College; but I did not complete my year there, for in October I was summoned back to the War Office as Deputy Director of Military Operations.

2

A YEAR'S RESPITE

1938–9

WHEN I went back to the War Office Mr. Hore-Belisha had been
Secretary of State for about two years. In his first year of office he
had, in effect, dismissed the military members of the Army Council,
because he considered them to be too old and too unprogressive,
and had installed a younger team, headed by Lord Gort as C.I.G.S.
He took a keen personal interest in all the higher military appointments, exercising, to the utmost, the Secretary of State's constitutional powers of individual selection through the Military Secretary. He was by far the most active Secretary of State the War
Office had had for many years. He did much that was good for the
Army, and he became popular with the rank and file. But he was not
regarded by the senior officers as a good Secretary of State; even
many of those who owed him their promotion disliked him and
distrusted his judgment. There was a widespread impression among
most of the highly placed and responsible officers, especially among
those who worked with him at the War Office, that he was too
much concerned with his own advertisement, and they regarded his
speeches on Army Estimates in the House of Commons as much too
optimistic: they looked on them as positively misleading.

When he made Gort C.I.G.S., Hore-Belisha no doubt considered
that it would help to 'put the Army on the map' in the public eye.
But the Army felt that Dill should have been chosen. Whether Dill
would have accomplished much more than Gort in those pre-war
years I very much doubt. He would probably have worn himself out
sooner than he did, in futile and frustrating struggles with the
politicians—and his temperament and character would have clashed
with Hore-Belisha's at every point. It is fairly certain, however, that
had he been C.I.G.S., neither Ironside nor Gort would have been in
key positions on the outbreak of war.

Hore-Belisha was aware, when he chose Gort, that he would not be the man for the kind of work the C.I.G.S. had to do in the Imperial Defence Committee, where the military advice given to the Government had to be discussed and defended. He discussed this difficulty with Sir Maurice Hankey, who told me about it later, and suggested that it might be possible for Gort to confine himself to outside activities with the troops, and to entrust his other duties to a suitable deputy. Hankey had explained to him that no C.I.G.S. could uphold his position under an arrangement of this kind, and that the C.I.G.S. himself must be the military spokesman of the Army in dealing with Ministers.

Gort's unsuitability for the post soon became apparent to all. In the War Office this fine fighting soldier was like a fish out of water. When I arrived, relations were already considerably strained between him and Hore-Belisha; their mutual dislike increased as time went on until, in the end, they were hardly on speaking terms at all.

One of the first jobs I was asked to tackle was to provide a memorandum for the Cabinet setting out the state of readiness of the Army for war; I was to make a case for equipping the regular divisions adequately and for putting four of the territorial divisions on a better footing. Pownall,[1] the Director of Military Operations, told me that he had written a draft himself, but that he had failed, in spite of several attempts, to get it into a form that would satisfy Gort. He did not think I would succeed either, but he wished me luck.

This seemed to me a fairly simple task. I read Pownall's draft which, as he explained to me, had become much too detailed as a result of Gort's amendments, and then rewrote it in a shorter and more forceful form. There ensued a series of long discussions with Gort, and at his direction I made extensive amendments and additions to my own draft. By this time it had suffered the same fate as Pownall's. When Gort finally approved it and signed it, it had grown to more than three times its original length and had become almost incomprehensible. I was not surprised when it was brushed aside by Ministers without being seriously discussed.

Hore-Belisha now announced that he would take the matter in hand. I sat with him in his room while he dictated a very clear and clever paper of a page or two, which presented exactly the programme of re-equipment that we wanted. He deliberately omitted any reference to the part the Army might have to play in a campaign,

[1] Afterwards Lieutenant-General Sir Henry Pownall.

saying, 'The Cabinet does not like strategy, you know.' The whole process of dictation and discussion, with me and another staff officer who was present, occupied some three hours.

Next day Hore-Belisha gave me a copy of his memorandum, and told me that he was going to discuss it with the Prime Minister in the afternoon. He asked me to find out what Gort thought about it.

When I went to see Gort after luncheon he was sitting in his room with Dill, then Commander-in-Chief at Aldershot, Liddell, the Adjutant-General, and Bartholomew, Commander-in-Chief of the Northern Command.[1] I handed him the memorandum and gave him Hore-Belisha's message, and they all read the paper together. Dill looked up, when he had finished, and said, 'I think it is *dreadful*.' I said, 'It may not be a strategical appreciation. Still it may be a very good move with the Cabinet.' But none of the three could find a good word to say for it. I asked Gort what message I should send to Hore-Belisha before he saw the Prime Minister. 'Send nothing,' he said.

Yet, as a result of Hore-Belisha's intervention, and despite the Generals' view of it, the Cabinet gave the Army £80 million a few days later, and we were authorized to go ahead with our re-equipment.

These, and other measures taken by the Government during the last year before the war, were not without value. Perhaps the most useful step taken by the Government was the expansion and re-equipment of the Air Force. But, on the whole, the so-called re-armament programme was not very effective. Sir Thomas Inskip, the Minister for Co-ordination of Defence, worked hard and conscientiously in a field that was entirely strange to him. But neither he, nor any other man in his post, could have accomplished much without greater powers than the Government were willing to concede, especially with regard to the control and reorganization of industry.

I had known Inskip since I was a boy. I regarded him with great affection and respect, and I had cause to be grateful to him for many kindnesses. When he gave up his office to become Secretary of State for Dominion Affairs, I wrote to him privately. I told him that we in the War Office had appreciated his efforts for the Army, and that we understood very well the reasons why it had been impossible for him to accomplish more. In reply he wrote me a letter, dated 9th March, in which he said:

[1] Generals Sir Clive Liddell and Sir William Bartholomew.

'I have had plenty of critics in the Press and in Parliament and I have not found it easy to answer them. Some of the criticisms were no doubt deserved; others were mere impatience. But my chief effort was to help the three Services to work together and to smooth out difficulties, and though my efforts would have been useless without the knowledge and skill of my advisers, I have little to regret. I don't think I care about getting any credit now things are seen to be going so smoothly and satisfactorily.'

As Army member of the Joint Planning Committee, I was involved, during the year before the war, in the preparation of numerous appreciations and plans. These studies were submitted to the Chiefs of Staff and some of them were communicated to Commanders-in-Chief. They served a useful purpose at the time. But our forecasts were, in the event, proved to be wide of the mark in many ways. For instance, in our consideration of the German war, we never took into our calculations so much as the possibility of a French collapse; and in our forecasts of the Japanese war, we could not, of course, foresee that both we and the Americans would be so weak in the Pacific at its outset.

A constant bone of contention in our discussions was the role to be played by the Air Force. Both the General Staff and the Naval Staff opposed the fanatical efforts of the Air Staff to press upon us their theory that the war would be decided by the action of air forces, almost unaided by the other two Services. We fought hard and unsuccessfully for the provision of adequate specialized air forces, properly trained and equipped for the support of naval and military operations. The introduction of such a policy was regarded by the Air Staff as a 'prostitution of the Air Force', so a senior officer in the Air Ministry once expressed it to me. This fight went on far into the war. The politicians were much attracted by the Air Force doctrine, and the soldiers and sailors could never persuade the Cabinet or the Defence Committee to settle the dispute in a way we thought right, either before or during the war.

In March 1939 the British and the French Governments agreed that military conversations should take place between their naval, general and air staffs, with the object of exchanging technical information, and co-ordinating plans for war with Germany. There was, of course, no military treaty between us, and the arrangements we might make were therefore to be purely provisional, implying no obligation on the part of either Government. In order to obviate reactions from Germany and possible political difficulties at home, the conversations were held in secret; but the Germans can hardly have failed to be aware at the time that talks were taking place.

The first of the series opened at the War Office on 27th March. Our delegation consisted of our Joint Planning Staff. Captain Danckwerts represented the Navy, Group Captain Slessor[1] the Air Force, and I the Army. General Lelong, the French Military Attaché in London, headed the French delegation, which included Colonel Noiret and Colonel Aymé of Gamelin's staff.

The first thing to be done was to exchange information about the strengths of our respective forces, their distribution at home and overseas, and the plans for mobilization. The unenviable task fell to me of disclosing to the French the real strength of our Expeditionary Force, and the rate at which we might hope to despatch divisions to France in the event of an attack by Germany. When I had done this, Lelong made a statement, evidently prepared beforehand in intelligent anticipation, in which he expressed the deep dismay of the French General Staff at the inadequacy of our arrangements.

The French officers told us, in general terms, the strength of their army in France, but they disclosed nothing of their plan of campaign. We did not press them on this point—indeed, we felt we had no right to do so.

I reported the French reaction to Hore-Belisha, and possibly Lelong's *démarche* had some influence with the Cabinet. In any case the British Government took the decision, very soon afterwards, to double the strength of our Territorial Army; and before the talks ended in May, they had announced the introduction of conscription as well.

The doubling of the Territorial Army sounded a big thing to the public, and it may have been a good political move; but it was by no means sound from a military point of view, because, although the number of our divisions was at once increased on paper, this was not the quickest way to get the Army ready for war. It pleased the French, however, as a public gesture that we were taking the situation a little more seriously; and conscription pleased them even more. We were also able to produce a bigger and faster programme for the despatch of divisions overseas, and a more effective but still not very good scheme for the expansion of the Army. We discussed plans for the colonial territories, and arranged various measures of co-operation, and of co-ordination of command. We also discussed in general terms how we might support the Belgians.

[1] Afterwards Marshal of the R.A.F. Sir John Slessor, Chief of the Air Staff.

As a result of these conversations, we were able to draw up instructions for British and French Commanders all over the world, which enabled them to make detailed arrangements for co-ordination in the event of war. We left over, for later discussion on a higher level, certain points, such as the system for the higher control of the war and the arrangements for command of the Allied Forces in France. All this would have been very fruitful—if only the French had stayed in the war.

One of the matters we discussed was a military route across Central Africa, to be used for reinforcing the Middle East in case the Mediterranean was closed. Kano in Nigeria was to be a staging point. Colonel Aymé, who was the French expert on the Colonies, said that he knew the route well. '*J'ai traversé l'Afrique par Kano*,' he said; which the interpreter rendered as: 'The Colonel says he has been across Africa in a canoe!'

One night after dinner, we took the French officers to the Tower to see the ceremony of the keys. Our guide told us that Ann Boleyn's ghost was said to walk on the green, with her head under her arm. One of our guests claimed to have read that she had been beheaded by a French executioner for a fee of £3, and suggested that this might be regarded as an early example of co-operation between the two nations.

At the beginning of May, Major-General Dewing was sent out to discuss the details of the plans for North Africa with General Nogués, the French Governor and Commander-in-Chief. On his return, he reported to Gort that Nogués did not consider our garrison in Egypt to be strong enough, and Dewing added that he agreed with this opinion. Gort was furious, and said to me afterwards that this was an example of the canker of defeatism of which he was determined to rid the Army. Any suggestion that the Italians were a serious enemy was enough to enrage Gort. We in the General Staff certainly felt no alarm about Egypt, so long as the Italians were the only enemy to be reckoned with; our only anxiety was that they might not advance far enough in the desert to come within striking distance. But the French always thought we rated the Italians too lightly.

One of my officers came one day to my room in the War Office and said that he felt he should report to me a very awkward thing that had happened. A new time-table for the despatch of the Expeditionary Force to France had just been prepared in his section, and so he had thrown the old edition into the fire. By a stroke of bad luck it had been wafted up the chimney without being burnt.

Although it was now out of date the old time-table still contained important secret information, and he had therefore asked the Office of Works to send over a chimney sweep to sweep the chimney and recover the document. The Office of Works had informed him that the chimney could not be swept without a requisition on the proper form and twenty-four hours' notice. But they had sent a man to close up the top of the chimney for the night with a slate. Next morning the chimney sweep arrived, but having probed the recesses of the chimney he reported that the document was not in it, and that it had probably been carried up by the draught and blown away. We never heard anything more of it, thank goodness.

The military conversations with the French were carried a stage further at a meeting in Paris between Gort and General Gamelin, at which I was present. We had been invited to attend the Fourteenth of July celebrations and we flew over to France on the 12th. Our party included Pownall, the Director of Military Operations; Gort's daughter; Major Gordon, his personal assistant; Captain Jeffreys, his A.D.C., and Jeffreys' wife. (Gordon and Jeffreys were both killed within the year in the first fighting.) We took off from Hendon on a lovely clear day, and, flying at about 3,000 feet, we passed over Eastbourne and crossed the coast of France at the mouth of the Somme. Then we flew over Abbeville, and over Amiens with its great railway sidings, which I had never before seen from the air. At Albert, I saw a glistening new gilt Virgin on the tower of the Cathedral. When I had last seen it in 1918 the Virgin was hanging precariously, almost cut down by a German shell. The scars of the trenches of the 1914-18 war were still plainly visible in the fields. The countryside seemed curiously empty, compared with England, and there was little traffic on the roads.

After a flight of two hours, we landed at Le Bourget at 5.30 p.m. Here we were met by Gamelin, whom I now saw for the first time— an insignificant little man, who shook hands flabbily, and without looking one in the face. Gort asked him the name of the commander of the battalion which was drawn up as a guard of honour, but Gamelin did not know it. We stayed at the Crillon, as guests of the French Government.

At ten o'clock next morning, we all went to the Ministry of Defence to meet Generals Gamelin, Georges and Huntziger. We were acutely conscious throughout the ensuing talk that we were in a poor bargaining position: the French were very much the senior partners because of their much greater initial contribution; but nothing was decided at the meeting which was not acceptable to us.

Gamelin struck me as a slick and clever talker, and rather a 'political' soldier; Georges, the Commander-in-Chief designate, as an agreeable, rather silent, man of strong personality; Huntziger I liked the best of the lot—intelligent, sincere and friendly. We were not to know that Georges was at loggerheads with Gamelin over the division of authority in the control of operations, and a convinced pessimist; still less were we to know of Huntziger that within a year it would fall to him to negotiate an armistice with the Germans.

The main business of the meeting was to ratify points which had been drafted beforehand, and there was no controversy. We agreed on Le Mans as the centre of concentration for the British Field Force, and we agreed that the British Commander-in-Chief should be subordinate to Georges, though with adequate rights of appeal to the British Government. There was no question of a British general having command at the outset; we all favoured a repetition of the system under which Foch and Haig had commanded in 1918, with the ultimate command in the hands of one man; and this was endorsed by the Cabinet on our return to London.

The meeting was followed by a heavy luncheon, and the luncheon by an afternoon off, which I spent in sight-seeing. Gort went up the Eiffel Tower. Then I had another meeting with Huntziger, who was leaving that evening on a special mission to Turkey.

Next day was the Fourteenth of July, and Gamelin took us, with some difficulty, through vast crowds to our seats in the President's stand. Mr. and Mrs. Churchill were in the seats next to ours. Churchill smoked two large cigars before 11 a.m. and kept up a stream of questions about the troops, their guns and equipment, as they marched past. He remarked that we could not have held up our heads that day, if we had not introduced conscription in England.

The French Army looked as magnificent as ever. It never entered our heads that their morale was rotten at the core. All the same, the most impressive event of the parade was the march past of some British Guardsmen; they looked splendid in their scarlet, and the cheer they got from the crowd as they swung down the Champs Elysées eclipsed even that accorded to the popular Foreign Legion.

Gamelin saw us off at 5.30 p.m. at Le Bourget, and we flew back to Hendon over lovely white clouds, at 10,000 feet. We were accompanied for a great part of our journey by a little circular rainbow which surrounded the shadow of our aeroplane on the clouds, a phenomenon I had never seen before.

I think it was during this trip that Gort spoke to me of his love of flying. He owned a Moth aeroplane, in which he used to go for flights at the week-ends—this, he asserted, kept his nerve steady in spite of the War Office routine. 'I often lose my way,' he said, 'but, if you keep on flying long enough, you always find it again in time!' Such a remark was vintage Gort.

Three days before our visit to Paris, General Sir Edmund Ironside had come to see me in my office. He had been commissioned by the Government to go to Poland to find out what military plans the Poles had made, and to assess their prospects of resistance if they should be attacked by the Germans. Ironside's official appointment was Inspector-General of the Army; but he spoke Polish—he was an interpreter in no fewer than six languages; he had made a deep study of and written a book about Hindenburg's Tannenberg campaign; and he was altogether an excellent choice for the mission on which he was being sent.

Ten days later, after his return, I dined with him at the United Service Club. He gave me a graphic description of his flight— three hours of it through thunder and lightning, 'with the aeroplane dropping a hundred feet at a time'. He described his talks with the Poles as having been very successful. Smigly-Ridz intended to fall back in face of attack—'that was the way to kill lots of Germans'. Ironside said that he had got hold of some Germans in Warsaw, and had told them that we really meant business this time, and that the Prime Minister had made that clear to him.

Five days later, on the 26th July, he came to see me again. He thought he might be required for the discussions which were to take place in Moscow early in August (these were the talks which eventually ended in the Russo-German Treaty), and he wanted to be briefed. He said in the course of conversation that he had asked Gort which seaports in France the Field Force would use; Gort had replied that he did not know, and that he had never asked for the information: he felt he should not do so, as the matter was so secret! It was obvious that Ironside was desperately anxious for active employment in the field; he made no secret of it.

The views held as to the possibility of war with Germany, a month or so before it broke out, were very varied. General Dill, for instance, who was still Commander-in-Chief at Aldershot, looked in to see me on the 31st July, and we discussed the situation for half an hour. Dill thought Hitler would not go to the length of war with us over his continental policy; but the danger, in his opinion, was that, in playing near the edge of the precipice, he might get a foot over, and be unable to recover. He thought it quite possible that Hitler might prove to be a greater man than Napoleon. If war did come, he said, it would find our Field Force very imperfectly trained—it could hold a defensive position and that was all; training had been set back by the sudden expansion; measures had had to be taken to teach the new militia. He felt, if war came, we would not be able to avoid having a big army in France; weakness there would expose us again to the risk we had run in March 1918, when Ludendorff's last big attack almost succeeded in breaking through to the Channel.

On the 24th of August there was a bombshell for us. The Russo-German Pact had been signed the night before. It was supposed to last ten years. Next morning, the 25th, there was a good deal of betting in the War Office on whether or not there would be a war. Gort offered 5 to 4 against; Adam,[1] the Deputy C.I.G.S., 6 to 4 against; Ironside was laying 5 to 1 on. The division of opinion continued right up to the actual outbreak.

I saw Ironside in my club after dinner that evening, and he expounded his theory at length, saying that he felt Mr. Churchill had been quite wrong, in a newspaper article published the day before in which he had given it as his view that Hitler could still step down. Ironside held that Hitler, being a peasant, and with his German mentality, would not do so. Ironside was going to see Churchill the next day, and he said he intended to tell him this. He felt sure he would be Commander-in-Chief, and that Dill would have the 1st Corps.

It will make it easier to understand some of the events which took place in the War Office during the following months, if I interrupt my narrative here to describe the personal relations existing among some of the leading figures in the Army, as I understood them from my level.

Hore-Belisha and Gort, by the time the war came, had been barely on speaking terms for many months. So far as I could see, Hore-Belisha bore no animosity to Gort, but he could hardly have failed to be keenly disappointed to see how unsuited Gort had shown himself to be for the post of C.I.G.S., and he was obviously well aware of Gort's distrust and dislike of himself. Hore-Belisha, largely because of the unhappy relationship that had grown up with the C.I.G.S., had formed the habit of dealing with junior officers in the General Staff. In my own dealings with Hore-Belisha, I never found him anything but courteous and charming (and he had considerable charm when he cared to exercise it), and I could not but admire his

[1] General Sir Ronald Adam, Bt.

subtle brain. But I was acutely conscious of the animosity felt towards him not only by Gort, who was my own chief, but by practically every senior officer.

Some time before the war, Hore-Belisha had further antagonized the generals by his association with Captain Liddell Hart, who was then the Military Correspondent of *The Times*. Hore-Belisha admired his clever writing, and found his advice stimulating and progressive. But Liddell Hart's theories of strategy and tactics were anathema to many professional soldiers, and it was greatly resented that he appeared to have become an unofficial adviser to the Secretary of State.

Relations between a Secretary of State for War and the senior officers of the Army could hardly have been more deplorable than they were in 1939. For a good many years the division of opinion between the General Staff and Ministers had been growing wider. But the relations between the soldiers and the Minister for War had always been friendly before Hore-Belisha's arrival, and the Minister had always been respected. Walsh, Hailsham, Halifax, Duff Cooper, Oliver Stanley were all liked, although it was felt that the first of these was rather out of his depth. My generation had been brought up to believe that Haldane was the best Secretary of State the Army had ever had, and that none of his successors had equalled him.

Mr. Chamberlain, Sir John Simon and Sir Samuel Hoare were all more or less unpopular with the General Staff because of the way they torpedoed many of our attempts to raise the state of preparedness of the Army,[1] but they were respected for their sincerity, even when they disagreed with us. Sir Thomas Inskip was always admired for his upright character, although he was not regarded as the right man to be Minister for Co-ordination of Defence.

It was, of course, nothing new that the relations between soldiers and statesmen should have been as unhappy as they were in 1939. The training and outlook of the politician are so fundamentally different from that of the soldier that clashes of opinion are always bound to be frequent and severe.

---

[1] Sir John Simon was Chancellor of the Exchequer; Sir Samuel Hoare had been First Lord of the Admiralty, and was now Home Secretary.

3

'A STATE OF WAR EXISTS'

1939

DURING the last weeks of August 1939 we were heavily engaged in a kind of partial mobilization. Overt mobilization must always be postponed till the very last moment, since the order to mobilize may precipitate a crisis, and looks like an irrevocable step towards war. We therefore set aside our carefully prepared plans, and resorted to all kinds of makeshifts, for manning defences, filling up the cadres of the staff, and so forth, so as not to run the risk of being taken at too great a disadvantage if hostilities were suddenly begun by Germany. My Club, the United Service, which will figure a lot in this book, was darkened after sunset by 24th August; and the bedrooms were converted into dormitories to accommodate the officers who were beginning to arrive to fill war appointments in the Service Ministries.

Germany attacked Poland at dawn on 1st September, and at mid-day representatives of Ministries were summoned to Colonel Ismay's[1] room in the Cabinet Office, to draft the 'warning telegram'. I attended on behalf of the War Office. Admiral Sir Dudley Pound, First Sea Lord, came for the Admiralty. The telegram was drafted by Ismay, in the first instance, to order precautions to meet war with both Germany and Italy. Then it was held up, to add a sentence qualifying the preparations to be taken with regard to Italy, and was finally despatched at 2 p.m.

'To Commanders-in-Chief overseas.

Warning telegram. You are to take all defence precautions in case of war against Germany and Italy. Italy's position is not yet clear and no action is to be taken which might be considered provocative by Italy.'

[1] Then Secretary of the Committee of the Imperial Defence, afterwards Lord Ismay of Wormington.

15

At 9.30 p.m. the first British ultimatum was sent to Germany. There was no immediate reaction; and just after midnight we sent off another telegram to Commanders-in-Chief:

'Germany has not yet replied. No time limit was given. Germany may of course open hostilities by surprise attack.'

There were no further developments, so far as we were concerned, on 2nd September. But at 9.30 a.m. on Sunday the 3rd, the second and final British ultimatum was despatched. Representatives of Ministries were again summoned to the Cabinet Office in Richmond Terrace, and we assembled in Sir Edward Bridges'[1] room at 10.30 a.m. expecting to learn, within an hour, whether or not war was to be declared.

While we waited, I wrote three drafts of telegrams to be sent to Commanders-in-Chief, covering the three possibilities: postponement, declaration of war from a certain hour, and immediate opening of hostilities. Remembering Moltke's dictum that, in military appreciations, there generally seemed to be three courses open to the enemy, but that he often chose a fourth, I kept one blank bit of paper on the table in front of me. I showed my three drafts to the Admiralty and India Office representatives, who were sitting on either side of me, and asked them if they would care to make a small bet on the probability of any one of the three. I had no takers.

At eleven o'clock Bridges came in, and told us that a message from Germany was being deciphered. I telephoned this information to Pownall, the Director of Military Operations. He told me, later in the day, that he had passed it on to Hore-Belisha, who had immediately telephoned to Simon that he hoped there would be no more negotiations with Germany.

At 11.15 a.m. Bridges came in again. He announced that the Ambassador's message from Berlin was to the effect that the German Government had sent no reply to our ultimatum; the Prime Minister's instructions were that the War Telegram was to be despatched immediately.

We broke up at once, and scattered to our respective Ministries, to send off the telegram. Small groups of anxious people were standing about in Whitehall as I walked back to the War Office.

I had just told Pownall the news and given instructions for the despatch of the telegram when, at 11.30 a.m., the air-raid sirens suddenly began to sound that memorable false alarm. 'The usual

[1] Afterwards Lord Bridges.

German efficiency,' we all thought. But the sirens had been set off by mistake. Some of our aircraft had flown over Holland, contrary to orders, on their return from a reconnaissance flight in the neighbourhood of the Heligoland Bight, and had been taken for Germans.

On hearing the siren, hundreds of officers, civil servants, clerks, and messengers now emerged from their rooms, in accordance with orders, and descended to the basement—at this time, and indeed all through the war, a very dangerous place in which to take refuge, for it was not properly concreted or protected. When I got to the ground floor it occurred to me that we might be kept in the basement for some time, and so I ascended the stairs again, battling my way against the crowd, to get my newspaper. When I got back, I went first to Hore-Belisha, in his allotted section of the basement, and reported to him that the War Telegram had been despatched. He seemed to be extremely cheerful.

For some time we hung about in the basement, waiting for the war to begin. We heard occasional bangs which we identified, quite incorrectly, as A.A. guns: they were in fact the slamming of some subterranean War Office doors. Then the All Clear sounded; and we returned, rather ignominiously and with some sense of anti-climax, to our respective offices.

The big event of the following day was the receipt of an official War Office Memorandum, dated twenty-four hours after our unceremonious invasion of the basement:

OFFICE MEMORANDUM No. 1897.
    The following information is circulated *for Office use only*.
H. J. CREEDY

The War Office,
    4th September 1939

OUTBREAK OF WAR

Notification has been received from the Offices of the Cabinet and Committee of Imperial Defence that a state of war exists between the United Kingdom and Germany with effect from 11 a.m. on 3rd September, 1939.

Of all the office secrets entrusted to me during the war, this one, on the whole, was the most difficult to keep to myself.

On the 3rd September, the Cabinet had decided that Gort was to be Commander-in-Chief of the Field Force, and Ironside to replace him as C.I.G.S. Adam (Deputy C.I.G.S.) told me this news at dinner in the Club. These appointments were a complete surprise to us all. I was sorry, on personal grounds, that Gort was to leave the War Office. His appointment as Commander-in-Chief must have seemed to the Cabinet a good solution politically in view of the strained relations between him and Hore-Belisha; and possibly as good a solution as any other militarily. The Army, after all, had, at that time, no single soldier with war experience of high command. Gort had been much in the public eye, and had been 'built up' in the Press.

I think now that the appointment of Gort to be Commander-in-Chief may be regarded as one of those strokes of great good luck which came our way more than once in the course of the war. Under any other commander, the Field Force might, for quite good reasons, have been manœuvred differently, and in such a way as to be cut off from the sea when the French Army collapsed—a disaster from which it would have been difficult to recover.

I believe Gort, as C.I.G.S., had advised the appointment of Dill as Commander-in-Chief. Lelong, the French Military Attaché, said the French would prefer Dill to Ironside as Commander of the Field Force, and so did Colonel Petibon of Gamelin's staff. But Dill was comparatively unknown to the British public as opposed to the Army; and if he had been appointed the problem of Gort's disposal would still have remained, which might well have been an embarrassment to the Government.

Ironside's appointment was well received. He was much in the public eye at that time, was *persona grata* with the Prime Minister, and was strongly backed by Churchill. Had he not been brought back by Hore-Belisha from Gibraltar, a year or so earlier, to be Inspector-General of the Forces, it is probable that he would never have been considered for a high command, and almost certainly not for the post of C.I.G.S. Somebody said to me, about this time, 'Hore-Belisha does not know it yet, but he has raised a regular Frankenstein's monster in bringing Ironside back from the dead.'

Most of us felt that the combination of Ironside and Hore-Belisha could not last. Some of us believed that Hore-Belisha would find himself overshadowed by Ironside in the Cabinet Councils, and that he would soon find a way to get rid of him. Others felt the betting was the other way, and that Ironside would get rid of Hore-Belisha. They were right.

On Ironside's first morning in the War Office I went to see him in his room to brief him for his first Chiefs of Staff Meeting. But before he looked at the papers he gave Adam and me an account of an interview he had had with Hore-Belisha.

Sticking out his enormous forefinger, and banging the edge of his table with it as he spoke, he delivered himself in terms something like these:

'I said, "Now, Mr. Belisha, I have formed a better opinion of you during the last few weeks. You have behaved extremely well during the crisis, and I have changed my mind about you. But understand this—and let us be quite clear about it—I never asked to become C.I.G.S., and I accept it only on condition that you are perfectly frank with me, that you never go behind my back, or speak contrary to or without my advice on any military matter. If I find you doing that, I will have you out, or I will go. These are my terms, and you must accept them." I always told Jack Gort,' he went on, 'that he should have had a charter like that with Hore-Belisha—it is the only way.'

Ironside did not take long to brief: he was quick at grasping the points at issue; but he asked me to accompany him to the meeting, in order to prompt him if necessary. So we went off together to the underground conference room in the Office of Works, and continued our discussion on the way. As we sat in the car he remarked, with characteristic self-confidence, that he knew the Chiefs of Staff Committee needed pulling together, and that he was sure he could do this before long.

We arrived at the War Room, and were told that the Cabinet would probably assemble there at the end of the Chiefs of Staff meeting. Ironside asked how it was proposed to arrange the seating plan. Ismay suggested that the three Chiefs of Staff should sit together across the top of the table. 'No, no,' exclaimed Ironside. 'We should be like three naughty boys—that won't do at all,' and he changed around the name cards so as to put each Chief of Staff beside his own Minister. In the end the Cabinet never came to the War Room, and the problem did not arise.

The business on the agenda was quickly despatched; Ironside was excellent. Then the three Chiefs of Staff went over their drafts of the reports on the situation which they were to make to the Cabinet; and after a meeting which had lasted an hour and a half, we walked over to 10 Downing Street where the Cabinet was to meet. It was a lovely summmer day and the sun shone into the garden, which we could see through the windows of the Cabinet Room.

Cabinet discussions are sacrosanct, and I cannot even now quote what was said; but I remember two things in particular. The one is a stony glance which Chamberlain directed at Churchill as the newly reappointed First Lord lit an enormous cigar; I guessed that it was not normal to smoke at Chamberlain's Cabinet Meetings. The second is a distinct impression left on my mind that three of the Ministers sitting round the table seemed to stand out head and shoulders above the others: Halifax, Churchill and Chatfield. The meeting ended, so far as I was concerned, with an agreement that Ironside and Newall, the Chief of the Air Staff, should fly over to Paris that afternoon to see Gamelin; and I went back to the War Office to arrange their trip, leaving the Chiefs of Staff still in session with the Cabinet. I saw the party off from Hendon in the afternoon.

Ironside got back from Paris next day, the 5th September, and joined Adam and me at our luncheon table in the Club. He had taken quite a liking to Gamelin, whom he described as a 'nice little man, with a well-cut pair of breeches'. Gamelin had explained that the French Army would not be on the frontier before mid-September; it was now advancing stealthily, covered by heavy artillery, forming salients and then filling up the gaps between them. On the 17th, he would 'lean on' the Siegfried Line, and bombard it. The question of action by the air forces was not yet settled, but Gamelin was averse from using them so soon.

Ironside said the French had been having fearful rows, especially Gamelin and Georges, about the division of reponsibility for the direction of army operations. He had discussed the command of the British Field Force. Gamelin had suggested putting it under Pretelat, with Georges in command of both the German and Italian fronts, but Ironside would not consent to the British Commander-in-Chief being placed lower in the hierarchy than immediately under Georges.

We got back to the War Office at three o'clock, and Hore-Belisha and Ironside went off to a Cabinet meeting. At about six o'clock Gort came into the War Office to see me. He was simply beaming and kept saying, 'Isn't it *grand* to be going to the War!' He was in the highest spirits, like a schoolboy going off for the holidays. He said he would love to be in action quickly, and would much prefer to be on the Siegfried front than on the Belgian sector, where there would probably be no Germans. Gort's general instructions were contained in a document which he himself, while still C.I.G.S., had edited with the greatest care, on 2nd and 3rd September, saying, 'This is an historic document, we must get the wording right.'

When I went to see Ironside the next morning (6th September) about 9.30, he was sitting in his room, with a big flask of whisky and a siphon of soda-water before him. He had been up till 1 a.m. at an Army Council meeting, discussing further 'civilian evacuation'—children and 'expectant mothers' had already gone —and 'industrial mobilization'. (These dreadful clichés were now general currency.) Ironside said he had told the Prime Minister he wanted to do a one hundred per cent evacuation of Government departments at once. Chamberlain had replied that this was a civil problem, to which Ironside had answered, 'No, Prime Minister, it is a *military* problem now.' Ironside was convinced the Germans would soon drench London with bombs. 'They all think they will be able to go on having their Cabinet meetings at three o'clock every day. They look funny enough now with their little civilian gas masks—what will they look like when the bombs begin to drop in Whitehall? It is madness to wait and then have a disorderly rush at the last moment.'

Ironside went off to see Hore-Belisha. When he came back he ordered a paper to be written asking the Government for 32 divisions in the first year of war, 32 more in the second year, and possibly 32 more in the third. A Cabinet 'Land Forces' Committee, under Sir Samuel Hoare, considered these proposals a little later, and recommended the formation of 55 divisions, which soon afterwards became our authorized 'target'.

While we were talking, Gort came in. Ironside addressed him thus:

'Now, I want you to go down to Aldershot, as an Inspector, and look after your force. You don't take command till they are in France. See that they dig in and are safe from air raids—we may be drenched at any time. I will get you over to France in a day or two.'

Gort: 'I will go down to Aldershot. But I don't want to go to France too soon—the Germans would get wind of it, and that would disclose the movement of the Field Force across the Channel.'

Ironside grunted and said he would consider that.

At 10.15 a.m. I walked to Downing Street with Ironside on his way to the Chiefs of Staff meeting. As I left him, he remarked: 'Now I am going to waste a morning educating these old gentlemen in the Cabinet in their job. Winston *must* be Prime Minister.'

The relations between Hore-Belisha and Ironside became no easier. I heard, about this time, an account of another brush. The two of them were engaged in some discussion when they were interrupted by the arrival of a certain duke of military age, who had come to ask Hore-Belisha to find him a half-time job, not out of his own county. No sooner had this been settled than another visitor arrived to see Hore-Belisha, upon which Ironside turned on him and said, 'Mr. Hore-Belisha, I can give you half an hour, or even an hour, occasionally, but I will not be interrupted, and arrangements must be made accordingly.'

On 7th September, Ironside sent for me to discuss strategy in the Middle East. After we had talked, he dictated to a shorthand writer a very clear and emphatic document, in which he urged two things: neither General Weygand nor any other Frenchman should be put in a position of control at the centre of the British Empire; and, secondly, we should not go to Salonika as the French appeared to desire.

He then commented upon the instructions that had been given to Gort, and said he did not like certain wording about his rights of appeal to the British authorities. He said that he (Ironside) meant to have the last word in the employment of the Field Force, and that it must not be under the French Government. 'Gort,' he said, 'is a boy—he has a one-track mind—quite rigid. He will play for the side, and that is all. That is not good enough for me. This force is the mother of the British Army. I do not want it to go into the line at first. I have told Gort that he is to *train* his army first when he gets to France.'

These encounters with Ironside were both amusing and stimulating, and he certainly inspired great confidence in us all.

4

THE ESCAUT LINE

1939

THE next fortnight was one of intense work on appreciations, completion of mobilization arrangements, and so forth. Major-General Dewing had arrived to be D.M.O., and I did not see so much of Ironside after this. But he told me one day, when I was briefing him for a Cabinet meeting, that the Cabinet were too much engaged in tittle-tattle, and spent much time in discussing such incidents as balloons breaking away or being destroyed by lightning, and mistakes made by our fighter aircraft in attacking each other. He meant to stop all that. He was also worried about the battle between the Army and the Air Force, and felt he would have to fight it all over again to get proper support for the Army. He had written a sharp letter to Gamelin about the publication in the French newspapers of reports of the movement of our Field Force across the Channel. Our newspapers had got it too, and when we discovered it, in the middle of the night, we had tried to stop it. Thousands of copies of papers were destroyed in Fleet Street before we found that the French had already published the news. In the event the Germans made no attacks on the Field Force transports, as we had feared they might.

The Joint Planning Committee, of which I was at this time the War Office member, produced a forecast of Hitler's possible courses of action. The only hope we could offer was that we should be all right if we could hold fast at the outset in vital places, and play for time to build up our strength. Scarcely a year had passed since Gort had been rebuked by Ministers for asking that four of the Territorial Divisions should be equipped for war, and had been told 'All that (i.e. the policy for the Army) was settled long ago—why re-open it?'

On 17th September the Russians entered Poland. This development, of course, put an end to any slight hopes that might have remained that the Germans would be engaged for long in active operations on their Eastern front. But we could hardly believe that the association of the Germans and the Russians would be a happy one, and we hoped most devoutly that it would not develop into a military alliance.

On the 19th I was lunching at the United Service Club, when Ironside came in and sat down beside me. I was struck by his changed appearance. He looked tired, his eye was not so bright, nor his voice so full, and, as he talked, he seemed depressed and pessimistic. For luncheon he ordered a curious meal—a boiled potato, some mashed potato, broad beans and carrots, no meat, and a bottle of ginger beer. An officer at the next table asked him if his boy was going to enter the Regiment.[1] 'We've got to win this war first,' replied Ironside. 'There may not be a Regiment after it.' He would not allow that there might be friction between the Germans and the Russians over Poland. When I suggested that we might at least hope for a breathing space, since the Germans might suffer from indigestion after swallowing Czecho-Slovakia, Austria and Poland in such quick succession, he replied, 'Indigestion is a slow process—it takes a long time to die of it.' He complained of having to labour at all the things that should have been done years ago, of the necessity of holding midnight sittings of the Army Council, and of the difficulty of picking up all the threads at such a time.

When we were alone in the smoking-room he ordered a cigar and some coffee, and then told me about a War Cabinet meeting he had attended that morning. 'I gave them a fright this morning,' he said. 'I told them that Gamelin now fears a German attack in the West. I explained to them that the French defences on the left are practically non-existent. Gamelin is the commander of the only army in the field—the British Army has not yet arrived; anyhow it is no good yet. I told them that our Army is not properly equipped, and that the men were thrown together just before they embarked. I gave them my opinion that the B.E.F. is unfit to advance into Belgium or to fight in the open, and that it could only dig in and hang on. I said that, therefore, we must oppose the French plan to put us on the Escaut. I said I had been at them in the Cabinet every day since I came in, to get the Belgians to agree to collaborate—and what had been done? Nothing. I told them that, if the Germans came through Belgium, the Government would be faced with ordering the bombing of Belgian towns to stop their advance. I

[1] Ironside, like the author of this narrative, was a Gunner.

reduced them to silence for ten minutes. You have got to frighten these people to get anything done. That is where Gort failed—he did not press his points home and scare them. It is not enough to put in your papers.' He went on to say that he did not like the look of things at all—especially if the Germans pushed home an attack on the French Air Force. Nothing I could say would change his gloomy mood.

I asked him if anything had been decided. He said the Cabinet now wanted to have discussions with the French on a higher level than between him and Gamelin—'that means the civilian level,' he added rather bitterly. So Hore-Belisha, Hankey and the D.M.O. were to go to Paris next day, to see Daladier and Gamelin. Hore-Belisha had asked him after the Cabinet meeting why he had attacked the state of the Field Force so fiercely; he had answered that he looked on himself in the same light as an auditor, and bound to report what he had found out.

Later in the day I heard that, far from impressing the Ministers, Ironside had annoyed them very much, apart from reducing Hore-Belisha almost to tears. His manner with politicians was much too brusque; on the other hand it was a joy to hear him give a straight-forward military survey in a military environment. Only a day or two after his diatribe in the Cabinet, I took General Arthur Smith, Wavell's Chief of Staff, who had just flown home from the Middle East, to see him; and the verbal appreciation of the situation which Ironside gave him was precise and clear, with some picturesque adornments for good measure. He put our current preoccupations into admirable perspective, and the gist of his talk might make at this stage a useful 'still' in a moving picture which was soon to move all too rapidly.

He said our first task in the West was to make up the French order of battle so that it could withstand the Germans, which meant a British force of some twenty divisions. The Germans could con-centrate in the West by mid-October; they might not venture on a land attack so late in the year, but they could fall upon and over-whelm the French Air Force. Of this prospect the French were terrified, and they would allow no air action for fear of retaliation. Our own Air Force still believed that their main objectives should be factories and similar targets; it was neither trained nor equipped to support land operations. We were trying as hard as we could to wean them from this conception.

On land, Gamelin had revoked on his promise to attack the Siegfried Line with the object of relieving pressure on the Poles; he did not wish to expose too many troops to the risk of counter-attack in front of the Maginot Line. The Germans had a big army; it was their main weapon and instrument of victory; their air force was largely designed to support it. This basic fact would govern the shape of operations to come.

Belgium remained a horrible problem. The Cabinet had had it impressed on them that if the Germans elected to come through the Low Countries they would be faced with the political problem of whether or not to bomb Belgian towns. (At this point in his harangue, Ironside sent for a glass of water: he said he had a sore throat from talking so much to the Cabinet, and trying to teach 'the old gentlemen' their job.) The British Army, he went on, must not be allowed to fight an encounter battle on the Escaut Line.

He now turned to the Middle East. We meant to put some twelve divisions there, but we could not yet say when: troops would have to be sent where the threat seemed most urgent. Overall strategy would have to be defensive at first; the offensive must be built up later. A door might open in Rumania, or Italy; we might have to send in small forces to put Poland and Czecho-Slovakia back on their feet. The armies available to do all this would be minute and under-trained for some time. The wastage of the lean years could not be restored by the wave of a wand. Turkey would be our front line and our bastion. We did not want to bring in weak Balkan states, which would only be a liability at the moment; Salonika could be occupied as the French wished, but only defensively and only if it became essential to complete the Turkish front. If Turkey failed as a front, we might need an alternative defensive line across Syria and Palestine. We must certainly contemplate operations in the Black Sea area later on.

In Ethiopia we might have to raise the country even before serious operations were begun: the right men should be selected now, and the spark fanned. We needed mobile columns, like those of Von Lettow-Vorbeck in East Africa during the First War. Deliberate operations based on Kenya could not be mounted, for want of roads and railways, which would take a year or more to build.

Tired though Ironside was, he delivered this statement with all his old vigour and clarity, and spoke for an hour or more. It was really masterly, and seemed to come from a different fount than the man who referred to Hore-Belisha as 'that little monkey', and complained of having to waste time in teaching the elements of strategy to the Secretary of State for War.

·　　·　　·　　·　　·

The problem of the Escaut Line, which Ironside had touched on in his briefing of Arthur Smith, was a burning one in the early stages of the war. It had not yet been finally settled whether, if the Germans attacked, we should fight on the French frontier, or move forward to the Escaut Line—Escaut being the French word for the Scheldt. On 19th September, after he had opened his heart to me in the Club about his scene with the Cabinet, I had walked back to the War Office with Ironside to discuss with him and the head of our Military Mission to Paris a letter to Gamelin on this very subject. It pointed out the dangers of putting the British Army in the Escaut Line, and asked Gamelin to agree to issue a joint directive to Georges and Gort, forbidding them to occupy that position other than with delaying troops.

Next day, as arranged, Hore-Belisha, Hankey[1] and Dewing, the D.M.O., discussed the problem with Daladier[2] and Gamelin, in the absence of Ironside, who had always consistently opposed the idea of an advance. Gamelin favoured the advance for two reasons: to gain more depth for the defence, and to secure the Belgian coast. No decision was reached during the meeting of 20th September, but on another point we got what we wanted: an initial position in front of Lille. This suited our lines of communication, and was agreeable to us.

Ironside now renewed his pressure on the subject of the Escaut Line. He spoke out afresh to the Cabinet, and he wrote to Gort. In his letter he pointed out the dangers of being caught in the open during a forward rush, particularly by the low bombing attacks which the Germans were known to favour; he stated his opinion that troops who were not dug in, in depth, before they were attacked were bound to be routed; and he maintained that an improvised defence on a line like the Escaut, unreconnoitred and unprepared, could only be linear, and would therefore be ineffective. He ordered Gort to discuss the whole project with Georges on these lines.

Yet for some reason within a few days Ironside's opposition had weakened. Gamelin had written him a letter setting out the case for the advance to the Escaut; and on 26th September, Ironside replied:

'I thank you for the explanation about the line of the Escaut. I agree with you as to its importance. I quite understand about

---

[1] Lord Hankey, who had been raised to the peerage in 1939, was at this time Minister Without Portfolio in the War Cabinet.
[2] M. Daladier was Minister of National Defence and War.

the necessity for covering the territory close to Great Britain from the installation of enemy aircraft, which could then bomb us at shorter range.'

This was our first indication that Ironside might be prepared to fall in with the French conception.

On 28th September, Germany and Russia signed their second pact in five weeks: Poland was partitioned, and Warsaw fell. *Punch* produced a cartoon of two seals, Stalin and Hitler, about to devour their respective platefuls of Polish fish, Stalin having much the bigger helping. The caption (*loquitur* Stalin) was: 'You eat *your* dinner, I'll eat *mine*.' We felt fairly sure that Russia would warn Hitler off the Balkans and the Black Sea; she had already anticipated him in the unhappy Baltic States. It looked as though the full weight of the first blow would now fall on France for certain, with the utmost strength of the Army and Air Force, together and not in separate operations. Gamelin expected a thrust through Belgium and Holland some time between 22nd October and 10th November; as the autumn wore on, the Dutch and Belgian Governments became convinced that it was fixed for the 11th November; we now know that Zero Day was in fact November 12th, but was postponed.

We were being strongly pressed by Gamelin to increase our air commitment in France, where we had only ten bomber and four fighter squadrons; but the Air Staff were loath to comply. Hore-Belisha asked me to his room in the War Office on 30th September, to discuss this subject, and he sipped a glass of milk as we talked. He was tired and confused; and he kept getting involved as to how many squadrons were fighters and how many bombers. He had a lot on his mind at the time; and the whole matter of air policy *vis-à-vis* the Army was in a mess. Our bomber force had never been designed to participate in Army operations, and was both unsuited and untrained for the purpose. The bombers could not operate in daylight without fighter escort, and the available fighters could not escort them very far. The Air Staff was pressing for approval of a night-bombing policy, against targets such as the Ruhr, when operations should at last begin. The General Staff had other views as to their proper use, which we urged in vain. The arguments became more and more academic—and more and more tiresome. In fact, the whole of October was tiresome. We studied plans and hypotheses; we churned out notes, briefs and memoranda on every conceivable subject. Never had so little fighting produced such a voluminous range of documents. All the traditional gibes at the staff welled up in our minds.

On 5th November, Ironside told me he thought it possible that the Germans might occupy Holland before the winter was over. He confided these misgivings to Gamelin in the following letter:

My dear General,

I am becoming increasingly anxious about an invasion of Holland during this winter. There have been persistent rumours about the collection of boats and of parachute detachments. A descent by parachutes followed by troops in aeroplanes would seem peculiarly suitable for an attack on Holland, followed by an invasion on land.

Hitler specializes in Blitzkriege and this would be after his own heart. It would be a preliminary encirclement of Belgium, just as was arranged against Poland by the occupation of Slovakia. It might well be Hitler's winter campaign, to be followed in the spring by an attack on Belgium. Hitler will stop at nothing and can easily tell his people that it is done with no intention of hurting Holland, but to break the encirclement of Germany now being arranged by the Allies.

One very serious result of such an occupation would be the closing of the port of Antwerp. I do not know if the Belgians ever had any idea of occupying the islands north and south of the Scheldt at its mouth in the event of Holland falling.

Should such an invasion of Holland take place it is likely to be a quick one. The consternation and confusion in Brussels and Antwerp will be great. It may even call for frenzied appeals to the Allies to help Belgium.

Have your Intelligence anything definite about such an invasion? I am ordering mine to redouble their efforts at discovering whether it is imminent or not. Have you considered such an eventuality as regards the possibility of making quickly a line with our left on Antwerp?

We do not relish another Walcheren Expedition of 1809 or a repetition of the Antwerp episode of 1914, but I should like to receive your ideas upon the subject of such a move and of air action from us should the Germans be in Holland.

A day or two later Ironside went over to Paris to discuss plans with Gamelin; and here the subject of the Escaut Line bubbled up afresh. At Ironside's request I prepared a brief for him in which we reiterated our point of view regarding an advance into Belgium. We held that the plan would have to be such that the Army should not be caught in the open before reaching a new defence line, and we were opposed to any attempt to occupy a new line which there would be no time to organize before the Germans attacked. We argued that, if the plan did not satisfy these two requirements, we would merely throw away the advantage of fighting in the well-prepared defences on the frontier and gain nothing to offset it. This meant, in fact, that no advance should take place unless we could be sure that the Germans would not move forward simultaneously—and certainty in such a matter was highly unlikely.

On the evening of 9th November, Ironside returned from France at about nine o'clock and was summoned at once to a Cabinet Meeting which was just assembling. He had been accompanied by Newall (Chief of the Air Staff) and Gort at a meeting with Gamelin, at which the latest French plan for meeting a German attack through the Low Countries had been discussed. The idea was to advance to a forward line in Belgium, if the Germans invaded the Low Countries and the Belgians called for help. We knew that the Belgians had made some very tentative and non-compromising approaches; the French Military Attaché in London, for instance, had told me in confidence nine days earlier that the Belgian Foreign Minister had buttonholed the French Ambassador in Brussels; and Ironside had been irritated, when I told him, that the Belgians should have done it in such a roundabout way. We knew also that Georges had discussed the projected advance with Gort; and that the more these approaches had progressed the less had the French dwelt on the necessity for *temps utile* to organize a new position. No new arguments had been marshalled by Gamelin to justify his contention that the Allied armies could reach more advanced lines in time to establish themselves before they were attacked by the Germans. I was dismayed, as anybody else in my shoes would have been, to be told that Ironside, Gort and Newall had nevertheless all accepted this happy-go-lucky French plan.[1]

When Gamelin's plan was sent next day to the Joint Planning Committee for our comments, we did our level best to shoot it into

[1] 'General Ironside reminded the Cabinet that the Commander-in-Chief had been expressly put under the orders of the French Commander; he had the right of protest to the Cabinet, but until he protested—which he had no intention of doing—they would be ill-advised to intervene. Gort had agreed to the proposed advance and he himself had accepted it. This assurance seems to have satisfied the Cabinet.' (p. 162, *Official History, Grand Strategy*, Vol. II, Professor J. R. M. Butler.)

splinters. We pointed out that the Louvain position, which was now being talked about, could not be quickly organized for defence; that air forces could not be deployed to support the ground forces in good time; that the flanks of the British Army would be open; that we did not think we could count on occupying the islands at the mouth of the Scheldt, and that even if we could it would not give us control of the river: neither the Germans nor we could use the Port of Antwerp without the control of both banks and all the islands of that inconceivably broad estuary. We admired the spirit of the French, but we deplored their buoyant, ill-founded optimism. Even as we built up our irrefutable case (as we sincerely believed it to be) against their propositions, we knew it to be doomed: we had little hope of persuading them to modify their plan. They, the stronger partners with the final say, could not see its weaknesses; we, the weaker partners, saw them all too well, but realized that we should be obliged to fall into step with as good grace as we could muster.

I gave a copy of our report to Howard-Vyse.[1] Somehow it came to the knowledge of Gamelin, who wrote to Ironside, saying that 'he objected to criticism of his plan by a Committee of junior officers; that it was his plan, it was a very good plan, and that he meant to carry it out'. Ironside replied that he agreed with Gamelin.

The Council in Paris also discussed the task to be given to the British Air Force in the event of a German advance through the Low Countries. Our representatives advocated the bombing of the Ruhr. They were forced to take this line because the Air Staff still argued that their bombers were unfitted for the support of military operations and that they should surely be used somehow. Gamelin was opposed to the bombing of the Ruhr. He maintained that this would not delay the German armies because they would have passed through the Ruhr before bombing could be begun, and he was anxious not to initiate unrestricted bombing which would be likely to draw retaliation in kind on factories in France. This point was left for further discussion, but I had grounds for feeling that the battle for the direction of the air effort was lost already. The Permanent Under-Secretary of State for War had warned me that the Air Ministry was bound to win this particular fight for one simple reason: Newall was ready to resign on the issue; Ironside was not.

During all these searing discussions, we still had our lighter moments. We were always delighted when the laugh was not on us, and the War Office was duly gratified by this story from across

---

[1] Major-General Sir Richard Howard-Vyse was Head of the British Military Mission with the French High Command.

the street. Sir John Simon had suddenly remarked, at a War Cabinet meeting, that no Foreign Office representative was present. A Secretary said that there was one outside; and a personage was brought in and put into a chair beside Sir John. The Cabinet was discussing the subject of neutral ships lying in Ferrol; and in due course Sir John Simon turned to his neighbour and said, 'What do you think?' The personage looked embarrassed; and Sir John Simon, with a sudden misgiving, said, 'You *are* the Foreign Office representative, aren't you?' 'No, no,' said the stranger, shuddering, 'I'm the telephone orderly.'

5

A VISIT TO FRANCE

1939

On 8th November, as I was going back into the War Office after dinner, I met Hore-Belisha on his way out. He said: 'You know, Kennedy, I think we've won this war if we only hold on and stick it out, and don't go in to help the Belgians and the Dutch. As you know, the C.I.G.S. has just gone over to see Gamelin about this. I'm going over to France myself next week: would you like to come?'

I said I would love to; and next morning Major de Guingand, Hore-Belisha's Military Assistant, came to my room to confirm the invitation. De Guingand, who was afterwards to become Chief of Staff to Montgomery—one of the most successful of such partnerships in military history—had been appointed to his present post because Hore-Belisha disliked reading memoranda; de Guingand's job was to master them for him, and to give him the gist of them. We arranged the trip together; and on the 17th we took off from Hendon in a new-type American aircraft called a Flamingo.

It was a very thick day; but at 5,000 feet there was sunshine, blue sky, and lovely stretches below us of billowing white clouds. When we dropped down through the clouds as we neared Paris, we flew very low over woods and fields. The oaks still had their brown and golden leaves, and the woodpigeons flying out of the branches seemed almost within shot. As we touched down at Le Bourget the throttle jammed and we could not stop; we sped across the airfield at great speed, took off again and cleared the rooftops by a few feet. A civilian mechanic on board put things right again, and we landed safely ten minutes later. Hore-Belisha smoked a cigarette throughout this episode, and showed no sign of nerves.

The Military Attaché met us. There was no love lost between him and Hore-Belisha. 'He's dull as ditchwater,' said Hore-Belisha;

'I can't think why Gort wanted him here.' The Military Attaché, on the other hand, told me that he felt it was good for his soul to meet Hore-Belisha occasionally; he disliked him so much that it was a very good exercise in self-control.

We motored to the Gare du Nord, and caught a train to Arras. In the train, Hore-Belisha talked at some length. He said he did not like the system on which the Chiefs of Staff worked. He felt it wrong that they, as a corporate body, should put forward views which might be contrary to those of their Ministers; he thought the Service Ministers should be consulted at a much earlier stage. I argued that it would be dangerous if opinions on purely military problems were coloured by political considerations; that the Chiefs of Staff views should be accepted by Ministers as the views of experts on the purely military aspect of each problem, and these views should then be considered, and approved, or rejected, or modified, by Ministers after being weighed in the light of political factors.

Hore-Belisha then drew my attention to his boots, which he had designed himself. They had a zip fastener up the back instead of laces.[1] (This reminded me of something Ironside had said in a lecture to the Imperial Defence College when I was a student there. When he went to see Hore-Belisha on taking up his appointment as Inspector-General, he noticed that he was wearing a very odd pair of boots with elastic sides and zip fasteners. 'Now, Gentlemen,' he said, with a twinkle in his eye, 'how can one get on with a Secretary of State who does that sort of thing? That is the sort of difficulty one is up against with this kind of politician!')

We dined on the train and eventually arrived at Arras, where we were met by Gort and Pownall, Gort's Chief of Staff. We drove to Gort's château, and talked for a bit before going to bed. Gort was full of vitality and as boyish and impish as ever. But one of our party thought he had aged, because the back of his neck had fallen in a lot, and that was always a bad sign.

On 18th November we breakfasted at 7.30 a.m., then motored through Arras to Douai. There we met Dill, who was commanding the 1st Corps. Douai was his railhead, and we had a look at a pack train with supplies for 52,000 men. This number was significant, as there were only 26,000 men in Dill's two divisions. It meant that his

---

[1] These boots impinged also on the notice of Major de Guingand, who described them as 'a sort of Wellington—wool-lined, with a zip fastener up the back. He was very pleased with them at first, but before long the water got in through the zip, and the inside became very unpleasant. He never showed his discomfort during the day, but confided his disappointment at the failure of his design that evening when we got in.' *Operation Victory*, p. 38.

Corps troops (i.e. supporting, ancillary and supply units) accounted for exactly half the total strength of the Corps.

We visited various points on the fronts of the 1st Division (Alexander) and of the 2nd Division (Loyd). The men were digging trenches, building pill-boxes, making anti-tank obstacles with mechanical diggers, and so forth. They all looked fit and cheerful. The frontage they were holding was very wide: one brigade had a front of 4,500 yards, and another 7,000 yards. In our peace training about half these frontages would have been regarded as quite enough; but the wet state of the ground meant that during the winter an attack would be confined to the roads, and wider frontages were permissible. Yet this was not intrinsically a strong position. Our front was in a salient, which could easily have been isolated by passing through the weak defences of the French sectors on the flanks; and this is probably what would have happened had it ever been attacked.

I talked with Dill for some time as we walked round. He was perturbed by the weakness of the Allied line. If the Germans had 160 divisions by the spring, and if they could put 120 to 130 of these on the Western front, as we calculated, then our line would be far too thin. There would not be time to produce enough new divisions by the spring to equalize the balance, and Dill knew this only too well.

We went next to the front of the 2nd Corps, commanded by Brooke, and saw Montgomery's and Johnson's 3rd and 4th Divisions. Gort had sent out orders that the men were not to parade, but to continue their work. Montgomery's men, nevertheless, were drawn up in lines on the roadsides. Gort was angry when he saw them, and said, 'Just like Monty—I will take it out of him for this.'

One of Gort's staff told me that Dill worried too much, and wore himself out. He said that Brooke was always bothering G.H.Q. about standing farther back, and continually asking for more anti-tank guns, etc. I felt that the truth of the matter was that the two Corps commanders understood the situation better than Gort. But Gort was in a predicament too, owing to the shortage of equipment, and he was trying to meet it by taking up the attitude that demands for greater resources were merely signs of defeatism. Gort himself gave the impression of a very gallant, cheerful, hardy commander. He often quoted Foch as he talked— '*Attaquez, attaquez*,' '*Tout le monde a là bataille*,' '*Pas de relèves pendant la bataille*,' and so forth.

I discussed with Pownall ways and means of ensuring the success of the plan for the advance into Belgium. But the only remaining hope was to enlist the help of the bomber aircraft, and that hope was dim indeed.

We motored back through Lens and Vimy to the G.H.Q. offices. Here Pownall showed us, on a map, the detailed and complicated arrangements for the advance into Belgium. Hore-Belisha had a talk with the Chief Engineer (Pakenham-Walsh)[1] about the programme for the construction of pill-boxes, which Hore-Belisha felt was far too slow.

We dined at Gort's château. Gort spoke much of the war of 1914–18, in which he was very well read. He criticized the handling of the British troops in 1914 at Le Cateau, on the Marne, and at the crossing of the Aisne. Once again he interlarded his comments with many old clichés, such as 'Sweat saves blood', 'Ask me for anything but time'.

After dinner we attended a conference of senior staff officers over which Gort presided. The first subject he raised seemed curious for a Commander-in-Chief's conference. It was the question whether a tin hat, when it was not on a man's head, should be worn on the left shoulder or the right. Hore-Belisha remarked to me afterwards that it also struck him as funny, but he added that it was good to see Gort so interested in details about his men. It was midnight before we got to bed.

Next morning, Sunday 19th November, we breakfasted at 7.30 before motoring to Arras, where Hore-Belisha addressed about forty pressmen in an hotel. He made some comments on his visit to the front, and in the course of his talk he remarked that 'we were winning the war comfortably'. Meanwhile Gort and Pownall were waiting impatiently outside.

It was a wet, cold, windy morning. We motored through the rain to the western side of the British salient, where the 51st French Division was holding the line, under Gort's command. On our way we crossed the Vimy Ridge. Gort got us out of our cars when we reached it. He made Hore-Belisha climb a very muddy bank and kept him shivering in the howling gale, while he explained the battle fought there in the 1914-18 war. In spite of his discomfort Hore-Belisha kept up a very good appearance of polite interest. By this time his patent boots must have been giving him hell. We stopped again, a few miles farther on, to hear Pownall

---

[1] Major-General R. P. Pakenham-Walsh was Chief Engineer to the B.E.F. For more about the 'Pill-Box' Controversy, see *Operation Victory*, pp. 39-42.

describe an attack on the Aubers Ridge which had been supported by his battery from that very position twenty-odd years before.

General Gillard, the commander of the 51st French Division, took us up to a top-floor room in a château, and spent a long time pointing out to us various places in the landscape. Gort opened a window and let in a piercing draught on Hore-Belisha; when we went out again into the rain, he shouted jovially, 'Isn't it a grand day!'

We then went on by car to Commines and Halluin, and made another long halt on a hill top, while Gillard and one of his officers pointed out chimneys and other landmarks *ad nauseam*. Hore-Belisha stood it all with the greatest patience. He remarked to me afterwards: 'I thought I would get pneumonia. Why did they want to keep on showing me all these places as if I were a student being taught map-reading?'

On the way back to Arras we ate bully beef sandwiches supplied by Gort's mess. When we reached the town, de Guingand suggested to Hore-Belisha that we should stop at the hotel and get some hot soup before setting out on our long drive to Paris. This we did, thinking that Gort and Pownall, to whom we had already said good-bye, would go on. But they hung about outside in the courtyard of the hotel. Hore-Belisha, on seeing them, asked me to go out and tell them not to wait. I told Gort that we were going to have some soup, whereupon he roared with laughter and exclaimed, 'Weren't my sandwiches good enough?' Pownall said: 'We'd better go—you are making Hore-Belisha feel awkward.' But Gort would not leave, and he tramped into our room with his staff, and chaffed us for half an hour.

We started at length for Paris at 2 p.m., and Hore-Belisha asked me to join him in his car. During the journey he spoke upon a variety of subjects.

He began by describing how he had got rid of the Army Council. 'They were an awful set of duds,' he said. 'You have no idea how impossible they were. They had to be got rid of. I wrote them all letters telling them they must go.

'Well, when that was over, I had to find a man the Army would look up to—a man I could build up so that he would be known to the public. I thought Gort was the man. I said to myself, "Here is a man that the public and the Army will accept as a soldier—with a V.C., three D.S.O.s and all that." I knew he wouldn't make a good C.I.G.S., and he didn't. But I wanted to get him known. The first time I saw Adam[1] I said to myself, "This is the man I want; he will

[1] General Sir Ronald Adam, Bt., Adjutant-General, 1941 to 1946.

do all the work, while I build up Gort as a public figure." I always meant to get Gort a command. If the war hadn't started so soon, I meant to put him into Aldershot, and Dill could have gone to India. Then nobody could have said that Gort had no experience of command. But the war came, and there was no time for that.

'When Gort went off to the B.E.F. I had to find another C.I.G.S. I took Ironside, in spite of all that people said about him, because of his personality. If Ironside comes into a room, everybody will take notice of him. Not so Dill. Dill is more the staff officer—he has not the personality. Everybody said that Ironside would want to dominate everything and run the show. I said I would see to that. Not everybody can handle a situation like that, but I can. I said that, if things went wrong, after all it was my funeral and nobody else's. Ironside is doing very well. He dominates the Chiefs of Staff. I like dominating personalities. He makes mistakes, but we all do. Look at his opposite numbers—nonentities.

'I knew we had to prepare for war when I came to the War Office. I can get things done, and I got them done. Look at all the concessions I got. I got the equipment. I said that, if I got the money, I was not going to spend it on uniforms. You fellows do not understand the politician's role. You remember that paper Gort put in last autumn, about equipping the Regulars and some of the Territorials. He insisted on putting it forward under his own name. I let him do it. I knew he would fail. And he did. Then I got it all, with a short note of one page.[1] I choose my moment. I go and see my colleagues when necessary. When I take up a thing, it gets done. You have no idea of the opposition I have met in the War Office in everything I have tried to do. It has been a constant struggle.

'My impression of the front is that they are working on quite the wrong lines. There ought to be hundreds of pill-boxes, every hundred yards if necessary. Pakenham-Walsh had an enormous file with six designs in it, and no pill-boxes have been built except two, although they have been in that position for a month or more. I sent them a good engineer to help them. I found him very crestfallen. He had not been properly used. It is always the same in the British Army. You are always looking for the best design. The best is the enemy of the good. That is why we have got no tanks or anti-tank guns. We must standardize pill-boxes for mass production.

'My next impression is that the organization is all wrong. It is one of the biggest things that has happened that Gort has agreed to a smaller and simpler division for defence. I should be able to get

---

[1] See page 5.

out fifty per cent more divisions in the first year than we thought. Why should we not have French units supporting British divisions— tanks, artillery and so on? We saw the amalgam working in the French 51st Division.'

As we got near the Marne, I pointed out some of the places we were passing where there had been fighting in 1914. But he had had enough of the last war while we were with Gort: he curled up for twenty minutes and went to sleep.

He woke up again as we entered the suburbs of Paris. 'I think Gort realizes I am out to help him?' he asked. Knowing that Gort disliked him, I had some difficulty in thinking of a diplomatic and yet not untruthful answer.

I left him at the British Embassy, where he was to stay the night, and went on to the Crillon Hotel. There I found Ironside, who had come over earlier in the day to see Gamelin. I thought it would be useful to him to hear about our trip to the front before he met Hore-Belisha at the Embassy, where he was to dine. While I waited for him to emerge from his bath I read a record of his inter- view with Gamelin that day, which his secretary handed to me. The point which interested me most in the report was that Ironside had promised Gamelin 10 British divisions by the spring and 5 more by the autumn of 1940.

As Ironside sat in his dressing-gown, smoking his pipe, I gave him an account of the points we had discussed with Gort. He asked how Hore-Belisha had stood up to the trip. I told him very well indeed, and added that I thought his discussions with Gort had been useful. Ironside retorted, 'Coffee-housing, I suppose.'

Next morning (20th November) I went to the British Embassy to collect Hore-Belisha. I was shown into his bedroom and there I found him half-dressed, sitting at his dressing-table. I went over the points he wished to take up with Gamelin that morning—the number of British divisions to be sent to France, the reorganization of divisions, the arrangements for air support of the advance into Belgium, the construction of pill-boxes. I felt very much that these —apart perhaps from the first—were strictly military matters, un- suitable for discussion by a Minister, and that Gamelin could hardly fail to be amused by British methods of dealing with technical military matters.

At Gamelin's request, the interview was strictly *tête-à-tête*, and I was therefore not present. After luncheon we flew home, and landed at Hendon at 3.30 p.m.

6

EUROPE AND THE MIDDLE EAST

1939

On 23rd November Pownall came over to London, and I had a long discussion with him about the plans for the B.E.F. I told him that I had been astonished and disappointed by our easy acceptance of the plan for the advance into Belgium. Nothing had been co-ordinated with the Belgians, and, as things stood, we could not expect their army to put up an effective resistance. Now that the plan for the forward move had been accepted, I added, we should at least enlist the support of our heavy bombers; but this had not been done, nor had any arrangements been made to secure increased fighter support. Pownall replied, 'If Georges orders an advance, how can the B.E.F. stand out and refuse to take its part?' But he agreed that we should continue to press for increased air support.

On 3rd December I had a long talk with Ironside after dinner in the Club. He had just returned from France, where he had been investigating the criticisms of the defences which Hore-Belisha had made in the Cabinet after his visit to the B.E.F., as well as further criticisms by Dominion Ministers who had also made a tour of the front. Ironside said that Gort had been especially angered by a message Hore-Belisha had sent him, to say the Prime Minister was very dissatisfied with the defensive measures taken in the B.E.F. and with the shortage of pill-boxes. 'Now that I have seen the defences myself,' said Ironside, 'I intend to tell the Cabinet quite straight that Hore-Belisha is wrong. I think he'll have to go. It is time we had a better chap in the War Office.' He said he had seen Hore-Belisha since his return and told him that he intended to report to the Cabinet that the front was in good order, despite the criticisms Ministers had heard. To this Hore-Belisha had agreed 'without a murmur', although he had been very much upset and had said he had made it clear that he cast no aspersions on Gort.

On the afternoon of 8th December, Wavell, who had flown home from Cairo, came to the War Office to discuss strategy in the Middle East with Ironside. As we were beginning to talk, Hore-Belisha sent a message to Ironside that he would like to see him. Ironside sent a reply that this would be inconvenient, because he was holding a military conference and could not be interrupted; but if Hore-Belisha cared to come to the conference, he would be pleased to see him. Hore-Belisha strolled in a few minutes later, and took a seat at the table.

Ironside explained that pressure was being put upon him by the French to reinforce France, but that his feeling was that the Middle East should be stronger than it was. The Middle East was the centre of the world and the Empire. It had now become necessary to clear up the French attitude. They were advocating a forward policy in the Balkans. But they could not have it both ways. We should not reinforce France if the French meant to transfer troops from France to the Middle East. That would mean that their strategy, which would not be our strategy, would become predominant there, and this in an area that was ours.

'If we let a Frenchman go and talk to the Balkan States, it will be done in a way to suit the French and not us. We ought to do it in such a way that the French do not take charge. This is our beat. In the last war the French did not do things in a way to suit us.'

At this point Wavell intervened, and said: 'I don't agree. I am afraid we have got to win this war as best we may. I don't care who does it.'

Wavell went on to say that he did not believe the Germans would attack in the West. They had nothing to gain by butting their noses into the defences in France. The East was the soft spot for them. If they went East, they would get oil and corn. The Russians might not like it, but they could not stop it. The danger would come in the spring. It was essential that we should be stronger in the Middle East. Weygand's optimum plan was to hold a line across Jugoslavia and Rumania. This we could hardly do. But, if we were to cut the German communications through Jugoslavia and put forces into Thrace and Salonika, we could safeguard our interests. We should not let the Turk fall down or run out.

To this Ironside replied: '*Tout le monde est égoiste*. The Turk will see that it is to his own interest to fight against Germany and Russia.'

Wavell answered, '*Tout le monde est égoiste*, and the Turk will see it is in his own interest to make the best terms he can.'

Ironside went on: 'We must not have an administrative disaster—nothing like Mesopotamia or Gallipoli or Tanga. Salonika was nearly a disaster, too—I cannot understand why it was not. But we must realize that the Turk may run out. Then Italy would come in against us to get her share of the spoil. The whole world would be against us. Therefore we must be strong in the Middle East in any case. We may have to fight in Syria or in Palestine. We could cripple the Germans by blowing up the Taurus tunnel.'

Then he returned to his point that we could not build up forces both in France and in the Middle East—the French appeared to have done a *volte face* and we must get out of them what they really meant. He added that the Cabinet had just received a telegram from France to say that Gamelin had far-reaching proposals to put before them. It was now necessary to find out what these were, and thrash out the whole business in the Supreme War Council.

Hore-Belisha took little part in the discussion, beyond remarking that the Germans might not come beyond Rumania, since they could get their oil and grain there.

The Chiefs of Staff and Wavell were to go over to Paris on 10th December to discuss Weygand's[1] plan for the Balkans, and I was to go with them. The day before we went, Hore-Belisha sent for me and asked if we were likely to see Gort in Paris. I said I thought not. But Hore-Belisha thought I might have a chance of getting a message to Gort, and he spoke at some length about the situation that had arisen as a result of his criticism of the defences of the B.E.F. He said he understood that Gort was angry, and that it seemed very unnecessary that the matter should be talked about by the whole Army as it had been. 'After all,' he said, 'if that line were broken by the Boche, I am the man they would blame. They would ask why I had not pushed on the construction of the defences. It is always the Minister they go for. Now, if Stanhope had still been at the Admiralty instead of Winston, he would have been sacked when that submarine got into Scapa and torpedoed the *Royal Oak*—although probably he would never have heard of the defence plan. Gort owes a tremendous lot to me,' he went on, 'I have done more for him than anyone. He is an ambitious man, too. I am only out to help him. I wanted to get him his pill-boxes and to get them as fast as possible.'

I promised that, if there were an opportunity, I would give Gort his assurance that he wanted to help him. But I felt—although I

[1] General Maxime Weygand was then Commander of the French Forces in the Near East.

could hardly say so—that it would be impossible to overcome the weight of prejudice against Hore-Belisha.

On 10th December, before taking off for Paris, I lunched with Ironside at the Club. He went over the points of the pill-box business, and told me Gort was furious, not only at the criticism of his defensive arrangements, but even more so because of the way in which the criticism had been made—not to him direct, but to the Army Council and the Cabinet in the absence of the C.I.G.S. Gort had become quite convinced that Hore-Belisha was trying to unseat him. Hore-Belisha had misunderstood what Gamelin had said to him about the time it took to build a pill-box—Hore-Belisha had thought he said three days, whereas Gamelin had said three weeks. 'I said to him,' Ironside continued, 'that he could not speak French well enough for military discussions. I told him that his French was Le Touquet French—all right for talking to Mademoiselle X on the *plage*, but no good for military conversations. Hore-Belisha said I could not be really serious, and I said, "Yes, I am." What he was really after was a Belisha Line joining up with the Maginot Line.'

Next morning in Paris we drove out to Gamelin's headquarters. We assembled in a mediaeval hall, on the walls of which hung a number of hideous and incongruous modern paintings. Among the French officers were Gamelin, Darlan, Weygand, Vuillemin (Chief of the Air Staff) and Lelong (Military Attaché in London). Our party consisted of Ironside, Pound, Newall, Wavell, Ismay, Howard-Vyse and myself.

I was especially interested to see Weygand for the first time—he was such a romantic and remarkable figure. But he looked old, and yellow, and unhappy. He spoke forcefully and with animation, and seemed a much more vivid character than Gamelin.

It was soon apparent that at this conference there would be no conflict of views. We had been led by the French note to expect them to advocate a forward policy in the Balkans, and to present us with a definite project for an expedition early in 1940. We had sent Gamelin our views in writing before we came over, and no doubt these had been fully discussed by him and Weygand before our arrival. In any case, there was no apparent difference of opinion between them at the meeting, and the discussion turned mainly upon vague possibilities for the future.

It was agreed that nothing should be done that might antagonize Italy, or precipitate an extension of the war to the Balkans. It was also agreed that there should be no overt negotiations with Balkan powers and that, further, we should take no action in their territories without their invitation and consent. It was decided that we should make preparations and work out plans for operations in Turkey and the Balkans, so that there might be no repetition of the administrative disasters we had experienced in the previous war. It was also decided that we should go into the possibilities of providing arms and equipment for possible allies in that part of the world.

Weygand took the line that the time might come when we would be forced to intervene in the Balkans. He agreed that there must be adequate preparation. He advocated secret diplomatic negotiations, despatch of equipment and administrative planning. He felt that a virile decision to act would produce a remarkable effect in the Balkan countries. He deprecated any attempt to get Italy to agree to our preparations, and said such an attempt could be likened to two soldiers who wanted to fight a duel—if they asked their colonel for permission, it would certainly not be given. As to lack of resources, he said, you could never have all you wanted in war.

Wavell was in full agreement with Weygand, but went further, saying that he felt it to be practically certain that we would be called upon to defend our interests in the Balkans in 1940. When one started building up a defence in a hurry, it had to be done from the rear. Therefore, we should start by getting the support of Turkey, and possibly by occupying Salonika. He felt that the Germans would attack the rear and the bases with air forces, and that, therefore, the first demand would be for fighter aircraft. He also explained that his forces were still immobile for lack of administrative services, and that they were particularly weak in artillery.

We broke up at twelve o'clock, had a quick luncheon, and then drove to Le Bourget, where we found that the engines of both our aircraft were out of order. We waited for some twenty minutes while the mechanics tinkered with them. Then Ironside said to Pound, 'It is the function of commanders to make decisions. I think we ought to decide that this is not good enough and go back tomorrow.' So we drove back to the Meurice, and, after an excellent dinner, went to the Casino de Paris to see Maurice Chevalier and Josephine Baker.

Next morning, 12th December, we rose at six o'clock, and were back in London at ten, after a stormy and bumpy flight.

A week later I was nearly killed by Captain Cecil Harcourt,[1] of the Admiralty staff, when his motor-car knocked me down outside the Cabinet Offices, in St. James's Park, in the black-out. I was walk-

---

[1] Afterwards Admiral Sir Cecil Harcourt; then Director of the Operations Division in the Admiralty.

ing up the white line in the middle of the road, thinking I was on the pavement, so it was my fault, not his. I had no recollection of being hit by the motor; and the next thing I knew I was lying on a stretcher in the Westminster Hospital.

A surgeon told me that I would have to be sewn up; but that first I must see a man from Scotland Yard because the War Office feared I might have been knocked on the head by someone who wanted to rob me of secret papers. A detective walked in and, bending low over me, he said, 'My name is Inspector Ferret.' Dazed as I was, his name struck me as delightfully appropriate. I assured him I had left my papers in the Cabinet Room, and was then wheeled off to the operating theatre.

The wags in the War Office said that Harcourt had run me over because of a difference of opinion between the War Office and the Admiralty over one of our plans. He sent me such a beautiful bunch of grapes that I bore him no grudge; indeed, I felt deeply grateful to him: for, after the life I had led in the War Office, four weeks in bed being dosed with bromide seemed an interlude of bliss. At the end of that time I found I had forgotten how to walk; and I spent another week in the hospital learning that art afresh, in company with Lord Lucan, aged 79, who was recovering from having fallen downstairs and broken a thigh. Two minute nurses supported us as we promenaded slowly up and down the corridor.

While I was in the Westminster Hospital, Hore-Belisha was superseded as Secretary of State for War. Ironside wrote to me, saying, 'Hore-Belisha's departure has raised a pall of discontent and we shall now get down to good work.'

Hore-Belisha also wrote to me in my hospital bed, 'I liked the Army, as you know, and tried to do something for it. I was working out plans for what it should be after the war. Never mind. It is all meant.' Eighteen months later I had a talk with him about the circumstances in which he went; I will record it in its proper place.

7

A PLANNER AND HIS OWN PETARD

1940

THANKS to Captain Harcourt and his motor-car, I was now out of the high life of the war for the best part of a year, and happy to be free of it. By the middle of February I felt fit enough to work again. I was passed by a rather perfunctory medical board, and had no after-effects from Harcourt, apart from occasional dizziness, which wore off after a year or so.

The night he knocked me down—and I still concede that it was my fault—I had been working in the Joint Planning Committee on a paper about possible military intervention by the French and ourselves in Scandinavia.[1] It was based on the assumption that the Germans might try to occupy Scandinavia, and that Norway and Sweden might call on us for help.

On 23rd February, Major-General P. J. Mackesy wrote to me saying that he had asked Ironside to appoint me to his staff; and I went to London to find out what the job was. I found that our hypothetical plan had become a reality, and that I was mooted as Chief of Staff to a combined Franco-British expedition to Narvik under Mackesy's command. I wrote to Mackesy, and said I would be delighted to come.

Ever since September 1939, Churchill had been prodding in vain for a decision to mine Norwegian territorial waters. The Cabinet had refused to act, partly on moral grounds and partly from reluctance to shock world opinion; but even on strictly military grounds it would have been a dubious undertaking. If the Germans should occupy Norway as a result, we would be worse off than before; and such mining would therefore only be effective if we first occupied the west coast Norwegian ports. But the matter was reviewed from time to time; and on 5th February, 1940, at a meeting of the Supreme

[1] See Official History, *Grand Strategy*, Vol. II, pp. 98, 99.

War Council in Paris, the project took a step forward. It was decided to ask the agreement of Norway and Sweden to a plan whereby we would send three or four divisions to occupy Narvik, reinforce the Finns, and, incidentally, get control of the Gellivare ore-field at the head of the Gulf of Bothnia. We had gone beyond the point of waiting for a Scandinavian invitation to intervene.

It was this project which had now come to the boil. The Narvik landing was to be carried out on 16th March, which was in three weeks' time. In addition to the Gellivare ore-field, where the plant was to be destroyed, Trondheim, Bergen and Stavanger were all to be captured. Pressure was to be put on Norway and Sweden to allow us to pass through their territory; and they were to be offered an additional four divisions or so to help protect southern Scandinavia if the Germans reacted violently, as they probably would.

Mackesy rang me up when he got my letter, and I went up to Yorkshire for twenty-four hours, to meet his commanders and staff and discuss the operation. 'Force Avonmouth', as his little army had been christened, was to consist initially of two British Brigades and a French Chasseurs Alpins Brigade, plus supporting units: about 20,000 men in all. Mackesy had hitherto been command-ing the 49th Division, and was going to use its headquarters as H.Q. Force Avonmouth.

I could hardly believe that the scheme was likely to come off, but we had to work on the assumption that it would, and I put in a fortnight's hard labour in London. On 11th March the whole affair suddenly looked more realistic. I had been lunching with Hugh Smith, who had been living in Narvik since the beginning of the war, and pumping him about the place. When I got back to the War Office, I was summoned to the Chiefs of Staff; and found them already in session.

Admiral Evans[1] was sitting with them, and was holding forth with immense enthusiasm when I went in. I had never seen him before. He looked very young, and he impressed me at once as a keen and daring officer. He knew Norway well; his wife was Norwegian, and he spoke the language. He was convinced that the Norwegians loathed the Germans and would not oppose us; he was certain he could put the Army ashore. He thought the plans as they stood were half-hearted, and was pressing a more dashing—and, as it seemed to me, sounder—plan of his own. As we broke up the meeting, after a long discussion, Pound said, 'I might let Evans

[1] Admiral Sir E. R. G. R. Evans ('Evans of the *Broke*', later Lord Mountevans) had retired from the Royal Navy in 1939, and was Regional Commissioner for London.

47

hoist his flag for this show.' Ironside, who had been almost as keen as Evans in discussion, said that the Army would welcome him.

But the meeting was far from unanimous. As we walked out, Newall said to me, 'I think the whole thing is hare-brained.' Ismay agreed with him. So did I. But I was no longer a back-room boy: I was taking part in the operation, and I did not think it seemly to express my doubts.

The weakest point of the plan was its dependence on Swedish agreement. The Swedes had only to cut off the electric current to bring the railway to a standstill, and the railway was the only means of getting into Sweden; there was no road from Narvik into Sweden, and the nearest was 150 miles east of the frontier. There was a good chance of seizing Narvik, and reaching the Swedish frontier, only 25 miles farther on, by a mixture of bluff, speed and persuasion; but beyond that point the prospects of a further advance were poor. I had no idea at this moment how the Foreign Office was proposing to cope with Norwegian or Swedish intransigence. Their ideas would have to be incorporated into the Cabinet's instructions to Mackesy. Before dining at the United Service Club, I roughed out a draft of what I thought they ought to be; and after dinner I walked back through the black-out with Ironside to the War Office, and discussed my draft with him until 10 p.m.

Mackesy and I met Ironside in his room at the War Office at 3 p.m. on 12th March. His opening words were: 'You don't know how unsatisfactory the Cabinet meeting was this morning. I can't tell you how disappointed I am. They want to cut out the whole thing, except possibly Narvik; or at any rate to postpone the southern landings until we see how Narvik goes.' The Prime Minister wanted to see the General and the Admiral, and we were all to go with him to No. 10 at 6.30 p.m.

We then spent some time going over the draft instructions to the Force Commander which I had written in the Club the day before. Ironside inserted a paragraph to say that I was to take over if anything should happen to Mackesy; he was not prepared to accept a French replacement when the headquarters set-up was British, and said he would write to Gamelin to that effect. He also asked us to draft a set of instructions for platoon commanders, exhorting them to use bluff and good-humoured determination as a substitute for force. If force had to be used, it must be the minimum necessary for the safety of the troops. If we could not make our way through Norway and Sweden without fighting, then the whole business would be called off.

At 6.30 p.m. Mackesy and I walked over to Downing Street. The Prime Minister was at Buckingham Palace, but the front hall was full of people waiting for the meeting—Chatfield, Hankey, Newall, Pound, Evans, Bridges and Ismay. Mackesy and I scribbled the finishing touches to our platoon commanders' instructions, to the effect that friendliness should be met with friendliness. Then we all chatted until the Prime Minister arrived, with Lord Halifax and Sir Horace Wilson.

The meeting began with Evans giving an enthusiastic exposé of the whole plan, with all its details. The Prime Minister looked tired and lugubrious enough when he began; but as Evans warmed to his subject, Mr. Chamberlain looked more and more horrified. Halifax listened in grave silence. The draft instructions to the platoon commanders were passed; they were hedged about with a great many provisos, and were based 'on the same principles as those which apply to military action in aid of the civil power': this phrase has an evil connotation in the Army, since it is popularly interpreted as 'whatever you do, you'll be wrong.'

We then went on to the instructions for the Force Commander. By the time these had come through the mangle they were extremely detailed, and gave the commander little discretion. They set out the tasks with clarity, but included such phrases as these:

> 'It is the intention of H.M.G. that your force should land provided it can do so without serious fighting. . . . Fire upon Norwegian or Swedish troops is only to be opened as a last resort. Subject to this you are given discretion to use such force as may be required to ensure the safety of your command. . . .
>
> It is not the intention of the Government that the force should fight its way through either Norway or Sweden. None the less, should you find your way barred by Swedish forces you should demand passage from the Swedish Commander with the utmost energy. . . .
>
> The decision as to the size of the force to assist the Finns and the time for its despatch is left to your discretion. It is important that the force to assist the Finns should be despatched as soon as possible.'

Ironside said the troops would get into the first train and go up the line. The important thing was to get hold of the railway quickly. Mackesy said that he proposed to go up to the frontier in person to demand passage. The Prime Minister asked what he would do if the way was barred. Mackesy explained that if he could not get through without fighting he would call it off. Ironside intervened to say that the Government would of course be in the hands of the general.

Then Lord Halifax said, 'Well, if we can't get in except at the cost of a lot of Norwegian lives, I am not for it—ore or no ore.' The meeting came to an end. The Prime Minister shook hands with us as we filed out of the room, saying, 'Good-bye, and good luck to you—if you go.'

Once again we resorted to betting, as we had on the day war broke out: this time at least we were not Sabbath-breaking. Bridges said he thought the chances were against it; Newall was laying three to one against; Mackesy a hundred. There were no takers, as usual.

This meeting was on 12th March, and we were due to join Evans in the *Aurora* in the Clyde on the 15th. The 13th was a very odd day. All day long I was putting the finishing touches to our orders, down to the minutest detail, while the news coming in from Finland about an impending peace with Russia made the expedition more and more unlikely. Ismay agreed to tackle the Prime Minister and persuade him that he must make up his mind: the ships were loaded, the troops were moving, and a decision was overdue. In the end, the thing fizzled out like a guttering candle: first all troop movements were stopped; then we were reduced to 48 hours' notice; finally the whole project was cancelled. Mackesy and I dined together flatly in an atmosphere of anti-climax at the Carlton Grill.

I slept at the Club, and next morning met Ironside at breakfast. I remarked, rather obviously, that it was odd to think that 48 hours earlier I had been rounding off the orders for landing at Narvik. He held up his hands in a characteristic gesture, and exclaimed, 'You know it wasn't my fault we took so long to make up our minds. We need more drive at the top.'

To add to the bathos, General Audet, with the French advance party, arrived that morning. We talked with him and his staff in the War Office, and then gave them luncheon at the Carlton Hotel. They gave me a message, for what it was worth, that Gamelin was 'charmed' that I should be Mackesy's nominated successor.

Next morning we should have been slipping down the Clyde in the *Aurora*. Instead I was digging my garden. I am not at all sure that I wasn't better employed.

This may well seem to be a long story for an operation which never came off. But it was important to me for several reasons. I was, for once, personally involved, instead of being only academically concerned in the chambers of the War Office; and the more so because, if anything went wrong, the command was to devolve on me. I learned how extremely difficult it is to say 'No' when such a stand might be construed as a confession that one's heart is not in one's job. I learned how futile the waging of war becomes when the higher command refuses to grasp the nettle and delegate command to chosen subordinates. I learned afresh the dangers of hesitation when embarking on a course whose only hope of success is to be bold. We know now that the plan would have been anticipated anyway; but our own assault on Scandinavia might have had a better chance of success if we had not been guilty of letting 'I dare not' wait upon 'I would'.

For me, as a staff officer concerned with plans, this experience of being planned for was probably both salutary and useful.

8

FRANCE FALLS

1940

In May Dill relieved Ironside as C.I.G.S. I had come to
know them both extremely well for an officer much junior to
them, and been admitted to their confidence to a degree which
I had no right to expect. I served under Dill for much longer,
and on more intimate terms, than under Ironside. I admired the
latter immensely. The post of C.I.G.S. was uncongenial to him, and
he made no secret of the fact. But during those bogus months
between September 1939 and May 1940, he had injected into our
preparations for war a virility and imagination and forcefulness
which would have been lacking in Whitehall but for his presence.
'His presence' may be the *mot juste*: he was powerful and impressive
in physique, compelling in counsel, devastating in criticism. He
had a more varied experience of the continental armies of Europe
than his contemporaries; he had made full use of his great powers
as a linguist.

But at the time of this change of office I had been out of the
War Office for more than three months; and on 3rd April, 1940,
I was appointed to Major-General James Drew's 52nd Scottish
Lowland Division, to command the artillery. I was delighted to
revert to my proper trade as a gunner, especially among my own
compatriots. When I joined the division at Melrose, it was on the
move to Dorset; and within a few days our headquarters were
established in Sherborne Castle. Our troops were mostly Territorials, good keen men, but undertrained and short of equipment. We
lay in Dorset all through April and May, training hard, and ranging far and wide in our exercises over the peaceful and lovely
Wessex countryside.

Nobody knew what the division's overseas destination might
be; but when the Germans occupied Norway on 9th April it looked

as though we might go there. I lectured my officers on the kind of fighting we might have to do, basing my talks partly on my recollections of the country round Trondheim, where I had once fished the Stoerdal for salmon, and partly on the studies I had made for the Narvik operation. The possibilities of Norway quickly faded, and the Middle East looked more likely; so I scrapped my Norwegian series, and subjected my officers instead to a new lot of lectures on the Middle East, based on my year's service in Egypt in 1937. Nothing came of this either; and their polite attention to what I had to say was ill-rewarded: indeed, it was not rewarded at all.

When the Germans invaded the Low Countries on 10th May, the day Churchill became Prime Minister, we felt that our destination was becoming clear at last. But we were still short of equipment, and had never yet fired live shell. The campaign was quickly over, and we were still out of the hunt; but suddenly, on 4th June, the last day of the Dunkirk evacuation, the Division was ordered to France. I surrendered two of my three field regiments in exchange for two from another Division which had finished their training, made up their equipment by shamelessly despoiling the two regiments I was leaving behind, and concentrated at Aldershot. On 9th June we began to embark at Southampton.

At Aldershot and in London we met many of the officers of the B.E.F. who had been taken off the beaches at Dunkirk. They were unanimous in their opinion that the French Army was finished and would not fight; they all thought that the despatch of more British troops to France was a mistake. We found it hard to believe that this was true.[1] We felt that there was plenty of room between Paris and the Pyrenees to carry out a fighting retreat and establish a line of defence. In fact we continued to be optimistic and confident until we had arrived in France, and had seen the situation with our own eyes.

Drew asked me to accompany him with the headquarters of the Division. So, having seen the movements of my regiments under way, I arranged to meet him at Southampton. I arrived there at about one o'clock on 10th June, and found that we were to take passage in a little Dutch boat, *Batavier IV*, which lay alongside one of the jetties. Our party was complete except for Drew, who had not put in an appearance. We waited for him until 2 p.m., and then the skipper came to me and said that, unless we pushed off at once, the gates of Cherbourg harbour would be shut, as they always were at dark, and we would not be able to land that day.

[1] But see the reaction of General Sir Alan Brooke—*The Turn of the Tide*, p. 159.

I agreed that we should go, but no sooner had we got into mid-stream than we saw Drew's car drive on to the jetty, and we went back to fetch him. He had had a puncture. We were now an hour late and consequently had to spend the night in the Channel. This did not matter much to us, but the Captain of our escorting des-troyer was anxious on account of submarines. The day was calm and sunny, and our passage uneventful. While at sea we picked up some wireless messages, one of which contained the information that the Germans were now on the Lower Seine, and another that Italy had entered the war.

Having spent the night cruising near the French coast, we landed at Cherbourg next morning, 11th June, at six o'clock We breakfasted with Colonel Gervase Thorpe, the Commandant of the port, who had come back from retirement, had dropped two ranks, and was enjoying himself hugely. Drew and I then set off by car for Le Mans, where the Division had been ordered to assemble. It was exhilarating to be in France again; I had never seen the country look lovelier. But soon we began to meet pathetic pro-cessions of refugees, some in motor-cars piled high with baggage, some in farm carts and wagons with their household goods stacked around them, many walking or riding bicycles—all making their way southward.

We lunched in a little restaurant at Vire, and arrived at Le Mans at about 5 p.m. There we met Major-General Philip de Fonblanque, the Commander of the British Lines of Communica-tion, and he explained the situation to us so far as he knew it. Sir Alan Brooke had been appointed British Commander-in-Chief, but he had not yet arrived. There was therefore no effective control.

The Germans were reported to be in Rouen, and to be across the Seine in some numbers between Louviers and Vernon. The 51st Highland Division had withdrawn to the Havre peninsula, which seemed a bad mistake. A large part of this Division had been cut off near Fécamp, but it was hoped that the remainder would be embarked at Le Havre.

That night, 11th June, we received a message from Weygand, which had been approved by the C.I.G.S., to the effect that we were to send our 157th Infantry Brigade, the only Brigade which had as yet arrived, to take up a position on the right of the French 10th Army at Conches. It was accordingly despatched with an Anti-tank Battery to support it.

Le Mans was crowded with French troops and refugees, but

we got rooms in the Hôtel de Paris, and went to bed in the dark, all lights having been extinguished because of an air-raid alarm.

Next morning, 12th June, as I was leaving the hotel to walk to de Fonblanque's headquarters, a nun came up to me, and asked if I could do anything to help her and her four companions who were standing in a group on the pavement nearby, surrounded by bundles containing their possessions. She said that she assumed we were on our way to the coast, and she asked if we could give them a lift. I explained we were going in the opposite direction but said I would ask de Fonblanque to do something for them. He found them a car later in the morning, gave them some money, and sent them down to Cherbourg. A few weeks later, when I was back in England, I received a letter from this nun, who was called Sister Ursula and signed herself 'Religieuse du Bon Secours de Troyes'. In this letter she enclosed a little illuminated medallion which was inscribed, '100 days indulgence each time'. I have never quite understood what this means, but I have kept the medallion as a souvenir of perhaps the only really useful thing I was able to do in the course of this excursion to France.

The news that morning was that the Germans were advancing southwest on Evreux, and that there was a gap twenty miles wide in the French line on our immediate front. It was still impossible to tell whether the Germans would continue to advance southwest, or wheel left and eastward to encircle Paris.

We were sitting in the officers' mess, talking, when a dishevelled young officer rushed in, and reported to de Fonblanque that he had just come from the front of the 10th Army; that there was an enormous gap in the line; and that the Germans were pouring through it towards Le Mans. De Fonblanque fixed him sternly with his eye, and said, 'And is it the custom in your regiment, may I ask, to come into the officers' mess with your cap on?'

A little later, Colonel Swayne,[1] the British liaison officer with Weygand's headquarters, arrived with an order from Weygand, directing that the 52nd Division should be put into the line by Brigades as they arrived. It was highly unsatisfactory that the Division should not be kept together, but the situation seemed to be desperate, and we were told that General Dill had agreed.

Drew and I motored in the afternoon to Orbec, and there we saw General Marshall-Cornwall[2] and General Altmayer, the

[1] Later Lieut.-General Sir John Swayne.
[2] Lieutenant-General (afterwards General Sir James) Marshall-Cornwall was on a special mission to the French Army.

Commander of the French 10th Army. We met streams of refugees and French soldiers on the roads, and it seemed clear that the situation was getting out of hand. The French soldiers were all stragglers; we asked some of them where they were going; they said they were lost, and that they were returning to their depôts. General Altmayer's staff were busy issuing operation orders, but we got the impression that these bore little relation to the facts of the situation—no doubt they were intended *pour l'histoire*. We completed our tour; and when we got back to Le Mans in the evening we visited the advance parties of our units, who were beginning to arrive in the concentration area a few miles outside the town.

On the next day, 13th June, General Brooke arrived. He was cheerful and full of vigour. He said that he intended to go to see Weygand at once, and he was anxious to get the British troops concentrated under his hand, so that they might be more easily deployed for a counter-attack, or embarked, as might be necessary.

I ordered my 71st Field Regiment up to support the 157th Infantry Brigade at Conches, selecting a route well to the west, because the Brigade was on the exposed right flank of the French 10th Army.

Next morning, 14th June, we heard a wireless announcement of the fall of Paris. The effect on the citizens of Le Mans was nothing short of stunning; and it must have revealed to the refugees, at last, that the French Army was a broken reed and their own flight useless.

Brooke returned from Weygand's headquarters in the afternoon. He telephoned immediately to London and gave Dill his opinion that it was urgent to withdraw the British forces if they were to be saved. While he was thus engaged, Drew and I sat under an apple tree in the garden and discussed possible methods of evacuating our troops.[1] The Division of that time was not provided with enough motor transport to carry all the men; therefore the infantry battalions and some other units always marched. We were 160 miles from the sea at Cherbourg, and it seemed fairly obvious that

[1] We did not realize that in the course of Brooke's conversation with the C.I.G.S., he found himself suddenly switched on to no less a person than the Prime Minister; nor did we appreciate, as we sat talking under our apple tree, that we were under his eye. When Brooke's telephone conversation was finished, and he summoned Drew, he never allowed us to know that the Prime Minister's conversation had been 'so infuriating that I was repeatedly on the verge of losing my temper. Fortunately, while I was talking to him I was looking through the window at Drew and Kennedy sitting on a garden seat under a tree. Their presence there acted as a continual reminder of the human element of the 52nd Division and of the unwarrantable decision, afterwards rescinded, to sacrifice them with no attainable object in view.' *The Turn of the Tide*, p. 173.

we should have to move quickly if we were to avoid being cut off. I therefore suggested that we should jettison ammunition, pontoons and other equipment, and put the men in the motor lorries which had been carrying them. If this were done the move to Cherbourg could be accomplished in one day. We also studied our maps and selected roads by which to advance to the 10th Army front in case the orders from London were to fight on.

Brooke soon sent for Drew, and told him that evacuation was to be carried out as quickly as possible. But the Brigade and supporting artillery in the line were to be left there for the moment, in order to avoid giving the French the impression that we were deserting them prematurely. Drew asked me to go at once to Cherbourg, to select a rearguard position to cover embarkation, and to dispose the Division upon it when it arrived. He intended to follow later. I made a quick plan from the map, and chose Tollevast Château as the place for our headquarters. Having explained the probable dispositions to the Brigadiers and Commanding Officers, I told them to come to me for orders at Tollevast when they arrived, and then, at 9 p.m., started to motor to Cherbourg, with my brigade major and staff captain. We drove all night and arrived at 5 a.m. on the 15th June. The drive was uneventful except for occasional delays to cross roads which were full of refugees; we also had to stop for a few moments to change cars when mine charged an unlighted road-block, head on, at about one o'clock in the morning. Luckily I had brought a spare car in case of accidents.

I went first to see Thorpe, roused him out of bed, and gave him the first news of the impending evacuations. I then had a look at the position I had selected from the map as a possible line on which to fight a rearguard action. It seemed quite suitable, but, before reconnoitring it in detail, I went into a field and lay on the grass under the hedge for an hour and tried to sleep, for I was very tired. But it was a bright sunny morning, and too hot to sleep.

By noon I had finished my reconnaissance of the position. Soon afterwards the Division began to arrive and, by the evening, the troops were in bivouac in their sectors for defence. The owner of Tollevast Château made us welcome to the spare rooms in his house and to some farm buildings in which we billeted our headquarters staff.

We began our embarkation on 16th June. Drew, who had now arrived, asked me to go over to England and take charge of the concentration of the Division as it disembarked. I accordingly went aboard the *Princess Astrid*, and sailed at 9 p.m. There had been no signs of Germans during the day, except for two small air raids. Luckily for us the German plan was to swing towards Paris, and no attempt was made to cut us off from the Channel ports.

Next morning, 17th June, we reached Southampton, and I disembarked my car, which I had brought with me, and drove up to London. I looked in at the War Office to tell Dill the latest news. He had just received a report that the French had entered into negotiations for an armistice. He took me to see Eden, who was then Secretary of State for War, and we discussed the situation. We felt that, all things considered, we might well congratulate ourselves on having got out of France without heavier losses, and that, if only the French Navy and Air Force would fight on from Africa, we would still have a good deal to be thankful for. In the afternoon of 17th June I motored down to Cambridge, where the Division was to be concentrated. I was given a delightful room in King's College, overlooking the river.

The Division duly arrived in good order, and settled down in Cambridge and in the neighbouring villages. Drew and I spent some days motoring round the Norfolk coast between King's Lynn and Cromer, and had a look at it from the point of view of meeting a German landing. This was rather a curious experience for me. I had often shot wild geese here, and watched birds, and sailed a boat, but never before had I thought of Norfolk as a possible battlefield. In the evenings we dined with the dons, and enjoyed their delicious wine and especially their excellent Château Yquem, which they drank instead of port when the weather was hot. The dons did not regard the war as a serious business, or as an interesting subject of conversation; and that was most refreshing.

9

DIRECTOR OF MILITARY OPERATIONS

1940

On 27th June I was appointed Chief of Staff to General Hubert Hudleston, who was commanding in Northern Ireland. He was a wholly delightful man, and I enjoyed serving under him. Among other preoccupations we had to make plans against the event of a German landing in Southern Ireland. We had a liaison staff who visited Dublin from time to time, and conferred with senior Irish officers. De Valera's position was quite simple and quite clear: if the Germans invaded, he would like our help to drive them out again; if we anticipated them and moved in ourselves, he would fight us. And that was that.

On 9th October I received a telegram appointing me Director of Military Operations at the War Office. I was far from pleased with the prospect of returning to the War Office; I had always disliked it. Service in Whitehall, in war, as I knew full well, was even more disagreeable than in peace. I knew, too, that the D.M.O.'s post was hard and exacting. I should have much preferred to get command of a division, for which I was in the running. But it was some consolation that Dill was C.I.G.S.

My first night in London I slept at the Club, but not very soundly, for it was a night of heavy bombing. While I was at dinner, a bomb demolished the Carlton Club, two hundred yards away; the curtains over the empty window-frames of the dining-room bellied out, as it exploded, and my table was covered with dust. Later, as we sat drinking coffee in the smoking-room, another bomb fell in Waterloo Place; a shower of bricks and broken glass fell among us, and we were covered with soot and cinders from the fireplace. Then, as the electric light was out of action, and as there seemed to be no point in settling down again in the smoking-room, I got a candle and went up to bed. The crash and thud of bombs, and the banging of guns, went on through most of the night, and the walls of my bedroom sometimes shook unpleasantly. The scene from my window was lit up by a bright moon and parachute flares. I thought to myself that this was really too much; it was bad enough having to put up with the horrors of life in the War Office, without having the horrors of war as well. I had not heard such a din since the Battle of Passchendaele.

Next day I began work on my new job. I found I was expected to be available at the War Office not only all day, except for meals, but up till midnight or later. Dill had always worked too hard and too long; and this fault was to wear him down and, in the end, to wear him out altogether. His capacity for good work was impaired before the end of his time as C.I.G.S., and even at this period he was already showing signs of great fatigue. It was he who bore the brunt of Churchill's fury when the latter's multitudinous ideas and projects were opposed by the Chiefs of Staff. On one occasion, after a long argument about some especially unsound suggestion, Churchill accused him to his face of being 'the dead hand of inanition'. On another, the Prime Minister, watching the Chiefs of Staff as they filed out of his room after a midnight sitting, remarked to one of his entourage, 'I have to wage modern war with ancient weapons.'

To cope with this routine, I had a bed put into my night room in the basement of the War Office, where the staff, at that time, worked at night. After dinner I used to go back to this room, work for a few hours, have a talk with Dill as soon as possible after 10 p.m., and then sleep there. This system had at least two advantages—one could work for a time without the constant interruption that was unavoidable during the day, and one could sleep in peace without hearing the bombs. The War Office basement was not a safe place, for it had not been strengthened, and a bomb falling near it would probably have flooded it with water and sewage; but, after all, it was no worse than a bedroom in the Club. I also arranged to spend one day each week out of London—I usually motored to my house near Andover every Friday night, and back to the War Office early on Sunday morning. When I had returned on Sunday, Dill would go off to the country and return in the evening.

One of my first impressions of the War Office was that a heavy strain was being imposed upon the Chiefs of Staff by the Prime Minister's habits. He worked in bed in the morning, slept in the afternoon, kept the Chiefs of Staff up at night, and went off to the country for long week-ends. This system suited him, if nobody else; and it certainly enabled him to remain fresh. I soon discovered that he was interested in the minutest details of everything we did, and that he poured out floods of memoranda upon all problems, great and small. Much time had to be spent in answering them. His usual hour for meeting the Chiefs of Staff was 9.30 p.m., and he often kept them up until one or two in the morning. Further, he had collected around him a number of men who gave him independent advice, which we thought to be sometimes irresponsible and often unsound; and their ideas had to be discussed and debated. Everybody realized and appreciated Churchill's great qualities. But there were few who did not sometimes doubt whether these were adequate compensation for his methods of handling the war machine, and the immense additional effort they imposed upon the Service Staffs.

When the Italians invaded Greece on 28th October, I had my first experience of the Prime Minister's technique. He sent us a rapid succession of notes in which he directed us to transmit detailed instructions to Wavell about the defence of Crete. One of these notes specified the number of battalions which should constitute the garrison of the island. Dill asked me to draft a reply to this note. I said to him that I thought it quite wrong that the strength of the garrison should be a subject of correspondence between the Prime Minister and the C.I.G.S., that the responsibility lay with the Commanders-in-Chief in the Middle East, and that we should not interfere with them. Dill agreed to this and he then telephoned to the First Sea Lord and suggested that the Chiefs of Staff should meet immediately to consider Churchill's message. When they had sat for an hour, they invited him to join them. A telegram was then composed and despatched to the Commanders-in-Chief, in which their attention was drawn to the importance of securing Crete, but making it clear that the responsibility for determining the size of the garrison was theirs.

Churchill was keeping up constant pressure on the War Office to send more troops to the Middle East. We also wanted to send them, but we were very short of ships. About the middle of November Eden sent a note to the Prime Minister in which he set out very clearly how this shortage was causing the reinforcement of the Middle East to fall into arrears; and soon after this more were provided. Churchill insisted on seeing the loading tables of all the ships. These had been drawn up with infinite care and in consultation with the Commanders-in-Chief, but every item had to be explained and justified to him.

Our policy in the General Staff, at this period, was to build up our resources, of which we were painfully short, and to refrain from all operations which were not essential. We wished to do nothing that would postpone decisive action; we considered it rash to risk unnecessary reverses merely for the sake of doing something. Churchill, on the other hand, thirsted for action, and his head was full of projects that had no attraction for the Chiefs of Staff. He fretted at the delays which are inseparable from the preparation of modern fighting forces, and he pressed us incessantly to 'grapple with the enemy'. He did, however, realize, as he himself put it one day at a conference assembled to consider the allocation of equipment to our allies, that 'there were too many little pigs and not enough teats on the old sow'.

Somebody said that Churchill was exactly like the horse in Job. Indeed the description of the horse in Job is a much better description of Churchill than it is of any horse—

'He paweth in the valley, and rejoiceth in his strength: he goeth on to meet the armed men.

He mocketh at fear, and is not affrighted; neither turneth he back from the sword.

The quiver rattleth against him, the glittering spear and the shield.

He swalloweth the ground with fierceness and rage: neither believeth he that it is the sound of the trumpet.

He saith among the trumpets, Ha, ha; and he smelleth the battle afar off, the thunder of the captains, and the shouting.'

But there was one plan being hatched, with the full blessing of the Chiefs of Staff. This was for Wavell's attack upon the Italian Army in the Western Desert. The essence of this plan was secrecy. No letters or telegrams were exchanged on the subject. Wavell had told Eden about it during his visit to Egypt in October. No one else in London knew of it except the Prime Minister, the Chiefs of Staff, and myself.

Churchill discussed the forthcoming battle nearly every day. He magnified the possible results out of all proportion, and he wished to extend the scope of the operations. He refused to recognize the hard realities of the problem of supply in the desert. He urged that operations should be begun against Abyssinia from Kenya, regardless of the vast distances, and, when Dill argued against this, he remarked that the successes of the Greeks against the Italians were becoming positively embarrassing in face of our inaction.

Then, in the beginning of December, he was pressing hard for an operation against Pantellaria. In this he was strongly supported by Admiral of the Fleet Sir Roger Keyes, who had been brought in to organize landing operations. Night after night, for many months, the Prime Minister assembled the Chiefs of Staff to discuss this operation, which he christened 'Workshop'. Pound, the First Sea Lord, was dead against it, and he was supported in his opposition by Admiral Andrew Cunningham, Commander-in-Chief in the Mediterranean. It was by no means certain that we could succeed in seizing the island; its capture, moreover, would bring us no advantage, for the Italians had another equally good base in that region, in Sicily. It would be an embarrassment to the Navy to be saddled with the maintenance of a garrison in Pantellaria; Malta was as much as they could manage. Dill also opposed the idea; he felt we should not risk failure for so small a prize. But Churchill had set his mind on Pantellaria, and a vast amount of time and energy was wasted on it.

On 4th December, after a long meeting on the subject of Pantellaria, Dill returned to the War Office about midnight, and came to see me in my room. I had just got into bed and was nearly asleep. I saw that he was agitated. He said: 'I cannot tell you how angry the Prime Minister has made me. What he said about the Army tonight I can never forgive. He complained he could get nothing done by the Army. Then he said he wished he had Papagos to run it. He asked me to wait and have a drink with him after the meeting, but I refused and left Anthony there by himself.'

I tried to calm him down, but without much success. I pointed out that this kind of thing was nothing new, and reminded him that Sir William Robertson had had to go through much the same sort of experience with Lloyd George. The really important thing was not to give way, to be patient in developing our strategy, and to remember that we could not afford to make mistakes. It was a pity, but we could not help it, that the Prime Minister did not devote his energy to the things he could do so well—like pushing on the organization of our resources and industrial production, negotiating with the U.S.A., and so forth. At last Dill went off to bed and I to sleep.

Next morning Dill said he could not get over the Prime Minister's behaviour the night before; he was still angry. I said, 'Could you not tackle him in this sort of way? It would be great fun. Could you not say to him something like this: "If you would like to realize how I feel, just think how you would feel if I said to you that your letter to Roosevelt did not go nearly far enough. Why have you not got the U.S.A. in the war? Why have you not got Spain on our side? Why have you not got the Balkan states and Turkey in with us? And what about the Far East, and the attitude of Japan? Everything is wrong and you must push on faster. But I would not say such things to you, because I know that our diplomacy is suffering from lack of strength behind it. So do our operations. Our lack of strength compels us to go carefully in both —we cannot afford to make a false step. But we may make a false step if you keep up this pressure on the soldiers and especially on Wavell—it is just this sort of political pressure that led to such disasters as Kut and the first failure at Gaza in the last war. We cannot afford that sort of failure now." ' We both began to laugh. I added that he must remember that he was in a weaker position than any C.I.G.S. in the last war, in that he had no commander in the field, with any prestige, to back him. Wavell's opinion did not carry great weight, because no one knew yet whether he was any good or not. The Navy were better off than the Army in this respect, because they had Andrew Cunningham to reinforce the First Sea Lord's opinions. There was nothing for it but to be patient.

We then discussed the papers for the Chiefs of Staff meeting. Among these was a characteristic note from the Prime Minister in which he urged that we should coerce Eire by blockade.

I saw Gort occasionally during November. He was anxious to get his despatches published, but for the moment there were objections, on political grounds. One day he came to discuss with me a report he had written on a visit he had paid to Iceland. He had under his arm a copy of a book called *The Black Baroness*, by Dennis Wheatley. This he put on the table, under his hat, until we had finished talking about Iceland. Then he took it out and showed it to me. He was absolutely furious about two passages which he showed me, criticizing him for not having cut his way through to Amiens, and for leaving Dunkirk before the last troops. Dill, who had seen him the same day, remarked to me later that he was tremendously sorry for him—he was like a lost soul. He added that, if Hore-Belisha had not picked him out for promotion, he would by that time have been commanding an Army Corps and would have been well cast and quite contented. Now he was a most unhappy man.

Gort was such a splendid and upright character, with such magnificent qualities of leadership and courage, that everyone sympathized with his sense of frustration when he failed to get another command in the field after Dunkirk. It was now almost impossible to place an officer so senior as he had become; but when, later on, he went to Gibraltar and Malta, he threw himself heart and soul into these tasks, and revelled in being at the head of a beleaguered garrison. Later still, when he went to Palestine as High Commissioner, he was a dying man; but the old heroic virtues in him never diminished.

One day in December, when I was having a cup of tea with Dill in his room, he said to me, 'Come now, you are the Director of Military Operations: I should like you to write a paper for me on how to win the war,' to which I replied, 'There's no need to write a paper—I can tell you my opinion now. I am sure we can make a plan for not *losing* the war; but the only way to win it quickly is to get America in—we must concentrate on that.'

Although as yet we had no master plan for 'winning the war', we were even then, in December 1940, working on plans for the occupation of the African shore of the Mediterranean, and the eventual descent on the Normandy coast.

I often dined with Colonel Raymond Lee, the American Military Attaché; and we used to discuss the course the war might take, and the chances of America coming into it. Lee was a very charming and intelligent man and a good friend of ours, and he was inclined to take an optimistic and philosophical view of the prospects. One night he asked me if I had read Ernest Hemingway's *Death in the Afternoon*. He told me that, in this book, there was a very good description of bull-fighting. The principle underlying the fight was to wear the bull out gradually; every move was planned to prepare the bull for killing by inducing him to exhaust himself, and it was considered a bad mistake to try to deliver the *coup de grâce* too soon. The Germans, he argued, could be compared to the bull: if we left them alone, they would finally exhaust themselves by offensives, although they might drive us back at first even as far south as the Equator. Next day Lee sent me a copy of the book in which he had marked various passages, a few of which I reproduce here.

... The three phases of the bull's condition in the fight are called in Spanish, *levantado*, *parado*, and *aplomado*. He is called *levantado*, or lofty, when he first comes out. ...

... When the bull is *parado* he is slowed and at bay. ...

... It is when *aplomado* that the bull is usually killed; especially in the modern bullfight. The extent of his wearing out, of his heaviness and tiredness, depends upon the amount he has charged, and been punished, by the picadors, and the number of times he has followed the capes, the amount his vigour has been lessened by the banderillas, the effect that the matador's work with the *muleta* has had upon him.

. . . the bull arrives at the final stage of the fight with his great neck muscles fatigued so that he holds his head neither too high nor too low, his speed less than half what it was at the start of the fight, his attention fixed on the object that is presented to him, and any tendency to hooking to one side or the other, but especially with his right horn, corrected.

. . . A bull that has successfully charged the horses and has killed or wounded one or several of his opponents goes on to the rest of the fight believing that his charges lead to something, and if he continues to charge, he will get the horn into something again. . . .

. . . If a bullfighter goes in to kill a bull in his *querencia*, rather than to bring him out of it, he is almost certain to be gored. . . .

. . . and many men have paid with their lives, or with bad wounds, because they did not bring the bull out of his *querencia* before they went in to kill.

I wrote to Lee:

'If you regard Hitler as a bull, and this war as a bullfight, then I regard you as a man in the front row of the stalls with a machine-gun. I want you to press the button now and shoot the bull. Remember that there is no barricade in this fight as there is in a bull-ring. Moreover, the bull will *not* be readier for killing if he gets the present bullfighter down—far otherwise.'

IO

WAVELL'S RUN OF VICTORIES

1940-1

On 9th December Wavell opened his offensive against the Italians in the Western Desert. We all walked with a lighter step as the news of his successes came in. We were thankful to have, at last, one fine feat of arms to place to the credit of our soldiers, and one general to prove that we could still produce great leaders in the British Army.

Wavell sent us a copy of his own notes on the preparations for the battle, which he had written on 15th December, and which we read with admiration and gratitude. In them he described the original advance of the Italians, the defences which he had been able to raise against them with his meagre resources, and the all-important arrival of three armoured regiments as reinforcements at the end of September.

'About the middle of October' [he wrote], 'when the enemy had been stationary for a month and there seemed no probability of his further advance, I began to consider the possibility of an early offensive action. The enemy's defensive arrangements, which I studied daily on a map fixed to the wall facing my desk, seemed to me thoroughly faulty. He was spread over a wide front in a series of fortified camps, which were not mutually supporting and separated by wide distances.'

It was in these circumstances that the plan had been conceived. Wavell had asked General Wilson[1] to consider the possibility of an attack; General O'Connor—like Wilson an old friend of Wavell's—

---

[1] Wilson—afterwards Field Marshal Lord Wilson of Libya—had been one of Wavell's brigade commanders in the 2nd Division at Aldershot in 1936–37, and had succeeded him as G.O.C., 2nd Division.

had produced a plan of his own; and Wavell and Wilson, sharing the same house on Gezira Island in Cairo, had accepted and adopted it. Not more than half a dozen officers had been 'in the know'; nothing had been put on paper until 5th December, when the one and only written instruction had been given by Wilson to O'Connor; to the authorities at home there had been nothing but a single verbal communication to Eden in person while on his visit. The troops were rehearsed for the operation without even their higher commanders realizing the purport of the exercises. The result of all this was the classic victory of Sidi Barrani.

About a week before Wavell launched his attack, we had a bad scare about a leakage. Colonel Richard Meinertzhagen had sent me a message asking if he could come and see me about a matter of great urgency and importance. Meinertzhagen, an old friend of mine and also of Wavell's, had been an outstanding Intelligence officer in the First World War; some of his exploits are described in *The Seven Pillars of Wisdom*, and it was he who was responsible for the famous deception ruse which so misled the Turks before Allenby's thrust up the coastal plain of Palestine.

Meinertzhagen was now aged sixty-two, and was serving in the Home Guard somewhere in Mayfair. He reported to me that a certain Minister had been dining with his platoon the night before, and had told them openly that an attack was about to take place in the Western Desert. Meinertzhagen said that he was not concerned to know whether or not this was true; but he felt very strongly that a Minister who openly discussed forthcoming operations in public was unfit to hold office, and if necessary Meinertzhagen would have a question asked in the House. As I have said, not more than half a dozen people in London knew of O'Connor's impending attack, so my feelings on hearing Meinertzhagen's story can be better imagined than described.

I at once told Dill and Eden, and we made enquiries. It turned out that the Minister knew nothing of Wavell's plans, but, as he put it, 'he just wanted to buck them up, and felt, anyhow, that it was about time something happened'.

Lord Cavan, who was head of the Home Guard, sent for Meinertzhagen and asked if it were true that he had been to see the Director of Military Operations without the permission of his commanding officer. Meinertzhagen freely admitted having done so, saying that experience had taught him that the fewer people who knew about such things, the better. Cavan was extremely angry, and so was Meinertzhagen; and after some sharp exchanges, the conversation ended by Cavan announcing, 'You're sacked, sir.' 'I am not going to be spoken to like that by an Irish Field Marshal,' said Meinertzhagen, and left the room. He jumped into a taxi which was hit by a bomb on his way home, and when he emerged from semi-consciousness a week or so later, the battle was over.

By 13th December most of the Italian Army had been rounded up, and it was evident that our troops would cross the Egyptian frontier at Sollum within a few days. Eden was asked by the Prime Minister to discuss with him the possibilities of exploitation of our victory and, before going to see him, had a conversation with me on the subject. I had a note prepared for him, in which I made recommendations which we hoped would influence Mr. Churchill to discard some of the wilder schemes which I knew were bubbling in his brain. It was a long and closely reasoned minute, which it would be tedious to reproduce; but I give the final summary in full, as representing in dehydrated form our feelings about the Middle East at that important moment.

'Until the result of the present operations on Italian morale is clear, it would be premature to make detailed plans, but a general outline of the strategy to be adopted can be drawn up.

The liquidation of Libya and Italian East Africa will be of greater direct benefit to us than operations in other areas. It will free our communications with the Eastern Mediterranean and release forces for subsequent employment, if need arises, in Greece or Turkey.

Our policy in Libya should therefore be to seize every opportunity afforded by a weakening of Italian morale to press forward, but to be prepared, should resistance be met, to consolidate our gains and build up administrative facilities for a further offensive.

In Italian East Africa we should foster the rebellion by all possible means, including converging advances towards Lake Tana from the Sudan and from Kenya. Necessary preliminary operations will include the freeing of the railway at Kassala and an advance to the line Kolbio-Dif on the border of Italian Somaliland.

It would be courting an administrative disaster to send formations to fight in Albania.

Though the defence of Salonika is important, it would be dangerous to attempt it with less than 20 divisions, which cannot now be made available.

The attack on Pantellaria should be abandoned; the Special Service units and landing craft should be placed at the disposal of the Cs.-in-C. Mediterranean and Middle East for raids on Libya, Sicily and Italy.

Spain's attitude should now improve and therefore any operation against the Canaries might now be postponed.'

Two important points which were treated in detail in the body of this paper, but which got squeezed out of the summary, ought perhaps to be added. The first concerned Pantellaria. About this, we said that, now that a striking success had been won in Egypt, there was no longer the same need as had existed previously for a victory over the Italians merely as a matter of prestige. The second point was that the next few weeks after the victory of Sidi Barrani would show what was possible. If I were to try and recall our sentiments on these matters, I would say about Pantellaria that it would be a nuisance to take, an embarrassment to hold, and not awkward enough to the enemy to justify our trouble. The sudden reversal of our fortunes in the Middle East following the success of Sidi Barrani demanded a completely new reassessment of what we might achieve, in the light of our resources. We rejoiced in, and took heart from, Wavell's victories in the field; we addressed ourselves in the War Office to the problem of how we could help him to exploit them.

It was on the night of 28th December that the Germans made their big incendiary attack upon the City of London. The bombing started early in the evening; and when I walked over to the United Service Club to dinner, the streets were lit up by fires. A gas-main flaring outside the National Gallery illuminated Trafalgar Square. When I went back to the War Office I went up to the roof to watch that extraordinary scene. The whole horizon was aglow over the City, and the dome of St. Paul's was silhouetted against the sky. Next morning, when I went out to breakfast, many fires were still burning. The people of London had become hardened to bombing by this time, and, no matter how bad the night had been, life always went on more or less normally next day. I never ceased to marvel how the waitresses in the Club, and the clerks and messengers in Whitehall, stuck to their jobs and their routine with such wonderful spirit and phlegm. It was even more remarkable, perhaps, that the staff officers in the War Office, many of whom knew full well how grim the military situation was at that time, were always full of fun and confidence.

General de Gaulle came into my life for the first time on 31st December. Major-General E. L. Spears, who was attached to his headquarters as liaison officer, asked me to go and see him to discuss a proposal he had made to carry out a military excursion from Tibesti into Southern Libya. De Gaulle seemed a very dour person; but he was courteous and forthcoming in his description of his plans. He had big ideas about sending Free French Forces from Tibesti into Southern Libya, and he reckoned that there were no more than about 200 Vichy French to oppose them. Our own information was that the potential opposition amounted to something more like 2,000, and I told him so.

On 2nd January, 1941, I attended a luncheon party given by the Government for De Gaulle at Lancaster House. De Gaulle turned up very late, and, while we awaited his arrival, we learned why he had been delayed. A letter had come into his possession which seemed to indicate that Admiral Muselier, who had also been invited to the luncheon party, had betrayed secret plans, for the capture of Dakar, and De Gaulle had placed Muselier under arrest. De Gaulle turned up eventually and the luncheon went off quite well, but without Muselier. (A fortnight later the incriminating letter was found to have been a forgery, and Muselier was reinstated.)

I saw De Gaulle again on the 21st January when he and I dined with Spears in his room at the Ritz. Spears' wife, Mary Borden the writer, was also there; she told me that she was hoping to go to the Sudan and Abyssinia with an American ambulance. De Gaulle was very cheerful and agreeable, and the party was pleasant. De Gaulle and Spears never saw eye to eye; De Gaulle thought him too domineering to be a good liaison officer; he remarked to someone, about this time, that he sometimes did not quite know who was running the Free French movement, himself or Spears. I had to leave early, and, as Spears walked with me along the corridor to the lift, he remarked that De Gaulle was a very suspicious fellow, suspicious like a French peasant; that he did not know how to deal with affairs in London, and needed careful handling. This struck me as odd, because of the two men we had always regarded Spears as being much the more difficult; but he was shrewd and intelligent, his French was perfect, and, as I wrote in my diary at the time, it was a good thing for the Foreign Office to have a few people like him who could speak to them bluntly.

Military policy in the Middle East and the Balkans was our

main preoccupation throughout January and February. To those in the know, the German threat to Greece was already apparent, although their invasion did not begin for another three months. On the surface everything was splendid, for Wavell's offensive was in full swing. On 5th January the forces under his command took Bardia, with 2,000 officer prisoners and 40,000 other ranks. Within the next five weeks, Tobruk, Derna, Cyrene and Benghazi had all fallen; Haile Selassie had re-entered Abyssinia; and British troops had crossed the frontier into Somaliland. By 27th March both British and Italian Somaliland had been captured in their entirety, and Keren had fallen.

But during these very weeks of victory some rather sombre planning was going on. On 9th January, after a late meeting between the Chiefs of Staff and the Prime Minister, a telegram was sent to Wavell to say that the support of Greece was now to take precedence of all operations in the Middle East. I did not see this signal until the following morning, when I told Dill I did not like it much; and at mid-day we received Wavell's reply, in which he said that the new instructions filled him with dismay. After luncheon I went to see Dill. I said I felt strongly that we ought to push ahead as far as possible in Libya—even to Tunisia, if the Italians broke. If our luck held, we might find ourselves in a position where we could pass our convoys through the Mediterranean, with fighter cover from the African coast; this would have an incalculable effect, apart from all else, on the morale of our enemies. We had not enough troops for intervention in Greece. We had calculated that at least twenty divisions, plus a considerable air force, would be needed to hold Salonika alone. The Germans could overrun Greece with the utmost ease if they wanted to do so. They would then be in a position to inflict much damage on our shipping in the Mediterranean. We, on the other hand, would be able to afford almost complete protection to that same shipping if we could win the control of most of the African coast-line. This prize was infinitely the more desirable. And we stood to gain more by winning the African coast for ourselves than by denying Greece to the Germans. On this issue, we should resist political pressure for all we were worth.

I was in the country on the 11th, but, when I returned to London on the 12th, I had another long talk with Dill about the project for sending troops to southern Greece and to Salonika, which had continued to take more definite shape in the Defence Committee.

Eden had drafted a telegram, intended to 'stiffen' Jugoslavia, in which he said that our offer to Greece, of certain army units and of aircraft, showed 'our determination and ability to help our friends'. I remarked to Dill that this would be more correct if it read 'our determination in spite of our inability'. In the end, we cut out 'and ability'. This incident brought back to my mind a conversation I had had with Eden at a dinner-party at Lord Craigavon's house in Belfast when I was serving in Northern Ireland. Eden had said that it was very wrong not to have organized the Balkan front earlier. I said, 'No, they are such a poor lot that they would only add to our commitments, and we should gain nothing. They have no proper military equipment or aircraft. It is not a sound military proposition, and it could not be effective. It might be possible to get a political front, but never an effective military front.' He said, 'I agree, if you put it on that ground,' to which I answered: 'No other ground matters in war.'

On 16th January Wavell and Longmore, his Royal Air Force opposite number, reported, with obvious satisfaction, that the Greeks did not want our units for fear that their arrival might provoke the Germans to attack them. A meeting of the Chiefs of Staff was summoned to discuss this turn in the situation. Attlee was in the chair, the Prime Minister being away. A telegram was drafted for despatch to Wavell, to the effect that we realized we could not force our help upon the Greeks if they did not want it; and that, if the Germans did attack, it might well be more important, as well as more correct strategically, to help the Turks rather than the Greeks. With unjustified optimism, I wrote in my diary, 'We are getting back to a sounder basis after a dangerous excursion.'

Meanwhile minutes on every conceivable subject flowed from Mr. Churchill's office in a never-ending stream. His strategic imagination was inexhaustible; very many of his ideas seemed to us to be wild and impracticable. 'Workshop' (Pantellaria) was dormant for the moment, but Wavell's offensive had stimulated him to intense activity in exploring strategical possibilities in the Middle East.

When Wavell was about to open his offensive in the desert, the Prime Minister had cabled to him that his task was to 'rip the Italian Army from the African shores'. But no sooner had Wavell's troops reached the outskirts of Tobruk, than Churchill had begun to urge that his main effort should be diverted to Greece and the Balkans. When these directions were sent, I said to Dill that I should have liked to see his dissent recorded. 'But,' Dill replied, 'I do not dissent—I consider that the limitation placed upon the first reinforcements to be offered to the Greeks a sufficient safeguard.' This seemed to me dangerous; we were not strong enough at that time to risk a dissipation of forces. There was another fortuitous safeguard, at this time, in the shape of the Turkish as well as Greek refusal of our offers of help. Graziani, as we knew, had only five divisions left, and their morale was at a low ebb. There still seemed to be good chances of making a long advance in North Africa, and of wiping out the remnants of the Italian Army.

On the last day of January Churchill sent for Dill and rebuked him about a statement he was supposed to have made at a press conference on the previous day. The *Daily Herald* had reported him as saying that Wavell might take a short cut across the desert to Benghazi. This was an obvious course to take, if practicable, and everybody concerned had always eschewed speculating about it in public, Dill included. Duff Cooper, then Minister of Information, said that the press conference had been a great success; they had enjoyed having access to a 'technician' as opposed to a 'politician'. To this Churchill had rejoined, 'Of course starving mice appreciate a Stilton cheese when it is set before them.'

Dill had been suffering for weeks from a heavy cold, but he would not take a day off. One night, when we were having a talk in his room, he said, 'I often wonder if there is something wrong with us, that all these people hate us—the Germans, the Italians, the Japs, the Russians and so many others.' We discussed the Prime Minister's methods of conducting the war and we agreed that his great qualities made up for the vast amount of work, often useless as we thought, which he imposed upon the staffs. Dill said that if he ever wrote his memoirs he would put him down as the greatest leader we could possibly have had, but certainly no one could describe him as the greatest strategist.

On 11th February Greece was still refusing our offer to send a few military units. In the General Staff we thought we were well out of it, but Churchill now returned to the charge. He urged that Turkey should be pressed to show her hand and not wait until it was too late. He also pressed again for assistance to Greece, and on a bigger scale. He put his idea into definite shape in a telegram to Wavell which suggested that he should make four Divisions available for Greece from the Middle East. Wavell in the meantime had telegraphed on 10th February to give us his views upon the possibility of a further advance into Tripoli.

'The extent of Italian defeat at Benghazi seems to me to make it possible that Tripoli might yield to small force if despatched without delay. I am working out the size of the force that would be required but hesitate to advance further in view of Balkan situation. But you may think the capture of Tripoli might have favourable effect on attitude of French North Africa.

As you will realize a further advance would also involve naval and air commitments and we are already far stretched. The Navy would hate having to supply us at Tripoli and air force to protect us. On the other hand the occupation of this coast might be useful to both.

I will make plans for the capture of Sirte which must be the first step.

Please cable me your views as to effect on Weygand and war situation generally. Will probably go Cyrenaica on 12th or 13th Feb to discuss matter with Wilson.'

On the morning of the 11th February Dill told me that he had been warned to be ready to leave next day, with Eden, for Egypt, Turkey and Greece. But he felt his place was in London, and he intended to ask the Prime Minister to send me instead. The aeroplane would leave Plymouth on the following night for Gibraltar, would make Malta on the night of the 13th, be in Alexandria on the 14th, then to go on to Athens, Ankara and back to Cairo. I went out and bought a light suitcase and some thin clothes.

When Dill returned from a War Cabinet meeting after dinner, he said: 'I tried to get them to agree to letting you go, and I lost a lot of prestige in doing it, because they thought I didn't want to go. I *am* to go.' Later that evening he said, 'I gave it as my view that all the troops in the Middle East are fully employed, and that none are available for Greece. The Prime Minister lost his temper with me. I could see the blood coming up his great neck and his eyes began to flash. He said: "What you need out there is a Court Martial and a firing squad. Wavell has 300,000 men, etc., etc." I should have said, Whom do you want to shoot exactly? but I did not think of it till afterwards.'

On the day of his departure I had a long talk with Dill. It seemed to both of us that the British Government was now trying to force an unsound policy down Wavell's throat, and down the throats of the Greeks and Turks. We felt that it would be playing into the hands of the Germans to send our forces to the European side of the Mediterranean at this stage of the war, and that, if they were sent, they were certain to be annihilated or driven out again. What was more, the dispersion of our forces would leave the vital centres of Egypt and Palestine unduly exposed to attack. It had been argued that our prestige would suffer in America if we did not go to the rescue of Greece, but we felt that it would suffer still more in the end when we failed, as we were convinced we would.

Dill told me that, much to his surprise, Portal and Pound seemed to favour the Greek project, and that he had had to bear the full brunt of opposing it. He said that Churchill regarded Portal as the real strategist among the Chiefs of Staff, and Portal had argued that the Air Force should be given a 'platform' in Greece from which to bomb the Germans in Rumania and in Italy. Pound had made no stand upon the difficulty of providing naval escorts and shipping.

I felt that there were good grounds for hope that our Greek policy would be corrected by him and Eden in the course of their visit. Eden, I thought, would become convinced that a military front in the Balkans was a chimera, and that a political front of itself would be useless. I could not see them off because, when they left London, I was sitting in a Chiefs of Staff meeting to discuss the possibilities of invasion of England. This was still a live issue—but only just.

Before leaving the War Office Dill had told me that the Prime Minister intended to ask me to stay with him at Dytchley; and he added that he hoped I would let him have my views on Greece very strongly.

11

THE FATEFUL GREEK DECISION

1941

I DULY received an invitation to stay a night at Dytchley, Mr.
Ronald Tree's country house near Oxford. It was here that the
Prime Minister spent week-ends when the moon was bright, as
Chequers was considered too dangerous at such times. I motored
down from London on 15th February and when I arrived at that
most beautiful of houses I found Mrs. Tree, Lady Diana Cooper,
Miss Mary Churchill and Mr. Bruce, an American, all having tea
together in the drawing-room.

We were to dine at 8.30, and, when we had assembled, the
Prime Minister appeared, looking cheerful and fresh. He talked
to me for a little, and then we went in to dinner; Lady Diana
Cooper sat on the Prime Minister's right, and I next to her.

Mr. Churchill was in good spirits, and his conversation was
scintillating. When the ladies had gone, he began to sing, waving
his cigar in time to the tune:

> *'I went in to pay the bill*
> *But, instead, I took the till.*
> *My wife and kids were starving'*

When the brandy came round I refused it. Churchill turned
to me and said, 'Ah, you are one of those abstemious fellows,
are you? Well, I can only tell you that I have always found liquor
of the greatest assistance to me—all my life.' When he continued to
talk of food and drink, I told him I remembered reading in one of
his books a description of the waggon in which he had travelled
in South Africa, and how he had had it fitted with a double bottom
in which to stow supplies. 'Yes,' he replied, 'our arrangements
were excellent.'

77

The Duke of Marlborough joined us after dinner with some other men who were staying at Blenheim and at other houses in the neighbourhood. When we went to join the ladies, Churchill insisted on the Duke preceding him as we walked out, saying, 'The head of the family must go before the Prime Minister.'

Someone remarked that he had visited Blenheim during the afternoon, and had seen the room where the Prime Minister was born. 'Yes,' he said, 'I chose it. My mother intended that I should be born in London. But I elected otherwise, and I arrived a month —no more than a month—before my time, while she was staying at Blenheim.'

Soon the lights were put out and we sat down to see some films. First came a news-reel, in which we saw Churchill inspecting troops, in a reefer jacket and yachtsman's cap, an Italian propaganda film depicting Mussolini making a speech, and, finally, a thriller. After that, we talked in the drawing-room, until, at last, the Prime Minister went off to bed at 1.30 a.m.

I had not been to a party on such a splendid scale for a long time. It was delightful, and the war seemed very remote.

Next morning, 16th February, I was summoned to the Prime Minister's bedroom at about 10.30. He had warned me at dinner the night before that he would do so, and that he wanted a general review of the situation. He was sitting up in bed in his famous gaily-patterned dressing-gown, with dragons, smoking a long cigar. Heaps of files and papers lay on the bed, and several telephones were on a table beside him. He said he hoped I did not mind his air-raid suit, and offered me a cigar. I told him I had brought no papers—only a map, which I spread on the bed.

From some notes on a postcard, which I had made over my morning tea, I reviewed the whole situation as it appeared to me. He listened attentively throughout, stopping me occasionally to discuss various points at greater length. When we came to the Balkans he seemed particularly interested; I gave him my views frankly and forcefully, and I expected that this might provoke him into anger, but to my surprise he argued most reasonably, and even seemed to accept my point of view. I was puzzled by this, remembering with what ardour he had pressed for a forward policy at recent meetings of the Defence Committee.

When we had finished talking about strategy, he spoke of Dill. He said that although Dill had many excellent qualities he had one great failing: he allowed his mind to be too much impressed by the enemy's will. I did not agree with this, of course, and thought to myself that Dill's powers of resistance to Churchill's will were proof enough of his moral courage. But I felt it was much too delicate a subject for me to discuss, and remained silent.

After we had been talking for nearly three hours, Mrs. Churchill came in, to say that she was going over to Blenheim for luncheon. The Prime Minister reached out for the big gold watch on the table beside his bed, and knocked it on to the floor. Mrs. Churchill picked it up, put it to her ear, and reported, in a phrase which took my fancy, 'Its little heart is beating quite strongly; it's all right.' And Churchill breathed a sigh of relief. I also left his room, most pleasantly surprised and considerably relieved at the way in which my *tour d'horizon* had been accepted. Never again was I to find him so easy.

General Sikorski and the Polish Ambassador came to luncheon, and afterwards Duff Cooper and I were hauled in to attend their talk with the Prime Minister. It went on for two hours, and ranged over such subjects as the employment and the equipment of the Polish forces, and the disposal of the Polish gold reserves. Churchill spoke fluently and expressively in schoolboy French. He was stumped at one moment, when he was trying to liken the Germans in Europe to maggots in a cheese; we all knew *fromage* all right, but not even Duff Cooper could interpret 'maggots'. The Polish Ambassador came to our rescue.

One of Churchill's phrases sticks in my mind. He held up his hand with the fingers spread out, and said, 'Do you play poker? Here is the hand that is going to win the war: a Royal Flush—Great Britain, the Sea, the Air, the Middle East, American aid.'

I had meant to go back to London that night, but the Prime Minister pressed me to stay. Sunday evening was a repetition of Saturday, and we were treated to another brilliant display of conversation—if a monologue can be so called. He said, among other things, that after the war he would give a lecture on strategy at the Imperial Defence College. 'It will be all animal stories—nothing else. You remember how Foch said, "I am like a parrot—*un perroquet*. First I grasp with my beak, then with one claw"—and so on. Then there is the tiger sprawled and the tiger crouched. I once had a horse that got badly rubbed in a ship coming over from Ireland. The inside of one hind leg was quite raw. It would have kicked a man's brains out if he had tried to doctor it. The vet. put a twitch on its nose, and then he could rub the leg with disinfectant and do anything he liked, while the horse stood trembling. That illustrates the initiative. I told them that story at the time of Gallipoli. Once you grab the enemy by the nose, he will be able to think of nothing else.'

Changing the subject, he went on: 'I have never known a case of a great athlete being a great general—no prize-fighter has ever been a good general. The only exception might be in the Italian Army, where a general might find it useful to be a good runner.'

At one point the conversation turned to Turkey. I said something about the Turks being a very doubtful quantity, and that their decision on entering the war or keeping out would turn entirely on what they considered to be their own interest. 'Yes,' he said, 'it is nearly always so with nations—but not with the Americans. They are moving into the war by sentiment. I could make out a very strong case to show why it would pay America to keep out.'

Speaking of the decisions that had been taken in the war, he said the two hardest were, first, to keep the fighter aircraft out of France, and, second, to send the tanks and other reinforcements to Egypt at a time when invasion still seemed likely.

To Brendan Bracken (who was then the Minister of Information), he said, 'You seem to be getting on very well with the Press. One always has to try to match the man to the job. When Duff was appointed I thought he was exactly the man for it. I said to myself, "Here is a man with a fine war record, with experience of politics and government, and a fine reputation as a writer. He is just the man for it." And what happened? He failed completely. It just shows that it doesn't do to harness a thoroughbred to a dung-cart.' One would not have thought that either Duff Cooper or Bracken would care for this much, but they both took it cheerfully.

I got up early next morning, breakfasted with the Duff Coopers, and motored back to London. It had been a stimulating break from routine.

Back in the War Office, I dictated a long note to put on record the gist of my talk with the Prime Minister the day before. In a short introduction I said, 'He would not admit the importance of Tripoli except as a stepping-stone to Sicily. With regard to Greece he seemed to me to be in considerable doubt as to the correct policy to follow.'

I reproduce this note in full because it represents the views of the General Staff at the time—16th February, 1941—and some readers may care to pause and take stock of the situation as we saw it. Those who wish may pass it over, and resume with the narrative on p. 85.

'We are regaining the initiative slowly. In fact, we have regained it so far as the Italians are concerned. But not yet against the Germans. We are still therefore in the position of having to await Hitler's next move.

There is no doubt that Hitler must be dissatisfied in many ways with the recent development of the position.

First. He was taken aback by the determined resistance of the British after the collapse of France. Furthermore our resistance has stiffened instead of weakening during the past six months.

Second. The German economic effort must soon begin to decline, probably in March or April, by which time the enemy will begin to be short of essential commodities, such as copper, sulphur, etc.

Third. The strong movement in our favour in America and the increasing volume of American aid must be a source of extreme dissatisfaction to Hitler.

It is doubtful if he can tide over another winter.

Hitler has in fact made many mistakes, and doubtless he will make more. His biggest mistake, of course, was in starting the war without a navy.

The German forces are at present massed in three big concentrations—in the north of France; in the south of France; and in the Balkans. His other big concentration (in Poland) is not an operational concentration, the bulk of the divisions composing it being garrison troops.

There are thus three main threats—the threat of the invasion of the British Isles, the threat of an advance into Spain, and the threat of an advance into the Balkans.

It seems unlikely that the Germans consider that the time for invasion is ripe. I think we may put this aside for a month at least.

This is a war of sea communications. It seems likely that the next phase will be an increase in the attacks on our sea communications. They will continue to attack our communications in the Atlantic by submarines and aircraft and raiders. The present threat of Japanese intervention is designed largely as a threat to sea communications. Our communications in the Mediterranean will also be the object of attack.

In the Mediterranean there are three points at which the attack may be developed by the Germans—Spain, Italy, and Greece. Spain seems unlikely at the moment. Attack from the south of Italy, and possibly from Tripoli, if we are not there first, will certainly be developed. Greece is also a likely point of attack in the near future.

With regard to the threat in the centre of the Mediterreanean what we should do is to push on to Tripoli before the opportunity to do so has disappeared. If we do not deprive the Italians of this last base in Africa it is certain that the Germans will build up forces there, particularly air forces. The threat to our sea communications in the central Mediterranean will be much increased if the Germans are based in Tripoli as well as in Sicily. If we had air forces in Tripoli we could protect our shipping to a considerable extent once it had passed east of the Sicilian Narrows. Our ships would then be able to sail along the African coast under cover of our own fighters. If we stay at Benghazi the scale of air attack which we may have to meet may well be as great as that we should have to meet in Tripoli. The distance from Sicily to Tripoli is the same as from air bases in Tripoli to Benghazi.

If we go to Tripoli we could hold the place quite lightly. The danger of overseas attack by Italians would not exist. Nor could the Germans develop a serious attack without command of the sea. In any case it would not be a place to defend like the British Isles. We could well afford to fall back and give up parts of it if necessary. If the enemy bombed Tripoli it would be his own property that he would destroy.

There is also the point that we should gain touch with Weygand in North Africa.

There is no question of course of a heavy operation. Communications are too long and difficult. But, if we move soon enough, the place may well fall to little more than a demonstration of force.

With regard to Greece, it seems fairly certain that the Germans have now put 20 to 25 Divisions in Rumania. It is more than likely that they will move south through Bulgaria as soon as weather permits, say about the end of March or beginning of April, perhaps even sooner.

It may be possible to form a political front in the Balkans. But a political front is of no use unless it can be backed up by an effective military front. It is impossible to form an effective military front because the Balkan nations are so ill-equipped and we have not sufficient forces to spare to do it ourselves.

Nothing we can do can make the Greek business a sound military proposition. The Greeks have not got reserves for more than a month or so of fighting against the Germans. The farther forward the Greeks get in Albania the worse will be their dispositions to meet German attack. If we put four divisions into Greece, a month's hard fighting there would suck the bulk of our reserves of ammunition, etc., out of the Middle East.

The locomotive and the petrol engine will always beat the ship, especially when the ship has to go round the Cape. The chances of our getting four divisions into Greece are in any case extremely small. It would take a hundred ships or more to put them in in one flight. And it takes time to organize bases. The prospect is that we should try to put our forces in piecemeal over a period of six weeks or two months. And it is inconceivable that the Germans would allow us to do this.

It has been argued that the country round Salonika is easily defensible. So was the country in Norway. For effective defence you want not only defensible country but an adequate force to defend it. We have discussed the size of the force required for Salonika on many occasions with the French and the Turks. Everybody has agreed that we should need a force of about 20 divisions (the front is 150 miles long). And everybody wanted everybody else to provide the 20 divisions.

Anything we put into Greece on account of the very important political aspect, we should be prepared to lose. We must not lose so much that our power of offensive action in the Middle East is killed, nor so much that our power of defence in the vital Egyptian centre is impaired.

It is admitted that the present forces in the Middle East are more than we need for defence against a German attack.

If the worst came to the worst, and the Germans were established in Turkey as well as in Tripoli, the scale of the attack they could stage would be severely limited by immensely long communications. Therefore we do not need a very big force for pure defence. But the point is that if we use up four divisions and a large quantity of reserves in Greece (in Thessaly or elsewhere), our power of offensive action is gone until we can replace them.

The strategic reserve in the Middle East might be used

for, say, three tasks. It is probable that we cannot do more than one of these tasks effectively.

The three possible tasks are : support for Greece, support for Turkey, and operations against Tripoli and Sicily. Of these, support for Greece is the least important.

If Greece is overrun we must hold on to the essential islands, and be prepared to support Turkey if she will fight. The loss of Greece will not be a disaster, although it will be an embarrassment. Support of Turkey is far more important since Turkey is the bastion of our position in the Middle East. If Turkey sees our reserves thrown away in Greece it may tip the balance against her resistance to the Germans.

The problem is, however, likely to solve itself. It is likely that Greece will see that we cannot hold her up and will make terms, or be overrun before we can arrive in strength. It is then quite possible that the Turks will endeavour to remain neutral. Such a development would not be too bad from our point of view, so long as we have not thrown away too much of our forces in the meantime.

It is of course extremely desirable to liquidate the position in Abyssinia at the earliest possible moment. The rains will come by April and operations will then be impossible. It must seem to the Italians in Abyssinia that their last hope of rescue has now gone. There are 300,000 Italians in East Africa: 200,000 settlers and 100,000 troops. They must be feeling very uneasy about their position. We must watch for a chance of clearing up the position as soon as they show signs of willingness to make terms.

After the campaign is over there can be no question of tying up large forces in the country. We might supply a gendarmerie and a few lower-grade troops. But the bulk of our forces from Kenya and the Sudan must be moved to the north.

To sum up.

We can hardly be too strong in the British Isles. The front to be protected is big. And the Boche has the initiative in the choice of the point of attack. Our plans must be based on stiff resistance on the beaches and on heavy counter-attack before any forces that may have landed can organize themselves.

All our strategy must be directed to safeguarding our sea communications. An immediate measure in which the Army can assist is the seizure of Tripoli.

In the Middle East we must not throw away our power of offensive action by adopting an unsound strategy in Greece. The real bastion of our position there is Turkey. If Turkey will not enter the war and accept our support we should hold our strategic reserves for other tasks, such as the seizure of Sicily.

Italian East Africa should be liquidated at the earliest possible moment, and forces released should be moved north.

The threat by Japan will doubtless be kept up. It is certain that this will have the effect of drying up the supply of reinforcements from India, Australia and New Zealand.

It is essential to cling to the things that matter, and not waste our strength on things that are not vital to our strategy.'

On 19th February Eden and Dill arrived in Cairo; on the 22nd they were in Athens; on the 23rd they were back in Cairo *en route* for Ankara.

At this moment opinions began to shift in a very curious fashion. The Prime Minister, who had urged the Greek venture from the outset, sent a signal to Eden on the 21st in the following terms:

'If in your hearts you feel Greek enterprise will be another Norwegian fiasco, do not consider yourselves obligated to it. If no good plan can be made please say so. But you know of course how valuable success would be.'

Now there happened also a thing that I had not expected. Dill changed his mind. So did Wavell. We began getting telegrams which showed that they both considered that there was a fair chance of success.

The Chiefs of Staff, after a meeting which lasted from 4.45 p.m. on Sunday 23rd February till 2.30 a.m. the next morning, produced a paper in which they advised that, on balance, the Greek enterprise should go forward. It seemed to me very wrong that the Cabinet had never asked for or received a purely military view from either the Chiefs of Staff or from Wavell. All the service advice given on this problem had been coloured by political considerations—a very dangerous procedure. The array of opinion in favour of the project was now formidable. I did my best to press my point of view without avail.

When the Cabinet discussed it on 24th February, the Prime Minister said that, on the evidence before them, he was in favour of the plan. It was then approved unanimously, subject to shipping being available and subject to the agreement of the Governments of Australia and New Zealand.

Armed with the decision of the Cabinet, Eden and Dill went back to Athens on the 2nd March, and stayed in Greece until the 6th. They were again in Athens on 28th March, on their way to Belgrade.

Eden had reported that the Turks would not enter the war yet, although they would fight if they were attacked. The Jugoslavs had shown no signs of wishing to fight with us—indeed they joined Germany and Italy three weeks later. In fact it was now becoming obvious that Eden's attempt to establish a Balkan front had been a fiasco. The Prime Minister had good reason to doubt the wisdom of his policy, but its momentum was now considerable, and no note of caution had been sounded by Eden and Dill or, latterly, by Wavell.

As the days went by, the telegrams sent to Eden from London became more and more discouraging. But neither he nor the Commanders-in-Chief showed any sign of having lost confidence, or of being influenced by the change of atmosphere in Whitehall. Presently the Chiefs of Staff produced a new appreciation, in which they gave it as their opinion that the plan now appeared more hazardous than before, and that they had come to view it with misgiving, although they felt that great weight should be given to Eden's and to Dill's advice, since they must be fully aware of local factors unknown to us. Menzies, who was in London at the time, became doubtful of the wisdom of going on, and told the Cabinet that he would have to consult the Australian Government again.

However, the first troops were due to disembark in Greece in the first week of April, and they began to land in accordance with the schedule. The effect of the Greek commitment had by this time begun to be felt in Libya. Our forces there had been so weakened, to provide for Greece, that they were unable to maintain their positions in face of German attacks. As our troops began to arrive in Greece the Desert Army was in full retreat from Benghazi to the Egyptian frontier.

The period from December 1940 to March 1941 had marked the height of Wavell's greatness as a commander in the field. The destruction of the Italian Army in the desert in December and January had been a brilliant feat of arms. Scarcely less remarkable had been the campaign in Abyssinia, which reached its culminating point with the occupation of Addis Ababa on 5th April, simultaneously with the opening of the operations in Greece. But Greece, in my opinion, can hardly be regarded otherwise than as an error of military judgment. It was the first of the series of major mistakes that finally led to Wavell's removal from his command. Wavell himself seems to have had some misgivings even then.[1]

Had Wavell advised against the Greek venture on military grounds, and had his advice been accepted, no doubt he would have been blamed later for missing a great opportunity. A commander in the field is always open to this kind of criticism, but that can be no excuse for failing to judge aright or for failing to give his Government an opinion in which the military prospects are clearly distinguished from political considerations.

It can of course be argued that we gained a great moral advantage in the eyes of America and of the world when we went to the rescue of the Greeks. It is arguable, too, that it would have been wise policy to send our forces to Greece even on a forlorn hope against military advice. But these were not the grounds on which the enterprise went forward. The military opinion tendered to the Cabinet by the Chiefs of Staff and by Wavell was proved wrong in every respect. Nor is there any truth in the belief, at one time widely held, that our intervention delayed the German attack on Russia, and helped to save the Red Army by shortening what remained of the campaigning season, before winter set in. It is clear from German documents that Hitler confirmed the 22nd June as the date for the offensive as early as 30th April, and that our operations in Greece caused no postponement. The most that can be claimed is that some forces were diverted.[2]

We had an extremely interesting visitor about this time in the shape of Colonel 'Wild Bill' Donovan. He was an American lawyer whom President Roosevelt had sent to Europe on a tour of enquiry, and who had been visiting all the uncommitted countries; he was afterwards to become the head of the American Office of Strategic Services, which corresponded to our own Special Operations Executive. On the 7th March he came by invitation to attend and address a meeting of directors of operations and intelligence from each of the three ministries, and talked about his trip.

He spoke first about the Balkans. For King Boris of Bulgaria

---

[1] In his *Letter from Grosvenor Square*, Winant, writing of the decision to support Greece, said: 'After reaching this decision Dill boarded his plane for England. As he stepped aboard Wavell turned to him and said, half laughing and half sadly, "Jack, I hope, when this action is reviewed, you will be elected to sit on my court martial."'
[2] See Official History, *Grand Strategy*, Vol. II, pp. 540–1.

he had the greatest contempt. Boris had said to him, 'We feel it a great injustice that nations like Bulgaria, who wish only to live in peace, should be condemned to death.' 'I do not call it sentence of death,' Donovan had answered, 'I call it suicide. If you let the Germans in, we shall not intercede for you at the peace.' He had spoken in the same sense in Jugoslavia, where he had seen the Regent. The small Balkan nations reminded him of children looking into a shop window full of modern toys—tanks and aeroplanes. They all complained that their military equipment was out of date. He had found a general feeling of helplessness everywhere, and a great fear of Communism if Germany did not win the war.

In Turkey he had been told that Britain had entered the war before she was ready, and that the Turks were determined not to make the same mistake. 'The new Prime Minister of Greece,' he said, 'is not half the man Metaxas was. He is a man of great integrity, but his stomach is weak, both morally and physically.'

In Spain he had seen Súñer, Franco's brother-in-law and Foreign Minister. While they talked, Súñer had taken notes. Súñer had said he believed Germany would win the war by strangling Britain's merchant shipping. 'I knew he would report to Hitler every word I said,' Donovan told us, 'so I said, "You can tell whoever you are taking those notes for that for every ship England loses America will give her two; and for every destroyer, another." '

He had seen Haj Amin el Husseini, the former Mufti of Jerusalem, and sized him up as a shrewd but second-rate crook. He had refused to argue politics with him which, as he said, was to an Arab like refusing him his daily bread. He had told him: 'I know nothing of Arab politics, and the Americans are not interested in them. I have only one thing to tell you—America is determined that England shall win the war.'

12

THE GREEK REVERSE

1941

On 10th April Eden and Dill returned to London. The situation
in Greece on that day was that the German armies had advanced
through the southern end of Jugoslavia, and they had also occupied
Salonika. The British forces, under General Wilson, had occupied
a position about Mount Olympus with their left flank drawn back,
a detachment having been sent forward to the Monastir gap. The
Greeks in Macedonia and Thrace had been cut off and had surrendered, except for some who had escaped into Turkey.

In Egypt the Germans had driven forward to Tobruk, where
the 9th Australian Division was concentrated. Wavell had lost
his Armoured Brigade and most of his Motor Brigade. Generals
Neame, O'Connor and Gambier-Parry and three brigadiers had
been taken prisoner. Practically all of Wavell's tanks, except for a
few at Tobruk and those with the Armoured Brigade in Greece,
were in workshops for repair and out of action.

This was not a pretty picture.

I saw Dill when he arrived in the War Office in the afternoon,
having missed him at Paddington, where I had gone to meet him,
because his train arrived early. He was very tired and said he had
not slept for three nights. I told him how operations were developing. He said, 'I am frightfully anxious about Egypt—it is a desperate
situation.' I said I did not agree; the German effort in the desert
seemed to be expended for the moment; Wavell had plenty of
room to manœuvre, with four or five hundred miles of desert
behind him, and he had everything to gain by drawing Rommel on.
Our talk was interrupted by a message from the Prime Minister
asking Dill to go and see him.

At about 6.30 p.m. Dill returned to the War Office, and came
to see me in my room. He asked me again what I thought of the

situation, and repeated, 'I think it is desperate—I am terribly tired.'
He spoke of the difficulties in Greece, and said he feared that a
bad mistake had been made. I tried to console him by saying that,
even if things went wrong, it would only be an incident—we must
regard this as a defensive phase, and hang on until we were stronger,
when things would be in our favour.

Dill asked me if I had seen a telegram that had been sent to
Wavell telling him to hang on to Tobruk. I said I had, and that
Wavell had replied that Tobruk was not a good position to defend.
But Dill said he was referring to a second telegram that had been
drafted that afternoon. We had had a lot of trouble while Dill
was away over signals being sent without our knowledge. This was
another instance. I sent for a copy and saw that it contained the
following passage:

'From here it seems unthinkable that the fortress of Tobruk
should be abandoned without offering the most prolonged
resistance. We have a secure sea line of communication. The
enemy's line is long and should be vulnerable provided he
is not given time to organize at leisure. So long as Tobruk's
garrison includes even a few tanks which can lick out at his
communications nothing but a raid dare go past. If you leave
Tobruk and go 200 miles back to Mersa Matruh may you not
find yourself faced with something like the same problem.
We are convinced you should fight it out at Tobruk.'

I said this was absolutely wrong; that we should not dictate
strategy and tactics from London to a commander in the field, and
that, if I were in Wavell's place, I should disregard it. Holding
Tobruk would be like letting go the anchor of a battleship in the
midst of a naval battle. In the desert the game to play was to fall
back, as we did originally with the Italians, and choose the moment
when the enemy was extended to fall upon him.

Dill said he would speak to the Prime Minister again. We
went along to his room, where he first spoke to Eden on the telephone in the sense of what I had said, and Eden agreed. He then
went back to the Prime Minister's annexe at King Charles Street, and
asked him to add a sentence to his telegram to the effect that we
left Wavell a free hand and would not dictate the course of action
from London. Churchill agreed to this. But, at this point, another
telegram arrived from Wavell, in which he said that he intended to
stand at Tobruk temporarily. I took it over to King Charles Street,

and sent it into the Prime Minister's room. He thereupon cancelled his original telegram and cabled back to Wavell that he cordially 'endorsed his decision'.

I was astonished by this decision of Wavell's. The force in Tobruk would not be strong enough to break out once it was surrounded, or to harass the German communications. But I could do no more. Dill went off to bed and I to dinner.

Next morning, 11th April, Dill still looked very worn and anxious. He was so tired mentally that he could not concentrate on the papers for the Cabinet, and more than once he asked irrelevant questions as we discussed them.

On 12th April, Dill was summoned to Chequers for the night, and, after luncheon, I spent a couple of hours with him to discuss points which might be raised by the Prime Minister. He was still very tired. Churchill had expressed a wish to send more tanks to Wavell, but we had advised that no more Tank Brigades should leave the United Kingdom for the moment. He had brushed this advice aside and Dill intended to return to the charge. It seems odd now that we were still regarding a German invasion of England as possible. Our view at that time was that it was a real, although diminishing, danger. It must be remembered that the Germans had not yet attacked Russia; comparatively few of their troops were engaged in active operations, and they had some 200 divisions available for new enterprises. Sir Alan Brooke, Commander-in-Chief of the Home Forces, stoutly resisted any further depletion of his command. Some of his Divisions on the coast were holding a front of over forty miles apiece, and a fairly strong tank reserve was essential for counter-attack. Brooke had said to me that he hoped we would not 'raid his orchard' any more to reinforce the Middle East. Churchill, in the meantime, was constantly urging the despatch of more tanks to Wavell. Many hours were spent in explaining to him the exact number of tanks with units, in repair shops, in factories, etc., etc. We know now that he was right. But the argument between him and the General Staff proved, in the end, to have been largely academic, because the number of tanks we could despatch was limited anyway by shortage of shipping.

Dill said again that he was desperately anxious about Egypt. The German tanks were moving on Tobruk; and it seemed inevitable that the 9th Australian Division would soon be cut off and besieged. In Albania the Germans had made contact with the Italians and were pressing forward. I said I was more anxious about our forces in Greece than I was about Libya. In the desert we did not depend upon the support of doubtful allies, and there were many possibilities for action.

Finally Dill said he thought it would be a good idea to send a telegram to Wavell. I said, 'Yes, and we must word it so as not to appear to be dictating his course of action.' Dill took up his pencil and began to write, saying, 'We must word this rather carefully.' This is the telegram he sent:

'From: C.I.G.S. to General Wavell (Private).

I have been studying your problem in Western Desert. I am convinced that enemy's supply difficulties must be immense. If his communications can be attacked by bombardment from the sea and possibly by blocking Tripoli and Sirte by bombing, including bombing of ports, and machine-gunning columns from the air, and by patrol raids through the desert to destroy his supply and petrol convoys, his advance must be checked till you can collect enough tanks to strike back. This is a time when great daring is needed and great losses accepted. I know you will not think that in this anxious time I am trying to interfere with your conduct of battle by sending you my thoughts. Good luck to you.'

We talked about Greece. I said I wished I could agree with him on this, and that I hoped very much I would be proved wrong, but I could not believe that I would. Dill replied, 'I still think the decision we took was right. If the Prime Minister attacks me, and claims that he checked Anthony and me and gave us an opportunity to draw back, my complete defence will be to point to the dates of the telegrams. The Prime Minister led the hunt before we left England, and by the time his telegrams were sent, it was too late. By the time he had begun to doubt, the momentum was too great. The offer had been made to the Greeks and the troops were in motion. All the same, if it had not been for the change in our programme, by which we went to Athens before Ankara, it is conceivable that the first telegrams might have reached us in time to affect the situation. Eden told me that he is prepared to resign on this, but I said to him that I could see no reason why he should resign, since his action was based on military advice.'

I told Dill that I had found myself in a most unhappy situation while he was away. But, I said, I knew that he wished that I should always give my opinion frankly, and this I had done, and I had made nothing of it; it was a pity we had had no strictly military appreciation.

He said that Wavell was a very lonely man, especially now that Wilson was away and Neame and O'Connor were prisoners.

It was a depressing interview. Dill was miserable. At 5 p.m. he went off to Chequers.

At this time it seemed quite possible that the war might be lost in Whitehall. The Chiefs of Staff were being over-driven; and they were having to compete for the Prime Minister's attention with a group of independent advisers with which he had surrounded himself. Principles of policy were in danger of being swamped by spates of paper and memoranda. It was difficult to keep the twin streams of military and political considerations pure and separate, and to prevent them from flowing together too soon. On 13th April, I wrote a minute to my staff, in which I said among other things:

'There is often a tendency to modify wording and the sense of papers which are being submitted to the Prime Minister with the idea of making them more acceptable to him. The authority of the Prime Minister is so great, and we all have such a tremendous admiration for him, and his personality is so overpowering, that this is liable to be taken to an extent which may be dangerous unless we watch it very carefully.

From what I have seen of the Prime Minister I cannot believe that he would not wish to have the most forceful and clear-cut opinion put to him on most occasions, so long as it is clear that the opinion is purely military in the broadest sense. The Chiefs of Staff must of course take very considerable account of political as well as military considerations. But the mingling of the two in a paper put forward by the Chiefs of Staff has to be most carefully done if things are not to go wrong. Political and other non-military aspects of any problem get more than their due weight in the levels above the Chiefs of Staff. . . . Papers that go forward should be mainly designed not as a comprehensive statement from all points of view, but rather as the military evidence which will be weighed with evidence supplied from other sources in the Defence Committee or War Cabinet.'

The very next day, almost as though it were to illustrate some of the points I was trying to make, Churchill circulated a directive which he had sent to the Commanders-in-Chief in the Middle East, and to C.-in-C. Malta. I reproduce it here, and in full. He has printed it himself in Volume III of *The Second World War* (pp. 186–8), and has added at the end a characteristically disarming comment in eight words, 'All this was easier to say than do.' Many years have passed since I first saw the original directive in the War Office, but my feelings about it remain now as they did at the time. It was cast almost in the form of an Operation Order by a Commander-in-Chief; and it included unsound and impracticable propositions which could only be dismissed after hours and days of unprofitable work by busy and responsible men who would have been better employed in getting on with their jobs. But it breathed a splendid spirit of courage, defiance and initiative. It appeared in our 'In Trays' at a moment when our fortunes had suffered grievous setbacks, and, even as we grumbled at the work it caused us, we could not but delight in its sentiments. Here it is:

DIRECTIVE

BY THE PRIME MINISTER AND MINISTER OF DEFENCE

THE WAR IN THE MEDITERRANEAN

April 14, 1941

If the Germans can continue to nourish their invasion of Cyrenaica and Egypt through the port of Tripoli and along the coastal road they can certainly bring superior armoured forces to bear upon us, with consequences of the most serious character. If, on the other hand, their communications from Italy and Sicily with Tripoli are cut, and those along the coastal road between Tripoli and Agheila constantly harassed, there is no reason why they should not themselves sustain a major defeat.

2. It becomes the prime duty of the British Mediterranean Fleet under Admiral Cunningham to stop all sea-borne traffic between Italy and Africa by the fullest use of surface craft, aided so far as possible by aircraft and submarines. For this all-important objective heavy losses in battleships, cruisers, and destroyers must if necessary be accepted. The harbour at Tripoli must be rendered unusable by recurrent bombardment, and/or by blocking and mining, care being taken that the mining does not impede the blocking or bombardments. Enemy convoys passing to and from Africa must be attacked by our cruisers, destroyers, and submarines, aided by the Fleet Air Arm and the

Royal Air Force. Every convoy which gets through must be considered a serious naval failure. The reputation of the Royal Navy is engaged in stopping this traffic.

3. Admiral Cunningham's fleet must be strengthened for the above purposes to whatever extent is necessary. The *Nelson* and *Rodney*, with their heavily armoured decks, are especially suitable for resisting attacks from the German dive-bombers, of which undue fears must not be entertained. Other reinforcements of cruisers, minelayers, and destroyers must be sent from the west as opportunity serves. The use of the *Centurion* as a blockship should be studied, but the effectual blocking of Tripoli harbour would be well worth a battleship upon the active list.

4. When Admiral Cunningham's fleet has been reinforced he should be able to form two bombarding squadrons, which may in turn at intervals bombard the port of Tripoli, especially when shipping or convoys are known to be in the harbour.

5. In order to control the sea communications across the Mediterranean sufficient suitable naval forces must be based on Malta, and protection must be afforded to these naval forces by the Air Force at Malta, which must be kept at the highest strength in fighters of the latest and best quality that the Malta aerodromes can contain. The duty of affording fighter protection to the naval forces holding Malta should have priority over the use of the aerodromes by bombers engaged in attacking Tripoli.

6. Every endeavour should be made to defend Malta harbour by the U.P. weapon (rockets) in its various developments, especially by the F.A.M. (fast aerial mine), fired by the improved naval method.

7. Next in importance after the port at Tripoli comes the 400-mile coastal road between Tripoli and Agheila. This road should be subjected to continuous harassing attacks by forces landed from the Glen ships in the special landing-craft. The Commandos and other forces gathered in Egypt should be freely used for this purpose. The seizure of particular points from the sea should be studied, and the best ones chosen for prompt action. Here again losses must be faced, but small forces may be used in this harassing warfare, being withdrawn, if possible, after a while. If even a few light or medium tanks could be landed these could rip along the road, destroying very quickly convoys far exceeding their own value. Every feasible method of harassing constantly

this section of the route is to be attempted, the necessary losses being faced.

8. In all the above paragraphs the urgency is extreme, because the enemy will grow continually stronger in the air than he is now, especially should his attack on Greece and Yugoslavia be successful, as may be apprehended. Admiral Cunningham should not therefore await the arrival of battleship reinforcements, nor should the use of the Glen ships be withheld for the sake of Rhodes.

9. It has been decided that Tobruk is to be defended with all possible strength. But holding Tobruk must not be regarded as a defensive operation, but rather as an invaluable bridgehead or sallyport on the communications of the enemy. It should be reinforced as may be necessary both with infantry and by armoured fighting vehicles, to enable active and continuous raiding of the enemy's flanks and rear. If part of the defences of the perimeter can be taken over by troops unprovided with transport, this should permit the organization of a mobile force both for the fortress reserve and for striking at the enemy. It would be a great advantage should the enemy be drawn into anything like a siege of Tobruk and compelled to transport and feed the heavy artillery forces for that purpose.

10. It is above all necessary that General Wavell should regain unit ascendancy over the enemy and destroy his small raiding parties, instead of our being harassed and hunted by them. Enemy patrols must be attacked on every occasion, and our own patrols should be used with audacity. Small British parties in armoured cars, or mounted on motor-cycles, or, if occasion offers, infantry, should not hesitate to attack individual tanks with bombs and bombards, as is planned for the defence of Britain. It is important to engage the enemy even in small affairs in order to make him fire off his gun ammunition, of which the supply must be very difficult.

11. The use of the Royal Air Force against the enemy's communications, or concentrations of fighting vehicles, is sufficiently obvious not to require mention.

Mr. Churchill was, of course, responsible as Prime Minister for deciding the allocation of manpower and of industrial production to the three Services. We in the General Staff were quite sure that the decisions he gave at this time were dangerously wrong. On 6th March he had issued one of his periodical directives, in which he instructed us to proceed upon the assumption that the

Army would never play a primary part in the defeat of the enemy. I reproduce here a paragraph extracted from this directive.

'The above considerations and the situation as a whole make it impossible for the Army, except in resisting invasion, to play a primary role in the defeat of the enemy. That task can only be done by the staying power of the Navy, and above all by the effect of air predominance. Very valuable and important services may be rendered overseas by the Army in operations of a secondary order, and it is for these special operations that its organization and character should be adapted.'

We attempted to reason with him on this issue, and sent him a memorandum in which we gave it as our view that he was adrift in his belief that the Army's part in achieving victory would be secondary. We pointed out that great results had already been achieved in the war, both by the Germans and by ourselves, by operations in which armies had played the predominant part. But, for a long time, he continued to believe that the war would be won by aircraft. So sure was he of this that the bombing policy of the Air Staff was settled almost entirely by the Prime Minister himself in consultation with Portal, and was not controlled by the Chiefs of Staff. Try as we would, we never succeeded in bringing this important but far from self-sufficient ingredient of victory under their direction.

On the night of 16th April London was heavily bombed. I was awakened by a particularly loud explosion at about 4.30 a.m., and when I walked across the Horse Guards Parade on my way to breakfast at my club, I saw that there was a large hole in the Admiralty.

That morning Dill told me that he had been dining with Menzies, the Prime Minister of Australia, and that Menzies was worried over the situation of two of the three Australian Divisions in the Middle East—the one shut up in Tobruk, the other in Greece. He had told Dill that he would hardly dare go home, and that he might as well go for a trip to the North Pole. Dill said to me that he, too, was anxious about the Middle East, and particularly because so many Dominion troops were involved. He felt he had made a mistake, when he was in Egypt, in not realizing the full extent of the danger in the Western Desert.

I had met Menzies on 10th April, when he came to the War

Office to get information about our future plans. He seemed to me to be an exceptionally shrewd and able man, with a caustic wit. He told us a story about Wavell and his proverbial silences. He had dined with him in Cairo on his way home, and had asked him what he thought of possibilities in the desert. 'That is a complicated matter,' Wavell had replied, and, said Menzies, 'I sat back expecting to hear an interesting exposition—but, after ten minutes' silence, I realized that the conversation was over.'

In Greece Wilson was making plans to withdraw to Thermopylae, and he was fortunately still free to manoeuvre. In the desert the Germans continued to drive us back, but there were signs that their lengthening communications were slowing down their advance. It now became necessary to consider whether we should evacuate our forces from Greece in order to save Egypt. Although Wavell still thought that Tobruk could not be by-passed by large forces, I believed he was wrong while devoutly hoping he was right. The garrison was in no position to make sorties against the enemy's communications; they had only twenty tanks, and such guns as they possessed were all essential for the defence of the perimeter, which was twenty-five miles long from sea to sea. We were further disquieted by a signal from Wavell in which he spoke of not being able to relieve Tobruk for some months.

At midnight on 20th April I dictated a note for my staff, to guide them in preparing a memorandum for the War Cabinet. It will be observed that I restricted it to purely military considerations.

1. Points in favour of early evacuation of Greece are:
    (a) We shall save a larger number of men for Egypt. The units will not be disorganized. Men are badly needed in Egypt as well as tanks.
    (b) We may get some equipment out if we move early, before the scale of air attacks on the Piraeus is too great.
    (c) The chances of successful evacuation will be greater because there will be less danger of the Greek Government disintegrating. General Wavell has stressed the need for Greek co-operation in his telegram. It is difficult to visualize an effective Greek Government after the collapse of the main strength of the Greek Army in the north, which seems imminent.
    (d) We shall save aircraft for use against the Germans in Libya—against both the German air force, and German preparations for a further advance in Egypt.

(e) We shall save ships, since we are bound to lose a large number if we do not get out early.

(f) We shall save further maintenance of the force from depleted stocks in Egypt.

(g) The effect on the Dominions, which has a military aspect as well as a political one.

2. If we fight a prolonged action at Thermopylae:

(i) We shall have to put much bigger forces forward because the scale of attack will become increasingly heavier and we must provide reliefs. It is probable that the best part of a division will be required to hold the Thermopylae position, and another division will be required to provide reliefs. The German mountain division was last reported about Larissa, and it may be in touch with the Thermopylae position quite soon.

(iii) It is a hundred miles from Thermopylae to the Piraeus. If we fight for long on the Thermopylae position there will be little chance of getting back the bulk of the force to the Piraeus. We do not know what the possibilities are of getting men out from beaches closer to the position.

(iv) The evacuation of casualties and provision of supplies will become increasingly difficult as transport gets knocked out.

(v) The longer we stay the less chance there will be of the Greeks being able to safeguard Athens from parachute troops. This will mean a dangerous dispersion of our forces in order to guard the rear.

3. Political considerations to be done separately.

Dill was out of London on 20th April, a Sunday, and I therefore attended a meeting of the Chiefs of Staff in his place. This meeting had been summoned, at the Prime Minister's request, to consider a note he had sent up from the country, in which he suggested that a hundred more tanks should be sent to Egypt. They were to go in a convoy which was due to leave on 24th April, and to proceed direct through the Mediterranean. We could not deal with this proposal without consulting the tank experts, because we did not know how many tanks there were in the country suitable for service in the desert. I said I would get a considered statement in a few hours, and we arranged to meet again at 10 p.m. Before we separated, I said to the First Sea Lord (Pound) and the Vice-Chief of the Air Staff (Freeman) that I felt we must face the issue whether we could spare more tanks from the United Kingdom; I reminded them that the Chiefs of Staff had quite recently given their opinion that we could not.[1] Ismay suggested a way of presenting a decision in this sense to the Prime Minister so as to make it 'palatable' to him. But I said, 'We must say frankly and clearly whether his proposition is, in our opinion, quite unsound.' This suggestion was received in dead silence. Ismay then telephoned to the Prime Minister and told him that we had postponed our meeting until 10 p.m., and he replied that he would send up Eden to take the chair.

When we assembled again, we first discussed the position in Greece. Eden argued that we should hold the Thermopylae line. Pound and Freeman were also in favour of this, on the grounds that, if we did so, we should be able to keep aircraft in Greece to cover the direct convoy which was about to leave for the Middle East. I opposed the idea strongly, and said there would be no hope of holding on long enough to cover the convoy, and that we might jeopardize our evacuation by holding on too long. We reached no decision, but the problem was solved for us next morning by the collapse in Greece and Wavell's decision to order immediate evacuation of our troops.

Eden, with great vigour, advocated the despatch of the hundred tanks to Egypt. This I did not regard as a very big issue, but I opposed the suggestion because I thought it wrong and because I knew that Dill was against it. We reached no conclusion on this point either. But, next day, Mr. Churchill returned to London and, after a talk with the tank experts, gave orders for sixty-seven more tanks to be loaded in the convoy. Events proved that he was utterly and completely right.

On 23rd April Dill gave me a copy of the record of his discussions with the Greeks. It made it clear that Dill and Wavell had examined the military implications of the Greek expedition most carefully, although their conclusions had never been communicated in any detail to the War Cabinet. When they had met Papagos on 22nd February, the plan he had propounded was that he should withdraw his forces from the frontier to the Aliakmon line, which was shorter and naturally very strong, and that the

---

[1] The opinion given by the Chiefs of Staff had been based on the calculation that the Germans would have been able, at this time, to deploy six armoured Divisions for the invasion of England, that is to say 2,400 tanks. In April there were in the Home Forces about 900 tanks which would be increased to 1,300 by June.

stand should be made there by both the Greeks and the British.[1] This was accepted by Wavell and Dill as 'a sound military plan offering a reasonable chance of stopping a German advance'. Wavell had thereupon ordered the movement of the British forces from Egypt to begin.

When Eden and Dill returned to Athens on 2nd March they found that Papagos had changed his mind; he had reverted to his original intention of fighting on the frontier, and had taken no steps to bring his forces back. After three days' discussion, Papagos agreed to concentrate three Greek divisions on the Aliakmon line to fight with the British troops. The risks in the new plan were obviously greater than those in the plan previously agreed, but it was Dill's and Wavell's opinion that 'on the Aliakmon position good troops under a capable and resolute commander should have a reasonable chance of checking and holding a German advance. At worst it should be possible to conduct a fighting withdrawal through country eminently suitable for rearguard action.'

Dill said that, on their second visit to Greece, when he was made aware of Papagos' breach of faith, he felt that the plan had become definitely unsound, but we were then so deeply implicated that we could not withdraw. I had not previously heard the details of the arrangements which had been made in Greece, but I felt that, even if Papagos had stuck to his first agreement, the ultimate result of the operations would probably have been the same. I think that Dill, too, agreed that this would have been so, now that we knew the true weight and the strength of the German attack.

It must be admitted, all the same, that the difficulties which confronted Eden, Dill and Wavell were considerable. The prizes of success would have been very great, and it could not be known, until later, that the resistance of the Jugoslavs would be so ineffective, and that the Turks would not fight.

Wilson was now on the Thermopylae line, and he intended to attempt to embark his troops on the nights of the 24th, 25th and 26th April. It seemed to me providential that we were being forced to go so quickly. If we had had to maintain a front in Greece, our depleted reserves in Egypt would have been used up, and the Nile Delta left unprotected from the German threat through the desert. At this time it seemed to us that the Germans would have

[1] Papagos maintained that he had never agreed to do this, but only that he should put three divisions on the Aliakmon line. He repeated this assertion in a book which he published after the war. The recollection of the British participants in the talks of the 22nd and 23rd February was quite otherwise. See Official History, *Grand Strategy*, Vol. II, p. 444, and *Operation Victory*, p. 58.

done better not to move so fast, and to have delayed their attack, both in Cyrenaica and in Greece, until we were more heavily committed in the latter country. Egypt would then have been exposed to invasion, and we would have suffered heavier losses in Greece. We were unaware, however, that the Germans had decided to attack Russia in June, and that they were pressed for time.

Wavell was now reassessing his numerous problems, and, on 24th April, he sent us a note in which he explained them. I reproduce some passages which are of special interest. After reviewing the various possibilities, which included attacks from Libya, through Turkey and Syria or from Syria alone, from Iraq by the Iraqi Army supported by German airborne troops, and air or sea attacks upon Crete and Cyprus, Wavell wrote:

'To meet the above possibilities we have a considerable number of troops, but the majority are not battle-worthy, being either unsuitable or insufficiently equipped. There is not at present in the Middle East a single formation complete in organization and equipment. We are fighting, as we have done since the beginning of the war, with improvisations, and insufficiencies. As the enemy is unlikely to give us any time to organize, train and equip, we shall have to continue to do our best in spite of these disadvantages.

Palestine. It looks as if the defence of the northern frontier of Palestine will become very much a problem now, and we shall have to establish a sufficient force when we can.

Crete and Cyprus. These outposts have now become a considerable problem. I hate locking up troops in them but it is disturbing to think of them in enemy hands. Our discussions of all these defence problems by the three Commanders-in-Chief run along a fairly normal line. The Navy say it is absolutely essential that they should be held, the R.A.F. say that the aerodromes are indefensible and that they have no aircraft to spare, and the Army is left to hold the baby with suggestions that anything from a brigade to a division is required, with about 50 A.A. guns. I explain that there is nothing in the cupboard at all, and we generally end by adding an extra battalion to the garrison, which almost invariably means some improvisation elsewhere, like using reinforcements to guard prisoners of war or Yeomanry to man searchlights. Some day, perhaps, we shall have enough of everything, but I doubt it.

It seems unlikely that the enemy will attempt a landing in

force in Crete from the sea. An airborne landing is possible but not probable, since the landing force would be isolated without sea support. Scale of air attack on Crete, will, however, undoubtedly be heavy. . . .'

With this letter, which came home by hand of a liaison officer, Wavell enclosed a copy of his 'Worst Possible Case', as it stood at the moment. This was an intensely secret document: only half a dozen officers on his staff and about the same number at home knew of its existence; it was revised from time to time. The general assumption in this paper was a failure to check the German advance, and the consequent loss of Egypt; later in the war, when Wavell was commanding in India, the assumption for his then 'W.P.C.', as he called it, was the loss of Assam and Bengal to the Japs. No commander ever had a more robust spirit than Wavell, and these W.P.C.s were merely soldierly precautions so that, if the worst happened, some sort of thinking to minimize the effects would already have been done; there was no question of a secret Achilles' heel of pessimism.

In this particular paper he faced the fact that the loss of Alexandria and Cairo would mean the loss of all troops in Greece, Crete and Cyprus, unless they could previously reach Palestine. The loss of Egypt would not mean the loss of the war, but the troops there would have to be evacuated: by the Nile Valley to the Sudan, overland to Palestine or by sea to other destinations. There were not enough resources to move everybody away, and many questions remained unresolved. How long could Palestine hold out, living on its own fat? Would an expedition from India into Iraq be necessary to uphold it? What could be done about civilians? And what about the Jews?

He foresaw the remnants of his forces falling back to the south, and helping Smuts and the Union of South Africa to build up an African Empire which would include the Sudan, and some of the British, Portuguese, French and Belgian African possessions.

13

FIREWORKS AT CHEQUERS

1941

THE Prime Minister had invited me to Chequers for the night of Sunday, 27th April; I motored down from London with Ismay and we arrived at about 7 p.m. I was talking to one of his secretaries when Mr. Churchill appeared in his 'rompers', as he called his strange one-piece dark grey suit fitted with zip fasteners. In his hand he carried a speech which he was to broadcast that evening. The secretaries were still working on it and were busy telephoning to London to check various points.

When I had had a bath and changed for dinner, I came downstairs to listen to the broadcast. A few minutes before 9 p.m. the Prime Minister walked through to his study, where the microphone was installed; he apologized for keeping us waiting for dinner, remarking that duty came first. When he had finished the speech, which he had delivered quietly and with little rhetoric, he joined us again, and we went in to dinner at 10 p.m. I sat on his left, Brooke on his right—the others were Margesson,[1] Ismay, Lindemann,[2] Mrs. Randolph Churchill, and two secretaries.

First we discussed the Prime Minister's speech. He said that, in this broadcast, he had had the Americans chiefly in mind. He had been keeping the Clough quotation, which Bracken had suggested, and which he had just used, until the proper occasion arose. Telegrams began to come in almost at once, and were brought to Churchill. The political reaction in America had been good, and messages of congratulation came from Winant and Harriman.

Presently the Prime Minister turned to me and asked me if I'd rather be in Wavell's shoes or in Rommel's. I replied, 'I'd rather be in any British General's shoes than in any German's— no matter what hole he might be in.' 'A very good answer,' said

---

[1] Captain, afterwards Lord, Margesson was Secretary of State for War.
[2] Afterwards Lord Cherwell.

Margesson, and the Prime Minister grunted approval. (When I told Dill about this later, he said that, on his advice, Churchill had cut out of his speech a sentence to the effect that he would rather be in Wavell's shoes than Rommel's.)

Churchill called continuously for more champagne, remarking it was very good stuff. He said he wanted to see the Germans out of Cyrenaica quickly—he had thought of giving up cigars till they were out, and then had decided to give up snuff instead. A few days later he said he had changed his mind, for he did not see why he should give up either snuff or cigars for any German.

He then tackled Brooke about the defence of the United Kingdom. Brooke repeated his estimate of the scale of German attack we should be prepared to meet. The Prime Minister brushed this aside, and said to him that he need not be frightened about his tanks and his equipment—very soon he would not have enough men to handle the stuff that was coming out so well from the factories. He then asked my opinion. I said I believed our forces at home were now below their proper level. I felt we should make up our minds how much we ought to have at home and then not send any more away, whatever the consequences might be in other places which, in the ultimate resort, were less important. He replied that I need not be anxious, because the limitation of shipping would prevent us from sending too much away. 'Your ships have already been enough,' said Brooke, 'to take too much away from home.'

The Prime Minister then turned the discussion to Egypt, and asked me what I thought of the situation there. I said I did not feel much anxiety about the immediate future. Eventually everything would depend upon what we could do to cut the German line of communications across the Mediterranean and through the desert, and I added that what we had done so far to interrupt their communications was not enough. He replied that he had ordered Cunningham to bombard Tripoli twice a week and that Cunningham's fears of fixed defences, and their effect on ships, had proved all wrong. He added that he had also ordered Cunningham to base a battleship and some destroyers on Malta. I said that, in time, if we did not interrupt their communications, the Germans might bring such a scale of attack to bear on Egypt, from East and West, that we would be unable to provide adequate forces for its defence—to take armoured Divisions alone, our estimate was that five would be necessary. (This estimate was of course based upon the assumption that the Middle East, and not Russia, would be the main objective for the Germans in 1941.)

Churchill flushed at this, and lost his temper. His eyes flashed and he shouted, 'Wavell has 400,000 men. If they lose Egypt, blood will flow. I will have firing parties to shoot the generals.'[1]

'You need not be afraid they will not fight,' I replied. 'Of course they will fight. I am only arguing that we should decide the price we are prepared to pay, and can afford to pay, for the defence of the Middle East.'

But his wrath was not appeased. He accused me of defeatism in thinking it possible that Egypt might be lost; he said that I must get such ideas out of my head—determination was what was needed.

When he paused at last, I said I fully agreed with what he said about determination, and that he had based his accusations upon a misconception of the thoughts that were in my head; that it did not mean defeatism to consider the worst case as well as other possibilities—that was a normal function of any commander or of any staff. I added that, surely, he was aware that Wavell had a plan for withdrawal from Egypt should it be forced upon him, and that, even in the unlikely event of our having to clear out of Egypt, it would not mean defeat, for there were other lines on which we could stand, to prevent the Germans breaking out on the Indian Ocean and the Persian Gulf.

At this he fairly exploded. 'This comes as a flash of lightning to me,' he exclaimed. 'I never heard such ideas. War is a contest of wills. It is pure defeatism to speak as you have done.'

'You would not consider General Smuts a defeatist, would you?' I asked. 'No,' he replied. 'Well,' I said, 'have you read the speech he made yesterday? He talked about these same possibilities. It is necessary to calculate them quite calmly in order to arrive at the price we are prepared to pay.'

The others had sat silent through all this and Brooke had not intervened on my side, although I knew I had said nothing with which he did not agree. Perhaps he felt it useless to do so. I thought of Haig's plans for possible withdrawals in France, and of other similar plans in other campaigns. But I felt that the argument had gone on long enough, and that we were having a row about a hypothetical case which was not of immediate importance. I also blamed myself for having started the argument at all, when the Prime Minister was obviously tired and unreasonable.

I managed to avoid being provoked into losing my temper. It

---

[1] It had become a well-known idiosyncrasy of the Prime Minister's to talk of shooting generals. But, of course, nobody took it literally, or as other than a vent for his feelings of exasperation.

was a new experience for me to be dubbed a defeatist, and I can remember, even at this distance of time, my blazing anger and the difficulty of repressing it. I had not yet learned that this was the Prime Minister's usual reproach, from which nobody was immune. I said no more, and we got up from the table.[1]

It was now about midnight, and we retired to the hall, where we stood round the fire, and the conversation went back to tanks. Presently, we went into the Prime Minister's study, and Lindemann produced some of his graphs showing the rates of production of equipment by the factories. Churchill walked up and down. From time to time he came up to me, and repeated what he had said at dinner about war being a contest of wills, and so forth. He then said, 'I will tell you an experience I once had. In April 1918, I was not in the War Cabinet—I was Minister of Munitions. But I put in a memorandum upon the action of the British Army. As you know, Haig wanted to fall back to the sea if the Germans broke through. I argued that he should fall back, with the mass of the French armies, on Paris. Then Foch swept all that aside. He said "We shall do neither"—he launched his counter offensive, and the situation was saved. That has always been a lesson to me.' I said, 'I think you were right to consider the plan for withdrawal—it did not necessarily imply that we would withdraw. It happened that that was the right moment to attack, and Foch had the insight to see it.'

Reverting to Egypt, he said, 'The German advance in Cyrenaica was the quintessence of generalship. It is generalship we need in Egypt.'

'My plan for winning the war is this,' he said a little later: '1,000 tons of bombs a night on Germany—we are only averaging 50 now—and 20,000 tanks or so, ready to land all along the coasts of Europe.'

At about 3 a.m. Churchill announced that it was time for bed, and, coming up to me, he said, 'I am going to have breakfast in bed—I advise you to do the same.'

I certainly came out of this evening very badly, and I blamed myself for having started such an argument at the dinner-table. I did at least learn that a discussion with the Prime Minister in the presence of others was a very different matter from one in private. Later, I realized the wisdom of the technique which Brooke acquired after many stormy passages with the Prime Minister.

[1] For Lord Alanbrooke's account of this stormy scene, see *The Turn of the Tide*, p. 254.

Brooke found it an invaluable rule never to tell Churchill more than was absolutely necessary. I remember him once scoring out nine-tenths of the draft of a minute to the Prime Minister, remarking as he did so, 'The more you tell that man about the war, the more you hinder the winning of it.' Nobody who knew Brooke or the Prime Minister would take such a remark as a hundred per cent serious, any more than I did; but we were all nervous at all times of feeding a new idea into that fertile brain in case it might lead us away from the main stream into irrelevant backwaters.

When I saw Dill on my return to the War Office on Monday morning, 28th April, I told him what had occurred at Chequers. I think he could not help being amused—he had had to suffer the same sort of treatment so often himself. Later in the day he attended a meeting of the War Cabinet, and when he came back he sent for me and said, 'My word, you have raised a terrific storm, and it was made worse by Menzies—he spoke in the Cabinet on the same lines as you did at Chequers.' The Prime Minister had asked Dill to send him a copy of Wavell's 'Worst Possible Case', and had said he intended to order it to be called in. It was perhaps fortunate for Mr. Churchill's peace of mind that we did not learn, until some weeks later, that Wavell had a plan for an even worse case, namely for carrying on the war in Africa in the event not merely of Egypt but of the British Isles being lost.

Later in the day the Prime Minister sent us a directive for the conduct of the war. This had been prepared without the knowledge or advice of the Chiefs of Staff, and had obviously been largely provoked by the episode of the evening before.

DIRECTIVE
BY THE PRIME MINISTER AND MINISTER OF DEFENCE

Japan is unlikely to enter the war unless the Germans make a successful invasion of Great Britain, and even a major disaster like the loss of the Middle East would not necessarily make her come in, because the liberation of the British Mediterranean Fleet which might be expected, and also any troops evacuated from the Middle East to Singapore would not weaken the British war-making strength in Malaya. It is very unlikely, moreover, that Japan will enter the war either if the United States have come in, or if Japan thinks that they would come in

consequent upon a Japanese declaration of war. Finally, it may
be taken as almost certain that the entry of Japan into the war
would be followed by the immediate entry of the United States
on our side.

These conditions are to be accepted by the Service Departments as a guide for all plans and actions. Should they cease to
hold good, it will be the responsibility of Ministers to notify
the Service Staffs in good time.

2. The loss of Egypt and the Middle East would be a disaster
of the first magnitude to Great Britain, second only to successful
invasion and final conquest. Every effort is to be made to
reinforce General Wavell with military and air forces, and if
Admiral Cunningham requires more ships, the Admiralty will
make proposals for supplying them. It is to be impressed upon
all ranks, especially the highest, that the life and honour of
Great Britain depends upon the successful defence of Egypt.
It is not to be expected that the British forces of the land, sea
and air in the Mediterranean would wish to survive so vast
and shameful defeat as would be entailed by our expulsion from
Egypt, having regard to the difficulties of the enemy and his
comparatively small numbers. Not only must Egypt be defended,
but the Germans have to be beaten and thrown out of Cyrenaica.
This offensive objective must be set before the troops.

3. All plans for evacuation of Egypt or for closing or destroying
the Suez Canal are to be called in and kept under the strict
personal control of headquarters. No whisper of such plans is
to be allowed. No surrenders by officers and men will be considered tolerable unless at least 50 per cent casualties are sustained
by the unit or force in question. According to Napoleon's
maxim, 'when a man is caught alone and unarmed, a surrender
may be made'. But Generals and Staff Officers surprised by
the enemy are to use their pistols in self-defence. The honour
of a wounded man is safe. Anyone who can kill a Hun or even
an Italian has rendered good service.

4. The Army of the Nile is to fight with no thought of retreat
or withdrawal. This task is enforced upon it by physical facts,
for it will be utterly impossible to find the shipping for moving
a tithe of the immense masses of men and stores which have
been gathered in the Nile Valley.

5. In considering reinforcements for the Middle East, the
question of the defence of Great Britain against invasion does
not arise, as the available shipping would be far less than the

ships which would contain the number of troops who could be safely sent.

·6. Should TIGER[1] succeed, the empty ships should be returned by the short cut, keeping their deck armaments for this purpose. It must be remembered that General Wavell has, with the troops returned from Greece, a trained personnel of eight or nine Tank Regiments, for which the Tanks now sent or in his possession are barely sufficient. Moreover, the personnel of the Tank Corps now going round the Cape will require other Tanks besides those already provided to await them on their arrival. Therefore we must contemplate a repetition of TIGER at the earliest moment. The situation must be judged, however, when and if the M.T. ships return.

7. DOUBLE WINCH[2] having succeeded again, should be repeated with the utmost speed, all preparations being made to the aircraft in the meanwhile.

8. There is no need at the present time to make any further dispositions for the defence of Malaya and Singapore, beyond those modest arrangements which are in progress, until or unless the conditions set out in paragraph 1 are modified.

I gave Dill a note upon this directive, which I reproduce here.

NOTE ON THE PRIME MINISTER'S DIRECTIVE OF 28TH APRIL

It seems to me quite wrong that a strategical directive of this kind should be issued by the Prime Minister without the advice of the Chiefs of Staff. Surely, the Chiefs of Staff should at least put forward firm recommendations as to the policy to be adopted in the Mediterranean. Then, if the Prime Minister wishes to overrule any of their recommendations on his own responsibility, it should be quite clear that he has refused to accept considered military advice.

The directive contains many statements which I consider to be not only unsound, but extremely dangerous. The chief points are indicated in the following notes:

Paragraph 1. The last sentence of this paragraph is quite unacceptable from a military point of view. It takes some three months to dispatch[3] and instal additional defences in Malaya.

---

[1] The direct convoy through the Mediterranean.

[2] Supply by air to Egypt.

[3] Even allowing for a proportion of the reinforcements to come from Australia and America this statement was still true because many of Malaya's essential requirements had to be supplied from the United Kingdom.

It seems to me inconceivable that Ministers are gifted with such foresight that they will be able to give us three months' notice of any change in the forecast given by the Prime Minister as to the possible action of Japan. Moreover, even if they can give us three months' notice, it might well be impossible to make available the reinforcements required for Malaya if in the meantime we implement the instructions given in the remainder of the directive as to the dispatch of our resources to other destinations.

Paragraph 2. I do not agree that the loss of Egypt and the Middle East would be a disaster second only to successful invasion. The Middle East does not come second in our priorities. It would be possible to evacuate the Middle East and still carry on the war successfully, provided that we had not expended so much of our resources in the Middle East as to prejudice the security of the United Kingdom, Malaya and the Cape, and consequently our main sea communications.

It is quite wrong to say that the life of Great Britain depends on the successful defence of Egypt.

It is also quite wrong to say that British forces, land, sea and air, in the Mediterranean would not wish to survive the evacuation of the Middle East. If they did not survive it we should have insufficient forces left with which to carry on the war successfully.

The directive refers to the enemy's difficulties and his comparatively small numbers. This is true of the immediate future, but we have to look farther ahead.

I agree with the last sentence of paragraph 2. It is quite correct that the troops themselves should be filled with the offensive spirit. It may well be possible to achieve a victory in the Middle East which will have far-reaching results. But in case this victory should not materialize, it is of course essential that the Higher Command, both here and in the Middle East, should take cognizance of other possibilities.

Paragraph 3. The first sentence can be agreed. In fact, this is the present procedure.

I do not agree that 50 per cent casualties should be the standard. It is quite wrong to interfere with the conduct of the campaign by the commanders-in-chief on the spot to this extent.

Paragraph 4. The first sentence is all right as a directive to the troops. But it is not all right as a directive to the Commander-in-Chief.

It is wrong to say that shipping would not be available for more than a tithe of the men and stores. It is to be anticipated that a great part of the forces would not move by sea at all.

Paragraph 5. This paragraph is most dangerous. It brings into prominence once more the fact that the Chiefs of Staff have as yet no firm policy regarding the size of the forces which must be retained in Great Britain against invasion. It would be possible, with available shipping, to send away to the Middle East so much that the safety of the United Kingdom would be jeopardized. In fact, it would be quite possible to win the Battle of the Middle East at such a cost as to ensure our ultimate defeat.

We cannot accept the doctrine that invasion is so unlikely that we need make no proper provision against it. Invasion remains the only quick way of ending the war. As American aid grows, particularly with regard to shipping, the possibility of invasion must be more than ever present in the mind of Hitler. It is also certain that, as our scale of air attack upon Germany increases, it will become more than ever desirable to eliminate the bases of our air forces in the United Kingdom. Finally, if Hitler feels that his position is becoming intolerable, either through being unduly sprawled, or because of economic difficulties, it is certain that he would not give in without a last gamble in the shape of an attempt at invasion.

We cannot therefore escape the conclusion that sufficient forces must be kept in the United Kingdom to provide an adequate defence. And we cannot accept the instructions to send away out of the United Kingdom as much of our resources as our ships will carry.

Paragraphs 6 & 7. These are paragraphs on which the First Sea Lord and Chief of the Air Staff must advise.

Paragraph 8. I have already dealt with this point in my remarks on paragraph 1 above. Paragraph 8 is quite unsound strategically.

Most of these points were duly embodied in a memorandum which the Chiefs of Staff sent to the Prime Minister six days later, though it was naturally not so outspoken as my note to Dill. They rubbed in the fact that it took three months for reinforcements to reach Malaya, they dissented politely from some of the more sweeping exaggerations, and they defended the action of Wavell in preparing plans for the Worst Possible Case. Indeed, in this last matter they went still farther, declaring it essential to prepare blockships at once in case they were needed for the Suez Canal. But in point of fact this particular exchange came to nothing: for on the 21st June Hitler attacked Russia, the dispute became academic, and our conflicting theories were never put to the test.

14

WAVELL AND THE PRIME MINISTER

1941

On 2nd May our forces were out of Greece and, according to our information, 45,000 or more men had been taken off, out of 60,000. But all the heavy equipment was lost.

In the desert, the Germans were attacking Tobruk, and had penetrated a big sector of the defences. Late on the night of 1st May I had a talk with Dill about Tobruk. I said I still thought the decision to hold the place had been wrong, and that it would have been sounder to withdraw the force towards the frontier, and to counter-attack the Germans when their communications were stretched. Dill said that Wavell had been influenced by the great quantity of stores he had collected there, which he did not want to abandon, and he hoped that Wavell had not given undue weight to this factor.

Wavell was uneasy about the defence of Crete; the Iraqis were shelling our aerodrome at Habbaniyah; and Malta had been heavily bombed, with much damage to shipping and to the harbour.

The whole situation in the Mediterranean had, in fact, deteriorated with extraordinary rapidity. If the Germans had concentrated on the Middle East for the next few months, it is very doubtful whether we could have held it. But Hitler, with his Russian plans, was about to come to our aid, as he so often did at critical moments of the war.

At this time, criticism of Churchill was bitter and general, and it was said that all was not well with the machinery for the military control of the war. The gist of the criticisms was that we were living from hand to mouth on a diet of improvisation and opportunism; that no clear-cut military appreciations were being laid before the War Cabinet, for their discussion and approval or rejection; that from their very inception, military opinions were being distorted and coloured by the formidable advocacy of the Prime Minister; in fact, that he was not only advocate, but witness, prosecutor and judge. He was also criticized for sending personal directives to the Commanders-in-Chief without professional advice, and for exhausting the Chiefs of Staff to the point of danger.

Among the most outspoken of his critics was Menzies, who was still in London, and he made no secret of his downright opinions. I never discussed the higher control of the war with him, but I often heard him pronouncing on it, and putting into words what many of us felt in our hearts, that only Churchill's magnificent and courageous leadership compensated for his deplorable strategic sense. When he heard Churchill describing Wavell's plan for a possible evacuation of Egypt as 'defeatist', Menzies said to him that a general who had not thought of this would not be fit for his job. Churchill had spoken to Menzies also about the poor performance of our troops on various occasions. 'He does not seem to realize,' said Menzies, 'that men without proper equipment, and with nothing but rifles, do not count in modern war—after all, we are not living in the age of Omdurman.'

I met Hankey one morning on my way to the War Office; he was one of the wisest men I knew, and although he no longer occupied an official position, and I could not reveal plans to him, he was the repository of many confidences. I told him that many of us were thoroughly uneasy at the way the machine was running; and he replied that I was the fourth person near the centre of things to tell him that in the course of a few days. He said it had been the same, in some ways, with Lloyd George in the First War; but Lloyd George, though a rogue elephant, had had two steady old elephants to push him in the right direction, in the shape of Smuts and Milner.

I know that Hankey, and I believe that Menzies, both tackled the Prime Minister direct concerning his methods of conducting the war; but they cannot have made any headway: for the procedure remained unchanged, and the struggle between personalities continued, with Churchill always in the ascendant, until Brooke became C.I.G.S. at the end of the year. Meanwhile he continued to play Tom Tiddler's Ground across the dividing line which should properly separate the sphere of the statesman and that of the technical advisers. Often, as in the matter of the reinforcement of the Middle East, he was proved abundantly right; but we sometimes longed for a leader with more balance and less brilliance.

Early in May, there was an exchange of notes between him and

Dill, initiated by a draft which I wrote for the latter, on the vexed question of the relation of the Middle East to the security of the United Kingdom. Dill's first note and the Prime Minister's reply to it are printed in *The Second World War*,[1] and I do not propose to reproduce them again; but some of the Prime Minister's points were effectively answered in our riposte, which he did *not* print. Dill made one or two amendments to my draft, fearing that I had made it read rather pertly. The Prime Minister had said, among other things, 'I never remember hearing a single British soldier . . . deprecate our occupation of Belgium'. To this we replied that very many had, and that some of their criticisms had reached Gamelin himself.[2] We also made a point which has a bearing on the whole relationship throughout the war between the Prime Minister and his military advisers and commanders:

> 'I am sure that you, better than anyone else, must realize how difficult it is for a soldier to advise against a bold offensive plan. One lays oneself open to charges of defeatism, of inertia, or even of "cold feet". Human nature being what it is, there is a natural tendency to acquiesce in an offensive plan of doubtful merit rather than to face such charges. It takes a lot of moral courage not to be afraid of being thought afraid.'

In this context, I am tempted to quote the judgment of Professor Butler, who, writing of this period, says of the Prime Minister, 'He was too much inclined to consider boldness a sufficient qualification for high command.'[3] With that post-war observation of an historian, we would all have heartily agreed at the time; but let me make it crystal clear that we never ceased to be aware of his stature, or to feel other than deeply privileged to serve him. He towered over us all like a Colossus; but this would not be a true account of the atmosphere in Whitehall, nor of the angle from which I saw the Prime Minister, if I were to shrink from recording our feelings at the time, and the effects of his constant bludgeon-strokes on our daily work.

On the morning of 6th May, when I went to see Dill, he said: 'There is a serious matter to be settled today. The Prime Minister wants to sack Wavell and put Auchinleck into the Middle East.' Dill intended to tell him that, since it was obvious that he had lost confidence in Wavell, it was right that he should get rid of him;

[1] Vol. III, pp. 373–7.
[2] See p. 31 *supra*.
[3] Official History, *Grand Strategy*, Vol. II, p. 562.

that he, himself, had not lost confidence, but that the Prime Minister was the man who mattered. He added that he considered that Wavell should not go to India, as had been suggested, but that he should come home, for he was certain to be brought into the war again.

In the evening Dill said that the atmosphere had changed. The Prime Minister had been especially irritated the day before because he had considered Wavell to be too weak in his attitude to Iraq; Amery had written to him to say that he thought Wavell had lost his nerve and to suggest that he (Amery) might go to the Middle East to hold his hand. But, on the 6th, we had received more optimistic messages from Wavell; we had also had news that the Iraqis had withdrawn from Habbaniyah after having shelled the place for some days. I said that, on reflection, I thought it would be a mistake to sack Wavell—it would shake public confidence, and it might appear that he was being made a scapegoat.

On this day, 6th May, Iraq was transferred from the Indian Command to that of Wavell. Wavell telegraphed to Dill, 'What a baby you have given me on my 58th birthday'. Dill cabled back: 'Yes, what a baby, but I hope you will soon kill the little brute. Many happy returns of your birthday, but not of the baby.'

On the night of 10th May there was a heavy air raid. On the morning of the 11th some big fires were still burning, the air was thick with smoke, and the streets littered with débris and charred paper. The rooms occupied by my Middle East section were wrecked, but luckily no one was hurt, and our papers were secure in their steel safes. Dill's flat in Westminster Gardens was also hit, and the room below his bedroom blown away. Dill was very pleased because he had lost nothing but some collar studs. The windows of his room in the War Office had also been shattered. The Prime Minister telephoned about something or other in the morning, and Dill told him his flat had been bombed. Churchill said it served him right because he should have been sleeping in the basement of the War Office.

In the passage outside the door of my room there was a pile of bricks and broken glass, and, when it had still not been removed on the following day, I telephoned to London District Headquarters, and asked them to send over a working party to clean up the mess. Half a dozen Guardsmen duly turned up and did the job. When I saw Dill soon after he said to me, laughing, 'You have made a real blob. X [naming a senior civil servant] has just been to see me to complain about you. He is furious with you for bringing soldiers in to do a job that lies within the province of the Civil Service, and says there has been nothing like it since Cromwell took his soldiers into the House of Commons.'

On 11th May there were indications that the Germans would soon attack Crete. In the desert they were in difficulties owing to the heat and the sandstorms, and their supplies were being interrupted by the Navy, who were sinking a good many of their ships. The threat from Cyrenaica seemed to have been scotched for the time being. In Iraq, our troops had arrived at Basra, and we hoped to get control of the country fairly quickly. The direct convoy (with 200-odd tanks) had reached Alexandria, having lost only one ship (with 50 tanks), sunk by a mine, and it seemed likely that Wavell would soon be able to return to the offensive.

Churchill was still thinking seriously of removing Wavell. Dill told me that the Prime Minster was infuriated by the advice he gave him—'You must back him or sack him.' Dill, so far, had refused to advise his dismissal on any other grounds.

Liverpool and other English seaports had been heavily bombed. Luckily the Germans did not stick to the seaports as targets long enough to incommode us seriously; if they had continued to bomb them, we should soon have been in difficulties.

I was working, on 11th May, on a general appreciation which we were preparing in the hope of getting a firm policy for the distribution of our forces between the British Isles, the Middle East, Malaya, etc. As I noted in my diary at the time, this was 'an endeavour to get away from the improvisation in which we have been indulging'.

During the following week the Prime Minister abandoned for the moment his talk of sacking Wavell. He was concentrating on details of the dispositions of forces in Crete, Tobruk and East Africa. He sent to the War Office for information, but many of the particulars he required we could not supply. In the end he drafted a telegram to Wavell, to tell him how he should defend Crete—'let the Germans in before counter-attacking, then kill the lot', etc., etc. He also asked us to produce detailed plans for the occupation of Syria, and many hours were wasted on this because we did not possess detailed knowledge of the dispositions of the troops in Wavell's command. For some reason, he would not ask Wavell, whose business it was, to produce the plan. By the end of the week everyone was worn out by this futile work.

We were now beginning to learn that the Germans were moving many divisions back into Central Europe. We also knew that preparations were well advanced for an attack on Crete, and that German aircraft were passing through Syria into Iraq. In Cyrenaica, fighting was continuing around Sollum and Sidi Barrani, but the Germans seemed to have outrun their supplies, and there appeared to be a fair prospect of driving them back before very long.

General Sir George Giffard, who was C.-in-C. in West Africa, came to see me, and I had a long talk with him about his problems. We had had to consider the possibility that the war might move down into his parish, if the Germans occupied French North Africa; but we hoped that, in this event, the Americans would relieve us of that theatre. In the meantime Giffard had had to be left very short of equipment, and he had no air forces at all.

Brigadier Whiteley,[1] of Wavell's staff, also came to see me, on his return from America. He had been sent over to report on the Middle East to the President and other high officials. He told me that Knox and others had said they reckoned that the U.S.A. would be in the war within 30 to 60 days.[2] The President had questioned him at some length. Whiteley had been optimistic in his forecasts, and had assured the Americans that Wavell was confident that he could hold the Germans. But he told me that, in Washington, they feared we could not hold the Middle East, and felt that we might expend too great an effort there, and not come out in time.

On 19th May the Germans launched their attack on Crete, and things were looking ominous in Syria. Wavell had been strongly urged by the Government to occupy Syria, but he had replied that he had no troops to spare for a serious operation.

After luncheon the Prime Minister sent for Dill to come to Downing Street and 'have a cup of coffee and a cigar' (in neither of which he ever indulged). On his return, Dill told me that Churchill had finally decided to get rid of Wavell, and to put Auchinleck in his place. He intended to send Wavell to India where, he thought, he would enjoy 'sitting under the pagoda tree'. Churchill had said he could not have Wavell hanging around in London, living in a room in his club. Dill had repeated his former advice: 'Back him or sack him.' Churchill had replied: 'It is not so simple as that. Lloyd George did not trust Haig in the last war—yet he could not sack him.' Dill had told him that Auchinleck, for all his great qualities and his outstanding record on the Frontier, was not the coming man of the war, as the Prime Minister thought.

[1] Afterwards General Sir John Whiteley.
[2] The U.S.A. entered the war in December 1941, or about 180 days later.

Later in the day, Dill saw Amery, who did not wish Wavell to go to India because he thought everybody would feel that India was being saddled with a cast-off, whether for reasons of failure or mere fatigue. Neither of these suppositions would be acceptable as a background for a new Commander-in-Chief.

Dill thought that Wavell's removal would rock the Government. He was the one big figure in the Services at that stage of the war; the public believed in him, and so did the soldiers.

On the 20th and 21st May the Germans developed their attack on Crete. There were parachute and glider landings on a heavy scale. We had a message from Freyberg[1] on the 21st, which he had despatched at 10.15 p.m. on the 20th: 'This has been a hard day. We have been hard pressed. . . . Margin by which we hold the aerodromes and ports is a bare one. . . .' While I sat with him after dinner, Dill drafted a telegram to Freyberg and sent it off: 'Our thoughts are with you and your gallant troops in the historic battle which you are now fighting. May complete victory soon crown your efforts.'

Wavell was now being pressed to seize Syria by a kind of political *coup*, if he was unable to find troops for a military operation. He telegraphed early in the morning of the 21st that he was making preparations for a combined British and French operation 'if situation favourable', and he added, 'but you must trust my judgment in this matter or relieve me of my Command'. He was of course quite unaware that his dismissal was already being considered. When we received this telegram, I discussed it with Dill, and he then sent a note to the Prime Minister, in which he said:

> 'It is my opinion that we have now come to the point where we must either allow Wavell to carry out the policy which he believes to be sound or relieve him of his command. My own feeling is that, at this juncture, we should trust Wavell. It is no time to make a change.'

When I returned from luncheon, I found Dill sitting in his car in front of the War Office. He had been summoned to a Cabinet meeting, and was waiting for some papers to be brought to him. He beckoned to me, and asked me to get into his car and drive with him to Downing Street. Dill said that the Prime Minister had received his note about Wavell 'very badly', and that he intended

---

[1] Major-General Bernard (afterwards Lord) Freyberg, V.C., Commander of the New Zealand Division, was G.O.C. Crete.

to *order* Wavell to carry out the instructions that had been sent to him with regard to Syria. Dill asked me whether I thought he had been consistent in his policy, since he had agreed to the instructions to carry out the political *coup*. I said that I considered his position perfectly right—it was not inconsistent to have agreed to the instructions and then, when he had become aware of Wavell's reaction, to have written to the Prime Minister as he had done. I also said that, if the Prime Minister considered this a suitable occasion to force the issue, it might be a very good thing to do so from the Government's point of view as well as Wavell's. As I got out of the car, the Prime Minister was walking across from the War Cabinet Offices, looking very glum and pale. I saluted him, and he turned, and smiled as he greeted me, then he put his head down again and stumped into No. 10.

The Cabinet did not sit for long. When Dill returned to the War Office, he showed me a telegram to Wavell which had been approved at the meeting.

'Nothing in Syria must detract at this moment from winning the battle of Crete, or in the Western Desert. Freyberg declares he is hard pressed. No troops needed to sustain him can be diverted. Presume you are now reinforcing him with all he may require to master airborne attack.

We do not object to your mixing British troops with the Free French who are to enter Syria; but as you have clearly shown, you have not the means to mount a regular military operation, and, as you were instructed yesterday, all that can be done at present is to give the best possible chance to the kind of armed political inroad described in our telegram of 20th May.

You are wrong in supposing that the policy described in our previous telegram of 20th arose out of any representations made by the Free French Leaders or by Spears. It arises entirely from the view taken here by those who have the supreme direction of war and policy in all theatres. Our view is that if the Germans can get Syria and Iraq with a few aircraft, tourists and local revolts, we must not shrink from running equal small-scale military risks, nor from facing the possible aggravation of political dangers from failure. We of course take full responsibility for this decision and should you find yourself unwilling to give effect to it, arrangements will be made to meet any wish you may express to be relieved of your Command.'

Dill would have preferred to omit the last sentence. Wavell, he said, might now ask whether he had the confidence of His Majesty's Government. This would be awkward to answer. He asked me: 'What if he asks if he has *my* confidence? In that case I would reply "Yes".' I agreed, and said he could add, 'But the issue is not that—it is whether you have the confidence of the Government.'

At about 10.30 p.m. Dill came to my room to talk about some other matters, and we discussed the Cabinet telegram again. I said that, if I were in Wavell's shoes, I should reply that interference in the details of my Command had become intolerable, and that, unless I could be assured that it would cease, and that, in future, I would have the confidence of His Majesty's Government, I would prefer to give up my Command. He would then be on strong ground, having regard to the number of occasions on which he had been overruled or over-pressed. Dill said that he did not think any bad mistakes had been made, up till that time, in our instructions to Wavell, to which I replied: 'Wavell has no cause for complaint on bigger issues. That is because he has acquiesced. But the interference in detail has been outrageous.'

To my astonishment, Wavell accepted the Cabinet instructions without a word of protest. I never thought he would. He sent, the next day, a reasoned and restrained reply, in which he gave it as his opinion that the threat from Syria might well become more serious than the threat from Cyrenaica, and that he was moving the 7th Australian Division from Mersa Matruh to Palestine for the operation. The intelligence on which the Cabinet had ordered the political *coup* proved to be unfounded, but Wavell naturally did not rub this in. He made no reference to the threat to relieve him of his command.

This decision of Wavell's constituted, in my opinion, another error of judgment. It seemed right, at that time, that Syria should be occupied, since the Germans would be too close to Egypt if they got there first; but from a purely military point of view, the timing was wrong. The operations in the Western Desert, which became known as 'Battle-axe', were to suffer from the dispersion of forces which now took place; it would have been better to postpone them until the Syrian business was cleared up.

Whiteley was about to leave London to resume his duties on Wavell's operational staff. He suggested to me that it might be helpful if he saw the Prime Minister before his departure, and I arranged an appointment for him. He told me afterwards that his interview had consisted mainly of a tirade by the Prime Minister, who had repeated to him what he had so often said before—that Wavell's command consisted of half a million men, and that there was little to show for it; that the Germans, on the other hand, were fine soldiers, ruthless, and capable of achievement.

We were still suffering from the effects of our national habit of neglecting to create an army until after the outbreak of war. It could not be denied that some of the performances of our soldiers had been distinctly poor. But Churchill could never make allowance for the fact that it took three years to train and equip an army; he preferred to abuse the generals, sometimes with justice, often without. Someone, about this time, said, 'I don't see how we can win the war without Winston, but, on the other hand, I don't see how we can win it with him.'

On 23rd May there was growing anxiety about Crete, where the Navy had suffered heavy losses. The Chiefs of Staff and the Defence Committee held several meetings on the 22nd and 23rd. Dill was sent for by the Prime Minister on the 23rd, and did not get to bed until 1.30 a.m. for the third night in succession. On the 25th the situation was getting worse. Freyberg was unable to dislodge the Germans in the west of the island, where they were being reinforced by air. Wavell was endeavouring, too late, to put more troops in. Having done our best to leave him the free hand a Commander-in-Chief should have, we now felt that he had been mistaken in not sending them sooner.

Wavell had great achievements to his credit, but, as I noted in my diary at the time, I felt that he had now committed three, and possibly four, major mistakes, viz.:

(a) In Greece, where he would have sent 5 Divisions (one of them armoured), and lost them, had the Germans given him a little more time;

(b) In Cyrenaica, where he failed to appreciate the danger of the original German attack;

(c) In the desert and in Syria, where he was about to undertake simultaneous operations which would lead to undue dispersion of force at a critical moment (though the pressure put on him from home was immense);

(d) In Crete, where he underestimated the force required for defence.

On the 26th the Prime Minister sent Wavell a stream of telegrams, in which he urged him on to take more active measures—'Victory in Crete is essential', 'Hurl reinforcements into Crete', 'What about a stroke in the Western Desert?', and so on. Dill said to me, 'Poor Wavell, I feel so sorry for him with all these difficulties.'

Few Commanders-in-Chief in history have ever had such a row to hoe as Wavell at this moment. His problem called for a most careful distribution of his forces and for a good sense of timing. The Navy wanted Cyrenaica to be cleared of the enemy if Crete had to be lost, so that we should hold at least one side of the Eastern Mediterranean. It was important, too, to hold Cyprus, which was practically undefended. The Cabinet were pressing him to occupy Syria before the Germans could get there. This, he had said, would require three divisions (one of them armoured), and he had only one division to spare. He had also been told to seize Iraq in order to forestall the Germans, and a column (under General Clark) which had been sent to do this, in conjunction with the troops landed at Basra, was stuck half-way to Baghdad. One thing seemed quite certain to us—that if the battles were to be fought from London, a mess would be made of them. But this was not the Prime Minister's view.

After a Cabinet meeting, on the night of the 25th, Dill said to me, 'Do you realize we are fighting for our lives now?' I replied that I thought the situation was certainly grim, but not hopeless, and I reminded him that, in Whitehall, we suffered from a great disadvantage, in that we knew too much about the appalling difficulties which beset the men who were trusted by the people and the soldiers. All the same, I felt that, if the Germans were to continue to concentrate their efforts on the Middle East, we should soon have to reckon with the possibility of not being able to hold it. The German attack on Russia was still a month away, and we were wholly unaware that it was pending.

On the 27th May I went to the War Office at 9 a.m. I found a telegram which Wavell had sent in the night, to the effect that the situation in Crete was hopeless, and that he had ordered Freyberg to take to the hills with what troops he could extricate from the fighting. The Prime Minister asked Dill to go over to see him and discuss this telegram. On his return, Dill asked me to dictate for him a short appreciation of the situation, which he could send to the Prime Minister. That afternoon, he asked me to let him have three more notes, on Cyprus, Syria and Iraq, which he could use as briefs at the meeting of the Defence Committee to be held that night. When I handed them to him, I remarked that, although things were in rather a mess, we might take some comfort from the fact that we would have suffered worse disasters, had it not been for German mistakes. The timing of the German operations in Norway, in France, and in Greece, for instance, had saved us from the far greater losses we would have sustained had it been slower. I added that it was quite possible that the Germans would make more mistakes before very long; this shot in the dark was soon proved to be quite a good one.

I label these three notes A, B and C.

A. *Note on the pros and cons of holding Cyprus.*

No one will deny that there are advantages in holding Cyprus. The advantages fall under two main heads:

(a) It would prevent close-range air attack upon the alternative naval base at Haifa, and would prevent an increase in the scale of air attack generally upon sea communications in the Eastern Mediterranean and upon Alexandria.

(b) It would force the Germans to move into Turkey, which would cause delay in mounting a heavy attack from Syria and add yet another occupied country to their present embarrassments.

Whether it is right for us to defend Cyprus depends upon the strength of the forces which would be required. It is most important that we should not detach to Cyprus so many forces that a collapse of the position on the mainland might result from their loss.

The strength of the forces required to hold Cyprus depends, of course, upon the scale of attack which the Germans can bring to bear upon the island. In my view the scale of attack which could be developed is quite heavy. Cyprus is within range of specially fitted dive-bombers based on the Dodecanese. Very considerable airborne forces could be landed in the island, which contains many natural landing grounds as well as a certain number of artificial ones. A considerable scale of seaborne attack is also possible, because the Navy, with all their other commitments, cannot undertake to prevent it.

The defence of the island, which is 100 miles long by 60 miles broad, could not be guaranteed unless we put into it forces of the following order:

2 Divisions,

3 or 4 squadrons of fighter aircraft,

50 to 100 anti-aircraft guns.

It is clearly impossible to provide forces on this scale.

B. *Note on action in Syria*

Anything that can be done to occupy Syria, before the Germans are established there, should be done.

There seem to be three possibilities:

(a) To occupy the whole country with the co-operation of the Turks.

(b) To advance to the line Damascus-Rayak-Beirut, which General Wavell thinks he might be able to do, if all goes well, starting the first week in June.

(c) To occupy a line a short distance over the Palestine frontier on which to carry out delaying and defensive action.

We should aim at (a).

If (a) is impossible, then we should attempt (b), the moment for action being chosen by General Wavell. If we were able to accomplish (b), we should be in a position to hamper German action from Cyprus, and we might even force him to develop his main attack through Turkey.

(c) would be the course remaining open to us if both (a) and (b) failed.

C. *Note on Action in Iraq.*[1]

1. In the appreciation which you sent to the Prime Minister this morning you made it clear that in Iraq the utmost boldness is required to complete the disintegration of Rashid's regime. In the letter attached, Mr. Amery makes certain suggestions for action from Basra which, if practicable, would contribute towards this end.

2. If the Defence Committee Meeting tonight results in the despatch of instructions of any kind to the Commanders-in-Chief in the Middle East, I suggest that Mr. Amery's proposals might well be included in any such telegram.

3. Connected with this question of operations in Iraq is that of the command of the forces there. General Wavell has given his views in the attached telegram, but we have so far received nothing from General Auchinleck as a result of his talk with General Wavell. In my view, General Wavell's proposals should be accepted. It is not possible to divide Iraq into two spheres of operations, nor can General Quinan control the whole country until he has established contact, presumably at Baghdad, with the forces coming from Palestine.

[1] On 2nd May, 9,000 Iraqi troops with 50 guns had invested the British cantonment at Habbaniyah. Rashid Ali fled the country, and his attempt to seize power collapsed, on the 30th.

15

AUCHINLECK RELIEVES WAVELL

1941

On 28th May Churchill sent another directive to Wavell in which he emphasized the need for victory in the Western Desert and for quick action in Syria. Dill wrote a note to the Prime Minister, when he saw the draft, protesting against this interference, which, he said, might upset Wavell's judgment in handling the very delicate problems with which he was faced. He also went over to Downing Street to speak to him about it, but the Prime Minister insisted on his telegram being sent.

On the 29th orders were sent from London to evacuate Crete, but Wavell had already decided to do this, and his telegram crossed ours.

A week later, on 6th June, I dictated the following note, to put on record the views I held at the time with regard to our failure to hold the island:

'Much criticism is now being directed against the conduct of the campaign in Crete.

During the first four days of the operations it would appear that the Air Force was able to provide no fighter cover for either the Navy or the Army. And, after the first four days, the fighter cover provided was very inadequate, consisting only of occasional brief flights made by aircraft based on Egypt. The Navy had never pretended that they could operate close to enemy shore-based aircraft without fighter cover. It is not clear whether the Navy realized, before the operation began, that fighter cover would not be forthcoming.

As soon as the Navy were forced out of the waters round Crete, it became clear that the Army could not hold the Island. The garrison provided would probably have been sufficient

127

to deal with airborne attack provided that it had some assistance from fighter aircraft in shooting it down. But it was not big enough to deal with seaborne attack, and seaborne attack became possible as soon as the Navy were driven off. The garrison required to deal with seaborne attack would probably have been in the region of three or four divisions. Such a force could not be spared from Egypt. Moreover, such a force (together with the civil population) could not have been maintained in the island without fighter cover to enable our ships to enter the harbours on the northern side.'

On the 30th May we had a gloomy telegram from Wavell. He said that prospects in the Western Desert were not bright, owing to the inferiority of our tanks and armoured cars. The Prime Minister telephoned to Dill at 9.30 a.m., while I was discussing with him some papers for the daily Chiefs of Staff meeting. He said that he considered Wavell's telegram the message of a tired and beaten man. He added that he was deeply disappointed with the fighting in Crete. Dill said, 'You must not forget, Prime Minister, that we started the war without an army. Although we are getting on, our army is not an army yet, except in name, and it is not too easy to build it up and to fight at the same time.' Churchill then suggested that we should send more reinforcements to the Middle East, to which Dill replied, 'No, Prime Minister, we cannot send more units. Of course we must maintain what we have got there, with reinforcements and equipment, as well as we can—but we cannot risk sending any more units from here.'

When this conversation was over, Dill and I had a talk about the situation. I said I considered we were not beaten yet in the Middle East, but I thought it very important that we should keep enough in hand to hold the outer ring if we were forced on to it, and that we should not lose the war in an effort to save Egypt. The real danger would come if the Germans were to begin a heavy air attack on Egypt, and it seemed that this might happen within a few weeks. We still did not know that Hitler was about to switch his air forces to Russia.

On the afternoon of the same day (30th May) Dill sent for the V.C.I.G.S. and myself, and said to us that the question of Wavell was becoming very urgent in the Cabinet. He, himself, was now in two minds about it. He added that individuals did not count now, and that we must not allow our judgment to be swayed by personal feelings. We were indebted to Wavell for such successes as we had had, and our admiration and affection for him had not lessened; but we came to the conclusion that Dill should advise that, if the Government could face the difficulty with the public, it would be best that Wavell should go: not merely because he had made mistakes, but because the Cabinet had lost faith in him.

On 1st June there were some brighter gleams in the Middle East. The Iraqis had signed an armistice; our troops had reached Baghdad. But, more important, the Germans were moving large forces from Greece to Poland, although for what reason we could not yet be sure. In fact, so far as the Middle East was concerned, it now became apparent that the Germans were about to repeat the mistake, which they had made more than once before, of failing to concentrate upon one objective for long enough to get decisive results.

Wavell had sent us a series of telegrams in which he had pointed out his need of reinforcements, and had drawn our attention to shortcomings in the delivery of material he had been promised. He had also given reasons which had led him to the conclusion that he should not undertake an immediate offensive in the desert. In spite of this, however, he now attacked at Sollum and undertook, simultaneously, the invasion of Syria. Dill had given Wavell a strong hint that it would be wise to postpone the desert offensive and to make sure of Syria first, but he elected not to do so, with the result that both operations suffered for lack of punch. The desert attack suffered most, and was, in fact, a failure; the occupation of Syria dragged on for a month, and was not completed until 11th July.

On 6th June, the day before our troops entered Syria, I dictated the following note which indicates how our thoughts were shaping with regard to the phase of the war upon which we were now entering.

NOTE ON THE NEXT PHASE OF THE WAR

During this summer, we shall still be on the defensive. The Germans will have the initiative, and we cannot choose the places in which we shall fight. We may suffer further heavy reverses.

At the moment the German effort seems to be directed

(a) against the Middle East;

(b) against Russia.

In the Middle East the situation for us is difficult, but with good management and a certain amount of good fortune, it is quite possible that it may turn in our favour. The Germans are now meeting with increasing difficulties. They have come to the end of easy advances. They are now meeting obstacles in the shape of the sea and the desert. They are becoming more and more extended, more and more of their forces will be required to hold down newly occupied territories.

They have been forestalled in Iraq, and with luck we may be able to forestall them in Syria. It seems more than likely that this would not have been possible but for the fighting in Greece and in Crete. The German programme is doubtless behind time, and time for them is short.

In order to restore the situation in the Eastern Mediterranean it is necessary for us to occupy Syria and Libya. If we were able to operate fighter aircraft from both these places the Fleet would be adequately covered. (It would be similar to the cover provided in Home waters where we hold one side of the sea only.) The Navy would be able to move freely enough for our purposes. They would also be able to keep open communications to Malta which otherwise might be closed.

In the conduct of any operations which we now undertake for the clearance of the Mediterranean shores, it will be necessary to provide a much heavier concentration of aircraft than seems to have been possible up to now. When the Germans undertake operations they always use an enormous concentration of air power to cover them. When we operate our air cover is never sufficient. The necessity for adequate air support has been rubbed in time and time again. Without such support neither the Navy nor the Army can operate with full effect.

The reasons for the German concentration against Russia, which has involved considerable withdrawal of their forces from Greece, are not yet clear. One of the greatest weaknesses from which Germany has suffered in this war lies in her relations with Russia. It seems possible that she has now found it necessary to clear the situation up. Germany may be able to get what she wants by a show of force. Failing this, she may have to carry out the occupation of the Ukraine and the oil-fields. The harvest will be in within a few weeks, and the moment will then be suitable for such an operation. Now that the seizure of the Middle East oil-fields must appear doubtful to Germany, it will be all the more necessary for her to secure her supplies from Russia. (No doubt the occupation of Crete had as one of its objects to ensure passage of oil by sea from the Caucasus.)

The setback to the German programme may well involve her

in great difficulties, with so much on hand that must be accomplished before the winter.

Germany's relations with Vichy France have suddenly become closer. There are indications that we may soon see a closer measure of co-operation between Germany and France. Indeed, it is possible that France may even attempt war-like action against us, although this would not be very effective in the present state of her fighting forces. Events in Syria may precipitate a crisis. (We shall enter Syria the day after tomorrow.)

If France moves further into the German camp the greatest danger for us will lie in the added threat to our Atlantic communications. We may be deprived of the use of Gibraltar, and a threat to Freetown may follow. Measures are under active consideration to ensure the occupation of Fleet bases to replace Gibraltar. But the situation in West Africa is not so satisfactory. In West Africa we should have far stronger defences at Freetown, and we should have sufficient forces on the spot to be able to advance to the line of the Senegal River, which is the best line on which to hold German penetration from the north.

The necessity for American intervention grows greater every day. It is to be hoped that America will enter the war before the summer is over. Provided we are holding out in the places which are vital for the security of our sea communications when America enters the war, there will be little need for anxiety.

It must be clear to the Germans that, failing a successful invasion of the British Isles, there is no prospect of an early victory for them. Indeed their present operations seem to be designed to secure the resources, particularly corn and oil, which will be necessary to them for the conduct of a long war.

The next phase of the war will probably see great efforts on each side to produce the heaviest possible scale of air bombardment on the other. To this form of attack the British Isles are, of course, somewhat vulnerable, lying as they do at the centre of the circle, the circumference of which is occupied by Germany—in part at any rate. On the other hand, we have always taken the line, in this country, that heavy air bombing was to be expected, the public has been fully warned, preparations made to deal with casualties, etc., on a heavy scale.

In Germany the reverse has been the case. The German people have been assured not only that the war would be over quickly, but that they would be more or less immune from bombing. The wider the German forces are flung, the more vulnerable will Germany be to air bombardment. When we arrive at the stage of being able to blot out one German town after another the effect on German morale should be devastating, and it should be quickly felt. The German people at home will have been separated from their menfolk for a long time and their absence will be felt when bombing becomes heavy. There will, moreover, be much dissatisfaction at the thought that the German fighting men are living in luxury and safety in foreign lands while the people at home have to suffer. And the German fighting men will be filled with anxiety for the safety of their families in Germany.

The execution of this policy demands the building up of a very large force of bomber aircraft, but the numbers required are well within the capacity of British and American production. To finish the war a well-equipped army will be required, in order to occupy Germany when morale is sufficiently undermined.

A point which requires very close attention is the preservation of our own morale during the period of retaliatory action on the British Isles. The arrangements made up to date are not adequate and much more remains to be done to safeguard the civil population.

A development of the struggle into bombing and counter-bombing, however, would be a tragic affair, and long drawn out. We must hope—and, in this war of surprises, the hope is by no means unlikely to be fulfilled—that some other dénouement may be possible.

The Prime Minister made a practice of telephoning, from time to time, to junior officers in the War Office. One night, during the Syrian campaign, he asked to be put through to M.O.5, the section of my staff which dealt with the Middle East. Presently he was told that M.O.5 was on the line.

The following conversation ensued:

Prime Minister: Is that M.O.5?
Voice: Yes.
Prime Minister: How do you think the operations are going in Syria?
Voice: Oh, I think everything is going all right.
Prime Minister: What about that turning movement the French are trying to make?

Voice: Oh, that seems to be all right.
Prime Minister: Who are you?
Voice: Corporal Jones, Duty Clerk, M.O.5.
    End of conversation.

On 10th June I attended the debate on Crete in the House of Commons and heard the Prime Minister's speech. He could not, of course, give all the facts, but his speech was well received, and criticism was uninformed.

I was on leave for a week from 14th to 20th June. When I returned on the 21st, I went to see Dill. The past week had been a disappointing one. The Syrian invasion was going very slowly (although Damascus fell that day), and the offensive in the desert at Sollum had failed with heavy loss. Dill said, 'I suppose you realize we shall lose the Middle East?' I was somewhat taken aback at this, but I replied, 'Well, that depends on the Boche. If he concentrates on the Middle East, I agree that we cannot put in sufficient resources to hold it. But he may not concentrate on it, and he may get into trouble elsewhere.' Twelve hours later, the Germans declared war on Russia.

On this day Churchill sent over to us copies of two telegrams which he had despatched. One was to Wavell and the other to the Viceroy; and they contained instructions for Wavell and Auchinleck to exchange commands. The blow had fallen on Wavell at last; Dill and I were both very sad for him, and we discussed at some length what had gone wrong. I felt his biggest mistake had been his failure to take the right line with regard to the instructions he had received from London. How far was a commander in the field justified in opposing directives from his Government with which he disagreed? We felt that he must expect to be abused, and to be reproached for lacking initiative, and that he must be prepared to resign if his advice on major questions were over-ruled. I thought that Haig would never have allowed his hand to be forced if he had found himself in Wavell's position.

We recalled Wellington's relations with his Government in the early days of his campaign in the Peninsula, and Dill pointed out the tremendous advantage he had enjoyed in the slowness of his communications with home. Reverting to Wavell, I suggested that, apart from his handling of the Prime Minister's directives, his biggest mistake in the realm of strategy was Greece, though I realized that Dill might not agree. 'Well,' said Dill, 'when I was out there, I was always hoping that the Boche would attack in Cyrenaica before we got committed in Greece.'

Dill showed me a letter he had had from Wavell. It said among other things that he felt tired; that he sometimes wondered if his judgment had become affected; and that, if he were told to go, he would go without making any trouble. He added that he hoped his successor would be more successful than he in dealing with the 'bold and hazardous courses' put to him by the Prime Minister.

Next day Dill sent for me. He had evidently been thinking over our conversation about Wavell's relations with the Prime Minister, and he was anxious that Auchinleck should be fully apprised of what he was likely to be up against. Together we drafted the letter which appears below. It has already been printed by Professor Butler;[1] but I reproduce it because I think it casts a useful light on the whole problem of relations between the supreme direction and the command in the field, and because it illustrates clearly the lessons which we were learning the hard way at that time. It also shows how solicitous, in the midst of all his own worries and preoccupations, Dill was, to ease the task of those who had to bear the burden of command.

26th June, 1941.

My dear Auchinleck,

On your taking over command in the Middle East, may I add to my congratulations, which I have sent you by telegram, a few words on the situation and perhaps of advice?

After Wavell had captured Benghazi, there was a possibility that he might have pressed on to Tripoli. He could only have done this with very small forces (as the so-called 7th Armoured Division was worn out), in the hope that the Italians were so demoralized that they could offer no effective resistance. But any hope there was of such a venture was ruled out by the decision of H.M.G. to support the Greeks. It then became a case of sending the maximum strength to Greece and leaving the minimum to hold Cyrenaica.

The result you know. We did not leave enough to secure Cyrenaica and the forces we sent to Greece and subsequently to Crete suffered heavily and lost much precious material—material which, as you will realize from your experience in England, is desperately difficult to replace. To right the situation, we did our best to send equipment at express rate and some 295 tanks were sent through the Mediterranean at great risk, and with great luck and good management on the part of the

[1] Official History, *Grand Strategy*, Vol. II, pp. 530–2.

Navy, 238 arrived, only one ship containing 57 was sunk. Then came a very difficult period. It was most desirable to clear the Germans back in Libya at the earliest possible moment, so that the Navy might be able to get the air protection necessary to enable it to attack the enemy's communications with Tripoli and also maintain Malta.

It was also highly desirable to act rapidly in Syria to forestall the Germans.

From Whitehall, great pressure was applied to Wavell to induce him to act rapidly, and, under this pressure, he advanced into Syria with much less strength than was desirable, and in the Western Desert he attacked before in fact he was fully prepared. The fault was not Wavell's except in so far as he did not resist the pressure from Whitehall with sufficient vigour.

You may say that I should have minimized this pressure or, better still, that I should have seen that, having been given his task in broad outline, he was left to carry it out in his own way and in his own time. I might possibly have done more to help Wavell than I did, but I doubt it. The fact is that the Commander in the field will always be subject to great and often undue pressure from his Government. Wellington suffered from it: Haig suffered from it: Wavell suffered from it. Nothing will stop it. In fact, pressure from those who alone see the picture as a whole and carry the main responsibility may be necessary. It was, I think, right to press Wavell against his will to send a force to Baghdad, but in other directions he was, I feel, over-pressed.

It is about this question of pressure which I particularly want to speak. You may be quite sure that I will back your military opinion in your local problems, but here the pressure often comes from very broad political considerations; these are sometimes so powerful as to make it necessary to take risks which, from the purely military point of view, may seem inadvisable. The main point is that *you* should make it quite clear what risks are involved if a course of action is forced upon you which, from the military point of view, is undesirable. You may even find it necessary, in the extreme case, to dissociate yourself from the consequences.

Further, it is necessary that such a Commander should not wait for pressure and suggestions or even orders. He should anticipate these things and put clearly before his Government in the most secret manner how he views the situation and the action he proposes to meet it. He should point clearly to the risks he is prepared to accept and those which he considers too great. He should demand the resources he considers strictly necessary to carry out any project and he should make it clear what he can and cannot do in their absence.

You, in your responsible Command, will never have in the near future all the resources which you would like to have to carry out your great task. You, having served here, know something of the situation and the immediate paucity of our resources. You know too what the essentials are in our great picture—to hold England, retain a position in the Middle East, maintain a firm hold in Malaya and keep open our sea communications, which last-named involves such things as continuing to be able to use West Africa. The time will come when we can strike out with effect and there is hardly a soul in the world outside Germany who will not rejoice at our success and join in our final victory. But in the meantime we have a grim fight to fight and we cannot afford hazardous adventures. So do not be afraid to state boldly the facts as you see them.

The second and last point upon which I would like to touch concerns 'air co-operation'. Nowhere is it good. Nowhere have we had sufficient training. You will find the 'Air' out to help, but they have no complete understanding of what is required of them from the purely Army point of view and how necessary training is. Also, to ensure that our military and air strategy works in complete harmony is uncommonly difficult. It is quite clear that Tedder has to serve the Navy as well as the Army, but his main mission in life is to support the Army to the nth degree in any operation it has to undertake and to support it in the manner most acceptable to the Army Commander concerned. When you have had time to look round, you may be able to let me know how you view the problem and whether I can do anything to help.

I would add that the telegrams marked 'Private from General Auchinleck to C.I.G.S.' are in fact private, whereas 'Personal' telegrams have a certain limited distribution. I may have told you this before.

God bless you.
Yours ever,
(Signed) J. G. Dill.

Meanwhile, at Dill's request, I had written a strategic review of the Middle East, which he had read before we composed the letter to Auchinleck. I also reproduce it in full. It dealt largely with the past; but it makes a useful summary at this moment, for it marks the end of a phase. The 21st June was the day that Wavell was told that he was being superseded; the 22nd the day that the Germans attacked Russia. We did not at first realize the magnitude of this German blunder; remembering the fiasco of the Russian armies in Finland, we were not optimistic about their ability to withstand the German assault. The most we dared to hope for was a temporary respite.

STRATEGY IN THE MIDDLE EAST

Whether we can now hold on to the Middle East depends on one thing and one thing alone—whether the Germans concentrate seriously against us there. If they do, they will be able to develop their attacks in considerable strength from the west through Libya, from the north through Turkey, and possibly from the north-east through the Caucasus and Persia. We cannot produce sufficient strength in the Middle East in the near future to secure our position in face of serious attack from even one of these fronts. Even if we had the forces available for dispatch to the Middle East, which we have not, we have not the shipping to transport them or maintain them. The fact of the matter is that the maintenance of the forces already in the Middle East constitutes a drain on our resources which we can ill afford in face of the threat to the British Isles and to ill-defended key points, in particular, West Africa and Malaya. If we hold on in the Middle East over an appreciable period it will therefore be only because the Germans are fully occupied elsewhere.

We are now relatively far weaker in the Middle East than we were at the beginning of the campaign last October. Reinforcements have been sent, both for the Air Force and for the Army, but these have been far outweighed by the losses we have sustained (taking into account German reinforcements). We have certainly inflicted heavy damage upon the Germans, and no doubt we have delayed their progress to some extent; here again, the balance is an adverse one for us.

In a retrospect over the last few months, even making allowance for the great difficulties with which Wavell has had to contend, it is clear that grave errors have been committed both in London and in the Middle East—but far more in the Middle East than in London.

The pressure exerted by London upon the Commanders-in-Chief in the Middle East has been far too great. There has been a constant flow of directives and suggestions regarding both major and minor policy. The Directives can be justified partially, and only partially, upon the ground that political considerations and other considerations of Government policy were involved. They might also be justified on the ground that they were not couched in terms of definite orders. But they have been pressed far too hard.

It seems to me, however, that the gravest mistake has been committed in the Middle East. This mistake—and it is an inexcusable one in my view—consists in the acquiescence by the Commanders-in-Chief in practically every suggestion which was put to them. On occasion they have expressed disagreement, but their disagreement has never been insisted upon.

It is probably true to say that every commander in the field has been subjected to pressure by his government to adopt this or that strategy. But the great commander, in this situation, must display, and in history he has always displayed, a considerable degree of toughness or stubbornness in resisting propositions which he believes to be unsound. This quality has never been displayed in the Middle East. It is inconceivable to imagine men like the Duke of Wellington or Douglas Haig acquiescing in a strategy such as that which has been, to all intents and purposes, dictated to the Middle East over the last six months. There have been at least four or five situations when a great commander would have preferred to resign rather than follow the course which has been suggested. Nothing can take the place of proper direction by the commander on the spot. Therefore, if what I have said is true, as I believe it to be, much of the blame for the present situation must be laid upon the shoulders of the Commanders-in-Chief, and of Wavell in particular.

The strategical errors which in my view have been committed are the following:

(a) *The failure to push on to Tripoli after the Italians were routed in Cyrenaica.*

At this moment the remaining Italian forces were inconsiderable, and their morale was at its lowest ebb. A small force rushed on to Tripoli might well have eliminated the enemy threat from the North African shore for the rest of the war. Occupation of this shore would have given us control of the sea communications in the eastern Mediterranean, which is now lost. Wavell did suggest sending on such a force, but rather tentatively. He was told from London to hold hard until the Balkan situation had been cleared up. This direction from London was a bad mistake, which I pointed out at the time, and again when the commitment in Greece became imminent. But the biggest mistake was committed by Wavell when he did not insist on sending at least a small force in a bold attempt to seize this great prize. The diversion of such a force would not have affected his ability to operate in Greece. Nor did the Naval Commander-in-Chief perceive this great opportunity and offer to co-operate in seizing it.

(b) *The commitment in Greece.*

There is no doubt now that this was a major error. From a purely military point of view, which was never given its proper weight, we could not afford to send a strong force to Greece. At best we might have held a front against the Germans in Greece. But the maintenance of this front would have drained away the resources of Egypt, and they could never have been replaced. It is inconceivable that the Germans would have confined their attack to Greece, and if they had attempted a flank attack on Egypt either by way of Libya or through Turkey, the forces remaining in Egypt would have been so weak that we could not have held the country. But it was clear to all, except the wishfully-minded, that we could never have held the Germans for long in Greece. Therefore the only sound basis for this adventure would have been to send only the minimum forces necessary to satisfy political requirements. (When the Greeks were first approached they actually said they did not wish British Forces to come to Greece, and we could have confined our effort to air operations on the mainland and to the holding of Crete, without any loss of honour.) And we should have been prepared to lose anything we sent. The political pressure put upon the Commanders-in-Chief, Middle East, was tremendous. A certain measure of disagreement was expressed in the early stages of the discussions. But when the plan began to take definite shape no protest was raised by the Commanders-in-Chief, except only by Longmore, who represented that his resources were insufficient. Wavell accepted, without a murmur, a proposition that he should send to Greece four infantry divisions and an armoured division. Had not the Germans attacked in Cyrenaica as early as they did, this large force would have been sent. It would all have been lost, and the Germans would have had a walk-over in their advance in Libya. It seems inconceivable that the Commander-in-Chief should have accepted and attempted to carry out such an unsound project.

(c) *The loss of Crete.*

This flowed directly from the adventure on the mainland of Greece. If the fully-equipped forces which were sent to the mainland had been put into Crete, there is little doubt that we could have held the island. We never imagined that the Germans would concentrate against Crete for long. This conception we now know to have been correct, for they had the Russian business on their hands, and they could not have afforded the losses of men, aircraft and of time which they would have incurred in prolonged operations against Crete.

(d) *The holding of Tobruk.*

I considered at the time that the holding of Tobruk was a strategical error. It now seems as if this view would prove correct. A directive to Wavell to hold Tobruk was stopped, just before dispatch, on the grounds that it was wrong to dictate action on such a matter from London, and that in any case the holding of the place might lead to a situation such as we had at Kut. The correct strategy in the desert seemed to be to fall back, the farther, within limits, the better, and to deliver a counter stroke when the enemy had overrun his communications and had hundreds of miles of desert behind him. But at the moment when the cancelling of this directive was being discussed between the Prime Minister and the C.I.G.S., Wavell telegraphed to say that he had decided to hold the place. Here again the decision lay properly with the commander in the field, and all one could do at this end was to leave him free to make his own decision. The decision, as far as one can gather, was largely influenced by the fact that large quantities of stores had been accumulated in Tobruk. The loss of these stores would have been regrettable. But the loss with which we now seem likely to be faced will be even more regrettable. There is now little prospect of reaching the place by land. Unless we are saved by some lucky chance, it seems certain that we shall have to take out by sea as many as we can of the men, and to leave behind their own equipment, in addition to the stores which were already there. Other reasons which influenced the decision to stand at Tobruk were—firstly, the check which would be placed on the enemy's advance by the threat of this large force on his communications, secondly, the effect it would have in holding back the enemy air bases, and thirdly, the denial to the Germans of the seaport. But all these objects would have been better accomplished by a defeat of the enemy in the open desert at a point east of Tobruk.

(e) *The simultaneous launching of the June attacks upon Libya and Syria.*

Here again considerable pressure was exerted from London. This was a mistake. But the bigger mistake was committed in the acceptance of the plan by Wavell. The double operation constituted a flagrant violation of the elementary principle of concentration. One operation or the other should have been undertaken with greater strength. The German threat from Libya was never regarded as immediate. There was of course the fact that the German force there might grow stronger the longer they were left. But one of the chief causes of failure is now said to be that the armoured division had not had time to train and settle down. This alone was a sufficient reason for the Commander-in-Chief to put forward for postponing the operation. Moreover, the Syrian operation was undertaken on the basis that it should be regarded as 'a gamble'. We could not afford a failure in Syria for many reasons. It was therefore a grave error not to concentrate a bigger force against Syria. On the information available, Syria could not wait, since it appeared that the Germans were establishing themselves there. Therefore the correct action would have been to allow Libya to wait, and to strike hard at Syria.

These are all grave errors of judgment and strategy.

Against them must be set, of course, the well-conceived and brilliant operations carried out against the Italians in Libya and East Africa.

At a meeting of the Defence Committee on the night of 25th June, the Prime Minister announced the forthcoming change in command in the Middle East and, as Dill told me after the meeting, he had criticized Wavell in bitter terms. He had evidently been at his most difficult. He had also attacked Dill upon his refusal to agree to the despatch of 100 more cruiser tanks to Egypt, by direct convoy through the Mediterranean, over and above the considerable number that we had already planned to send. Dill felt that, with the Germans racing towards Moscow, invasion of the United Kingdom might be the next item in Hitler's programme after a quick victory over Russia and that it would therefore be wrong to send these tanks away. Churchill had said, 'You would see Tobruk brought down, with all those Australians there, you would see the whole position in the Middle East crumble, rather than send the tanks.' Dill had been quite firm, but, he told me, he had received no support from the other Chiefs of Staff.

On the 26th, the Prime Minister summoned another meeting, at 5.30 p.m., to continue the discussion with regard to the despatch of the tanks. Dill asked me, before the meeting, whether I thought he should resign if he were over-ruled. I said, 'Yes'. Dill said he thought so too, and that, if the Prime Minister were to refuse his resignation and at the same time insist on sending the tanks, he could say that he wished to state his case to the War Cabinet.

On the following day Dill told me that the Prime Minister had once again been in one of his worst moods. He had attacked Dill afresh about the cruiser tanks for Egypt. Dill said, 'I just smiled and sat silent. Then the Prime Minister said, "Well, I won't send them—not because of the reasons you have given, but simply because the Navy can't take them." ' 'Well,' I remarked, 'it doesn't matter what the reason is, so long as he does not send them.' 'That is exactly what I feel,' said Dill. He repeated that he was prepared to resign on this issue, and that, if the Prime Minister refused his resignation, he would appeal to the War Cabinet. He added that he had twice before offered to resign.

The Prime Minister had also spoken at length of the premature offensive in the desert earlier in the month. He was still bitterly disappointed and angry at its failure. It had now become evident that our attack at Sollum had been badly timed, not only strategically, but tactically as well, for no adequate time had been allowed to the crews and the units to train with their new tanks before they were put into action.

On 13th July, Wilson and Dentz[1] agreed upon the terms of the armistice in Syria, and we felt that it had not been a bad performance to wind up this campaign in a month, considering the inadequacy of

[1] General Dentz was the Vichy French Commander-in-Chief in Syria.

the forces with which it had been undertaken. There now seemed to be a good prospect of consolidating our position in the Middle East, although, owing to the shortage of shipping alone, the forces there could not be substantially reinforced. We had indeed been lucky in that the Germans had switched off their attack; but for this, we should not have been able to occupy either Syria or Iraq, and we might well have lost Cyprus, and a good deal more besides.

Dill was much harassed by the Prime Minister's interventions in the minutiae of Service affairs. One day when he returned from a particularly difficult interview with him he said, 'The Prime Minister was quite impossible today.' Then, looking up at Sir Henry Wilson's portrait which hung among others in his room, he remarked, 'One cannot condemn Henry Wilson so heartily as one used to, now that one has had first-hand experience of politicians.'

When Wavell received the telegram which informed him of his dismissal, he wrote to Dill and said he 'was sorry he had not done better'. He also sent us a very frank account of the withdrawal from Cyrenaica in April. In it he admitted freely that he had not appreciated the possible weight of the German attack at Benghazi, and he described the series of mistakes and misunderstandings on the part of his subordinates which led to the *débâcle*. Never once in his official communications had he blamed anybody but himself.

Dill sent a copy of Wavell's report to the Prime Minister, who thereupon circulated it to the Cabinet, with a covering note, in which he criticized Wavell strongly and, as I thought, unjustly. When a copy of the Prime Minister's note was brought to me I took it to Dill, and said that it seemed to me to be very unfair. Dill read it and then said he had not seen it until that moment, and that he was horrified. He at once wrote to the Prime Minister as follows:

PRIME MINISTER.
1. I have only just seen your note of 11th July covering the report of the action of the 2nd Armoured Division during the withdrawal from Cyrenaica.
2. I feel I must let you know how shocked I am that you should make such an attack on General Wavell as you do in paragraphs 3 and 4 without giving him any chance to make an explanation. One of the clearest impressions I get from General Wavell's statement is that, as is his habit, he is taking blame to himself which properly belongs to his subordinates, particularly those who were taken prisoner and are therefore unable to state their case. I would certainly have been disposed to unmask such subterfuges

had I known that an attack was going to be made on him.
3. In particular, I must take exception to your statement that
the Commander-in-Chief and the General Officer Commanding,
Cyrenaica, were 'resigned to disaster' should the enemy press
hard. The sentences from paragraph 8 of General Wavell's report which you quote refer only to the task of the 2nd Armoured
Division, not to the Commander-in-Chief's intentions for the
whole force in Cyrenaica.

As you have emphasized yourself, the value of armoured
forces is most apparent in the offensive, and it was with the idea of
conserving the armoured force in Cyrenaica for an offensive blow
at the enemy, as soon as opportunity arose, that General Wavell
directed its preliminary withdrawal if faced with superior forces.
4. This is clearly shown in the directive (copy attached) which
General Wavell issued on 19th March as soon as he returned
from a visit, upon which I accompanied him, to General Neame
in Cyrenaica. From this directive it is clear that General Wavell
intended to defend Cyrenaica by a mobile action in which the
enemy, if he advanced in superior strength, should be lured
forward along the coast whilst the 2nd Armoured Division
operated at all times on the enemy's inner flank until a suitable
opportunity presented itself for a counter stroke. Such a counter
stroke against the flank and rear of the enemy would compel him
to beat a retreat, or to be cut off and captured.
5. It was recognized by General Wavell, and explicitly stated
in his directive, that the flat plain south of Benghazi offered no
position which could be held. General Neame was told, therefore, to examine whether a position could not be organized
immediately South of Benghazi between the escarpment and the
sea. If, however, the enemy strength made this impossible, he
was to hold the road leading up the escarpment immediately east
of Benghazi and the defile where the road to Barce enters the
hills. This position, with the 2nd Armoured Division on its
southern flank, would still have allowed a counter attack to be
made against the enemy's rear and flank where his communications ran parallel to General Neame's front east of Benghazi.
6. It is clear to me from this directive that General Wavell had
issued the orders best calculated to enable the forces in Cyrenaica
to defeat an enemy advance, and I submit that the account of the
battle which has now been received should be read in the light of
these orders before blame for what happened can be fairly
apportioned.

7. General Wavell unquestionably under-estimated the strength in which the Germans were likely to advance into Cyrenaica. This mistake he has freely admitted. But I can assure you that nothing could be further from his mind than to deceive His Majesty's Government as is implied in paras. 3 and 4 of your note.   14 July, 1941.

Two days later Churchill sent a note in reply in which he said, 'I must retain the right to address my own Cabinet colleagues as I think fit upon such information as is before me at any time.' He denied that anything in his paper suggested that Wavell had 'deceived the Government', the charge he was making against Wavell was that he had not informed the Government accurately, or sufficiently fully, about the position in the Desert. The decision to send the Army to Greece, he added, was 'freely taken by the men on the spot' without the slightest pressure from home, but that he certainly had had no idea till now that the Western flank had been 'left so hopelessly under-insured'.

Dill's acknowledgement of this note closed the correspondence.

PRIME MINISTER.

Thank you for your note No. M.747/1 of 16.7.41.

I sincerely hope that you do not think that I for one moment wished to question your obvious right to address your Cabinet colleagues as you think fit. I am sure, for your part, you will not take it amiss if I seek to defend commanders who I think have been criticized without a full hearing.

General Wavell's failure to appreciate the strength in which the Germans might advance and his very imperfect knowledge of the fitness of his own troops to meet such an advance are serious mistakes which brought serious consequences. The other faults which you attribute to him were, in my opinion, not his.

17th July, 1941.

Thus Wavell's command in the Middle East came to an end. We knew well, in the War Office, the great things he had to his credit, which far outshone his failures. It was a remarkable achievement, with the resources at his disposal, to have destroyed the Italian Army, and to have occupied Abyssinia, Syria and Iraq, even though he failed against the Germans in Greece, in Crete and in the Desert.

Reflecting upon the controversies that agitated us in London during the last months of Wavell's command, the reader of this narrative may well come to the conclusion that Churchill was right, and that we in the General Staff were wrong, on at least two questions which had engendered much heat. He was always for reinforcing the Middle East and for taking a chance on the security of the British Isles. We, on the other hand, believed the importance of the United Kingdom in our strategy to be so great that no risk there should be accepted so long as there was still a real danger of invasion.

The second point of difference was whether it was wise or not to prepare plans for a possible evacuation of Egypt. Churchill felt that the risk of neglecting to make such plans was more than counterbalanced by the danger of fostering a defeatist outlook in the minds of the Commanders-in-Chief and their staffs. As things turned out, it would not have mattered if no plans had been prepared.

In both these matters we were endeavouring to base our action on a reasoned appreciation of what the Germans might do. Churchill seemed to move by impulse and by intuition, and we therefore regarded him as a gambler. In each case it must be admitted that the gamble would have come off. As we now know, it was not put to the test.

All the same, the atmosphere in the General Staff, as we toiled at our tasks in the War Office, was invariably one of calm cheerfulness; our confidence in ultimate victory was complete even when things went wrong, though at this moment it was certainly difficult to make a definite plan that would bring it about. The charges of defeatism which Churchill hurled at us all continually and which were so fiercely resented at first, came to be regarded as time went on as a matter of course, and were even taken lightheartedly. But, though we would probably have denied this hotly then, there is no doubt that his taunts and exhortations and his criticism of every detail of our work, kept us continuously on our toes.

16

HITLER TURNS EAST

1941

When we heard, early on the morning of 22nd June, that Hitler had declared war on Russia, we did not think the Russians would stand up for long. But, even so, it was obvious that this new commitment would at least afford us a respite, extend the Germans, and dissipate their strength. I see that I wrote in my diary: 'The thieves have fallen out. This Russian business may stretch the Boche and help us. We shall have to try to keep it going.'

Dill said that he regarded the Russians as so foul that he hated the idea of any close association with them; soon afterwards, Eden telephoned to me from the Foreign Office, and said he had just come out of a room where he had been talking to Maisky, and that he wanted to ask me what my ideas were about a Military Mission. I told him about my conversation with Dill, and asked him if he could tell me what sort of functions the Russians would allow a Mission to perform. There would be little or nothing that we could do, for some little time, in the way of sending in supplies; but a Mission might be useful if it could have some influence on Russian strategy, or if it were to be allowed to do something towards keeping the war going in Russia. Eden said he was not at all clear what a Mission could do; he could make no suggestions, but would ask Maisky to enquire whether one would be received in Moscow.

On the following day, 23rd June, Maisky told us that Moscow would receive our Mission. In the meantime Major-General Mason-Macfarlane had been nominated for the job. He was rather highly strung, but keen, clever, courageous and tough. He came to see me in the evening, and did his best to get out of it. He said he could see no light—nothing that he could do, and he suggested names of others who might go in his place. It is amusing now to read the notes I made of our interview, and to see how wrong we all were in our estimate of the Russians.

I said to Mason-Macfarlane: 'We don't think this is anything more than an off-chance. But we can't afford to miss even a poor chance like this. Your job will be to do what you can to help to keep the Russian war going, and so exhaust the Boche. Even if we only manage to keep it going in Siberia, as we did with the White Russians after the last war, that will be something. Another job will be to do what you can to ensure that demolitions are carried out by the Russians as they go back—it would be especially important to demolish the Caucasus oil-fields if they have to be given up. Another job, of course, will be to send us intelligence reports and let us know what is happening.' Mason-Macfarlane was very unhappy about it all. But he set about making preparations for his departure; and luckily for us all, my forecast proved to be unfounded. The Russians surpassed our expectations in every respect except in the provision of intelligence reports. They remained extremely reticent about what was happening on their front until the end of the war.

On the 26th June I made a note: 'Little news from Russia. We are all hoping that this business may prove to be a great blunder of Hitler's, but we cannot yet be sure. Winston has issued a directive ordering air attacks upon Germany while she is engaged with Russia, winding up, 'Make hell while the sun shines.' This directive was, of course, in accordance with our own views, but it was hard to do anything effective, especially in the air, because of the short June nights.

On 29th June it was still impossible to assess the Russian situation. According to the communiqués, both sides were winning. But it seemed to us likely that the Germans would soon break through towards Moscow, although they would be faced with immense administrative difficulties in a 500-mile advance. No one could say what would happen. Mason-Macfarlane had arrived in Moscow, and was telegraphing for large quantities of equipment, especially of fighter aircraft.

My next note was made on 13th July. The Russian front was still wrapt in mystery. Mason-Macfarlane had got nothing out of them about their dispositions or plans, or about the development of operations. The Germans were within 50 miles of Leningrad, and 25 of Kiev, and were surrounding Smolensk. We were still hoping that they would be involved in Russia until the winter came, but we had no facts on which to base an estimate. The Russians now urged us to carry out diversionary operations in order to relieve the pressure on them, and we were already considering the possibility of doing this.

A Russian Military Mission had arrived in London headed by General Golikov and Admiral Karmalov. They were a hard-looking lot. Dill forced himself to be friendly out of a sense of duty, but he said to me, after his first meeting with them, 'They look like a lot of pigstickers.' We gave them a cocktail party at the Ritz on 10th July, at which the theme of their conversation was the need for active intervention by us to help them. They were full of righteous indignation that we could not do more; they seemed to have entirely forgotten how they had ratted on us in 1939.

I stayed a night at Wrotham Park about this time. In the dining-room was a portrait of Admiral Byng, 'the unfortunate Admiral', as my hostess Lady Strafford called him. I inspected this picture with particular interest because Churchill had more than once referred to Admiral Byng when he had talked of having unsuccessful Generals shot by firing parties. The Prime Minister, joking, had once got the First Sea Lord, Pound, to admit that the shooting of Byng had had a salutary effect on the Navy in 1757.

When I dined with Colonel Raymond Lee, the American Military Attaché, as I often did, he always asked me to tell him how we proposed to win the war. I used to take the opportunity of rubbing into him that the Americans must not rely upon us to win it alone. Lee did not require to be convinced of the need for American intervention, and he explained, as indeed we realized only too well, that Roosevelt was still unsure of public support. Roosevelt had sent a Brigade of U.S. troops to Iceland, to relieve our garrison there; and we were all surprised, as I think he must have been himself, that this move had been so calmly accepted by the American public.

On 16th July Hore-Belisha, whom I had seen a few days before at a luncheon party at the Savoy, invited me to lunch with him at his house in Stafford Place. After luncheon we sat in his little garden behind the house. Hore-Belisha talked a great deal about his removal from the War Office eighteen months before, but without bitterness.

Referring to our visit to France in 1940, he said, 'I remarked to Gort that I did not think very much of the defences. Gort replied that he had seventeen designs for pill-boxes, but that he had not yet been able to get a decision as to which should be adopted. I said that that was the story of tank design over again. When we went to Paris I told Gamelin of this, and Gamelin said that the French had a quick method of making pill-boxes. On my return to London, I sent for engineering experts, and I asked them how defences could be made quickly. Ironside said, "You can't make a Maginot Line with mud," but the engineers suggested various ideas—one of them thought that the best way to do it would be literally to use mud, by freezing it. I then summoned the Army Council to discuss the problem. Just before the meeting Neville Chamberlain sent for me, and told me that he had had criticisms from Dominion visitors to the front about the state of the B.E.F. defences. I replied, "Curiously enough, the Army Council is sitting at this moment to consider the whole question, and I will see it put right." At the meeting Ironside said, "Jack Gort knows nothing about defences. Let me go and see the front and report."

'Ironside then sent a telegram to Gort, "Secretary of State wishes me to inspect and report upon defences." Naturally this telegram upset Gort. When Ironside came back he came immediately to see me, and said, "All France is in an uproar at your criticism of the defences." "Well," said I, "I hope you will put them right." Then, to my astonishment, Ironside said, "No—I agree with them," and he produced charts of the defences which showed a great number of completed works.'

I told Hore-Belisha that I had not heard the details of the dispute until now. I added that, the stronger the British defences had become, the greater would the danger have been of the British Army being surrounded and cut off, had we stood on the frontier; the French would undoubtedly have been swept away on our flanks because they had made no proper defences. As for his removal, I said that I thought the question of the defences was, in a sense, a side issue, because it seemed to me clear that the attack on him was the culmination of a long series of differences; if he had not fallen out with Gort and Ironside over that, some other occasion would have been found for a test of strength.

Hore-Belisha remarked that it was curious to reflect that both Gort and Ironside were his selections. Then he asked, 'Whom do you think I should have chosen as C.I.G.S. originally?' I replied, 'Dill.'

We talked about Churchill for a bit. Hore-Belisha said that he could not have served under him as a Minister even if he had been invited to do so: he could not have tolerated never being allowed to exercise the proper functions of a Minister. He had a poor opinion of the quality of the then House of Commons, but he thought that if feeling in the country against Winston became strong enough, the House would 'rise to the occasion'. I declared that I thought Churchill's régime had entirely justified itself, in spite of mistakes, if only for two things: the first, the way in which he had stiffened the people all through a difficult year, as nobody else could have done; the second, the manner in which he had handled our relations with America. Hore-Belisha conceded this; but he still thought that Churchill would fall.

Hore-Belisha then spoke about the future course of the war. He thought it would last a long time, and that the Russians would be out of it in three weeks. He remarked that, in thinking thus, he was guided by intuition as he always was. It was not one of his better hunches.

We then talked for a little about the difficulty of creating mutual trust between politicians and soldiers, and how it might be possible to overcome the idea that they belonged almost to different species. Hore-Belisha was charming, and I, at least, enjoyed our talk. I had never seen the side of his character that caused him to be disliked by so many soldiers.

There has been a good deal of speculation about Hore-Belisha's career as Secretary of State for War, and the circumstances surrounding his departure which in some circles has been viewed as a 'downfall' engineered by a 'conspiracy of brass hats'. In a sense I suppose it was. It seemed to me obvious that he had no natural aptitude for getting on with his military colleagues; they were suspicious of his undoubted personal ambition, and what they regarded as his passion for publicizing himself and his achievements. His actions in the so-called 'Pill-Box Controversy', for instance, were absurdly distorted; and although I am quite sure, from what I saw of it at first hand, that he was out to help in every way, these actions came to be regarded as symbolical of his reputed itch to interfere.

But he was always extremely kind to me; for all his fads and affectations, I never found him anything but easy to deal with. And I am in no doubt that the Army was deep in his debt. He brought the Army and the nation closer together in many respects; he improved conditions of service where his predecessors had failed to do so, although they had tried; he had the knack of handling Chamberlain's Cabinet; he made some changes at the top of the Army at a time when the operation was overdue. Whether he was wise in his filling of the vacancies which resulted is open to doubt. It may well be true that the best of his work was done by the time he went; it is hard to believe that he would have survived for long into the Churchill administration; but I have always felt that he has had less credit than was his due. Yet although the Generals may have handled him more roughly than he deserved, I am perfectly sure he was not the man for the hour.

On 17th July, the Prime Minister said to Dill that he would like to meet the Chiefs of Staff at 10.30 p.m., to discuss the question of reinforcements for the Middle East. Dill remarked that that was rather late. 'Not at all,' said Churchill, 'it is only eight-thirty by the old time.'[1]

On 21st July I dictated a note for record, which I reproduce here to show what we thought of the war then, or at least what I thought of it. I am loath to include too many such notes, but I think this one is important, for two reasons. It shows how uncertain we were of the ability of the Russians to hold out; and it illustrates the growing interest of the United States in our problems.

'The German advance into Russia continues, but progress is apparently slower than had been anticipated by the Germans. It appears that the Germans have now reached a point about half way between Pskov and Leningrad in the north. They have probably penetrated east of Smolensk, and are endeavouring to continue their advance towards Moscow on a wide front. In the south, they have reached the vicinity of Kiev and are turning south in an endeavour to round up the Russian armies on the Dniester. We have practically no information of the advance of the German *main* armies, and the points reached by their Panzer divisions are probably far ahead of the infantry advance.

The Russians are still extremely optimistic. They have given Mason-Macfarlane no information as yet about their dispositions or about the details of the fighting. They claim to have inflicted a million casualties on the Germans, and say that some of the German Panzer divisions are reduced to 40 or 50 tanks. They have carried out effective bombing raids on the Rumanian oil-fields.

The issue is therefore still in doubt. Stalin yesterday assumed supreme direction of the war. We have hopes that the Germans will be heavily involved in Russia for a long time to come. But our hopes have no reasoned foundation.

On the outcome of the Russian operations depends the next development of the war. There is still time for the Germans to finish the Russian campaign and to turn on Great Britain before the winter. If it is their plan not to try invasion, but to attempt to drive into the Middle East, they have the whole winter before them as a suitable season for operations.

In a few weeks we shall be able to assess the possibilities more clearly. We are still a long way short of minimum requirements

[1] It will be recalled that 'Double Summer Time' was in operation.

for defence at home, especially in tanks. Therefore we cannot yet dispatch a large number of tanks to the Middle East. The Prime Minister has ordered 150 tanks to be prepared for dispatch should the situation permit in two or three weeks' time. This number can be prepared only by taking them out of the hands of the troops in this country.

An appreciation has just been cabled from the Middle East—the first appreciation we have had since General Auchinleck's arrival. From this it is clear that an offensive against Cyrenaica cannot be attempted for two months at least. Even if the enemy forces now in Cyrenaica are not increased, Auchinleck estimates that he will require over 300 additional tanks. It will be impossible to provide them. On the assumption that the Germans will turn their attention to the Middle East within the next few months, Auchinleck estimates that he would require about five armoured divisions, not to mention 90 squadrons of aircraft. It is quite impossible to provide forces upon this scale for a very long time to come, if ever.

The Americans are fairly well informed of the facts. Mr. Hopkins, who has just arrived here, has asked for a military appreciation of the situation in the Middle East. He tells us that the chief military advisers in the U.S.A. hold the opinion that our Middle East policy is a mistaken one. They think our position there is quite hopeless, and that to send further reinforcements there is like "throwing snowballs into hell". As a result of this, he feels that the U.S.A. will not be willing to provide large numbers of tanks, etc., if we mean to allot them to the Middle East, especially in view of the fact that the British Isles and other vital areas on the sea communications, such as West Africa and Malaya, are still inadequately defended. He says that they would prefer to keep the equipment for themselves rather than let it go to the Middle East.

We are now going to prepare the appreciation he requires. We shall point out to him that, a year ago, and on several occasions since, it might have been proved conclusively on paper that we had no chance of operating successfully in the Middle East. It might have been argued on many occasions that the situation was so hopeless that we should do better to walk out. But war cannot be conducted successfully this way. The Germans have difficulties which we know only imperfectly. When everything appears hopeless, these difficulties may well cause the enemy to make some unexpected move which reduces the expected pressure—for example, when the Germans had to divert their forces to Russia. Our vital interests should not be risked unduly. It is true that we have taken risks to maintain the Middle East. The difficulty is to calculate these risks correctly. I feel that this American intervention into the sphere of strategic thought will be very wholesome in restoring a proper balance.

Another point, which the Americans do not seem to have appreciated, is that our difficulties are by no means over if we walk out of the Middle East. We would still have to hold the Germans on an outer ring, which must include India, the Persian Gulf, and the southern end of the Red Sea. The German communications would certainly be very stretched if they had to follow us so far. But we should still have to provide very considerable forces to hold the outer ring. It is right, therefore, that we should fight on the inner ring, that is to say in the Middle East, so long as we can do this without too heavy a drain upon our resources.

Japanese action may prove to be the determining factor in our policy as regards the Middle East. If the Japs enter the war, it is more than likely that we shall have to reduce our effort in the Middle East in order to hold Malaya.

There is one American criticism which is more difficult to meet. They say that the enormous air forces which we divert to the Middle East would be far more effectively employed in hammering Germany from bases in the British Isles. I think this is one of the disadvantages which must be admitted.

The situation in Iran is not too happy. A large number of German agents are established in the country. We are now in communication both with India and the Middle East as to action which might be taken in the diplomatic, and possibly in the military, sphere to secure their expulsion and establish ourselves in a controlling position. If the Germans were to appear in force in Iran by way of Russia, our whole position in Iraq would be threatened and our communications in the Persian Gulf might be cut.'

On 22nd July, the Russians were still optimistic and the Germans were slowing down. In the Middle East we now had a golden opportunity to strike in Libya, before the Germans could strengthen their forces there. But unfortunately we had not the means. Auchinleck had said that he wanted another armoured division before he could attack. We still felt we could not safely spare another one from England, and, in any case, it could not have been sent to him in time.

17

AMERICANS, RUSSIANS AND PERSIANS

1941

ON 22nd July I dined with Dill at his flat to meet Harry Hopkins. Hopkins was a man of great charm, and I took to him at once. He talked well and easily with great intelligence and spirit, though he looked a physical wreck; and I suppose that even then he was dying on his feet. Dill went off after dinner to a meeting of the Defence Committee, and I stayed and talked with Hopkins until about eleven o'clock.

Smoking cigarettes incessantly, he spoke first about America and Roosevelt. He said, with conviction, that the U.S.A. would be in the war within six weeks (he was 13 weeks out in this forecast). He told us that Roosevelt could not walk, which I did not then realize, and that he sat in a chair all day, and worked up to 6 p.m., when he had a swim, and a rub down. That, said Hopkins, was the best time to do business. He very often saw him at dinner, and they talked. 'The President,' continued Hopkins, 'is very like Winston in some ways —very temperamental. I regard my job as being to keep those two in close and friendly relations. If they were put together, in a ship for instance, they would be sure to have terrific rows.' He referred to a telegram which Roosevelt had sent the Prime Minister, casting doubts on the wisdom of hanging on to the Middle East, and suggesting that we should get out before we had wasted our resources too much. Churchill's reply to this telegram had made Roosevelt 'hit the roof'. 'But,' said Hopkins, 'I smoothed the President down. I said to him, "Remember you sent that telegram to a man who is fighting for his life. Think of the blitzes in London and all that and the United States still sitting outside the war." He softened at once, and sent a very friendly telegram back to Winston.'

We talked at some length about the Middle East, and before Dill left us, both he and I explained the British point of view. We told him that our constant problem was to strike the right balance in taking risks. Hopkins then said that the Prime Minister's present proposal to send 150 tanks to the Middle East would be 'like dynamite' to Roosevelt and Marshall. Marshall's argument was that, if the U.S.A. was to be in the war soon, he would want the tanks and other equipment for the American Army. He had given up things that were like gold, in order that we might have them. If we sent these tanks to the Middle East, he would feel they were being wasted and would want to keep them. Marshall, he added, was not convinced of the soundness of our Middle East strategy; and no one had talked to him about it in such terms as Dill and I had that evening.

I suggested to Hopkins that he should get the President to ask us for a military appreciation by the Chiefs of Staff. This might clear the air a bit. I said I realized there was much to be said in support of Marshall's views about the Middle East, but that you could not rely altogether on a bare comparison of military strengths. If we had worked on that basis, we might have cleared out of lots of places which we were still holding successfully. The enemy had difficulties we knew nothing of; courage was needed, risks had to be taken.

Hopkins then turned to the subject of the Prime Minister. I said that, in dealing with him, I had learned that it was important to realize that he hated looking on the worst side of things; he felt that even to speak of failure was half-way to bringing it about. Hopkins said he had noticed that, when he had stayed at Chequers. He described a harangue that Churchill had delivered, in which he had spoken at length about defeatism. 'I listened to him for a bit,' he said, 'and then I said, "Now, Mr. Prime Minister, I don't want a speech—I want something I can take back to convince the President you are right."'

When I bade Hopkins good-night, I felt that, in him, we had a good and powerful friend.

On 23rd July, we were working on a plan to get the Germans out of Persia. The idea was to try diplomatic pressure first, and then, if necessary, to deliver an ultimatum, backed by a threat to bomb Tehran and occupy the oilfields. This entailed concentrating a division and a half near Basra, which would take a week or two to do.

That evening General Chaney, who had been sent to London from Washington as a 'special observer', dined with me at the Club. He spoke of the situation in the Middle East. He thought we should give up the idea of an offensive in Libya, and merely defend the desert front, keeping the remainder of our forces in hand to meet the threat from the North, through Turkey or Persia. He also held very strongly that we should send no tanks out of England until the middle of September, basing this on the assumption that the latest possible date for invasion of the British Isles was the middle of November, by which time the weather would be too bad. Chaney and Hopkins were to meet the Prime Minister and the Chiefs of Staff on the following day, to discuss the Middle East. For this meeting we prepared an *aide-mémoire*, of which I have not kept a copy. But I made a note, at the time, of the chief heads.

Aide-mémoire on Middle East

1. Advantages of holding Germans off Indian Ocean. Retention of economic resources in M.E., especially Iranian oil in view of shortage of tankers. Cover for India. Effect on Arab world of withdrawal, etc.
2. By holding Middle East we can interfere with Axis trade in Mediterranean, increase effect of blockade. Later we can attack Italy, N. Africa, Greece, etc.
3. Turkey can be bolstered up if we join hands with Russia through Iran.
4. Adverse reaction on Spain, if Middle East given up.
5. Material loss involved in withdrawal.

Conclusions.

(a) We must balance, day by day, risk to run and disposition of available resources between United Kingdom and Middle East, the security of the U.K. being a first charge on our resources.
(b) If Germany becomes involved deeply in Russia, there is a good chance of holding on in Middle East.
(c) Americans should supply large numbers of tanks and aircraft for the Middle East, before the end of the year.

On 29th July someone told me that the Prime Minister had commented on the bomb-proof building which the Admiralty had erected near the Horse Guards Parade: 'They have put up a very strong place there—masses of concrete and tons of steel. Taking into account the fact that their heads are solid bone, they ought to be quite safe inside.' We were cheered enormously by this sally against our naval colleagues, who, we thought, usually got off more lightly than we on our side of Whitehall.

On 3rd August the prospects of invasion were fading fast, and it began to look as if Russia might hold out. It was therefore becoming safer to send reinforcements to the Middle East, but shipping was still the limiting factor. On that day Dill went off with the Prime Minister to join the *Prince of Wales* for the meeting which had been arranged with Roosevelt off Newfoundland. He telephoned to me from Chequers, and told me it had been decided to send the 1st Armoured Brigade to the Middle East, and that the rest of the Division was to follow later.

Before the Prime Minister left London, Auchinleck arrived from Egypt for consultations. Stolid and staunch, he made an excellent impression on the Cabinet. Churchill pressed him hard to start an offensive in the Desert. He said that he would certainly do this if an opportunity offered, but that he could not see any prospect of moving before November, when the strength and the training of his forces would be adequate. He was, of course, in a strong position to resist War Cabinet pressure after the failure of Wavell's premature attack at Sollum in July. He spent some time with me and described his plans for a far-reaching offensive.

On 7th August the Russians were still holding the Germans fairly well, and slowing up their advance. We estimated that the German casualties, since the beginning of the campaign, must have amounted to between half a million and a million, but we had no definite information, despite the presence of our Military Mission. Kiev had not fallen, and the Germans were still 60 miles short of Leningrad. On the southern front, however, they were making progress towards Odessa.

In the first week of August I attended two meetings which were called by Attlee, as Acting Prime Minister, to discuss the Persian situation. Eden, Anderson, Sinclair and Amery[1] were present, as well as Auchinleck. As I have already explained, we were anxious to get the German 'technicians' out of Persia, and we wanted to get control of that country in case the Russian front broke up in the South: in which event German armies would soon reach the Caucasus and, perhaps, the eastern side of the Caspian. If this happened, Persia would then become the essential bastion of our right flank in the Middle East, and an outpost for the defence of India; moreover, it was necessary to be sure of Persia if we were to continue to draw the vital supplies of oil from the Gulf. We were still anxious to accomplish our aim by diplomacy if possible; but in case that failed, we had arranged to concentrate a force at Basra by 12th August, consisting of one division, one cavalry brigade and two armoured regiments, designed to move into the Persian oilfields. Two more infantry brigades were due to arrive from India on 20th August, and our view was that we should not move before that date, in case there should also be fresh trouble in Iraq.

[1] Mr. Amery was then Secretary of State for India, and Sir John Anderson Lord President of the Council.

At these meetings I urged the advantages of avoiding the use of force, and I felt strongly that the diplomatists should be able to accomplish what we wanted without it.

In any event my views about diplomatic action were over-ruled, the Foreign Office and their Ambassador declared themselves impotent, and our troops marched on 25th August.

About this time I accompanied Margesson to a meeting of the Defence Committee. We discussed Persia again, and also the question of sending a force to Spitzbergen. The Admiralty staff had said they would need Spitzbergen as a refuelling base for the Russian convoys, and we had actually embarked two Canadian battalions to hold it when they changed their minds. We discussed an alternative plan to take the coal miners off the island and to put the mines out of action. This was successfully executed, a few weeks later, by a detachment of 500 Canadians.

Another item for discussion was the position in Malaya. On 29th July the Japs had signed a protocol with Vichy France, under which they were permitted to occupy Indo-China, thus obtaining a closer jumping-off point for an attack on Singapore. To meet this new threat, it had been suggested that we should seize a short defensive line in the Kra Peninsula inside Thailand. But the Admiralty was anxious to avoid any action which might precipitate war with Japan; they could do nothing in the Pacific while still engaged with the Germans, and the Americans had still given no sign that they would intervene.

On 8th August Auchinleck came to see me to say good-bye—he was to fly back that night. It was impossible not to like and admire Auchinleck. He had great charm, a strong personality, and a fine presence. Had he been a little more fortunate, he might well have been one of the great figures of the war. But three things were to bring him down. He had got his command at the wrong time, before we were very strong in Egypt; he was a 'frontier' soldier, one of the very best we ever had—but he knew little of European war; and we felt in the War Office he was not a good picker of men, nor would he take advice in selecting his subordinates. Probably this last fault was the most serious of the three. But with this criticism he would never agree, because if ever there was a man who was loyal to his subordinates it was Auchinleck.

On 14th August we were still working on plans for Spitzbergen, Persia, Malaya and the Canaries, and we were beginning to plan the further reinforcement of Singapore. On this day I had an unusual visitor in Monty Marx, a cinematograph magnate, whom Margesson had asked me to see. He had been in Spain for some months making a film of Christopher Columbus (of all irrelevant subjects). He told me that it was his impression that the Spaniards would resist a German invasion, and they would equally resist us if we entered Spanish territory before the Germans. This view had already been given to us by Colonel Torr, our Military Attaché in Madrid, and we saw no reason to think it wrong. Franco, in fact, seemed to be taking up the same kind of attitude in this matter as de Valera had adopted in 1940, when we thought there was a possibility of a German invasion of Ireland. The Canaries plan remained in being for some time in case of a German move against Gibraltar; then it eventually faded out.

On 18th August, Mr. Fraser, the Prime Minister of New Zealand, sent me a message that he would like to see me, and I went over to his room at the War Cabinet Offices after dinner. Like a true New Zealander, he ordered tea, and then settled down to a chat, which lasted for two hours, about past events in Greece, Crete and the Desert. Some of his people had been criticizing Freyberg, and he was very much exercised whether he should ask for another man to command the New Zealand Division. He had had a talk with Wavell on the subject, and now, he said, he felt more or less satisfied to leave Freyberg in charge. I told him that, if he still had doubts, he should ask Auchinleck and Dill to advise him; that I had known Freyberg as a fine battalion and brigade commander, but did not know him well enough to be able to advise on his capacity for his present job. Fraser consulted Dill and Auchinleck, and luckily for the New Zealanders Freyberg did, in fact, remain in successful command throughout the war.

On 19th August the Prime Minister's party returned to London. Dill told me that the meeting with Roosevelt had been most valuable politically, and very useful in establishing personal contacts, but that nothing much had been accomplished on the military side beyond clarifying our respective points of view upon the war. The Americans, Dill thought, had cooled off a good deal, possibly on account of Russia being now our ally, and it was quite clear that Harry Hopkins' forecast that they would very soon be with us in the war had been too optimistic. If the Germans got thoroughly bogged in Russia, it was unlikely that America would feel it necessary to come in, for the present at any rate. Dill had liked Marshall very much, but had found him less interested in strategy than he had hoped. Marshall, he said, carried out many of the duties that fell, in the

United Kingdom, to the Secretary of State, and he was more concerned, at the moment, with the production of equipment, and with organization, than with the conduct of operations—which, as America was not yet in the war, was hardly surprising. Dill had enjoyed the trip, and he looked better for it, although he had slipped in his bathroom when a heavy sea was running, and hurt his shoulder.

There was as usual a great deal of chat in Service circles in London about personalities. Churchill's critics sincerely believed at that time that it would be impossible to win the war so long as he controlled our strategy. Others held that his leadership was the greatest asset we had, that the people regarded him almost as a god, that the Chiefs of Staff were quite futile and that, without his drive, nothing whatever would be accomplished.

Dill was regarded by many as being completely worn out. They said his brain was anyhow not agile enough for his job, that he had no drive, and that he was always half asleep at meetings of the Defence Committee and of the Chiefs of Staff. Beaverbrook had remarked that Dill, although no doubt a very sound soldier, was the sort of man who made no impression when he came into a room; but that, in any case, there were no outstanding soldiers in this war such as there had been in the last. Others maintained that Dill had great moral courage; that he was strong on points of principle; and that he was straight, sincere and respected by the Army.

Dudley Pound was believed by some to be too old; but the Navy had complete confidence in him. He was sometimes criticized for being slow and going to sleep at meetings. We know now that he was suffering from a mortal disease, so it is remarkable that he was able to do so much for so long, and there is no question of his ever having failed to be wide awake and very much on the spot the moment the Navy was mentioned.

Portal, the Chief of the Air Staff, although greatly liked and admired in the War Office, was deemed to be altogether too persuasive, and to have an undue influence on the Prime Minister. But there was never a shadow of doubt that he was a magnificent Chief of the Air Staff; we sometimes ruefully reflected that from our point of view he was much too good.

In spite of this mutual criticism, all worked together loyally, and strained every nerve to achieve the best possible direction of the war. Once decisions were taken, previous disagreements were forgotten.

On the morning of 20th August, Dill came into my room, and said, with a wry laugh, that he did not think we had touched bottom yet. The news from Russia was bad. Mason-Macfarlane, in Moscow, had reports of a major disaster and of chaotic conditions in South Russia, where the Germans were believed to have crossed the Dnieper, and to have cut off the Crimea. Dill said that he felt we were in for a difficult time in the Middle East, and that pressure was certain to be put upon Auchinleck to move before he was ready. He asked if I thought he could tell the Cabinet definitely that invasion of the United Kingdom was off for this year. I said 'Yes.'

Dill then discussed his own position. He said he thought he would be open to justifiable criticism if he remained as C.I.G.S. after the age of sixty, which he would reach on Christmas Day, the more so as he had removed a good many Generals on grounds of age. He intended to write to the Prime Minister, or to the Secretary of State, whichever might be more correct, and offer to go. I said I thought it would be right to do this, but I hoped very much he would not be allowed to fade away. I added that if he were to continue as C.I.G.S., he would have to adopt a less severe régime; to take a day off every week, and go away on leave occasionally. He replied that he did not feel tired.

He went on to say that he had been wondering who should succeed him if he were to go at Christmas. He did not think the Prime Minister would have Wavell, and, in any case, Wavell had no aptitude for putting his ideas into words, which would make it difficult, if not impossible, for him to be C.I.G.S. Brooke, he thought, was too narrow. This view was perhaps well founded at that time, but Brooke was eventually to develop in a quite remarkable way, as so many good men do when given responsibility.

At 10 p.m. on the 20th, the Russian Military Attaché came to see me in the War Office, and I took him to Dill's room, where I gave him an outline of our plan for the operations in Persia. We asked him what the Russian plan was, but he did not know it, and he promised to transmit to Moscow the questions we had asked him. We hardly expected answers, for we had already failed to get any information out of Moscow ourselves through the Embassy or our Mission, despite repeated requests.

When the Russians had gone, Dill and I sat and talked for some time. We discussed a project which had been put forward for a big raid on Cherbourg. I was against it for several reasons. It could not help the Russians, since it would not draw off any German forces from their front; we should lose a great deal of heavy equipment which we could ill spare; it was unlikely that we could damage the Germans seriously; and it was possible that our prestige would suffer, since our withdrawal after the raid would certainly be represented as a defeat. I thought that the correct raiding policy at this period of the war was to harry the enemy with small detachments on a wide front, and thus force him to maintain troops all along the coast-line for the purposes of defence.

We were now arranging to move two more Divisions from England to the Middle East, and Churchill had asked Roosevelt to provide the necessary shipping. There was no longer any difference of opinion on the question of reinforcing the Middle East, since the danger of invasion had now receded so far.

On the afternoon of 24th August the Russian Military Attaché came to see me again, to tell me that Maisky had heard from Moscow that a Russian force would cross the Persian border at dawn on the next day. He knew nothing of the plan or the strength of the force, but he thought that the Military Mission which the Russians had just sent to Mosul would know it. He added that in Moscow they believed that we had underestimated the Persians, and that they were about twice as strong as we had calculated.

The Persian affair did not take long to settle. On the morning of the 25th, the diplomatic representations having failed, our troops occupied Abadan, Khurramshah and Nafti Shah without appreciable opposition, and the Persian population showed no great hostility. Two Persian gunboats were 'disposed of' at Bandar Shahpur. When the Russian Attaché came to see me next day, I gave him this news. He asked what I meant by 'disposed of', and I said 'liquidated', whereupon he gave a loud guffaw. The Russians produced their plan for North Persia at the last moment; they intended to occupy Tabriz and Ardebil, using 3 infantry divisions, 2 Tank divisions and 2 cavalry brigades. They told us nothing, however, of their intention to bomb Meshed and to go there too.

The Prime Minister telephoned to Dill on the evening of the 25th, and said he was perturbed to discover that the Indian Division at Basra contained no British battalions, and that he thought we should move more troops to Persia. Dill replied that he considered our force to be adequate, because the Persians were badly fed, ill paid and incapable of prolonged resistance; but he said he would order Auchinleck to hold further troops in readiness.

On 9th September Dill and I were drafting an order for the occupation of Tehran, when Eden telephoned to say that the Shah had consented to meet our demands. We were much relieved not to have been saddled with a more serious military commitment. But there was a very general feeling that this short war had been unnecessary, and that our diplomatic action had been bungled.

18

A SURVEY BY CHURCHILL

1941

ON the 24th August Rear-Admiral Sir Henry Harwood telephoned from the Admiralty, and swore heartily for five minutes on end about a note Churchill had just sent to the Chiefs of Staff, in which he had suggested the despatch of another direct convoy through the Mediterranean, to take more tanks to Auchinleck. Harwood said he had rung me up to blow off steam, and that, now he had done it, he felt much better.

The Prime Minister now began to put pressure on Auchinleck to start his offensive before November, which Auchinleck considered to be the earliest date on which he could move with good hopes of ensuring a far-reaching success in Libya. On 25th August he delivered a diatribe in the Defence Committee, referring in scathing terms to the '600,000 useless mouths' in Egypt, and to the lack of activity in the Desert since June. Dill told me that he had said, in reply, that it should not be forgotten that we had pressed Wavell, against his own judgment, to attack in June, and that he now felt that he himself had been equally to blame for this. He had warned the Prime Minister against repeating the mistake, and had added that, but for the possibly premature attack in June, it might now have been feasible to take the offensive with success.

Auchinleck stood firm, and after a fortnight or so Churchill appeared to accept the situation with good grace. When Shearer, Auchinleck's Chief of Intelligence, left London for Cairo in the first week of September, the Prime Minister gave him a letter to take to Auchinleck in which he surveyed the prospects in the Middle East situation. There was nothing in this letter with which we disagreed, except for one statement, in which he referred to the foolishness of those who had doubted the wisdom of holding Tobruk. In my view, Tobruk had been saved only because the

Germans had unexpectedly switched their effort to Russia, and by nothing else.

In Russia the German thrust south of Kiev seemed to be progressing, and Leningrad was being invested. But there were now good grounds for hoping that the Russians would hold out until the onset of winter began to slow up the German operations. On 4th September Stalin had sent another appeal for help. In reply Churchill explained that, in spite of the most searching examination, we had been unable to discover any method of making an effective diversion. At this time we had only 26 divisions in the United Kingdom. Maisky, who probably did not know this, urged that we should land 15 or 20 divisions in France. It was clear to us that the Germans were strong enough there to be able to overwhelm any force that we might land or attempt to land. Nor did we possess the shipping for an operation like this, at that stage of the war.

On 9th September, Dill and I attended an official luncheon party at the Russian Embassy. The Russian officers as usual were a crude lot. Trying to make conversation with my neighbour, I said something about Fabergé, the former Court Jeweller. 'Ah yes,' he said, 'isn't that a night club in Paris?' Perhaps he thought I had said 'Folies Bergères.' The Russians ate caviare off their knives; my neighbour held his bread with both hands as he tore pieces off it with his teeth. I could not help feeling that they were odd allies.

On 19th September Lord Trenchard sent us a memorandum on winning the war by the bombing of Germany. He urged that we should confine our land operations against the Germans to North Africa and the Middle East, and that our main effort should be put into the breaking of German morale by bombing. He entirely dismissed alternative strategies. All of us admired Trenchard, his legendary prescience and his notable record; but he was no longer completely *au courant* with the progress or potentialities of the war. It was a curious chance that he and Sir Roger Keyes had married sisters. Each had contributed enormously to the build-up of their respective Services. Each, although belonging to an earlier generation, was crowding advice upon those responsible for the higher direction of the war. Each had been closely associated in former days with the Prime Minister, both in politics and in the field.[1] Each was out of date; each had something of genuine value to offer; neither was on speaking terms with the other. Both, in their respective spheres, were great men.

[1] Trenchard and Churchill had both served in the Royal Scots Fusiliers.

The main feature of the first week of October 1941 was a strong drive by the Prime Minister to attack Trondheim. The opinion of the Chiefs of Staff was that this was not a practical proposition, and that any attempt to carry out the operation would end in disaster. Churchill was not satisfied. On 3rd October he held a midnight meeting at Chequers, and, when it broke up at 2 a.m., he instructed Brooke, who had been present, to make a fresh and independent study of the project.

Dill told me on 5th October that he was going to marry again in the course of the following week. He had asked for a week's leave, but the Prime Minister said he could have only one day; in the end he got three. Dill remarked, with a laugh, 'You and I are undoubtedly the two most unpopular men at No. 10.'

Dill was married at St. Stephen's, Vincent Square. He had invited the Prime Minister, the Army Council, and a few private friends. He went off after the wedding, looking very happy; he had certainly had little happiness these last few years.

Next day, 9th October, the Prime Minister asked me to luncheon at No. 10, and he also invited Davidson, the Director of Military Intelligence. When we arrived, the Cabinet was still sitting, and we were shown into a sitting-room on the basement floor, on a level with the lawn behind the house, which might originally have been a servants' hall. Now it was strutted up, and nicely furnished. Churchill came in after a quarter of an hour, and apologized for being late; he said the Cabinet had been gossiping at the end of their meeting. He asked us if we had ever seen this floor of No. 10 before, and, when we said we had not, he took us along a passage and showed us a stronghold with steel doors which he had had prepared as a bomb shelter for the Cabinet. Then, after a glass of sherry, we sat down to luncheon.

Churchill was in a good mood. He first asked Davidson what news there was from Russia. Davidson told him that the Germans were now 100 miles from Moscow and were pushing on in the south towards Rostov, but that, as usual, we had little information of the real state of the Russian armies. He asked me if I thought Moscow would fall; and I said I thought it quite likely, but that that would not matter much so long as the Russians went on fighting. Even guerrilla fighting would contain large German forces. From a strategic point of view, the Ukraine and the Don mattered more. It did not seem to me that there were as yet any signs of a Russian collapse, and Stalin's whole interest, personal and otherwise, would be to keep the war going. Churchill agreed, and added that he thought Stalin, quite sincerely, and quite apart from personal motives, wanted to fight on.

I said I knew most of the ground over which the fighting was now taking place in Russia, because I had been with Denikin's army in the Bolshevik war. 'Ah,' said the Prime Minister, 'that was one of *my* ideas.' He asked why I thought Denikin had failed. I replied that Denikin had almost succeeded, and might have done so had he had more political sense. The country had risen against him behind his front because he had refused to declare his domestic policy, and, in particular, his intention regarding the ownership of the land. The peasants, in consequence, primed with Bolshevik propaganda, came to believe that he was fighting to re-establish the old régime, and nothing more. Added to this, Denikin had tried to hold too long a front, which had entailed great dispersion of his forces; and Budienny had been able to break through by making concentrated attacks with his Cavalry Corps. 'Yes,' said Churchill, 'I remember somebody told me that Denikin only had about one man to a verst.' He asked me if Denikin was still alive, and I told him that he had died in Belgium a few years before. He said he believed that, if Denikin had been alive, he would have been with Russia now.

He asked what I thought of our policy of sending tanks, aeroplanes and other military equipment to Russia. I said it was certainly a good policy, for we would get a better dividend out of keeping Russia in the war than we could by sending the equipment elsewhere. Then, for a little, we discussed the quality of the Russian generals and soldiers.

He next raised the subject of Libya. He said it would be a wonderful thing, and far-reaching, if we could smash the Afrika Corps. He hoped we might get our attack in before the Germans could be strongly reinforced, and while they were still weak from the effects of their long sojourn in the Desert, but he was afraid that we might miss our opportunity. I refrained from comment, for I knew how thoroughly the question of the date of our offensive had been thrashed out between him and Dill.

He then discussed our methods of work in Whitehall. He complained that official papers were nearly always too verbose, especially those written by the Foreign Office. I agreed with him, and asked whether he ever sent papers back to the Foreign Office to be condensed. 'That is what I should do if I were in a Department,' he said. 'Now I get my secretaries to distil a few drops of sense from them.'

He went on to say that, now, he never used a shorthand writer, and that he always dictated direct to a typist. 'That,' he said, 'is perhaps more of a strain, because you have to be sure you are giving the final wording. You do not like to spoil what has been typed. For that reason I am thinking of going back to shorthand—it takes a little longer, but you can change it more freely.' I asked if he ever used a dictaphone. 'No,' he said, 'I do not like them.'

I told him that Raymond Lee, the American Military Attaché, kept a dictaphone beside his bed into which he dictated ideas he might have during the night in case he should have forgotten them in the morning. 'That reminds me of the story of the philosopher's dream,' said Churchill. 'A philosopher dreamt one night that he saw the whole secret of the universe revealed and, realizing it was a remarkable dream and that he might forget it, he wrote it down on a piece of paper. When he woke in the morning he reached for the paper to read what the secret of the universe was, and found he had written "A strong smell of turpentine pervades the whole"—which illustrates the point that bright ideas in the middle of the night are not always very bright in the morning.'

He talked about the fighting spirit of our Army, which he thought was improving, and he told us a story of an ancient battle in which the warriors had cut the throats of their horses, before going into action, in order to remove the means of retreat.

When we went back to the drawing-room, he opened fire on the subject of Trondheim. I said that Brooke's report would be ready by Monday, but he was not to be put off in this way. He said he had summoned the Chiefs of Staff, the Commander-in-Chief Home Forces (Brooke), and the Commander-in-Chief of the Home Fleet to Chequers on the previous Sunday to discuss the operation. (This, of course, I already knew.) Then he proceeded to expound his view of the problem.

'Surely we can land parties, with Bangalore torpedoes, and light guns to haul up the hills, and attack the defences from the rear? The German commander in Trondheim would be exceedingly embarrassed if detachments of troops were landed all along the coast, with ships going alongside in every possible place, and with landings in certain selected places from special craft. The Army must do something—the people want it. Surely this is a thing within our power. The effects might be enormous. The Germans are engaged in Russia—now is the time. Sweden will come in, on the Germans demanding passage for their troops. We could blow up hundreds of miles of the Norwegian railways. We should have an impregnable position in Trondheim. The Americans might well come in, and send us troops to relieve those we had despatched to the attack. Wars cannot be won by sitting still and doing nothing. Even if we lost two or three thousand men it would be well worth it. What do you think, General?'

I said I agreed that we could probably take the place but that the price we should have to pay would not be worth it, especially in warships and merchant shipping.

'I was prepared to use the Navy against Trondheim last time we considered it,' said Churchill, 'but the First Sea Lord came to me and assured me that the military were confident of the success of their pincer attack from Namsos and Andalsnes, and that there was no need to risk ships. I therefore agreed, reluctantly, not to use them. After all, in the end it was a good thing, for the more we had got into Trondheim, the more we should have lost eventually.'

He went on to say that, of course, the responsibility was for him to shoulder. He would be willing to shoulder it, and he believed the country would be with him. I agreed the operation might have to be done some time, but I doubted if this was the right moment.

'I think it *is* the right moment,' he said. 'But, if we do not use the force for this, it can be kept in readiness for North Africa—for Casablanca, in case of need.' I did not reply to this, and he did not continue the discussion, which, considering the extent to which I had had to disagree with him, had been surprisingly amicable.

It was now 3.45 p.m., and the Prime Minister was looking sleepy. He said he always went to bed in the afternoon, when he could, and took all his clothes off, and slept for an hour. This enabled him to continue work until 2 a.m. or 3 a.m. He considered an afternoon sleep very important unless, of course, one was young, and there were many advantages in adopting the recumbent position while working. With a mournful expression, he bade us good-bye, remarking, as he did so, 'Yes, I am afraid Moscow is a gone coon.' Then he stumped along the passage to his bedroom.

Next day, in Dill's absence, I attended a meeting of the Chiefs of Staff, and gave Pound and Portal an account of my talk with the Prime Minister about Trondheim. The Defence Committee was summoned, on 12th October, to consider Brooke's report, which was a closely reasoned and detailed condemnation of the project.[1] Churchill, however, gave a last kick; he wrote a minute to the Chiefs of Staff instructing them to study how the difficulties

---

[1] For an account of this meeting, see *The Turn of the Tide*, pp. 261–2. 'The Prime Minister, looking angrily at Paget and Brooke, remarked, "I sometimes think some of my Generals don't want to fight the Germans!"'

raised by Brooke could be overcome, and he added that neither Brooke nor Paget (who had collaborated in writing the report) were 'to be troubled further in making such plans'. He also sent a note to Dill to say that Brooke should not again be admitted to our counsels. I often remembered this with amusement in later years, when he was the mainstay of our deliberations.

On 16th October the Defence Committee met again, and the Chiefs of Staff reported that the difficulties could not be overcome. Trondheim was now effectively scotched. A great deal of time and effort had been wasted. At last we were able to begin the series of raids on the Norwegian coast, which we had advocated months before.

19

BROOKE RELIEVES DILL

1941

AT about 6 p.m. on 14th October, the Prime Minister sent me a message that he wanted to see me, and would I bring with me the V.C.I.G.S. (Pownall) and the D.M.I. (Davidson). We found Mr. Churchill pacing up and down in the Cabinet Room, in a zip romper suit of Air Force blue, stained with snuff. I thought he looked rather disgruntled, and I felt we were in for a difficult time.

He asked us to sit down at the table, and he took a chair opposite us, and lit a cigar. He then proceeded to discuss the coming offensive in the Desert, to which he had given the code name 'Crusader'. It fell to me to conduct the discussion on our side, because Pownall and Davidson did not know Auchinleck's plan.

'This battle,' he began, 'will have a great effect on the war, if the attack succeeds. It will be the first defeat inflicted on the Germans by the British. It will have a far-reaching influence upon sentiment throughout the world. It has been an anxious time. We have been fortunate to have got the four months we needed for preparation, without being attacked by the Germans. Now there is another fortnight to go. What I have been turning over in my mind is this: when the movement goes forward, it will not be enough to sweep round the enemy's rear. There will be hard and bitter fighting. Infantry formations will be required. Are you satisfied that Auchinleck is going to use a big enough force? Everything should be thrown in.'

I said there could be no doubt that the only limit to the size of the attacking forces should be that imposed by the quantity of transport available for their supply and maintenance. I felt sure that Auchinleck must realize this. But, if he wished to be reassured, we would ask Auchinleck, or, if he preferred it, we could tell him to send a staff officer to London to explain the details of the plan, of which I knew the outline only.

He then continued, 'There will be actions at Tobruk, at Bardia, and at Benghazi. The correct method will be to contain the garrisons[1] of these places. We need not assault them, but we must be able to hold them in. Let them starve—those animals.

'Now, there is Tobruk. It has held out successfully for four months. And yet, when it was decided to stand there, I was told it was a mistake.'

Here I intervened and said, 'One thing, and one thing only, has saved Tobruk.'

'What?' he asked.

'Russia,' I replied.

At this he got up, and walked about the room.

'Why,' he said at last, 'we have been sinking fifty per cent of their shipping.'

I thought there was no point in pursuing the subject, although my information was that we had sunk only 17 per cent of their shipping, and this in the absence in Russia of German air forces which might otherwise have been operating from Greece and from Sicily to cover the enemy's lines of communication across the Mediterranean.

Sitting down again, Churchill went on, 'Now let us build castles in the air. What if we get to Tripoli? The aged Marshal may then give the word to Weygand that the Germans have no forces to spare to overrun France. We may get into North Africa, especially if the Germans try to use Bizerta.'

I said that that was a possibility we had been considering, and that we had also been studying how best we might take advantage of a collapse in Italy.

'We have had word that Mussolini is very unpopular,' he continued. 'The Italians might even ask us for protection against the Germans. We must think about these things, and have plans ready.'

I had given a note to the Chiefs of Staff that morning upon these very points, but it seemed to me better not to anticipate the deliberations of the Defence Committee, by entering on a discussion at this moment.

'Well,' continued the Prime Minister, 'let us have an outline plan for the Defence Committee tomorrow night.'

I said I would see to this, and then I added, 'I hope you will

[1] At Tobruk the German troops were, of course, an investing force.

not mind my saying this, Prime Minister. Our staffs are very fully occupied in studying other projects which you have ordered to be examined. In my opinion we should switch them on to these more likely and more important plans of which you have just been speaking. If we fail to take advantage of possible developments in the Mediterranean and in North Africa, we may miss opportunities for offensive action, and for improving our whole strategic position.'

'I want the *General Staff* to put up a plan,' he said. 'Committees always give me the difficulties.' (Well, I thought to myself, that is because you ask them to examine impossible projects.) 'If I get your plan,' he continued, 'then I will see how the Navy and the Air Force can help.'

Portal arrived at this juncture, and he read out a telegram from Tedder, the Commander of the Air Force in Egypt, to the effect that Auchinleck would not have air superiority in the coming battle. Churchill signified his disapproval, but Portal quickly read out his reply, in which he had told Tedder that he was wrong and pessimistic, and that he must think again. The Prime Minister said that Portal's reply was excellent. Then he thanked us, and we took our leave, at 7.15 p.m.

After dinner, I assembled the three Directors of Plans, and set them to work on outline plans for exploitation of a successful offensive by Auchinleck, to include Turkey and the Caucasus, Tripoli, Sicily, and Spanish and French North Africa. This paper was taken by the Defence Committee on 16th October, and was well received.

We hoped now that our work could proceed upon more balanced and orderly lines, but Churchill decreed otherwise.

There ensued a difficult and irritating phase. Auchinleck's attack had been scheduled to start at the beginning of November; he now postponed it until the 18th, and the Prime Minister was extremely disappointed. His reaction was to turn frantically to all kinds of other possibilities for offensive action. Whenever an idea, however wild, was thrown up, he ordered detailed examinations, or plans, or both, to be made at high speed. Our stables were so full of these unlikely starters that we were hard put to it to give the favourites the attention they deserved. To cope with the situation adequately, it would almost have been worth while to have two staffs: one to deal with the Prime Minister, the other with the war. His domination over the Chiefs of Staff seemed greater than ever; and Dill, on whom fell the brunt of opposing him, now began to show signs of great exhaustion.

When Churchill's projects were finally thrown aside, after the useless expenditure of much labour and energy, he obviously did not realize that he had been saved from disasters. On the contrary, he seemed to think he had been thwarted by men who lacked initiative and courage. At such times as this, we often felt that we would give almost anything for a less colourful occupant of No. 10.

I was lucky in my staff. I had a team of splendid officers, and I can never hope to describe their loyalty and devotion to duty in what was one of the most exacting tasks of the war. Some were temporary soldiers; others were professionals of the highest calibre; and of these last, four, all men of outstanding quality, were killed before the war was over—Dykes, Stewart, Vogel and Mallaby. Others have since filled a wide variety of responsible posts—if Commander-in-Chief, Member of the Army Council, Director-General of the B.B.C., and Chancellor of the Exchequer can be so described. Lieutenant-Colonel Isaac, who had been Personal Assistant to a succession of D.M.O.s for many years, was one of the 'characters' of the War Office; he was known to hundreds of officers whom he had befriended and initiated into the mysteries and rituals of the General Staff.

In the preliminary study of the exploitation of Auchinleck's offensive, to which I have referred, we had suggested that we should work out a number of plans to cover the various contingencies which we had defined. But we had made it clear that we could not yet forecast which of these might materialize, and we had emphasized the danger of making a false move by committing our meagre reserves prematurely. Yet the Prime Minister at once focused his attention on one of our suggestions, namely, the capture of Sicily. Our staffs were kept up most of the night of the 16th in order to produce a more detailed study of this operation, which he ordered the Chiefs of Staff and the Defence Committee to consider on 17th October. He christened the plan 'Whipcord', and we cursed it heartily for ten days and nights.

On the 17th, I lectured the Secretary of State for an hour before luncheon on the strategy of the Mediterranean and North Africa, and at 1.30 p.m., I saw Dill to discuss 'Whipcord', before he went off to the meeting of the Defence Committee. The view I held, which was also that of the planning staffs, was that an early attack on Sicily would be premature. The obvious counter, for the Germans, would be to move into unoccupied France and into French North Africa or Spain. We thought Sicily should be attacked later, perhaps in the spring of 1942, when we might be in possession of

Tripoli, Benghazi and other ports in North Africa. These ports would be required as bases from which to launch the attack. North Africa would be worth a thousand Sicilies, and it would be wrong to hold back troops and ships, for Sicily, which could be better employed to support Auchinleck's drive along the coast.

When, at 5 p.m., Dill returned from the meeting, he told me that the spotlight was more strongly than ever on 'Whipcord'. The Prime Minister regarded Sicily as virtually taken already, and had summoned Alexander to London to take command of the operation.

On this day we learned that the Germans were 50 miles from Moscow, and that the Russian Government had cleared out. We believed, however, that the German effort in Russia was now near its peak, and that it would fail unless the Russian armies were encircled, which did not seem likely.

On 20th October the Defence Committee met again to discuss Sicily. We had asked Auchinleck and the other two Commanders-in-Chief in the Middle East to send us their views, but they had not yet replied; so our study was confined mainly to the effect the operation would have on our resources of shipping, reinforcements and equipment. Obviously if we were to mount an attack on Sicily, convoys to the Middle East would have to be stopped, almost entirely, until the end of the year. That meant that we could do little to nurture Auchinleck's offensive, or to provide forces for the Caucasus, Persia and Turkey in case the Germans broke through the Russian front.

Dill asked me if I thought it sound to *prepare* for the attack on Sicily, without deciding as yet whether it should be launched, or whether shipping should be held up at once. I replied that, in my view, we could not afford to hold up the shipping, but that there would be no harm in preparing the attack on Sicily *on paper*. I added that Sicily was now being considered out of its proper strategic order. I asked if he would allow me to put the case to him in the form of questions, and he assented.

'Well,' I said, 'would you, if you had a free choice, hold the Germans up in the Caucasus and Persia, or allow them to come on there and have Sicily instead?'

D.: 'I would hold the Germans up in the Caucasus and Persia.'

K.: 'Would you prefer to get Tripoli, or fail to get there and have Sicily?'

D.: 'I would prefer Tripoli.'

K.: 'Would you prefer to hold Turkey up, if she is attacked, or have Sicily?'

D.: 'Hold Turkey up.'

K.: 'Would you prefer to push on into Tunisia, if the Germans began to land in Bizerta, or to have Sicily?'

D.: 'Push on into Tunisia.'

K.: 'Would you prefer to have the Canaries, if the Germans went into Spain, or to have Sicily?'

D.: 'The Canaries.'

K.: 'Would you prefer to forestall the Germans in Casablanca or Spanish Morocco, or have Sicily?'

D.: 'I would prefer to be in Casablanca or Spanish Morocco.'

'Then,' I said, 'we are in complete agreement. If we attack Sicily now, we shall not have the forces we would need for any of the possible alternatives I have mentioned. Sicily is not at the top of the list in strategic priority. We must try to get it back into its right place. We must remember that the taking of Sicily would not open the Mediterranean. The Germans could still close it to troop transports and regular traffic, by stationing air forces in Southern Italy, in Greece and in Crete. The way to open the Mediterranean is to get possession of the whole North African coast—we could then move our shipping close inshore, under cover of our own fighter aircraft. We have a big battle front—from the Caspian to the Canaries—and very meagre resources, and we cannot afford to waste them by making mistakes.'

Dill agreed with all this, and he added that Alexander had told him he could not be sure of holding Sicily, after he had got it, unless we gave him bigger forces.

Next day, 21st October, Dill came to see me in my room and said that the Prime Minister seemed to be immovable about Sicily. I had just dictated a note on the lines of the conversation I had had with him on the previous day, because the question of Sicily had been raised in a telegram from the Commanders-in-Chief in the Middle East; and I gave him a copy. Dill sat down and put his feet up on another chair, and read it. He then said that he agreed with it, and that he would try to convey the gist of it at the meeting of the Defence Committee which had been summoned for 10 p.m. that night.

Next morning Dill told me that Churchill was still apparently unshaken by the arguments against an early attack on Sicily, but that he thought he was beginning to see the red light. Alexander had attended the meeting. He was of course unaware of the wide implications of the problem, and he did not know how much all of us, and especially the Prime Minister, had been chafing at the delays

in launching Auchinleck's offensive. After listening to the discussion for some time he had said, 'You know, Prime Minister, I
think if we could get Auchinleck to postpone his offensive so as to
fit in better with the attack on Sicily, it would be much better.' He
was considerably taken aback by the loud laughter which greeted
this intervention.

Auchinleck now sent Brigadier Whiteley of his operations
staff to London to expound his point of view, and I saw him when
he arrived on the morning of the 22nd. Auchinleck's opinion was
that Sicily might be ripe for attack in the following summer. His
order of priority for operations was:

    (1) Tripoli,
    (2) Turkey and the Caucasus,
    (3) Sicily.

This coincided with our own ideas.

Whiteley told us that Auchinleck's intention was to try to
get Tripoli, and to recover his balance as soon as possible, in
any case before the spring, so as to be able to counter any German
move through Turkey and the Caucasus. He considered that if
we pressed on and captured Sicily as well, we should then be
faced with the problem of holding it; this would involve using
all the forces earmarked for stemming a German invasion from
the North, and might therefore entail the loss of Egypt. It
had taken five months for the Desert Army to recover from the
premature attack at Sollum, and to assemble resources for the new
offensive.

Whiteley's other task was to explain to the Prime Minister
the reasons for the delays in mounting 'Crusader', and this I did
not envy him.

The controversy over Sicily continued to rage throughout the
following week. Churchill ordered Admiral Sir James Somerville,
commanding Force 'H', to come home to discuss the operation,
and he talked over the plans with him and Alexander at Chequers.

Next day, the Chiefs of Staff were in continuous session on
'Whipcord' until 7 p.m., and the Defence Committee was summoned
for 9.30 p.m., to hear the result of their deliberations. I went to
see Dill before dinner, on his return from the Chiefs of Staff, and
I gave him yet another note on Sicily. Then we sat down together,
and drafted a statement which summed up all the arguments against
the operation, which had been repeated so often at previous meetings. He then went off for a hasty dinner, before going on to the
Defence Committee. He remarked that all the others seemed to be

in favour of the operation, and that, once again, the brunt of opposition to the Prime Minister seemed likely to fall upon him. But next morning, 28th October, Dill told me, to my immense relief, that 'Whipcord' was dead, and that the Navy had killed it in the end. The Prime Minister, he said, had been very disgruntled and had said that he now intended, for a change, to criticize the proposals of the Chiefs of Staff.

But the Prime Minister did not stick to this resolution for long. On the morning of the 28th the Chiefs of Staff were chatting about the meeting of the night before, and Dill had just remarked, 'I wonder what the next spanner will be that the Prime Minister will throw into the machinery?', when the door opened, and in he came, and said that he wished the Chiefs of Staff to study 'Gymnast'. 'Gymnast' was the code name he had given to our plan for seizing French North Africa—a plan which depended, at this time, on the unlikely event that the French would co-operate.

Now for a short time we actually had a lull. We had various visitors: General Giffard from West Africa, to discuss plans against a possible German incursion into French West Africa; Sir Philip Mitchell from Addis Ababa, fuming against Foreign Office policy there; a Portuguese Military Mission, vainly seeking assurances of protection in the event of an attack on them. The Russians were holding, except in the south, where they were having to give a little ground: we were sending them every month 250 tanks and some aircraft, which we could ill spare. In the Middle East we were managing to build up a new armoured division, partly with American tanks.

We had some discussions in the War Office on the role of the Air Force, but these came to nothing. Our chief complaints against the Air Staff were, first, that they would never submit their general bombing policy or programme to the Chiefs of Staff for discussion; and secondly that they were violently opposed to the provision of proper air support for the Army, which they regarded as a diversion of effort from winning the war.

On 18th November Dill sent for me earlier than 9.45, our usual hour for meeting in the morning. When I went into his room he said: 'The world is upside-down for me. I am to go. The Prime Minister told me last night. Brooke is to be C.I.G.S. He almost put in Nye instead. Paget is to succeed Brooke as C.-in-C. Home Forces. Pownall is to go to Singapore instead of Paget. I knew, some days ago, that all this was going on.'

I was sad to hear Dill's news. My admiration and affection for him had never waned; but I could not help feeling that he was now much too tired to give of his best, and that it was right he should go before he became completely worn out. For a year and a half he had borne a heavy burden, which would have been almost intolerable anyway; but he had had in addition to bear the brunt of opposing the many madcap projects put up to him, during a period when it was our duty to hold our own and to husband our slowly growing resources. Considerate of others and sensitive in himself, he was more affected than most other men would have been by the constant railing to which he had been subjected; he had not the enviable gift of his successor of being able to grow a shell. His achievement, none the less, had been considerable, especially in the critical months when Britain was threatened with invasion. No one, and least of all himself, could guess that his greatest and most splendid work was still to come.

It had been touch and go whether Dill's mantle might not fall on somebody else. Paget and Nye were strongly backed for the job. Much as I admired and liked them both, I was thankful that Brooke had been chosen. One Minister who had been closely involved in the discussions told me at the time that they felt they '*had* to appoint Brooke, but very much to their regret, and it was hoped it would only be for a year at the outside'. Margesson, no doubt influenced by Dill, had backed Brooke strongly, as he told me himself later on. In this he certainly rendered a great service.

Before I went out to dinner that evening, Dill asked me to help him draft a statement for the Press. It was obviously a wrench to be leaving the Army, but he was, I thought, not really sorry to go; he was glad that Brooke was to succeed him. I said I was glad too, but that I thought the politicians did not, perhaps, realize what they had taken on, for Brooke was tough and impatient. Dill then wrote his statement, and, with his approval, I added the last sentence, which was what he had said to me.

'I have always been anxious that the young men in the Army should get on. That can only happen if the older men give way to them. You all know General Brooke and his fine record. I hand over the duties of C.I.G.S. to him with the greatest confidence. General Paget you also know and he is certainly one of our finest generals. The new V.C.I.G.S. is an officer in my old Regiment, whom I had long marked out for rapid advancement. He, as you know, replaces General Pownall, who is required for a very important appointment which will be announced before long. Of course I need hardly add that I leave the Service, which I have loved, with the deepest regret but, I am glad to say, with no bitterness.'

It was on this day, 18th November, that Auchinleck began his long-awaited offensive, but in the evening we had no news beyond the fact that his preliminary dispositions had been successfully carried out. Rommel was away in Greece when Auchinleck began to move, but he flew back immediately.

On the 19th, the Prime Minister sent for me to come and see him at No. 10, and he came over from the House soon after I had arrived. I showed him the dispositions of the two forces on my map, and told him the news, which did not amount to much, except that there had been a heavy rainstorm which might hold up our advance. We discussed the dispositions and prospects for half an hour, while he smoked a cigar. He said he hoped that he would be able to tell the House something on the next day. He remarked that my map was much better than his, and he asked if he might have a copy of it. He added that he would like to have a scale on it. I said I would have one put on, but he said he could stick it on himself, and pointed to his pot of paste.

Two days later, 21st November, the Prime Minister again sent for me at 12.45 p.m., and I found him sitting in his chair in the Cabinet Room. We were still without news of the progress of the battle. For half an hour we speculated on the course of the operations. He made a sweeping movement over the map with his cigar, and said that the Germans should be cut off by a turning movement at Agedabia, and so forth. He said he agreed with Auchinleck's idea that the first essential was a tank battle. He had decided not to go to the country that week-end, in order that he might keep in close touch with the progress of the operations.

Auchinleck's offensive had begun very stickily. No great progress was reported in the first few days. On the 23rd November, Churchill, unable to control himself any longer, sent him a telegram pointing out the possibilities of bold and far-reaching action in the enemy's rear.

On the 24th the battle in the desert seemed to be reaching a crisis. The Germans and Italians were counter-attacking heavily with tanks, and we were a little anxious because Cunningham appeared to have used up most of his reserves.

The 26th was not a good day. When I arrived in the War Office in the morning I was given a telegram from Auchinleck in which he announced that he had removed Cunningham and had put Ritchie[1] in his place. He gave as his reason that Cunningham had begun to think defensively mainly because of our large tank losses. We heard later that Cunningham was worn out, and had not slept for weeks. He had contributed so much to our fantastic victories in East Africa.

Dill was no longer taking part in our work, but he still came to the War Office on most days, to talk about the war. He told me, on the 26th, that he was not very well; he was suffering from shingles and was very run down. It was sad for him that his last days in the War Office were clouded by the disappointments of the battle in the Desert.

Brooke, to whom I had sent some papers to read, wrote to me to say that he would assume duty on 1st December. In his letter he said that he regarded Dill's departure as 'nothing less than a calamity'. I was to have gone with Eden to Moscow, but Brooke wanted me to be in the War Office when he started work as C.I.G.S., so Nye went instead.

The battle in the Desert took a turn for the better on the 27th. Rommel seemed to be in difficulties, and Ritchie had made contact with our garrison in Tobruk. I suggested to Dill that he might speak to the Prime Minister about Auchinleck taking command himself, and this he did. After their talk Churchill sent a telegram to Auchinleck in which he suggested that, having saved the battle once, he should now go up and win it; but, properly, he left the decision to Auchinleck, who did not like the proposition.

Brooke arrived on 1st December. It was a delight to work with him. He was quick and decided; his freshness made a new impact; he infected the War Office and the Chiefs of Staff with his own vitality; the change of *tempo* was immediate and immense.

On the 3rd Brooke, surveying his new sweep of responsibilities, told me that the Prime Minister was very depressed. He had built up such great hopes on the offensive, and now it was turning out a fiasco. He had spoken gloomily of going back to Mersa Matruh, and giving up the battle. Brooke said he intended to impress upon the Defence Committee that night the importance of going on with the offensive.

After the meeting, about midnight, Brooke asked me to send a telegram to Auchinleck to enquire what was in his mind about

[1] Afterwards General Sir Neil Ritchie.

181

bringing up further troops in view of the prolongation of the operations. This message was intended to convey to Auchinleck that the forces earmarked for the Caucasus would have to be drawn in; there was indeed no good reason for not using them, because there was no firm prospect of their being accepted by the Russians, and, in any case, the Caucasus could wait till the spring.

On 3rd December there were sudden indications that Japan might soon be involved. On that day I made the following note in my diary: 'Japan looks like coming into the war at once. If we get America in, we shall gain, on balance, in the long run.'

On 4th December the Prime Minister summoned the Chiefs of Staff to discuss the plans we had drawn up for raids on the coast of Italy. The First Sea Lord said that these raids could not be carried out because the Admiralty was preoccupied with Japan. Churchill thereupon banged his papers on the table and walked out, saying, 'You frustrate me in all my offensive projects.' Next day the Prime Minister sent for me at one o'clock, just as I was going out to luncheon. Maisky was with him in the Cabinet Room and was taking his leave when I arrived. Churchill sat with his back to the fire, wearing his blue rompers, and with an extinct cigar in his hand. He seemed to be in fairly good heart.

He asked me what I thought of the situation in the Desert. I said that the setback we had suffered seemed to me to be due to bad leadership. All the same, I continued, our forces had another kick in them and this might tip the balance. If it did, then the whole thing would slide quickly. If it did not, then we should have to stage another offensive, which would take some weeks.

He agreed with me, except for the last point: he thought there need be no delay in staging another attack. He could not understand why, with 750,000 men in the Middle East, more could not be deployed in the battle. I said that the size of the force was limited by the means of supply and maintenance.

He asked for information about the contents of the recent convoys, and particularly how much transport had been sent. He also asked how we stood for tanks in the Desert as compared with the Germans. I had brought some particulars with me which I showed him.

He spoke for a moment of the Japanese, and said they would be fools if they joined in the war. 'Hong Kong will be a gone coon, I suppose, if they come in,' he added with a mournful air. I said that, on balance, we stood to gain if America came into the war, and he agreed. Then I went off to luncheon.

20

PEARL HARBOUR AND THE FAR EAST

1941

On 7th December the news about Pearl Harbour began to come in. The Americans were now well and truly in the war, and there was no lingering doubt about the eventual outcome. I happened to meet Dill, and reminded him how he had once, half-joking, asked me for a plan for winning the war; and I had replied that we could not do it until America came in. 'Now,' I said, 'we can get on with it.' But none of us was under any illusion but that we were in for a bad time of it in the immediate future. We ourselves were very weak in the Far East; the American Navy on whose help we had been relying in these circumstances had been crippled; and the supply of American equipment would now be largely diverted in favour of their own forces.

The Chiefs of Staff sat all day to discuss the idea of sending a force forward into Thailand, in order to shorten the line of defence for Malaya, but it was felt that we should not violate the neutrality of Thailand unless the Japanese were to do so before us. In the end the problem was solved by the arrival of the Japanese inside our own frontier. It would in any case have been a doubtful venture to go forward, because they could have landed on the beaches behind us.

The Prime Minister was about to leave London for Canada, to meet the President and the American Chiefs of Staff. Dill, who had been paying farewell visits to troops up and down the country, was recalled to accompany him, and while he was in London he came to see me several times. We discussed the state of our forces in the Far East, and we agreed we could not have done much more to reinforce them in face of the urgent needs of other theatres. We felt that there was little hope for Singapore, for the naval and air forces essential for its defence were lacking, and the army was very short of tanks, and of anti-aircraft and anti-tank weapons.

On 10th December we got the news that the *Prince of Wales* and the *Repulse* had been sunk with the loss of 1,000 men and officers including their gallant Admiral, Tom Phillips, who had gone down with his flagship. This was a shattering blow which stunned us all. A naval friend of mine said that Phillips would have preferred not to survive, for he would have been tormented by the feeling that he had committed an error in handling the ships as he did. A week after his death I received a letter he had written to me, on 15th November, during the voyage to the Far East, in which he said, 'It is grand to be at sea again.'

Churchill called several meetings of the Chiefs of Staff before he went off. At these meetings there was some argument about the destination of the 18th Division (then on passage to the Middle East). Brooke had pointed out that, organized and equipped as it was, it would have been useless in the jungles and mountain ranges of Burma where it had been suggested it might be sent. This unlucky Division was therefore diverted to India. Later, on Wavell's request, it was redirected to Singapore, where it was promptly rounded up by the Japanese.

We felt, at this time, that Hong Kong could not last long. We thought the garrison might hold out for a month or six weeks at the outside. The only hope for Hong Kong had been that the American Navy would intervene, but Pearl Harbour had now eliminated that possibility. We also realized that Singapore was insecure, to put it mildly, and that it would now be difficult to send in reinforcements, since Japanese aircraft would soon dominate the Malacca Straits. We could only conclude that we would have to do our best, fighting where we could, and as long as we could.

We were a little anxious about the Middle East, even though at the moment Rommel was in retreat. We had not been satisfied, before Japan came into the war, with the amount of the reinforcements and equipment we would be able to send there before the spring. Now there would be less to send, and there was also the possibility that, if the Japs got into the Indian Ocean, convoys round the Cape would become a precarious line of supply. This made it more important than ever that we should get a firm hold of all North Africa. If we could occupy the whole of the North African shore, we would be able to supply the Middle East direct through the Mediterranean.

On 12th December Dill came to say good-bye, and, though I knew it was right that he should go, I hated to think that our very happy partnership had come to an end. In the War Office it had been a year fraught with anxiety and continual setbacks and of exacting and unremitting toil. And for me it had been a time of personal sorrow as well. Dill's friendship had done much to make it bearable; and I shall always think of him as one of the best and truest men I have ever had the good fortune to know.

On 14th December I gave Brooke a note on the probable effect of Japan's entry into the war, which I had dictated to clear my own mind. I reproduce it here, with Brooke's marginal comments in italics.

Note on the Situation 14.12.41.

The situation in the Far East has developed with startling rapidity. The Japanese, taking full advantage of surprise, not to mention treachery, have succeeded in isolating, for the moment, the region of the Far East in which they wish to operate. The possibility of serious interference with their plans by either the British or the American Fleet must be ruled out for a very considerable period.

The immediate objectives of the Japanese will probably be the capture of the Philippines, the capture of Singapore, the capture of Hong Kong, and last but not least, the capture of Rangoon. It is unlikely that their operations will extend for *I agree* the immediate future beyond these places. The East Indian islands will doubtless be their next objectives. If they could consolidate all these gains they could afford to sit down and assume the defensive.

We have to face the fact, on our side, that our position in the Far East is by no means satisfactory, quite apart from the serious turn which it has taken at sea.

Luzon, the main island of the Philippines, is about as big as England. Its garrison consists of one American division and the Filipino Army. The Japanese have already got a footing in the *Yes* north of the island, and appear to be attacking Manila in force. An early evacuation of the Philippines is therefore a real possibility.

Singapore is stocked up for six months. But when plans were made to hold the Naval Base for six months, which was the period required to ensure the arrival of the Fleet, they were based upon the assumption that the proper scale of defence would be installed. For various reasons, mainly unavoidable in view of our commitments elsewhere, the defences have not been brought up to scale. The chief deficiencies are in the most vital items, namely aircraft, of which we have less than half the proper number, tanks, anti-aircraft and anti-tank guns. To reinforce Singapore now is a very difficult matter. Furthermore, the arrival of the reinforcements, after the lapse of some weeks or months, is no effective remedy for their absence at the beginning of operations because the main opportunities for the use of the defending forces arise during the approach and landings of the Japanese forces. Once these are ashore, the use of aircraft, in particular, cannot be of such telling effect. A difficult feature of the problem is that reinforcements would come in the main from the Middle East. They would be out of action during the time of transit, which could not be less than two months, and their withdrawal from Middle East would weaken the present offensive and set back our preparations in that theatre to meet further attacks, especially from the North, in the spring. But there is also the difficulty of running ships into Singapore, since it is practically certain that the Malacca Straits will be dominated by Japanese aircraft and other approaches will be by no means easy. Moreover, it is to be anticipated that operations in Malaya itself will have developed very considerably before the reinforcements have arrived. A large Japanese convoy is at this moment moving towards the east coast of Malaya—it may contain two or three Japanese divisions. If the Japanese can operate some 8 to 10 divisions in Malaya, backed by considerable forces of aircraft, the fact must be faced that the defending troops may soon be driven back upon the island. The island defences have not been designed to deal with this situation, and the defence from the north has always been founded on the conception that there will be very considerable delay to the attacking forces on the mainland itself. There is therefore a strong possibility that Singapore may have to be given up in a much shorter period than the six months originally envisaged. This of course is not a certainty, but account has to be taken of the possibility.

Yes

The garrison of Hong Kong is now in process of withdrawing to the island. Here the only hope of a protracted defence is based on the feasibility of pressure by Chiang Kai Chek's troops on the mainland. This is not a strong hope. If a strong Chinese offensive does not materialize it seems fairly certain that Hong Kong will be captured within a month or six weeks at the outside.

Yes

The situation of both Malaya and Hong Kong is very much affected by the initial reverses inflicted on the American fleets and ours. The results of the opening moves is that the Japanese sea lines of communication are practically free from interference or threat of interference; their fleet, instead of having been weakened, is relatively stronger than ever and can cover both Malaya and Hong Kong while their land and air forces attack these places.

Regarded in this setting, Rangoon assumes perhaps even greater importance than Singapore itself. If the Japanese get Rangoon they will have closed the Burma Road, and with it, the only entry into China. Thus we might be deprived not only of a most useful ally, now containing such a great part of the Japanese effort, but also of a vital point of re-entry into the Far Eastern theatre when the moment comes to assume the offensive against Japan.

The importance of the East Indian islands to Japan lies mainly in the fact that they form a defensive screen; a chain of bases for further offensive action against Australia and New Zealand, should this be contemplated; and finally a source of of supplies in the shape principally of oil. Rubber supplies of vital importance to Japan, and of the greatest importance to us, will be lost, of course, if Malaya is captured.

This does not make a very pretty picture.

On the other hand, the fact remains that if Germany is defeated, Japan will also be defeated in the end. It is particularly unfortunate that Japan has inflicted this setback upon us at a *Yes* stage of the war when Germany seemed to be showing signs of weakness. In Russia the Germans may still collapse. They are in great difficulties and the Russians appear to be pressing them hard. If the Germans were once forced back in Russia, especially during the winter, their retreat would be a far greater *Not much* disaster than Napoleon's. There is still hope that this may *hope, I am* come about. *afraid*

In Libya, too, the Germans are cracking. They are now well west of Tobruk, and with luck their retreat may become a rout. These developments had not become clear at the time when Japan entered the war a week ago. No doubt the Germans felt that time was short, and put pressure upon Japan to enter the war before the situation in Russia and in Libya came to be known to her. And no doubt they were able to convince Japan that all was well in Russia, and that our offensive in Libya was indecisive. It is a thousand pities that the Libyan battle had to be postponed so long, mainly on account of the abortive attack in June, and that, when it did begin, it was so slow to show results.

The importance of North Africa has suddenly become greater than ever. The possession of the North African coast in its entirety would enable us to keep the Middle East going with far less effort, and in consequence would ease the situation as regards the reinforcement of the Far East. The hope of getting the North African coast, however, now seems remote, although we must not give up all hope yet. The Germans no doubt will grasp the significance of North Africa and it is to be anticipated that they may make some effort before long to instal themselves in French North Africa either by way of Tunisia or possibly by way of Spain. This would indeed be a serious embarrassment at this moment.

The problem before us now is to decide how far we can strengthen our position in the Indian Ocean and in the Far East without weakening ourselves unduly at home and in the Middle East. It would be right to strengthen the Navy in the Indian Ocean, not only because the Americans can take a greater share of the Naval commitment in the Atlantic, but because, without a strong fleet in the Indian Ocean and apart from the difficulty of maintaining our convoys east of the Cape, we may lose our position, not only in the China Sea, but in the oceans around our Indian and African Empires, not to mention Australia and New Zealand. How far we can reinforce Malaya and Burma and the East Indies is a matter which will require the closest consideration and nicest calculation but it is certain that we must do something for Burma, and it is certain that we must do something for Ceylon as a naval base, but it is not quite so certain how far we can afford to help Malaya and how far it would be practicable to do so. The problem of deciding how far the United Kingdom can be denuded also becomes more difficult. If we withdrew a large portion of the fleet from home waters it follows that the land and air forces must be correspondingly stronger.

We have already taken certain measures to meet the situation. The 18th Division, which was already approaching the Red Sea, has been diverted to India. The 50th Division which was destined for Iraq has been handed back to the Middle East. The 17th Indian Division which was about to embark for Iraq from

India is to be retained in India and may possibly be used in Burma. In addition, a number of anti-aircraft and anti-tank units and some squadrons of fighters have been diverted to India. A M.N.B.D.O.[1] is being sent from Middle East to Ceylon. These are preliminary measures, but the further implications of the situation have not yet been examined.

There is no doubt that we are faced with a difficult period in which we must expect heavy reverses. But, taking the long view, I believe that the entry of America into the war will more than counter-balance the successes which Japan has gained and is about to gain. As I said before, Japan must go down if Germany goes down. A year ago we were fighting alone. Now we have on our side both Russia and America. This is a tremendous combination and must, in the end, spell defeat of the Axis combination. It is unfortunate that so much time is required for the development of the full power of the British Empire and of America. But this has to be accepted. And we must find consolation in the fact that it is the last battle that counts. We have all the resources and the power to win this last battle, even though it may be long delayed.'

When Brooke had read this note, he sent it back to me with the following minute:

I agree with your paper in so far as it goes. But it does not solve the main problem:
(a) Must we skimp the Middle East to save the Far East?
or
(b) Skimp the Far East to ensure success in the Middle East?

No doubt Brooke smiled as he penned these questions. The problem remained with us until the Germans were out of Africa, and its solution was reached, meantime, by slow and painful stages.

The third week of December was entirely devoted to improvising arrangements for the Far East. We diverted convoys, originally intended for the Middle East, to India and Malaya. Burma was put under the command of Wavell, who was still Commander-in-Chief, India—he did not take over the South West Pacific command until 3rd January.

Our troops were being pressed back in Malaya; but they were

[1] Mobile Naval Base Defence Organization.

350 miles north of Singapore, and *qua* land forces they could well afford to give ground. But in the absence of adequate naval and air forces, the eventual outcome was horribly obvious.

The Australian Government was naturally very anxious indeed, not only for its forces in Malaya but for the safety of Australia itself. The British Chiefs of Staff, since before the war, had always accorded to the defence of Singapore a higher priority even than the defence of the Middle East; but this had been lost sight of by the British Government during the last year and a half, and our attention had been focused (though not without many a glance over our shoulder) on the problems of Cairo rather than Canberra. The Australian Government had responded magnificently to our needs, and no fewer than three of their Divisions had been fighting in Libya, Greece, Crete and Syria; but they had always had more than half an eye on Japan. The 8th Australian Division was in Malaya.

When Menzies was in London in May, seven months before, he had visited the Foreign Office, and not been much impressed. He had told me about his interview there. When they had all sat down, Sir Alexander Cadogan, the Permanent Under-Secretary, enquired of him whether he had any questions to ask; to which he had replied, 'I have come from the other end of the world: I thought *you* might have something to tell *me*. But yes, there *is* a question I'd like to ask: what is your policy towards Japan?' He told me, 'I could sense their reaction. They were thinking, "What a cad to ask a question like that!" Anyhow, they seemed to have no ideas, so I said, "I'll tell you mine. One thing the Jap won't do is lose face. He'd rather fight. If you don't want to fight him, don't get him into a corner he can't get out of without losing face. He is now pushing forward gradually. Make up your minds how far you're prepared to let him go. Draw a chalk line—it can be a broad one—and say Thus Far And No Farther. Otherwise he will be over it, and unable to go back without loss of face; and in that case he'll fight." '

I do not see how the diplomatists could have handled Japan other than the way in which they did. We could not offer a show of strength; we did offer a teaspoonful of appeasement, in the closing of the Burma Road. In any case, the Japanese were now in the war, and flooding outwards fast in all directions.

On 18th December, I attended a conference which had been called to meet Sir Earle Page, the Australian envoy to the British Cabinet, and Bruce, the former Prime Minister who was now High Commissioner. We met at 10 Downing Street. Attlee, as Acting

Prime Minister, was in the chair, but took little part in the discussion. Attlee in the chair always provided a complete contrast to Churchill. He would have a neat agenda, and adhere to it strictly, making sure that every point was dealt with, that everybody's views were heard, and that the meeting finished in good time. Churchill would disregard the agenda, do most of the talking himself, often afford no facilities to anybody else to make their points, and sometimes allow the meeting to run on for hours without reaching a conclusion. But we always came away, however rebuffed or frustrated or even angry, feeling that we had been present at an historic occasion.

When, this time, it came to my turn to speak, I explained that the defences of Malaya were far short of what we considered necessary, but that this could not have been otherwise, on account of our other commitments, especially in the Middle East. Owing to the naval disaster and our shortage of aircraft, we must face the fact that the Japanese would be able to concentrate, without interference, on both Hong Kong and Malaya.

Bruce raised the question of setting up inter-allied machinery for control of the war. Ismay then described the measures which had already been taken for co-ordination of action—the conversations with the Americans, the Dutch, and so on. He also explained the duties assigned to Duff Cooper, who had been sent out to Singapore as Minister Resident.

The meeting lasted an hour and a half, and was far from cheerful.

On 16th December I had a talk with Brooke about the reinforcement of Singapore. He was inclined to think that it would be throwing good money after bad. I said we should strain every nerve to save it, and that we would lay ourselves open to blame if we did not try, although the chances of success were so slender. Next day the atmosphere had changed, and we were instructed to go full speed ahead with arrangements for reinforcements. The effect which this would have upon the Middle East was realized and accepted.

On Sunday, 21st December, I was on duty in the War Office, and Brooke was in the country. In the course of the morning we received a message from Hong Kong which indicated that the garrison was *in extremis*. We had to decide whether to order the troops to fight it out, or give the Governor permission to surrender, as he wished to do. Attlee rang me up and asked my opinion.

It was a miserable task, trying to form an objective judgment, as a non-combatant, 7,000 miles away from where many lives hung on whatever decision was taken. I said that, judging from what the Governor had said in his telegram, resistance could probably not be continued for more than a few days, and would be on a small scale. Therefore, it would have practically no direct influence on operations in the Far East, in the way of tying up Japanese forces which might otherwise be released for use elsewhere. On the other hand, I said that, in this situation, the psychological aspect was of overriding importance, particularly with an Oriental enemy. If we fought to the last round and the last man at Hong Kong, we should gain an indirect military advantage, in that the Japanese would judge our powers of resistance elsewhere by the same standard. Therefore my opinion was that, although it was an unpleasant decision, the garrison should be told to fight it out. Attlee agreed. Churchill, having evidently foreseen the situation which would arise at Hong Kong, had, that same morning, sent us a telegram, from Arcadia, directing that the garrison should fight to the last. All that was necessary now was to forward his telegram to Hong Kong, with an endorsement to the effect that His Majesty's Government agreed; and this was done at 3.30 p.m.

A little later, at the request of the Admiralty, I sent a second telegram, 'By all means in your power including gun-fire endeavour wreck oil installations and storages.'

Before these messages were despatched, Lord Moyne, the Colonial Secretary, telephoned to say he considered that the Governor should be empowered to surrender, in view of the suffering which would be inflicted upon the civil population by continuing the fight. I pointed out that our original conception had been that Hong Kong might have held out for four months, which would have entailed far greater sacrifices than the civilians would now be called upon to face over a period of a few days. The Secretary of State agreed with me that Moyne's suggestion was not sound, and he sent a message to Attlee to say so.

The garrison of Hong Kong fought on until Christmas Day, when they surrendered. So ended an unfortunate and unhappy episode.

We were busily engaged, for the next few weeks, in working out the redistribution of forces which had become necessary. A considerable reshuffle was begun in all three Services, but the Navy was more deeply affected by the Japanese War than either the Army or the Air Force.

Military thinking had always maintained, as I have said before, that the defence of Singapore had a higher priority than that of

Egypt, and that its loss would be even more disastrous. Perhaps the event proved that military thinking was wrong in this respect, so far as the actual winning of the war was concerned; on the other hand, the total loss of stability in South-East Asia since the war ended may be ascribed largely to the disasters which befell us there. The early embroilment of the Middle East in the war, and the comparative quiescence of the Far East, had led to the weakening of our ability to resist in the latter; and the Prime Minister had always fiercely opposed any attempt to rob our Middle East Peter to pay our Far East Paul. We summarized our policy over the last two years for the benefit of the new C.I.G.S., and the following points are taken from a note which we gave him on 23rd December.

1939: The defence plan contemplated only the defence of Singapore Island.

August 1940: The Chiefs of Staff decided that all Malaya must be held if Singapore was to be adequately defended; that the forces needed would be 6 brigades and 336 aircraft; that, until the latter could be built up, 9 brigades (or three divisions) would be needed.

September 1940: *7th* Australian Division, available for Singapore, was sent instead to the Middle East. The Prime Minister felt strongly that: 'The defence of Singapore must be based upon a strong *local* garrison and the general potentialities of sea power.' He pointed out that Malaya was almost as large as England, and that a single extra division could not contribute much.

October, 1940: The Chiefs of Staff recommended a garrison of 26 battalions (still the rough equivalent of three divisions) with supporting arms, and the same figure of 336 aircraft. Commenting on this in January 1941 the Prime Minister had minuted: 'I do not remember to have given my approval to these very large diversions of force. On the other hand, if my minutes are collected they will be seen to have an opposite tendency.' He wrote three further minutes in the same strain in April 1941.

September 1941: G.O.C. Malaya's estimate of his requirements had risen to 46 battalions, the equivalent of 5 divisions, a figure which the Chiefs of Staff accepted as reasonable, but unforeseeable.

In the event, when Malaya was attacked in December 1941, the respective strengths of land and air forces were 31 battalions and 158 aircraft.

21

SINGAPORE AND THE AFTERMATH

1942

THE war had now entered on another sombre phase, and the sun was to remain behind the clouds for six or seven weary months of disappointment and frustration. At times disasters threatened us which were even worse than those which actually befell us; and these were bad enough, in all conscience.

One immediate effect of Japan's entry into the war was the instant weakening of our forces in the Middle East. Two Australian Divisions, and the seasoned British 70th Division (in which every battalion but one was a Regular unit, and all were battle-hardened), were soon to be removed from that theatre, and sent to Australia, New Guinea, India or Ceylon. Reinforcements *en route* for Egypt were diverted to India, Ceylon or Malaya, in hopes of stemming the Japanese advance. And as we had foreseen, American supplies dropped to a trickle: their own forces had now to be equipped.

We were still quite uncertain of the outcome of the campaign in Russia. Would the Russians stand up to the German attacks, which were certain to be renewed when the snows melted in the spring? Or would they collapse? We had to bear in mind this second possibility. If it came to pass, could we hold the Middle East, with its garrisons depleted, against German attacks through Turkey and Iraq and Persia? Could we defend the oilfields in the Persian Gulf without which our fleet could not operate in Eastern Waters? Could we prevent a junction of the Germans and the Japanese on the shores of the Indian Ocean? And would we have to face, once more, the possibility of a German attempt to invade the British Isles?

Our forces were, as yet, inadequate in numbers, poorly trained and badly equipped. As their failures in battle mounted, it became more and more difficult for Churchill to maintain his position as

Prime Minister. Criticism was wide and bitter. Our victories later in the year came only just in time to save him.

When Eden returned from Moscow at the end of December, he confirmed our assessment of the situation on the Russian front. The Germans were not retreating in confusion, as the Russian communiqués alleged, but were merely withdrawing to a winter line. Their plans had gone wrong, and their armies had suffered and would still suffer heavy losses; but there was no reason to suppose that they would not be able to renew their attacks in the spring.

I was amused to hear the accounts of Stalin which were given by various members of Eden's party. One said he was like a clergyman, another thought him like a respectable old farmer, and a third said he was like a great cat. Yet another thought that the most sinister thing about Stalin was his peculiarly gentle voice. It was during this visit that Stalin, seeing one of his marshals being carried out, dead drunk, from a banquet, asked Eden whether British generals got drunk too, and added, 'I find that, the more my generals drink, the better they are.'

We made some adjustments in the system of command in consequence of the extension of the war to the Far East. On 3rd January, Wavell was appointed Commander-in-Chief South West Pacific, and, a little later, Iraq and Persia were transferred from the Indian Command to that of the Middle East. Wavell was against this last change, arguing that Iraq and Persia were ramparts of India. But the decision was given against him, because they were equally ramparts of the Middle East; and the forces that would defend them, if they had to be defended, could come only from there. With the threat of a German attack looming up from the North, it seemed essential to us that operational control should be centred in Cairo.

By the first week of January it was clear that Ritchie, although he was still advancing westward, had failed to inflict a decisive defeat on Rommel. Hopes of getting to Tripoli had now faded away to nothing. Our forces had been weakened by their long advance and by the lengthening lines of supply; and there was no prospect of reinforcing them, although we knew that Rommel would soon be strong enough to make a heavy counter-attack. There was no escaping the fact that we would have to take a risk in the Middle East, and we had our eyes quite open to this. It was certain that the Middle East would be very much short of requirements in the coming spring and summer, and that our position there would become precarious if the Germans managed to disengage themselves from Russia, or to break up the Russian front.

The reinforcements we sent to Wavell were sadly deficient of naval and air elements. We realized that Singapore might be lost, but we still had hopes that we might be able to hold a line somewhere in the Dutch East Indies. We hoped too that Rangoon and the road to China might be held. We waited impatiently for the Americans to enter the fight. We had made elaborate plans with them for the co-ordination and control of operations. As Dudley Pound put it, we had 'plenty of harness but no horse'.

The Prime Minister returned from America where he had left Dill behind as his personal military representative with the President, on 17th January. He immediately directed a jet of telegrams on Wavell as from a fire-hose. At a Chiefs of Staff meeting, he spoke regretfully of the neglect to make the defences of Singapore Island face northwards, as well as to the sea. Our view, however, was that the 'last ditch' would have to be on the mainland in Johore, and not on Singapore Island. The island had never been considered defensible from close attack—the channel was narrow, mangrove swamps impeded the fire of the defences; and the aerodromes, water supply and other vital installations were within artillery range from the mainland. It was our opinion that the forces at Singapore, or as many of them as could be extricated, would be better employed in holding the islands to the southward, where they might be able to hinder a further advance on Australia, than in trying to hang on to the island, once it had been isolated and invested. Churchill, however, stuck to his view that Singapore Island should be held to the last man; and Wavell acquiesced.

As January drew to its unhappy close, Rommel began to roll up our forward troops in Cyrenaica. There was nothing we could do to help. We considered cutting down our supplies to Russia, but this idea was not accepted by Churchill. We also asked the Americans for more of their tanks, since the British tanks in the Desert were still outgunned and outranged by the German tanks. There had indeed been many muddles in our design and production.

There can be little doubt that the loss of confidence in Auchinleck's leadership, which now began to be apparent in Whitehall, was accentuated by his over-optimistic forecasts and reports of operations. On 27th January Brooke remarked to me: 'If we had judged Rommel's condition by Auchinleck's reports and nothing else, we would regard him now as a prize-fighter in the last stages of exhaustion, lying back, practically unconscious, in his corner of the ring, with his seconds fanning him. It is quite funny, in a way, to see him rise up and deliver such a crack on Auchinleck's jaw.'

In Malaya we were fighting under even more unequal conditions than in the desert, so far as equipment and training were concerned. Wavell cabled to say that he would be falling back on the island of Singapore on 30th and 31st January. Beckwith-Smith's 18th Division, after its erratic voyage of some three months, was finally directed to Singapore by Wavell, with the Prime Minister's approval, and it disembarked there. On 30th January I made this note in my diary:

> 'There will be the equivalent of three divisions in the island, but many of the troops will·be tired and untrained and without equipment. I hope Wavell will use the fresh troops to cover the extrication of the others and will not fight in an untenable position. I feel that we should save what we can, to make sure of Sumatra, Java, Burma, etc.'

Such a policy would never have been endorsed by Churchill and was never suggested by Wavell. A withdrawal would have been difficult to justify in the eyes of the world, especially while MacArthur was fighting on in the Philippines; and it would have been hard to meet the criticism that we could have held the place had we tried. All the same, we had regarded it as almost certain, once the Japanese were established in Northern Malaya, that Singapore was doomed. We received the news of its fall on 15th February.

Wavell sent us a note, dated 17th February, from which the following is an extract:

> 'I realized from the first that the whole thing was a race against time, and that the critical theatre was Malaya and Singapore. If we could hold out there long enough to build up a strong air force in the N.E.I., I felt fairly confident that we could gain the upper hand of the Japanese air force, in which event we could keep his ships and convoys from approaching Java or Sumatra or the other parts of the island barrier from Malaya to Australia, and that after that we could gradually push him back again. I also had to see that our vital flanks in Burma and the part of Australia for which I was responsible would remain secure.
>
> It looks as if we had lost the race against time by a month, by the failure of Malaya and Singapore to hold out for at least

that much longer. I feel that it ought to have done, and yet the Malayan front seemed to crumble in my hands whatever I could do. . . .

The trouble goes a long way back; climate, the atmosphere of the country (the whole of Malaya has been asleep for at least two hundred years), lack of vigour in our peacetime training, the cumbersomeness of our tactics and equipment, and the real difficulty of finding an answer to the very skilful and bold tactics of the Japanese in this jungle fighting.

But the real trouble is that for the time being we have lost a good deal of our hardness and fighting spirit. I am sure that you realize this, and that in your training and teaching at home you are doing everything possible to restore it. Until we have again soldiers capable of marching twenty to thirty miles a day for a number of days running, and missing their full rations every second or third day, and whose first idea is to push forward and to get to grips with the enemy on any and every occasion and whatever the difficulties and odds, we shall not recover our morale or reputation.'

We had cause on many previous occasions to be uneasy about the fighting qualities of our men. They had not fought as toughly as the Germans or the Russians, and now they were being outclassed by the Japanese. There were two reasons for this. The first was that we had only begun to form our army in earnest after the war had broken out, and it may be accepted that it takes about three years to organize and train troops, and to produce modern equipment for them. The second reason was that we were undoubtedly softer, as a nation, than any of our enemies, except the Italians. This may be accounted for by the fact that modern civilization on the democratic model does not produce a hardy race, and our civilization in Great Britain was a little further removed from the stage of barbarity than were the civilizations of Germany, Russia and Japan.

I had some talks with Brooke about ways and means of raising the standard of leadership, morale and discipline in the Army; and I drafted a letter for him to send to Commanders-in-Chief. He preferred in the end not to send it out in writing, but to grapple with the problem at conferences with his subordinate commanders, and by setting up special schools to indoctrinate troops in tougher forms of training. But here is the draft letter, to illustrate the lines on which he was thinking:

'Whilst I fully realize the efforts made so far to raise the quality of the Army, recent events render it essential that Commanders-in-Chief should consider and initiate further special and more drastic measures to this end.

In the German and Japanese armies we have antagonists who have been trained in the hard school of war itself. The bulk of our army is still untried. The tempo of warfare has so increased that we can no longer season our troops by degrees on the field of battle. If they do not stand up to the first onset of the enemy, they will seldom be given a second chance. Therefore special measures are needed in preparation for battle.

First, there is the question of leadership—the most important of all.

I wish all Commanders-in-Chief to devote particular attention to the selection of Commanders. Too many officers have been, and are being, promoted even to high command because they are proficient in staff work, because they are good trainers, because they have agreeable personalities, or because they are clever talkers. I do not underrate the difficulties of selecting the best leaders without the test of active service. Mistakes are bound to be made. But let us make as few mistakes as possible. We must be more ruthless in the elimination of those who seem unlikely to prove themselves determined and inspiring leaders in the field. It is essential to select the best men to fill their places. You can rely on my full support.

Secondly, the morale and the discipline of the Army must be vastly improved.

There are strong hopes that the Government will now put a stop to the pernicious criticism of the Forces and the higher command which characterizes certain sections of our Press. This will remove one of our difficulties.

But there is much that we can do ourselves to raise morale and tighten discipline. It is, I fear, true to say that our troops have not always in this war fought as well as they could and should. The reason, in my opinion, has been directly due to a low standard of leadership and true fighting morale.

I might define this kind of morale as well-founded pride in fighting efficiency. To possess it our men must be physically hard and fit and capable of withstanding both mental and bodily reactions to extreme fatigue. They must possess a high sense of duty, of comradeship and of discipline; and they must be taught to love the spice of danger and to know its various aspects.

To produce the standard we require, troops must be trained as far as is possible to all the characteristics of war, and must be taught to foster a pride in their powers of endurance and achievement.

I desire Commanders-in-Chief to keep these aims before them in all training. Every artifice is to be employed. Hardening courses of all kinds are required. Artillery must shoot and field firing be practised close to troops to accustom them to the blast of explosions and other noises of battle. Long marches and exercises, practices over obstacle courses, river crossings, etc., will be organized to inure men to fatigue and hunger. By such means our men can be prepared to withstand the stresses and shocks of fighting in modern conditions.'

On 16th February, just after we had received the news of the fall of Singapore, I gave Brooke a note for the Chiefs of Staff meeting.

NEW SITUATION IN THE FAR EAST

General Wavell's telegram, followed by the news that both Singapore and Palembang have been captured, brings us up against the hard facts of an extremely unpleasant situation.

We are now faced with a decision as to what points we are to hold in the immediate future.

1. It is clear that, however hard we try, we shall be unable to hold the Netherlands East Indies; we should now harden our hearts and tell the Dutch that we do not propose to send any more reinforcements to Java. We should also start at once to remove land, air and naval forces, including such of the Dutch forces as they might agree to evacuate from the Netherlands East Indies. Anything left in the East Indies for more than a very few days will inevitably be lost. This would be wrong strategy in view of the nakedness of the land in Australia, Burma, Ceylon and India. Military considerations must now override the 'most serious moral and political repercussions' mentioned by General Wavell in paragraph 7 of his telegram.

2. We should concentrate our efforts on holding:

India and Ceylon;

Burma;

Australia.

INDIA. There is not a single complete trained and equipped fighting formation in India, and air forces are practically nil.

CEYLON. There are two brigades of raw troops and negligible air forces.

BURMA. Early reinforcement is urgently necessary.

AUSTRALIA. Contains a collection of newly formed and incompletely trained and equipped formations.

3. It is difficult to place these areas in any definite order of priority. The whole of our position in the Indian Ocean depends upon control in India and the retention of Ceylon. If India goes, the loss of the Middle East and Burma and the subsequent defeat of China will be inevitable.

With Singapore and Sumatra in Japanese hands, it is quite possible that within the next few weeks the Japanese will land small raiding forces on the East coast of India to exploit internal unrest. These may be accompanied by attacks on cities such as Madras and Calcutta by carrier-borne aircraft. Should this occur we shall be faced with an extremely difficult situation.

4. *Possibility of reinforcements.*

Army

(a) 6th, 7th and 9th Australian Divisions.

For political reasons the Australian Government will undoubtedly wish to send the Australian Corps complete to Australia if it is not to go to Java. General Wavell has suggested that one division might go to Burma.

Taking the time factor into consideration, the best strategical use for the two leading Australian divisions (6th and 7th) would be for the first to go to Burma and the second to Ceylon. The destination of the 9th Division can be left open for the time being, although a firm decision should now be taken to withdraw it from the Middle East.

(b) Further withdrawal from Middle East.

For the early reinforcement of India I strongly recommend the immediate withdrawal of at least one division from Iraq. Should the potential threat to Iraq and Persia develop, the forces which we shall be able to put into that area will be quite inadequate to meet it; any forces over and above those which are required for internal security are therefore wasted and would be of far greater value in areas more immediately threatened.

R.A.F.

R.A.F. reinforcements at present planned are quite incommensurate with the real needs of the situation. We should most seriously consider the despatch from this country by all means of strong R.A.F. reinforcements for India, Ceylon, Burma and Australia.

The immediate need is for fighters in large quantities and we should not hesitate to take twenty to thirty squadrons out of this country. This will necessitate giving a greatly increased allotment to the R.A.F. in Convoy W.S. 17 at the expense of the Army, and I consider that this must be accepted.

Secondly, an examination should be made into the capacity of the air reinforcement route from this country to the Middle East and beyond. I am by no means satisfied that the capacity of this route is being fully exploited.

Thirdly, we must consider the abandonment of the policy of bombing Germany, at any rate for the time being. The saving in personnel and ground establishments, and possibly of aircraft, should go a long way to make good the deficiencies in the Middle East and Far East.

To sum up, four major issues should now be decided:

(a) No further reinforcements should be sent to the Netherlands East Indies, from which area land, sea and air forces should now be evacuated.

(b) The earliest possible reinforcement of Burma and Ceylon, preferably by Australian divisions.

(c) One further division should be withdrawn from Iraq for India.

(d) Strong R.A.F. reinforcements should be despatched in W.S. 17 to India, Burma, Ceylon and Australia.

It very soon became clear that we could not hope to make a stand in the East Indies. By 20th February we had given up the idea of reinforcing Java, and were concentrating our efforts on Ceylon, which was now our main naval base for the Indian Ocean, and on Burma and Australia. We continued to rob the Middle East in our endeavours to save the Indian Ocean. In doing this we fully realized that we were gambling on the Russians standing up through the summer of 1942; if they failed, we knew there would be little chance of holding Egypt with its depleted forces. Even on the assumption that the Russians would be able to continue the fight, the defence of Egypt was now being weakened to a dangerous degree. But there was nothing else for it. We were in a bad patch of the war, and we knew it must continue for some months.

This was a trying time for the Prime Minister and for the

Chiefs of Staff. Brooke was standing up well to the strain, supported by his sense of humour. He was rapidly acquiring an effective technique for dealing with Churchill. He told me, one day in February, that he no longer attempted to reply when the Prime Minister declaimed. 'I just sit silent,' he said, 'and put up an umbrella.' When Churchill found that he could not start an argument, he always became more reasonable.

By this time Brooke was settling into the saddle which Dill had always found so uncomfortable; he was scarcely feeling comfortable in it himself, but he was finding, by trial and error, a *modus vivendi*. I was myself becoming something of a connoisseur in the various ways of dealing with the Prime Minister, having witnessed so many different approaches. Lord Salisbury seemed to be the most expert performer. He had the initial advantage that he so often produced what one quickly realized was the right answer. He had a gentle almost diffident manner. He would smile and he was always infinitely courteous. But behind his gentleness was a quality of steel and everybody, including the Prime Minister, knew that it was impossible to deflect him from whatever he thought right. More than once I saw him turn a discussion completely round when it was about to reach an opposite conclusion. By totally different methods, Bevin could achieve almost the same effect; in his case, his persuasiveness was due to the combination of blunt and bluff opinions, allied to honesty, courage and common sense. Attlee's staccato, matter-of-fact approach was different from both of these, but was also extremely effective. Some other Ministers, although acutely intelligent and of strong character, rarely carried their points in these open discussions.

Brooke once told me that when he was a subaltern in India his battery commander, the future General Wardrop, gave him as a watchword or rule of life the advice to 'live dangerously, live hard, and live straight'. Another motto, which I once noticed hanging in the bathroom of his house at Hartley Wintney, was 'Life consists of Monday to Saturday, not Saturday to Monday'. Brooke certainly had an immense zest for living, which could only have been nurtured by a commensurate store of vitality. It applied to his hobbies as well as his work: he was a keen ornithologist; his colour-films of birds rivalled those of professionals; he was a good shot and a good fisherman. He once caught a hundred salmon in a season.

He displayed the same characteristics in his work. He was quick, decisive and methodical; he was not afraid to decentralize, and he was so little seen in the War Office that it was said of him that he knew his way to only two rooms there: his own, and the lavatory. He quickly adjusted his routine to Churchill's, and used to disappear for three hours in the afternoon, during which he pursued his own avocations, chiefly nosing round the book-shops for bird books, or for new gadgets for his cine-camera. As a rule, he never came back to the War Office after dinner. In these respects he was far better equipped for the rigours of his job than Dill, who had not the same facility for skimming the cream off the work, and whose only pastime—riding—was not easily indulged in from the War Office. And whereas Dill was sensitive to a fault, Brooke was able to grow a thick skin in which the Prime Minister's *banderillas* did not stick.

By this time the campaign in Burma had begun to look pretty hopeless, and it was decided to send out Alexander to replace Hutton in command. Before going off, Alexander spent a few days in London reading papers and reports. He was cool and imperturbable as always. When Brooke and I bade him good-bye and wished him luck, he smiled, and said, 'I will do my duty. You must help me all you can.'

On 19th February, P. J. Grigg, the Permanent Under-Secretary for War, relieved Margesson as Secretary of State. On 5th March, Wavell was back in Delhi as Commander-in-Chief, having handed over command of the remaining forces in Java to the Dutch General Ter Poorten. We evacuated Rangoon on 7th March, and it was occupied by the Japs on the following day. The picture was, indeed, not a pretty one. Strategically, we were still living beyond our means, and we were woefully short of shipping to move our forces. If we could save Ceylon and India, or at least part of India, we would still be able to restore the situation in time. The Japs were becoming very extended, and it seemed likely that their advances were now nearing their high-water mark.

The policy of supplying Russia with military equipment once more came in for a good deal of discussion. We were sending to Russia, every month, some 200 aircraft and 250 tanks. Wavell was desperately anxious to get more fighter aircraft for the defence of India, and, at about the end of February, the Chiefs of Staff proposed to withhold 70 fighters from Russia and send them to him. But the Cabinet refused to approve this suggestion. It was, indeed, difficult to strike a proper balance, militarily as well as politically. It was of very great importance that Russia should be strong enough to survive the German drive to the Caucasus which was bound to come in the spring; it was equally important that we should not suffer a landslide in India, which was practically empty. We could hardly weaken the Middle East further without inviting disaster; we had already withdrawn from Egypt one British and three Australian divisions, all with hard-won experience, not to mention considerable air forces. In fact, the time had come to make an attempt to reinforce Egypt afresh. In this situation we considered, with anxious care, the load and destination of every individual ship in our convoys.

The course of the operations in the Desert, since Auchinleck had taken over, had failed to inspire the Government with great confidence in his leadership; but his position was still strong. Now, at the beginning of March, there began a chain of events which culminated in his removal five months later. It was in March that he sent us an appreciation of the situation, which indicated that his outlook had become defensive. It was true that Rommel's forces had been strengthened, while Auchinleck's had been depleted by withdrawals to the Far East. But the view we took in London was that, the longer he waited before he attacked Rommel, the poorer would be his chances of holding his position. And the Navy were desperately anxious that Auchinleck should regain aerodromes in Cyrenaica from which our aircraft might be able to cover the passage of convoys into Malta.

The Chiefs of Staff sent Auchinleck a telegram. They told him their considered opinion: that he should adopt a more offensive attitude. This telegram was sent instead of one that Churchill had drafted himself, and was couched in more courteous language. We agreed with the tenor of the Prime Minister's draft, but we thought it better to omit such remarks as that 'armies were not intended to stand about doing nothing', that 'soldiers were meant to fight', and so on. Auchinleck sent an unsatisfactory reply. He argued that the issue which he faced was far bigger than the security of Malta, and that a premature offensive would jeopardize our whole position in the Middle East. In fact he stuck to his previous opinion. He also refused to agree to our tentative correction of his comparison of the number of tanks possessed by Rommel and by himself, which we thought inaccurate.

At the same time Auchinleck sent a private telegram to Brooke in which he said he felt sure that Brooke could not have approved the terms of the telegram which had been sent to him by the Chiefs of Staff, since it implied that Auchinleck and his officers were incompetent. Brooke and I drafted a reply to him to say that his feelings would have been much more hurt if he had got the telegram the Prime Minister had intended for him; and we repeated that we could not reconcile his comparison of tank strengths either with our own estimate or with the figures he himself had previously sent us.

Churchill now decided that the impasse could not be resolved by correspondence, and on 8th March he cabled to Auchinleck asking him to come to London for consultation. Auchinleck replied that he did not want to come, and that he could see no good reason for coming. Brooke, at Winston's request, sent Auchinleck a private telegram in which he tried to impress on him that it would be best for him to come to London. Auchinleck replied with a suggestion that Brooke and Portal should go out to see him instead. Churchill was very much incensed by this, and sent Auchinleck a telegram to say he was considering sending 15 squadrons of fighters to help the Russians in the Caucasus if Auchinleck could not attack soon. Brooke advised the Prime Minister not to send this, but he insisted, saying, 'It will be a whip to him.' Churchill then decided that he would send Nye to Cairo to see Auchinleck. Nye went off on 12th March, and, in due course, reported that he agreed with Auchinleck's appreciation of the situation. This, to put it mildly, did not please the Prime Minister; but it gave Auchinleck a slight respite.

From time to time Brooke had advocated the appointment of a Supreme Commander for each theatre of operations and for each operation, and the abolition of the system of triumvirates under which the Commanders-in-Chief of the three Services were, in theory, equal to each other in status. But when he broached the subject in the Chiefs of Staff Committee he was opposed by both the First Sea Lord and the Chief of the Air Staff. After a lengthy sitting, Brooke said, 'Well, this discussion is itself a good example of the weakness of our present system. Here is a simple issue which any one of us alone could have decided in a few minutes—yet we have been arguing about it for two hours.' There could be little doubt that the triumvirate system had led to undesirable compromises in the past, each compromise tending to be the lowest common denominator of three different conceptions.

The Prime Minister now took a hand in the matter; and early in March he sent a note to the Chiefs of Staff in which he declared himself in favour of the unification of commands. Brooke then put his views into writing, and the decision to appoint Supreme

Commanders was taken soon afterwards. The following is an extract from his paper.

I am in general agreement with the Prime Minister's comments in so far as they relate to command. The committee system is not conducive to firm, decisive and quick action, which is essential to success in war. When a commander has to modify his decisions to meet the views of colleagues with an equal right to give decisions he is in effect merely a member of a Council of War, the evils of which have been proved in history. Resulting action is both weakened and slowed up.

In an active theatre a commander must possess an overriding and co-ordinating authority. For this reason I consider that there should always be a Supreme Commander in a theatre where active operations are in progress. His role should be:
(a) to direct operations with unity of purpose, decision and drive;
(b) to give the broad strategic decisions required for such direction;
(c) to co-ordinate the activities of the fighting and civil services placed under his orders.
He should seldom, if ever, exercise direct command of his own Service. He should require only a small personal staff. . . .

I do not however consider that the above principles apply to planning and staff work. Here it is essential that the limitations and characteristics of each Service should be thoroughly appreciated and related to each other.

(sgd) A. F. Brooke.
C.I.G.S.

22

STRIKING A BALANCE

1942

By the beginning of March Brooke seemed to be wilting a little, although, as Margesson remarked, he had the great gift of (as it were) shaking himself like a dog coming out of the water, after awkward interviews with Churchill. But he was showing signs of wear and tear; he was inclined to be irritable; he did not laugh so much as he had during his first weeks in office. It did, in fact, take him some months to adjust himself and establish a satisfactory relationship with the Prime Minister.

There was still no sign of any strong American movement against Japan. I often discussed the possibilities with the American officers in London. On 9th March, General Bolte, the American Chief of Staff in London, dined with me at the United Service Club. Among other things we discussed Roosevelt's generous response to the Prime Minister's appeal for ships, and the feasibility of advancing the date of the relief of the British garrison in Iceland by American troops. Bolte thought that our unsuccessful endeavours to hold Java and Rangoon would, in the end, stand us in good stead politically. And he thought that the Germans could and did subordinate the political to the military aspect of their operations; this was an inherent weakness in their system, which might lead to their downfall, in spite of initial successes.

On 5th March, Dill had sent a telegram to the Chiefs of Staff from Washington, in which he said:

'As we see it, now is the time to concentrate on essentials. These appear to us to be:
(a) Security of Britain.
(b) Security of U.S.A.
(c) Continuance of all possible assistance to Russia.

(d) Prevention of junction of German and Japanese forces, i.e.
    Germany reaching the Indian Ocean.
    Do you agree?
    These simple rules might help us to stick to things that
matter in these difficult days.'

Churchill was much annoyed by this telegram, and he sent Dill
a reply which implied that he was 'defensively minded'. I saw
the draft before it was sent, and was unsuccessful in an attempt
to alter its terms. I noted in my diary at the time: 'Winston is
very touchy about the offensive and defensive spirit, and any
hint of the latter always rouses him, even when quite fair. It is a
fault on the right side.'

On 12th March, Dill again telegraphed, expressing anxiety for
the Middle East. He suggested that we should make an effort to
get the Americans to reinforce the Middle East strongly before it
was too late. He asked for authority to go to the Americans and
say, 'Unless the Middle East is reinforced strongly and fast, we
shall be defeated there, and our combined efforts will not enable
us to win the war for years.'

About this time Roosevelt put forward a proposal to divide
the world into three main theatres of war—the Pacific for the
United States, the Indian Ocean and Middle East for us and the
Atlantic and Europe for combined effort. This plan seemed to
us to be a good general division, but we were anxious that it should
not lead to over-concentration of American effort against Japan to
the detriment of the war against Germany. Brooke sent for me to
discuss the draft of the reply to Roosevelt's telegram, the Prime
Minister having summoned the Chiefs of Staff for 10.45 p.m. to put
it into final shape.

In March the controversy over the allocation of the Air Force
was approaching a fresh crisis. The Navy and the Army continued
to urge, with little success, that a share of the air forces should be
trained for and assigned to their operations. But the Air Staff still
fought hard, with strong political backing, for what they sincerely
and obstinately believed the quickest and most effective way to
win the war.

In the first week of March, Alexander gave orders for the
evacuation of Rangoon. This meant that the last hope of maintaining
considerable forces in Burma had gone, for we calculated that the
single road from Assam would take no more than 30 tons of traffic
per day, and we had only two months' reserves of stores in the

north of Burma. We were lucky that the line of retreat northward of our 17th Division, 36th Brigade and Tank Brigade had not been cut.

A fortnight later, Wavell telegraphed his advice that Alexander should be directed to fall back into China. If this had been accepted, our troops would have been almost entirely cut off from supplies, and could have had nothing more than a guerrilla value. We felt that Alexander should make for Assam, and that, if we were given a few months' respite, roads could be put through from there to Northern Burma.

Admiral Furstner, a very agreeable and cheerful person, who was acting as Minister for War in the Dutch Government in London, came to see me on 9th March. He asked that the Dutch troops evacuated from the East Indies should be concentrated in Ceylon, and used to reinforce our garrison there until they could be sent back to the Dutch Colonies to take part in guerrilla warfare. I arranged to have this done.

The idea of establishing a front in France was being canvassed actively in the Press about this time, and there was some political support for it also. The General Staff opposed the suggestion for a number of reasons. The front proposed was a line across the neck of the Cherbourg peninsula. This line was about twenty miles in length, and the great stretches of sea coast behind it would also have had to be defended. Twelve divisions, at least, would have been required for defence alone, and at that time we could not have spared enough troops for an offensive. During the landing, we should have been at a great disadvantage in the air, for the range of our fighter aircraft was so short that they could have remained over Cherbourg only fifteen minutes before turning back to England to refuel. There seemed to us to be no point in the operation as a means of relieving the pressure of the German armies on the Russians, for the German troops already stationed in France would have been strong enough, without reinforcement, to deal with a landing on this scale. For all these reasons we argued that it would be wise to defer an operation in France until we could land in sufficient strength to be able to attack.

I had a talk with Paget about it at his Headquarters on 16th March. We agreed that offensive operations on the Continent were quite beyond our powers at that time, and that the most we could hope for, if we were forced to undertake the operation, would be an air battle which might, for a time, divert a part of the German Air Force from the Russian front.

Another complicated problem about now was what kind of direction we should give to industry, in order to ensure that we should have the right kind of equipment, in the right quantities, for the later stages of the war. Enormous masses of equipment were being produced in America which we did not think would ever be wanted, and other things that we believed would be required were not being made. Both British and American production had obviously to be carefully related to the probable form of our various campaigns all over the world; and so in March we wrote a special study for the Chiefs of Staff, largely to clear our own minds as to the priorities in which we needed equipment.

Until the entry of Japan into the war, our objects had been quite clear: to maintain our essential communications, to tighten the ring round Germany, and to wear her down by air bombardment, naval blockade and subversive action. From these objects it had not been difficult to deduce our needs in the way of production. They were tabulated in our study as follows:

(a) *Sea*: maximum concentration on merchant shipbuilding, and the means of protecting trade;

(b) *Land*: the production of enough material to equip the largest Army our manpower could support. The figures included provision for some 60 Divisions in overseas areas of British strategic responsibility, quite apart from the creation in the United Kingdom of an Army intended ultimately to return to the Continent;

(c) *Air*: subject to the provision of an essential minimum of fighters and certain other special types, the building up of a great force of heavy bombers (over 7,000 first-line operational aircraft) to undertake the process of wearing down Germany.

But with the entry of Japan, and for the matter of that of America, into the war, the problem had changed overnight. America now had her own requirements, to equip an army expanding at a rate which the world had never seen before, a navy designed to fight on two oceans, and an enormous air component in both. Our objectives had changed also, although we ourselves were not faltering in our belief that the defeat of Germany must be encompassed first, while we merely held Japan. We had always considered hitherto that a Japanese attack would at once be counter-balanced by American action; but Pearl Harbour and the loss of the entire East Indies had changed all that. It was not in our power to vary by much the forces and equipment which would become available during 1942; but it was obvious, now that the shape of the war against Japan could be seen, that our previous ideas needed modification.

'1942,' we said in our paper, 'will almost certainly be a critical year for Germany. Broadly there are two hypotheses:

(a) that the German offensive against Russia fails. In this event the collapse of Germany will only be a matter of time, provided we do not meanwhile lose command of the sea. The creation of a vast force of heavy bombers in the United Kingdom for use in 1943 or 1944 may hasten the issue, or it may be too late even to do that. The creation of a great American Army will not affect the issue at all;

(b) that the German offensive against Russia succeeds and that the German Army, by one route or another, reaches the Caucasus. In this event we shall be faced not only with a threat to the Indian Ocean from the West, but we shall also inevitably have to face invasion of this country.

We can only defeat invasion by having command of the sea and air round the British Isles. This will demand naval forces and aircraft of the type to support them.

In the East there is only one possible hypothesis—that Japan will continue to dispute with us the control of the Indian Ocean, and with the Americans the control of the Pacific. All history shows that the nation which commands the wider seas will ultimately emerge victorious. Enormous efforts will be required to regain our position in the Indian and Pacific Oceans and to bring about the collapse of Japanese sea power.

These efforts will demand the creation of fleets, of the wherewithal to launch combined operations and of large numbers of aircraft of a type suitable to attack Japanese shipping and to work with our own Navy and Army.

We shall not want—indeed we could never use—a big army to overcome Japan; nor shall we want large numbers of heavy bombers although we shall probably need a multitude of transport aircraft.

One can of course vary the above hypotheses almost indefinitely. Nevertheless I believe that their basic conception is right. As far as we and the Americans are concerned, this war is essentially a struggle for the control of sea communications, and I am more than doubtful whether we are developing our resources on the right lines to meet it. Are we for instance sure that we shall have enough naval and air forces of the right type to make certain that we can defeat invasion in 1943, or to enable us to carry the war into Japan's sea-girt Empire? Can the great quantities of army equipment to be produced next year ever reach a war zone?

These are questions which must be answered. I recommend that the Joint Planning Staffs both here and in Washington be instructed to examine them as a matter of the greatest urgency, and to draw up a revised list of requirements.'

Soon after this, it became a matter of routine to draft, every few months, a forecast of operations or 'hypothesis', which the appropriate sections of the staff translated into terms of equipment likely to be needed for the operations we envisaged. This task of foretelling the future, so far as the Army was concerned, fell in the first instance to me and my staff. On the whole, our soothsaying was fairly successful—so much so that we became liable to re-criminations from the production staffs on those occasions when it was not.

In the third week of March we had two operations on the stocks in London: the raid on St. Nazaire, and the capture of Madagascar. The first of these ('Sledgehammer') was strongly supported by all three Services. For over a year we had been trying to persuade the War Cabinet that we needed an active raiding policy to tide us over until we had the capacity for offensive action on a bigger scale. Keyes had been against such raids on the grounds that they would fritter away resources with which he hoped to be allowed to carry out bigger projects—projects on which he had set his heart, but which we regarded as wild, or unprofitable, or even impossible. Mountbatten, who had succeeded Keyes as Chief of Combined Operations, had been instrumental in winning Churchill to our way of thinking; and he displayed immense drive in organizing the descent on St. Nazaire, which was carried out in the first week of April, and was a resounding success.

'Ironclad', the Madagascar operation, cost us much discussion; the troops had already been embarked and were on their way, although their precise role and destination were still undecided. The decision to launch the actual attack on Diego Suarez had not yet been taken, and it would still have been possible to postpone it, put the troops ashore at Durban, and leave them there for a time in case we wished to mount the operation again at a later date.

The occupation of Madagascar had been arranged for one reason and one reason alone: to secure our sea communications round the Cape of Good Hope. Japanese raiding ships and submarines must be prevented from attacking our shipping in the Moçambique Channel; and if a danger arose that the Japanese might seize a base in Madagascar, then, of course, we must gain control of the island. This was a matter for the Naval Staff to advise on. If they did not press for the occupation of Madagascar, we would be glad to avoid running the risk of a break with the Vichy Government. We did not want to give the French a pretext for offering the Germans the use of their North African ports, especially Dakar and Bizerta. Nor were we anxious to create a new commitment to be defended, at a time when our resources were already so heavily strained.

When the expedition sailed, the view of the Naval Staff was that it might be necessary to establish a base in Diego Suarez; but they changed their minds more than once while the force was on its way. On 21st April, they stated that Kilindini, Ceylon and Zanzibar would suffice for the control of the Indian Ocean; so it looked for a moment as though the bottom would fall out of the case for the occupation of Diego Suarez unless a real threat developed to Ceylon. The Naval Staff pointed out, moreover, that the Japanese could operate effectively against our shipping on the East coast of Africa from bases in the East Indies, and did not need a base in Madagascar.

The Prime Minister called a meeting of the Chiefs of Staff on 24th April to discuss the pros and cons of 'Ironclad'. I thought we should oppose the occupation of the island, since the Naval Staff no longer thought it necessary: the chances of disagreable repercussions in North Africa had increased now that Laval was in power. It would be very awkward, for instance, if Gibraltar were to be bombed, in retaliation, from bases in French North Africa. I felt it would be best to send the force on to India where reinforcements were badly needed.

It is interesting to observe how the momentum increased as the days went by. It was originally argued, when the expedition sailed, that the mere fact of its sailing in no way committed us to the operation; the forces would in any case be handier for the various battle-fronts. But Churchill showed an increasing tendency to assume that we were already committed; perhaps he was influenced by the fact that he had informed Roosevelt and Smuts of the plan, and obtained their approval.

I discussed the whole business with Brooke again on the morning of the 28th April. He had put our view to the Defence Committee the day before, but it had been decided to postpone a decision until the last possible moment, which would be 3rd May. He was not inclined to make a major issue of it; Pound and Portal were apparently in favour of going ahead; and I was in a minority of one, and on a humbler echelon at that.

On Sunday, 3rd May, in Brooke's absence, I attended a meeting of the Chiefs of Staff. They had been assembled to consider a minute from the Prime Minister in which he asked us to examine the possibilities of reducing the scope of the occupation of Madagascar, so as to meet Wavell's request that the 5th Division could be sent on to India quickly. We agreed that this was sound, and instructions to that effect were duly sent to the Force Commanders.

'Ironclad' was launched when the expedition arrived at Madagascar, and on 7th May we heard, with considerable relief, that Diego Suarez was in our hands. The occupation was completed without difficulty, and there were no repercussions from Vichy. So the only price we had to pay was some delay in reinforcing India.

An intriguing feature of the Madagascar business was that some of the newspapers, quite unconscious of the fact that the expedition had been sent off from England, started a campaign of their own in favour of seizing a base at Diego Suarez. We had to consider whether, in the interests of secrecy, they should be asked to stop their public advocacy of the operation. But we felt that the newspapers might in fact provide additional 'cover' if they were not interfered with, since both the Japanese and the Germans would doubtless think that not even the British could be such boobies as to allow the Press to proclaim an operation which was in fact to be undertaken.

I do not know whether the Naval Staff, looking back on 'Ironclad' at the end of the war, would have considered that the possession of a base at Diego Suarez had been proved necessary. If so, I was quite wrong in opposing the scheme. But I didn't think so at the time. The objections we made to 'Ironclad', reinforced by Wavell's strong opposition to it, did at least produce one good effect, in bringing about a reduction of the extent of the occupation of Madagascar and the consequent early release of forces for despatch to India.

23

DELAYS IN THE MIDDLE EAST

1942

Aᴛ the beginning of April it was evident that we were fast approaching a crucial phase in our strategy.

Ever since the beginning of the war we had been trying to do too much with too little. The necessarily wide dispersion of our effort on exterior lines stultified all attempts to apply the most effective of all principles of war—concentration at decisive points. Now it was becoming particularly difficult.

In Europe, our intelligence indicated that the Germans were only awaiting the spring to launch a heavy and perhaps overwhelming attack upon the Russians. This was to be followed by an advance into the Caucasian oilfields, and perhaps farther south into the Middle East. In North Africa, Rommel was still undefeated, and it was becoming increasingly hard to supply the forces necessary for a successful attack in the Desert. The Japanese were pressing on in Burma, and might soon attack India and Ceylon, which were practically defenceless. The Americans were not yet ready to take the offensive, our reserves were small, and ships to transport them hard to come by. We needed quick decisions and quick action.

We could give little or no direct help to Russia, beyond continuing to send her supplies of war equipment. And we were unable to meet more than a fraction of the demands which now poured in on us from our own commanders.

Wavell, in a series of strong and well-reasoned telegrams, advocated the reinforcement of India. In particular, he was woefully short of aircraft;[1] he had only about a sixth of the number he

[1] When he arrived in India in July 1941, the first signal he sent was to his late colleague Tedder, A.O.C.-in-C., Middle East. It read: 'Have just seen on my way here India's most up-to-date fighter squadron armed with Audaxes. Does not this make your heart bleed?'

needed. His whole position might collapse if we did not defend Calcutta, which was at the moment practically naked; the Japanese were concentrating in Burma, and presumably preparing to descend on Assam and Bengal; Alexander was hard pressed in Burma, and without supply routes; our fleet could not operate in the Bay of Bengal for lack of fighter cover; the Japs had occupied the Andamans, from which we had evacuated our minute garrison; Ceylon, now our main fleet base, was not strongly enough held, but Wavell advised that we should accept a risk there. With this last we could not agree.

From Auchinleck came blunt statements of our weakness in the Middle East. The transfer of considerable army and air forces from his command to India and Australia had compelled him to postpone the offensive planned against Rommel. Now it had become doubtful whether the offensive should be undertaken at all. Could we spare the precious resources and ships which would be required for it, and should we not rather devote them to the defence of vital positions elsewhere?

Pressing demands for help came also from Australia and New Zealand, to meet possible Japanese attacks. And Giffard, in West Africa, was pleading for reinforcements, and, above all, for an air force, to enable him to meet the German penetration into French North Africa which he considered likely.

Here are extracts from two notes, dictated on 6th and 7th April, which will show the shape our thoughts took as we brooded over our problems.

6.4.42.

THE RELATIVE IMPORTANCE OF THE MIDDLE EAST AND INDIA

It is necessary to clear our minds as to the relative importance of the Middle East and India, and as to the relative importance of the various places within these two theatres, in order that we may be able to allot our resources correctly in this critical phase of the war. . . .

Although resources are so short, a great deal of attention has been focussed on the possibility of an offensive in Libya. Broadly speaking, our resources in the Middle East will probably be sufficient to carry out this offensive in the early summer. But, while it is being mounted and carried out, and for some considerable time after it has been carried out, there will not be sufficient resources left over to protect the Syria-Persia front. This latter front will require no protection so long as the Russians hold out. But, if the Russians fall down, a serious threat will develop from the north by the late summer.

The ideal, from our point of view, would be to carry out a successful attack on Rommel about May, destroy his forces or damage them so heavily that the defence commitment on that side would be negligible for many months afterwards; then to have sufficient time to reorganize and reinforce; then to deploy on the Northern Front and stand ready to meet any attack from that quarter.

But if the sequence of operations is not like this, the offensive may prove to have weakened us too much. When one is short of resources it stands to reason that a costly offensive is not the best prelude to a protracted and arduous defensive against heavy odds.

This side of the problem tends to be lost sight of. It is very attractive to consider the advantages of a successful offensive in Cyrenaica. It is only by seizing air bases in Cyrenaica that the Navy will have any freedom of manoeuvre in the Eastern Mediterranean. And it is only under cover of air bases that we shall be able to keep up supplies to Malta with any degree of ease.

It is necessary however to regard the Middle East and India not as two separate theatres but rather as two parts of one vast front. This front stretches from Malta on the one side to Burma on the other.

The whole front is very thinly held. But the left is stronger than the right. The Middle East, in spite of deficiencies, is stronger than India.

Looking at this long line, one way of assessing the relative values is to visualize the situation in which we should find ourselves if one point or another had been lost. It is by no means certain that any of them will be lost, but one cannot base one's plans on this best case.

Going from left to right:

Malta. The loss of Malta would be a terrific blow to our prestige. It would remove a considerable commitment for the Germans and Italians who are at present forced to keep a strong air force and navy in the vicinity. It would give free passage for enemy reinforcements to Tripoli and Benghazi. It would be a heavy blow to our whole naval position in the Eastern Mediterranean. It would deprive us of an essential staging point for air reinforcement not only of the Middle East but also of the Far East.

Cyrenaica. If we fell back to the frontier region our commitment for the defence of Egypt on the Western side would become heavier both for the Army and for the Air Force, owing to the closer approach of the enemy forces to the Delta.

The Delta. If we lost Egypt, this would be an even greater blow, both psychologically and militarily. The only front on which we are engaging the enemy actively would be gone. The effect would be felt at once in Russia. The threat to our whole position in the northern half of Africa would be immeasurably increased, for the Nile and the Red Sea are far the best line of attack into Africa.

Syria. If Syria were lost, our position in Egypt might well be untenable owing to the close approach of the enemy forces, both land and air, to the Suez Canal. It would probably be impossible to pass supplies and reinforcements into Suez.

Iraq and Persia. From the purely military point of view, the retention of Iraq and Persia is perhaps more important to us than the retention of Egypt itself. This is so because the holding of these two countries is necessary for the protection of the oil at the head of the Persian Gulf. Without this oil we should be unable to carry on the war in the Indian Ocean.

Ceylon. Ceylon is the only base, except Madagascar, from which we can operate a fleet in the Indian Ocean. If Ceylon were lost, and the Japanese were able to establish a fleet and air force there, it would be impossible to defend India. We should not be able to put essential supplies or reinforcements into India. Moreover, it is doubtful whether we could draw supplies of oil from the Persian Gulf if the Japanese were established in Ceylon.

India. If the Japanese were established in India—even on the east coast alone—it is doubtful whether we could hold Ceylon. If we held Ceylon, and had lost part of India, it might be possible to maintain our position in the Indian Ocean, but it would be difficult. It is very doubtful whether we could hold the remainder of India if we lost the Calcutta area—the effect on the people, added to the loss of the chief industrial area from which the fighting forces can be supplied, might well cause a complete collapse.

The whole structure is to a great extent interdependent. Without Cyrenaica, we may not be able to hold Malta, although there is a chance that we might. Without Malta, we may not be able to reinforce the Middle East and Far East with aircraft. Without destroying Rommel, we may not be able to free forces to meet a threat from Turkey and the Caucasus. By destroying him, we may be caught, unrecovered, by an attack from the north. If the Russians are not defeated, there is a good prospect of holding the Middle East. If they are defeated, there is a poor prospect of doing so. We may then be reduced to defending the key points only. These are: (a) the oil supplies in the Persian Gulf, and (b) Ceylon and such part of India as is necessary to ensure the security of Ceylon. These two are again interdependent. It is probably impossible to hold one without the other.

The threats to all these areas cannot arise simultaneously. The threat to India and Ceylon appears to be the more imminent. Therefore our immediate efforts should be to make them secure. Even now we may be too late. If this is accepted, the Cyrenaican offensive must be postponed, for air forces, essential to it, will have to be sent to India at once.

The threat to the Middle East is more remote. In fact, it will never materialize in serious proportions if the Russians stand up to the spring attack. If it does come, we should have time to send in further forces from home. If the war against Japan were to take a favourable turn, even if only to the extent of diverting Japanese attention to the Pacific, we might even be able to move forces, later on, from India to the Middle East.

There can be no question, to my mind, of deciding definitely in favour of a Libyan offensive at this moment. This offensive can only be launched early by leaving the defence of India and Ceylon to chance. The advisability of undertaking it will have to be assessed and reassessed up to the last moment.

Regarding the situation as a whole:

(1) We are faced, in a more acute form than ever before, with the problem of trying to do too much with too little. The dispersion, forced upon us, is worse than ever before.

(2) Our fortunes, especially in the Middle East, are bound up, more than before, with the course of events on the Russian front.

(3) We are in urgent need of some relief in the Indian Ocean, which can be provided only by a more active policy on the part of America.

J. N. KENNEDY.

ADDITIONAL NOTE ON THE SITUATION

The policy of dispersion, which is now forced upon us, will be justified only if Germany proves, in the coming Russian battle, to have been on the point of collapse. Then our tenacity and far-flung dispositions may prove to have been worth while.

But, if Germany is not on the point of collapse, we are bound to suffer heavily from our lack of concentration.[1]

In the Indian Ocean our naval position is fundamentally unsound; our fleet is inferior to the Japanese fleet. At this moment Somerville is seeking to evade them somewhere west of Ceylon. He cannot use his base at Ceylon so long as the Japanese fleet is operating within a few hundred miles of it. It is nothing like the base which the Germans had in Heligoland Bight in the last war, since it affords him no appreciable degree of security. Sooner or later, our Indian Ocean fleet is bound to be sunk unless something can be done to reduce the strength of the Japanese fleet operating there. The only possibility of bringing this about is to drive the Americans to a more active naval policy in the Pacific, or, alternatively, to take over the Atlantic, and allow us to reinforce the Indian Ocean.

The Air Force is the other big problem in the Indian Ocean. Wavell estimates that some 70 squadrons are required for India, and about a dozen for Ceylon. He has now about a dozen in India. Ceylon is operating about as many aircraft as it can maintain, but casualties are bound to be heavy. It therefore appears that, while there is some chance of building Ceylon up to its proper air strength, there is no chance whatever of building up India. And Ceylon can only be built up quickly at the expense of the Middle East.

I do not see how we can prevent the Japanese getting into India. If they do, it will be a very big commitment for them, and they must be fought hard, and as much of India retained as may be possible. I believe their high-water mark will be in India. Whether we can hold Ceylon with the Japanese in partial occupation of India is a doubtful matter, but we must try.

It may turn out to be a lucky stroke that we sent off the IRONCLAD force in good time.[2]

J. N. KENNEDY.

7.4.42.

Another big issue, which we considered at this time, was the future development of our Air Force. If the Air Force was to

---

[1] This was not one of my better forecasts. It would have been more correct to say that the failure of the impending German offensive in Russia would justify our policy, which, in fact, it did.

[2] Madagascar would, of course, have assumed great importance if Ceylon had been lost.

fulfil its role in the Middle East and in India, there would be nothing left for carrying on the bombing of Germany. Nor would there have been much left for bombing Germany if the demands of the Army and the Navy, for direct co-operation, had been met. The air policy could not easily have been changed at that stage of the war. Even if we had reduced the production of heavy bombing aircraft, there would have been no result in other directions for a year or more.

There was, of course, no cut-and-dried answer to any of these conundrums which I have described in this chapter. The solutions were evolved bit by bit over weeks and months as events unfolded; and each solution proved inevitably to be a compromise between conflicting opinions and demands.

Churchill was more concerned with Auchinleck's offensive than with anything else, as was natural to him. We were at one with him on the desirability of taking the offensive; we were all getting heartily sick of inaction. Yet the attack in the desert had to be postponed until the last reasonable moment; and then it was launched sooner than Auchinleck himself would have wished.

Throughout April we made an intensive study of the possibility of opening a 'second front' in Europe, to help the Russians. Pressure to open this front was applied not only by Stalin, but also by the Americans; and Marshall came over from Washington to urge the case. There was also a strong feeling in favour in the Cabinet and the country.

Norway was now accepted as being out of court, if only because of the impossibility of providing air cover. The French coast was the only other place worth examination. Air cover would not have been adequate there either, and the most we could have hoped to do would have been to establish the 20-mile front near Cherbourg, which I have already mentioned, and which the Germans could have overwhelmed at their leisure.

Brooke felt that the best way to convince Churchill and the Cabinet of the stupidity of the idea would be to show them a map of Europe with the Russian front and the possible 20-mile front at Cherbourg marked on it, and then to argue that the latter would appear so ridiculous in comparison as to make us the laughing stock of the world. I had this map made for him, and also another of the Old World, which showed the very considerable number of German forces we were already containing, either by operations already in progress or by the threat of operations which the Germans had to guard against.

We also examined the idea of carrying out a limited landing operation to draw off German air forces from Russia. This would have had to be done in a place where we could be sure of marked and sustained superiority of strength in the air. The Straits of Dover alone fulfilled this condition, but the French coast there was impossible for a landing.

On 2nd April, Colonel Skliarov, the Russian Military Attaché, dined with me at the United Service Club. We exchanged reminiscences of the fighting in Russia in 1919 and 1920. Skliarov had served in an infantry regiment of the Bolshevik Army which had driven Denikin's forces back through Rostov while I was with them. Several British officers who had been taken prisoner by the Bolsheviks at Rostov had been brutally tortured and then shot. It was certainly incongruous that, 20 years later, Skliarov and I should be dining together amicably in London.

Immediately dinner was over Skliarov broached the subject of the 'Second Front'. I was surprised he had managed to keep off it for so long. He said that efforts should be concentrated on knocking out the Germans in the spring of that year, and all risks taken. 'Why do you not open a front in Norway?' he enquired. I explained the naval and air difficulties. 'Well, what about France?' he asked. 'Why not put over fifty divisions? The Germans will then have to move big forces away from Russia, and we shall defeat them.' It showed how little idea the Russians had of our true strength—or weakness.

It would have been impossible at that time to find more than about a tenth of the force he suggested; and we had nothing like enough ships to transport and supply it. Skliarov maintained that we could not be making full use of the numbers of tanks that were being produced, as we were only sending a quarter of them to Russia. I tried to educate him a little, but I do not suppose that he believed me. He felt very strongly, I could see, that it was a mistake to bother about the Japanese 'who could easily be knocked out once the Germans were defeated'. And, evidently not realizing that fighter aircraft could not fly from Gibraltar to Malta, nor that there was some difficulty in sending in convoys of ships, he thought it strange that we did not use Malta as a base for cutting off Rommel's supplies more effectively. Having finished his harangue at 10 p.m., he took his leave, and we went our ways. I rather enjoyed the evening. He entertained me in turn, a few nights later, at a Russian film show.

By the second week of April, our shortage of ships was becoming still more obvious, which helped to damp the ardour of the advocates

of the Second Front. We were planning, in the course of the following four months, to despatch to the Middle East and India one
armoured and four infantry divisions. In the same period, we hoped
to move two American divisions from the States to the United
Kingdom. We would have liked to move more, but there were no
ships to do it.

Marshall arrived with his plan in the third week of April. I did
not see him on this occasion, but Brooke told me that he had found
him most reasonable. The talks he had during his visit certainly
helped him to a more realistic view of the practical difficulties of an
early invasion of Europe. Before he returned to Washington, we had
reached substantial agreement in principle as to the date when a
landing in France might be possible. We gladly accepted the first
stage of Marshall's plan, which was for the movement of American
forces into the United Kingdom. An American concentration in
Britain would, of course, fit all eventualities—a landing in Europe,
the despatch of expeditions elsewhere, and, in the last resort, the
defence of the United Kingdom in case things went wrong in Russia.

Marshall had brought with him particulars of American industrial production. Prospects for the later stages of the war were
brightening fast. But we still had to face a period of widespread
critical effort in the immediate future.

Harwood was now appointed naval Commander-in-Chief in
the Middle East. I was very sorry that we were to lose him. His
work in the Admiralty had often brought me into touch with him.
I admired him very much for his solidity and stolidity, and his
comments on Churchill's interventions in Admiralty affairs were
always amusing. In the course of the talks we had before he went off,
it was borne in on us, once more, how incredibly lucky we were to
have the Italian and not the German Navy in the Mediterranean. We
had a farewell luncheon together; and he said he had handed over
to his successor at the Admiralty with the words, 'The chief feature
of my period of office has been a steady and continuous deterior-
ation of the situation.'

Harwood very kindly made me a present, for the remainder of
the season, of a rod he had taken in a fishing syndicate on the Pang.
My best day there was Sunday, 24th May, when I had the water to
myself, and the mayfly was up. It was a cold windy day with frequent
heavy showers of rain. There was a strong downstream wind, and
sometimes I had to wait ten or fifteen minutes for a lull before I
could cast over a rising fish. My catch was three trout of about 2 lbs.
each, and two of about $1\frac{1}{2}$ lbs. A small boy appeared in the afternoon

and saw me catch a fish. He told me he had never seen a trout caught on a fly before, so I gave him a fish to take home. An hour or so later he turned up again, equipped with a rod of his own. As I was packing up my tackle about five o'clock, an old man came out of his cottage and said to me, 'I have lived here twenty years and I have never seen anybody fishing on a Sunday before. Have they changed the rules?' This was the first I knew that I had broken them.

In the War Office, we constantly discussed the prospects of the offensive in the Desert. On 7th April, I noted in my diary, 'Reading between the lines of Auchinleck's telegrams, I don't think he will do it—anyhow in May.' My own view was that the attack should be carried out, but that it should be postponed to allow the transfer of air forces from Egypt to India and Ceylon, where they would be desperately wanted if the Japanese attacked.

Arthur Smith came to see me on 7th April. He had just been succeeded by Corbett as Chief of Staff to Auchinleck. I asked him what he thought about the Desert offensive, and he said he thought the heat would probably rule it out in May.

It will be remembered that Nye had been sent out to Egypt, to reconcile the differences between our appreciation of the situation and Auchinleck's. He returned in the first week of April, having cabled a number of useful reports from Cairo. On all material points of controversy he had backed Auchinleck. This did not satisfy the Prime Minister, and he talked of sacking Auchinleck and of putting Alexander in his place.

With May came further indications that Auchinleck did not wish to attack Rommel. On 4th May, he sent us a telegram in which he said he was disturbed about India, and suggested that he should cancel his offensive and send reinforcements there instead. I was talking to Brooke in his room when Churchill rang him up and asked his opinion of this telegram. Brooke said that Auchinleck had not got up-to-date information of the situation in India; he did not know that we now considered it more likely that the Japanese would continue their operations in China and endeavour to capture islands to the north and northeast of Australia, rather than press on in the Indian Ocean.

A day or two later, on 7th May, Auchinleck said definitely that he did not want to attack on the date arranged. He backed this decision with a detailed statement of the comparative strengths of his own and Rommel's forces, particularly in tanks. Churchill's reaction was to ask us to produce our version of the strengths.

Brooke and Nye spent some time doing arithmetic with the

Prime Minister on 7th May. Next morning Brooke asked me what I thought about it all. I said we were approaching the same sort of situation with Auchinleck as we had had with Wavell towards the end of his régime, when Dill had said repeatedly to Churchill, 'You must either back your Commander-in-Chief or sack him.' I said it would be wrong for the Cabinet to order the offensive against Auchinleck's judgment—that would put everybody in a false position. If there was reasonable doubt about the soundness of Auchinleck's appreciation, then he should be removed. Brooke said he had come to precisely the same conclusion in bed the night before. But as the days went by, we both modified our opinions.

The Cabinet now ordered Auchinleck to go ahead with his offensive, saying they would accept responsibility for the consequences. On 10th May, Auchinleck cabled his reply. He argued, first, that the loss of Malta would not greatly affect our position in the Middle East. This was an incredible misconception. Apart from any question of prestige, the military value of Malta was great, not only as a check on traffic from Italy to North Africa, but as a staging-point for aircraft in transit to the Middle East and India; moreover, we had some 30,000 soldiers and airmen in the island, and they could not be sacrificed. He went on to say that, in any case, it would take a long time, even if he were able to advance, to get himself sufficiently established in Cyrenaica to provide air cover for convoys. Rommel, he continued, would place himself at a disadvantage if he were left to attack first, whereas, if we attacked prematurely and had our armour destroyed, it would be impossible to defend Egypt.

Auchinleck had stated his case badly. The manner in which he had conducted the long discussions had lost him the confidence of both the Cabinet and the Chiefs of Staffs.

We were now in a very tricky situation. On the one hand, it was dangerous that the Cabinet should direct the operations, and over-rule the advice of their Commander-in-Chief. On the other hand time was short, and the delay inseparable from a change of command might well entail the loss of Malta. It could be argued with some reason that an exceptional situation had arisen, in which the Cabinet would be bound to assume a greater degree of military responsibility than would normally be justified.

When Churchill had read Auchinleck's telegram, he summoned a Cabinet meeting for six o'clock on Sunday evening (10th May). Brooke was at his house in the country. I rang him up and sent him a copy of the telegram. He asked me to arrange for the Chiefs of Staff to meet an hour before the Cabinet, and came up to London in the afternoon. When he arrived, I went to see him in his room; and we discussed the impasse for an hour and a half.

Brooke said that he would like to get Wavell back in the Middle East, and send Alexander to India. I thought it most unlikely that Churchill would be willing to have Wavell there again, and besides, he was probably not fresh enough to undertake the command. In the end Brooke said he felt inclined to hold Auchinleck to his estimate that the offensive might be possible in the middle of June, which was a month later than the original date we had aimed at. A convoy was due to be run into Malta in mid-June, and an offensive then would provide some cover for it.

Brooke's view was accepted by the other Chiefs of Staff and the Cabinet. Churchill drafted a telegram to Auchinleck in which he was given a direct order to engage Rommel in time to assist the passage of the Malta convoy at latest. The Chiefs of Staff withdrew from the Cabinet meeting to amend this draft, and it was then approved and sent off. The Cabinet reiterated that they would accept the risks to the safety of Egypt which Auchinleck had pointed out. This order was duly acknowledged by Auchinleck without further comment.

We all felt at the time that no other solution was possible, in the light of all that had passed. But, obviously, it left Auchinleck in a thoroughly bad position *vis-à-vis* the Government. If his offensive had been successful, his position would have been largely re-established. But he failed.

24

'LORD HANKEY WILL BE AFTER US'

1942

ON the 25th March, before these events in the Middle East, there had been a debate in the House of Lords on Lord Addison's motion for an enquiry into the loss of Singapore. In the course of it, Lord Hankey and Lord Chatfield had attacked the machinery set up by the Prime Minister for the conduct of the war, and, in particular, the constitution and functions of the Defence Committee. They also criticized the assumption by Churchill of so much power, and his habit of keeping the staffs at work at night.

Here are some points from Chatfield's speech:

'It is much better to do away with the extraordinary position as it has grown up and to merge it into the War Cabinet, so that the brains of several men can be applied to the task of making these very vital decisions, which are going to affect us for all time, instead of the burden resting so largely on a single pair of shoulders, however broad, however able, whatever confidence we may have in these shoulders. . . . The only other point I wish to support Lord Hankey on is this matter of going to bed early. I feel that the remark he made is worthy of promulgation and repetition, and I do not apologize for saying that I strongly support him. I can assure Your Lordships that I have had representations made to me by those who work in Whitehall that the hours they have to work are perfectly intolerable. It does not lead to efficiency, as the noble Lord said. Nobody is at his best in the Middle Watch. . . . I believe it is the height of inefficiency and bad administration to work such hours, which really cannot be necessary, and it only wants a certain amount of sacrifice on the part of different people in order to get a proper working arrangement, efficient in all respects.'

We read these speeches with amusement, but we did not expect them to produce much effect, nor did they. There was one momentary reaction. The night after the debate Brooke told me that the Defence Committee had ended exceptionally early, and that, as they were putting away their papers, the Prime Minister had asked Ismay to prepare for him a statement of the exact number of hours spent in late sittings during the previous six months. Then he had said, 'Now it is half past eleven. We'd better break off or Lord Hankey will be after us.' After that the old routine resumed its course, and one night the Prime Minister offered the First Sea Lord a whisky-and-soda at 2 a.m. 'I never drink spirits in the morning,' said Dudley Pound, 'I'll have a glass of port.'

At the end of March, Churchill issued a declaration to the effect that, if the Germans used gas on the Russian front, we would use it, too. This was a point on which the military staffs might properly have been consulted in advance. As it was, we produced a study on the subject the following week, so that the cart was well and truly before the horse. The British Isles were more vulnerable to gas attack than Germany; German air bases were closer to our industrial areas than ours were to theirs, and our seaports were tender spots. In overseas theatres, such as Egypt, we were comparatively unprepared for defence against gas, and even more so for using it offensively. And we believed that the Germans had a new odourless gas, for which we had no detectors.

A secret session was planned for 23rd April, and Churchill's draft of his speech was sent to us for comment. I thought it was brilliant, and I was much impressed by his skill in skating over thin ice when dealing with failures and errors.

On 24th April, Sikorski gave a tea-party at the Dorchester Hotel. As Brooke and I drove to it together, he told me about a visit he and Sikorski had paid to the Polish forces in Scotland. As they sat together in a motor car, Sikorski, in very bad French, discussed Polish politics and, in the course of his discussion, he mentioned the Magyars. He then went on to say that he had had much trouble with the 'Hangars' (pronounced 'HANG-GARS') whom Brooke took to be the Hungarians. Arriving soon afterwards at some remote village, a parade of uniformed figures came into view and Sikorski exclaimed, 'Ah, here are the Hangars.' Apparently in Sikorski English it meant Home Guards.

Frank Naylor and I went down to St. Ives, in April, with our two boys, Kit and Bill, for a week's holiday, and we put the war out of our minds as much as we could. The weather was perfect, with sunshine every day and fresh winds off the sea, and we took some long walks along the cliffs. We saw about 80 species of birds, including some of the newly arrived migrants—wheatears, chiffchaffs, stonechats, etc. There were also shearwaters and purple sandpipers, and, one day, we flushed an osprey from a cliff face, and watched it circling away out to sea. We also motored to Mullion to see the sea birds which were already collecting at their nesting sites; to St. Michael's Mount where we went over the Castle and had tea; to Land's End; to Trengwainton, where we had a Tweed salmon from Floors for luncheon; and to Lamorna, where we spent two delightful hours with Lamorna Birch and saw some of his pictures. I thought his rough sketches were mostly better than his finished ones.

When I got back to the War Office, I found that the situation had not changed much while we had been away. There were, as yet, no definite indications of the strength and scope of the expected German offensive on the Russian front. But the Russian communiqués continued to be as optimistic and misleading as ever. If one had read them without a map, one might well have thought that the Russians had made long advances, although, in fact, their line had remained practically stationary. The German reports were indeed equally misleading. Both Russians and Germans claimed to have annihilated each other several times over. If only they had!

It was still hoped that Auchinleck's offensive would be possible. Malta was in the same critical situation, and there was talk of sending Gort to replace Dobbie,[1] who was said to be tired. The Fleet was still too weak in the Mediterranean. The Japs were still pushing north in Burma, and it was becoming obvious that Alexander would not be able to protect Mandalay. The controversy about the Second Front in Europe was still dragging on.

On 30th April, Brooke, Portal and I lunched at Claridge's with Sikorski and Anders, the Polish Commander-in-Chief. Anders, whom we regarded as a remarkable and able man, spoke at some length about the Russians. He considered that they hated the British with a much greater hatred than they had for the Germans.

Gort, who was still Governor of Gibraltar, sent me some long and detailed appreciations of possible eventualities. He set out the various possible forms of attack in a paper which he had entitled 'The Riddle of the Straits'; he felt we should guard especially against bombing attacks on the dockyard and naval base, and against a 'Trojan horse' surprise attack. In a letter which he wrote to me on

[1] Lieut.-General Sir William Dobbie.

1st April, he explained that he was examining his local problem in order that he might be 'ready to meet the otherwise unexpected situation which is the usual occurrence in war'. He asked for another battalion and for reliefs for the soldiers of the garrison who had been there since before the beginning of the war. I spoke to Brooke in support of his requests, and we sent him what he wanted.

At the beginning of May, Gort was appointed to Malta, and Dobbie returned to London. Dobbie came to see me on the 11th. He looked rather drawn and tired; he was not bitter at being relieved, but he said, rather wistfully, 'I could have stayed perfectly well.' He told me that he had just seen the Prime Minister, who had said to him that he believed we had broken the back of the attack on Malta. This was our opinion, too. The weight of the air attacks was decreasing, and U.S.S. *Wasp* had delivered a second lot of fighters, which were taking a heavy toll of German and Italian aircraft. This was *Wasp's* second trip, and Churchill sent her a message, 'Who said a Wasp could not sting twice?' A few days before, a fast supply ship had also managed to get into Valetta, unnoticed, with a cargo of ammunition, flour mills and so forth. I lent Dobbie a car to take him to Buckingham Palace to get his G.C.M.G. from the King, and I promised to send him news of Malta once a week.

The 11th May stands out as a red-letter day in my memory; but for gastronomic rather than historic reasons. I dined with Pug Ismay at Wilton's oyster bar in Jermyn Street, which was run by an old ex-waiter of Buck's, and his wife. Brendan Bracken and others were there. We had sherry, *chablis*, prawns, turtle soup, lobsters from Oban (which were collected off the Scotch express every morning), cheese and coffee. As he paid the bill, Pug remarked that eating was almost the only pastime busy people could have, and that it was a good idea to concentrate on it.

Churchill broadcast on 10th May. I thought it his best up to date, although he seemed to me to stress the importance of bombing Germany rather too much. We were always sensitive about this, because it increased our difficulties in our attempts to provide for the essential needs of the Navy and the Army. All the same, it was an excellent speech, and the general impression in Whitehall was that his prestige was waxing again. There was also a feeling that his judgment was growing more balanced. Looking back on this period, I have a suspicion that it was Brooke's influence beginning to bear fruit.

On 13th May, I had a talk with Hankey in the United Service

Club. He told me he had been asked to give a lecture, at London University, on the war organization of the Government. He promised to send me a copy, and this he did a few days later. It consisted of a detailed description of the system he had built up in the 1914–18 war. Hankey also said he had sent two memoranda to the Prime Minister: the first on the error of devoting such a great part of our effort to bombing as would be detrimental to the needs of the Army and the Navy, the second on the unsoundness of our naval dispositions in the Indian Ocean, where he considered that the weakness of our fleet exposed it to annihilation by the Japanese. He had also urged that our main task should be to regain command of the sea, and that the provision of aircraft for this purpose seemed to him to be a first necessity. Hankey no longer had access to official information, but he always managed to keep fairly closely in touch with the situation. He collected what details he could from the newspapers and from the guarded conversation of officers and officials in Whitehall; and, every three months, he regularly wrote a lengthy appreciation, of which he sent copies to me and to other friends. These appreciations were remarkably accurate so far as they went. He looked very fit, and he told me that he was enjoying his leisure.

On the 15th, I met him again outside the War Office and we walked over to the United Service Club together. He spoke of the coming debate in Parliament on the subject of a Combined General Staff. He realized it would be useless to prescribe ideal systems of organization, since the system in force must always be built up round the personality of the Prime Minister of the day. I told Hankey that the Prime Minister and the Chiefs of Staff now seemed to be seeing eye to eye to a far greater extent than before, and that Brooke was proving an excellent chairman. I said that nothing would be gained by appointing a professional chairman over his head even if a suitable one could be found, which was unlikely; and I thought it would be futile to appoint a politician as chairman with the object of exercising some control over Churchill; such a person did not exist.

The Americans had sent some of their new tanks to London for us to see, and, on 12th May, they were brought to the Horse Guards Parade. I walked over from the War Office to have a look. There were several types on view—Sherman, Lee, Grant, all with .75 guns, and some lighter models. The Prime Minister presently emerged from the garden of No. 10, and walked over to join us. He swept off his black felt hat in response to our salutes, laughed and joked with the American officers, and then climbed into a Sherman tank. He was the only person there with a gas mask. It was on the previous Sunday that he had given the pledge to Russia about the use of gas.

On 25th May, I made a note in my diary:

'The Parliamentary debates on the Combined General Staff and the higher direction of the war have fizzled out. . . . In the end Winston has been left supreme, and stronger than before, and it has been demonstrated again that all the other politicians are pigmies compared with him, and that his hold on the country and his place in the eyes of our allies, are such that a change in leadership at this time is unthinkable. And there is no doubt that, despite his strategical vagaries, he is a great leader.'

Churchill, imbued as ever with a strong desire to take the offensive, had demanded plans for an advance into Burma in the autumn. (Alexander had just got out of Burma with 30,000 men.) He had also discussed plans for the invasion of Europe for three hours over luncheon with Brooke and Mountbatten.

In the last week of May, I had a long discussion with Brooke about the organization of the forces for 'Round-up', which was at that time our code name for the invasion of France. Our forces in the United Kingdom had to be converted to an offensive basis, and we still had to take account, in our plans, of the possibility of a revival of a German threat to England. Staffs had to be organized and augmented; and all these things had to be co-ordinated with the American plans. No Supreme Commander had as yet been appointed, and I suggested that the time had come to nominate one; it was not very satisfactory that the command should remain in the hands of a three-service, two-nation soviet. I did not realize that Brooke was hoping to get the command himself. Brooke said that he was against asking for a Supreme Commander at that moment because he did not think one could be spared from other duties. If we pressed the matter, we might get somebody—MacArthur, for instance—who would be more of a nuisance than anything else before the plans were further advanced. I argued that the plans were already taking shape, and it would be difficult to hand them over at the last moment to a commander who had had no share in making them, and who might not approve of them; but Brooke stuck to his point.

Molotov came to London in the middle of May, with two

generals, to urge action to relieve the pressure on Russia. Churchill dealt with him, and he got no change. In the Crimea, the Germans alleged they had driven the Russians out of Kertch, and claimed to have killed or taken prisoner 170,000 of them; the Russian offensive about Kharkov had been held up by German counter-attacks. It was still early in the campaigning season for Russia. The Russian front as a whole was not to be expected to be suitable for operations until June.

Our forecast was that the Russians would not be knocked out in the summer offensive, but would be considerably battered. If they could keep going until the following year, we should be able to help them effectively; but if, contrary to our expectations, they were to collapse, then there would be nothing for it but to go back to the defensive for some time longer. We were still anxious about the continued heavy losses of ships from submarine attack, especially on the American seaboard, where we were losing six a day.

But in spite of difficulties our thoughts were turning more and more to the offensive. On 25th May, I noted in my diary: 'The defensive phase of the war seems to be drawing to a close.' As the time came nearer when the initiative would pass to us, it became necessary to co-ordinate and intensify our plans for the deception of the Germans and Japanese. It was Wavell who drew the attention of the Chiefs of Staff to this matter, and we took it in hand seriously. The special deception staff was augmented and reorganized, and soon began to play an important part in our operations. Some of their early efforts were a little amateurish. One day, about the end of May, a telegram was brought to me, which referred to arrangements for a meeting in London between Auchinleck and the War Cabinet about the time fixed for the forthcoming Desert offensive, and I was told that it was a bogus message, arranged by the deception staff, and intended to be a 'leakage'. I asked what else was being done, and was told that letters were being sent to his club marked, 'To await arrival'. I asked whether a bedroom had also been booked for him, but the reply was, 'Finance would probably not run to that.'

On 15th May, Margesson came to see me in the War Office to discuss the coming debate in the House of Lords upon a motion to set up an enquiry into the loss of Singapore. I said that I thought no good could come of an enquiry and possibly much harm. It could probably be demonstrated that the despatch of the *Prince of Wales* and *Repulse* had been an error, since a fleet could not be 'built up' in face of a superior enemy. But the loss of Singapore had been simply due to the fact that we had not been able to provide the naval and air forces which we knew very well were necessary for its defence. The enquiry into the Pearl Harbour disaster was a different matter altogether, and was being held with the legitimate object of condemning or clearing the commanders on the spot. Margesson agreed with all this, and said that, if he spoke in the debate, he would oppose the motion.

On 14th May, a long letter arrived by hand from Auchinleck to Brooke, in which the former repeated arguments he had already advanced in his telegrams. He said he thought the situation in India dangerous, and asked whether it would not be wise to give up the offensive in the Desert in order to strengthen India. This letter naturally caused some anxiety, the more so because it went so far as to say that even the evacuation of Egypt might be necessary if the safety of India were at stake. As I have already said, the possibility of having to relieve Auchinleck had been discussed in London for some time; now we began to feel that the change would have to be made fairly soon.

In the end, Rommel moved in the Desert before Auchinleck. He advanced on 26th May, and drove a wedge into our positions. Auchinleck sent us fairly optimistic reports and we formed the impression that he was much happier now that the period of suspense was over.

Churchill had been concentrating a great deal of attention on the situation in the Desert as the crisis drew nearer. A few days before Rommel attacked, he had drafted a telegram to Auchinleck comparing his situation to that which had existed before Austerlitz, and suggesting that, if Rommel attacked, he should deal with him as Napoleon had done with the Allies. He telephoned to Brooke late at night and asked if he had any comments to offer on this draft. Brooke replied that he would like to think it over. Next day, as they drove away together from a luncheon for Molotov at the Russian Embassy, Brooke advised him not to send it. He reminded him that Auchinleck had been considering and pondering this battle for weeks and that all his plans were laid. He said that the telegram might have some harmful effect in influencing Auchinleck to alter his dispositions at the last moment. Churchill thereupon withdrew the draft.

But he blew off steam in other ways. Streams of minutes on a great variety of subjects flowed out on us from No. 10. When his imagination failed him in the matter of the coming operations in the Desert, he re-opened the question of an autumn offensive in Burma.

In my diary for May there is a story of Churchill told me by Major-General Evetts. When he was a boy, Evetts and his brother once accompanied their father to a shoot at Blenheim, at which Churchill was present. At one of the stands a hare galloped past him at about eighty yards' range. He shot at it, and some fur flew, but the hare went on faster than ever. Evetts' brother then asked him, 'Why did you shoot at it—it was well out of range?' 'Young man,' Churchill replied, 'I wished that hare to understand it was taking part in these proceedings.'

25

THE FALL OF TOBRUK

1942

O_N 29th May, I met Eisenhower for the first time. He was then
holding the post in Washington which corresponded roughly to
mine as Director of Military Operations in London. He had flown
over for a few days, and he came to see me at the War Office. We
talked for an hour or so about the general situation, and I remember
that we also discussed the various systems then in vogue for the
control of air forces. I told him of some of the difficulties which had
arisen out of the independent position of the British Air Force, and
how we had failed to get a proper allocation of aircraft to the Navy
and the Army. He impressed me as a very pleasant, intelligent and
forceful person, and I liked him immensely. I drew his attention to
the map of the world which hung on the wall of my room. I had had
it made up to show America twice—on the right and also on the
left, in order that one might comprehend the great extent of the
Pacific Ocean more easily than when it is cut through the middle, as
on normal British maps. He looked at it for a few moments, and then
said, 'I have had my maps of the world cut through India, because
that is the place in which I am least interested.'

On 2nd June, Bolte, the American Chief of Staff in London,
came to discuss the plans for stationing American troops in Ulster.
These were eventually altered so that Americans came direct to
England. The thoughts of the Americans were becoming more and
more concentrated on 'Round-up' (the landing in Europe), and we
also felt that our arrangements should be shaped mainly with this end
in view. But I see I wrote in my diary after this discussion:

> 'If things go wrong in Russia, of course the programme
> will have to be modified again—we are proceeding now in
> the hope, although not the certainty, that invasion (of England)
> may soon be written off as a contingency to be allowed for.'

On the same day, I lunched with Admiral 'Turtle' Hamilton.[1] He was considerably perturbed, as I was, at the extent to which the bombing of Germany was being boosted. The Air Force had just carried out two successive raids, with over 1,000 bombers, on Cologne and Essen. These had given rise to much jubilation and wishful thinking in both the American and the British Press. It was not realized what a big price we were paying for the bombing of Germany. Both Hamilton and I felt very strongly that if even ten per cent of the effort devoted to bombing could be diverted to the air support of the Navy and the Army, the war situation would be greatly improved.

On 1st June, Mason-Macfarlane came to see me. He had just given up his appointment as head of our Military Mission in Moscow, and was about to take over Gibraltar. He was convinced that world revolution was still the long-term policy of the Kremlin, and that this accounted for the reluctance of the Russians to accept military instructors from us. All our people in Russia were regarded as intelligence agents. He told me that the spirit of the Russians was good, and that he believed they would not be knocked out by the Germans. True, the Russian armies had just been severely shaken south of Kharkov, where vast numbers had been cut off by the Germans. But the Russians had dislocated the German offensive, and our impression was that, on the whole, they had had the best of it.

Molotov came to London in June and reinforced Maisky's continuous pressure on us to be more active; but Churchill told him firmly that no big landing operation would be undertaken by us in 1942 unless the Germans had first begun to crack.

Auchinleck's reports of the operations in the Desert continued to be optimistic for the first week after Rommel's attack—so much so that on 1st June, I wrote:

'It is clear that Rommel's plan of attack has failed. He has been heavily damaged, as we should doubtless have been had we moved into his defences. But his force is not cut off, and lines of supply have been opened through minefields, which will be hard to close.'

Next day the position did not seem quite so good. I wrote:

'Rommel has fixed a big wedge in the left flank of our desert position north of Bir Hacheim, and has destroyed a good brigade,

[1] Admiral Sir Louis Hamilton.

the 150th. There will be much hard fighting here to prevent the Germans rolling up our positions. . . . Auk is optimistic, and speaks of the possibility of a decisive victory. But, as things appear today, one would not bet heavily on a big advance.'

A week later, the battle still dragged on and we remained on the defensive, while Rommel retained the initiative. It was now clear that the course of the fighting would not help us much with the May convoys, and the prospect was growing dim of gaining air bases, farther to the West, from which to protect our ships. We were even getting anxious for Malta. It was decided to try to run in two convoys in June simultaneously, one from each end of the Mediterranean. If no ships got in, we calculated that Malta would starve in a month or so.

Churchill's personal position was stronger than it had been a few months back, though perhaps still not strong enough to survive great reverses. Prime Ministers need luck as well as Generals; Prime Ministers who usurp the role of Commanders-in-Chief need a double dose of it. His boldness had certainly been justified on several occasions, and had strengthened his position *vis-à-vis* the Chiefs of Staff. He had sent a hundred tanks to Wavell and the May convoy to Russia against naval advice; the first had got through, and only five or six ships out of forty had been lost from the Russian convoy. The capture of Madagascar had been largely due to his insistence. And these were not the only instances.

On 4th June, Ismay dined with me at the Carlton Grill. We were indeed fortunate to have Ismay to take so much of the initial shock of the Prime Minister's impact on the Staffs. He never claimed that he influenced Churchill to any extent, and probably he did not. No man with the inclination and capacity to deal seriously with Churchill could have retained Ismay's post for very long. He was always charmingly frank in admitting that his chief function was to act as whipping boy, and as a person to whom Churchill could blow off steam at all hours of the night and day. We all felt we would not have had his job for anything in the world. He was, in his own right, one of the most remarkable men of the war.

On the morning of 10th June, the Prime Minister sent me a telephone message that he wished to see me at No. 10 to discuss the strengths of the opposing forces in the Desert, and he asked me to bring with me the Director of Military Intelligence (Major-General Davidson). I guessed that he might want to go into minute details, and I did not want to be drawn into them myself; so I asked the Director of Staff Duties to come with us, too. He was not only head of the department that dealt with details, but he had also lately served on Auchinleck's staff in Egypt. But this device proved unsuccessful, for Churchill did not address a single word to him, nor did he open his mouth.

We were ushered into the Cabinet Room at about eleven-thirty and there was Churchill in his zip suit, sitting with his back to the fireplace. He looked well, and as we settled ourselves on the opposite side of the table, facing him, he lit a big cigar.

The first half hour was spent in going over recent reports of German losses and reinforcements.

He then turned to a sheaf of papers which dealt with the British forces, and began to do sums. I was anxious to avoid getting involved in arithmetic, so I summarized our Desert strength in this way: Auchinleck had, roughly, $5\frac{1}{2}$ divisions fit to fight in the Desert, and the equivalent of another in the Delta, making about 100,000 men in all. The other formations in his command were unfit to fight because they were being re-organized and re-equipped, except for approximately two divisions in Syria, Iraq and Persia. Rather to my surprise, the Prime Minister said he had made the figures exactly the same, and this part of the discussion came to an end.

He then read out the draft of a telegram which he proposed to send Richard Casey, who was at that time our Minister in the Middle East. It was a reply to a communication from Casey in which he had set out the views of the Middle East Defence Council, consisting of himself and the Commanders-in-Chief. They maintained that, if the Germans were to break through the Russian front, we should be faced with a choice between two alternative policies: either to hold the Delta, or to concentrate on the defence of the Abadan oilfields. We would not be strong enough to do both. Casey had made a second point: if we were to win the impending battle, the extent of the advance we might subsequently make into Cyrenaica would be governed by the situation on the Russian front.

Churchill's draft said that if Auchinleck won his battle, all might be well; but that, if he lost it, nothing could save him. He had added some suggestions for new dispositions of the forces in the Middle East.

I suggested that Casey was right to consider the worst contingency, but that, with luck, a full-scale German attack from the North would never materialize. They had a long way to come; they could not arrive in great strength; they had to endure another

Russian winter first; and the Russians ought to be able to hold a front farther East, even if they were driven back.

Churchill then held forth for nearly an hour about past events in the Middle East, and about the situation of Auchinleck's forces. He got up and walked to and fro as he spoke, exclaiming repeatedly, 'I don't know what we can do for that Army. All our efforts to help them seem to be in vain.' He went over all the attempts he had made to strengthen the Middle East—he had sent fresh divisions out to them, he had got Sherman tanks out of the President for them, and so on. 'Nothing seems to help them. And I am the one who gets his neck wrung when things go wrong.'

He asked me why the divisions arriving in the Middle East could not go straight into action. 'Why should they not have officers and men attached to them who know the desert? Why can arrangements not be pushed on to man the three hundred Sherman tanks coming from America, so that they can go straight into action when they arrive? These tanks should be the tin-opener. I will have to account to the President for their use. Is all this being done in the best way? What exactly are the units who are to get the tanks? Why are there not more men in the fighting line? They all come up for their rations, but not to fight.'

I felt that there was substance in his criticisms, but I also felt it was for the C.I.G.S. to deal with them, not me. I said it was more than likely that Auchinleck was pushing on with all these matters, but, to make sure, I would have a telegram drafted and give it to the C.I.G.S. to bring with him to the meeting of the Defence Committee later in the day.

Churchill then asked whether there was any reason why we should not attack the Italians in the Desert at once. I said that this could hardly be done outside the general plan of attack.

'I doubt that Army's offensive spirit,' said the Prime Minister. 'Do you think Auchinleck really means to attack?' I answered that I was sure of that.

'I quite realize that Auchinleck has much more at stake than Rommel,' he continued.

'Yes,' I said, 'he must not be pushed into a false move.'

As he bade us good-bye at one o'clock, he repeated, 'I don't know what we can do for that Army.'

At the meeting of the Defence Committee, the situation was discussed for two hours, and, in the end, two telegrams were sent off, one to Auchinleck telling him that the real solution of his problems was to defeat Rommel, and another, to his Chief of Staff

(Corbett), asking for full details of the plans for reorganizing and re-equipping the Divisions which were temporarily out of action.

Next morning, on my way down to the War Office after breakfasting at the Club, I met Charlesworth, Brooke's A.D.C. He told me that Brooke had retired to bed the night before with the remark, 'Well, that is one of the bloodiest days I have had for a long time.'

Under 16th June, there is a note in my diary, 'The Mediterranean situation is in rather a mess.'

The South African Division had retired from Gazala into Tobruk, and the 50th Division was starting a march of 100 miles behind the German lines near Bir Hacheim, in an attempt to escape. The Germans had claimed 12,000 prisoners and many tanks and guns.

Our operations appeared to have been piecemeal in character, and there seemed to have been no real effort to organize a concentrated counterstroke after Rommel's first attack. We fully realized the heavy disadvantage Auchinleck suffered in the poor quality of our tanks, which were inferior to those of the Germans. We had sent him tanks in large numbers; but quantity was no substitute for quality.

As the battle developed, Churchill sent a succession of telegrams of advice and exhortation to Auchinleck. These were usually read over the telephone to the Chiefs of Staff before being despatched, but, despite this precaution, it seemed certain that the conduct of the operations would be unduly influenced by the personality of the Prime Minister. I wrote in my diary at the time, 'It is such a pity that Winston's fine courage and drive cannot be harnessed to the war effort in a more rational way.'

On 16th June, another entry reads, 'A more dangerous matter at the moment is his pressure on Auchinleck to hold Tobruk.' I had a talk with Brooke on 15th June, and I explained to him what had happened when this issue had cropped up before in Dill's time, and how the risk Wavell had run in holding Tobruk had been justified, in the end, only because of the unexpected withdrawal of the Germans from the Mediterranean for the Russian war. The limelight had been on the place so much that its political and prestige value had now become very great; that was bound to be a real difficulty for the Prime Minister.

Auchinleck had first considered the question of holding Tobruk in January 1942. In his Operation Instruction No. 110 dated 19th

January, which dealt with the contingency of a retreat from Agheila, he had included the following paragraph:

'It is NOT my intention to try to hold, permanently, Tobruk, or any other locality West of the Frontier.'

I sent this Instruction to Brooke on 6th February, with a minute in which I said:

'Tobruk might, last year, have proved another Kut had it not been for the outbreak of the Russian war. It was moreover a great strain on the naval and air resources in the Middle East. In particular, the losses suffered by the fighter escorts to convoys had begun to have a bad effect on the morale of the R.A.F. pilots. In my opinion, it would be right to avoid such detachments in future.'

On 11th February, Auchinleck issued another Operation Instruction, No. 111, which was as follows:

PERSONAL to Lieut.-General N. M. Ritchie
1. I intend to resume the offensive in Libya as soon as possible with the aim of defeating the enemy forces in the field, occupying Cyrenaica and subsequently Tripolitania.
2. The enemy, however, may try to drive us back from our present positions round Gazala, and from Tobruk, before we are ready to launch our offensive.
3. It is essential to retain Tobruk as a supply base for our offensive. Our present positions on the line Gazala–Bir Hacheim, will therefore continue to be held, and no effort will be spared to make them as strong as possible.
4. If, for any reason, we should be forced at some future date to withdraw from our present forward positions, every effort will still be made to prevent Tobruk being lost to the enemy, but it is not my intention to continue to hold it once the enemy is in a position to invest it effectively. Should this appear inevitable, the place will be evacuated, and the maximum amount of destruction carried out in it, so as to make it useless to the enemy as a supply base. In this eventuality, the enemy's advance will be stopped on the general line Sollum–Maddalena–Giarabub, as laid down in Operation Instruction No. 110. . . .

The orders contained in this Instruction were still in force when the battle began in May. It will be seen that an element of doubt had been introduced in Instruction No. 111, as compared with Instruction No. 110, since the holding of Tobruk, according to the second Instruction, was to depend on whether 'effective investment' was considered possible or not when the moment came to make the decision.

I made some notes at the time on the correspondence between Churchill and Auchinleck in June.

'On 14th June, the P.M. cabled Auchinleck and asked to what position Ritchie wanted to withdraw the Gazala troops, adding that "he presumed there was no question in any case of giving up Tobruk; that, so long as Tobruk was held, no serious enemy advance into Egypt was possible; and that we went through all this in April, 1941".

On 15th June, Auchinleck replied that, although he did not intend that the 8th Army should be besieged in Tobruk, he had no intention whatever of giving it up.

On the same day, the P.M. cabled to ask if the War Cabinet should interpret his telegram to mean that, if the need arose, Ritchie would leave as many troops in Tobruk as were necessary to hold the place for certain.

On 16th June, Auchinleck replied that this was a correct interpretation, that the situation was quite different from last year, as we now held fortified positions on the frontier, and could operate fighter aircraft over Tobruk, and that, moreover, Rommel was not strong enough to invest Tobruk and to mask our forces on the frontier.'

(In this telegram as will be seen, Auchinleck had not summed up the pros and cons at all adequately. Churchill cabled, in reply, that he was very satisfied with the decision.)

'17th June: If Auchinleck does not stage a counter-offensive soon, the prospects for Tobruk are not good.

18th June: Rommel seems to have pretty well got round Tobruk to the South East. . . . Auchinleck intends to hold it, and, from what we know here, this is, in my opinion, a wrong decision, and I should like to question it, rather than do what has been done, namely, to express gratification that he intends to stand there. . . . However, the fact remains that the defence

of Tobruk must come from outside rather than inside, and, if
Auchinleck judges that he can provide the outside defence in the
shape of active operations, he is on good ground. We cannot say
here what his position is.'

On 21st June, we received a telegram from Auchinleck in which
he stated that the Tobruk garrison was adequate, and that he would
be able to stage a counter-offensive from Sollum in such a way as
to make Tobruk secure. This telegram was laid on my table simultaneously with another which reported the fall of Tobruk.

At this black moment, Churchill and Brooke were both away in
Washington, and each has described how he heard the news—
Churchill in the presence of Roosevelt, Brooke in that of Marshall.
On 25th June, Sir John Wardlaw-Milne, M.P., put down his Vote
of Censure on the conduct of the war; and Churchill dealt with it in
the House of Commons on the 2nd July. He sent Brooke a draft of
what he intended to say. On my suggestion, Brooke sent him the
following comment:

'In fairness to Auchinleck, and in order to obviate any
further allegation that your statement is not complete, it is
suggested that a sentence be included, to the following effect:

"When the possibility arose of having to withdraw
from the Gazala positions, I and the C.I.G.S. expressed to
General Auchinleck a strong hope that Tobruk would be
held, but no order to this effect was ever sent from London." '

But Churchill, so Brooke told me later, took the opinion of
Ministers who had seen all the telegrams, and did not feel that it was
necessary to make the proposed amendment. He carried the House by
475 votes to 25.

By the middle of June, before he left for Washington, Churchill
had given us, in considerable detail, plans of campaign for the
reconquest of Burma, for the occupation of the northern end of
Norway, for rolling up the Germans by an advance from Northern
Europe, and for an invasion of Germany from the West.

The project for Burma was impracticable because the means
were lacking, especially naval and air forces. The Norwegian idea
was impracticable for all three Services; so were the proposals for
the invasion of Germany. We consumed a great deal of time and
energy in pointing out these facts.

On Sunday, 14th June, I attended a conference at the Admiralty, with Admiral Brind, Assistant Chief of Naval Staff, and General Hamsteen, the Norwegian Commander-in-Chief. We decided on a plan for sending a second Norwegian detachment to Spitzbergen. There were already some 40 Norwegian soldiers there whom we had sent in April; and we arranged to make this garrison up to a strength of 100, since it would be useful to have meteorological information and to get reports of the facilities for refuelling ships. The Norwegians were also given the task of dealing with the Germans who were believed to be in the island, and of interfering as much as possible with their meteorological activities.

Lord Swinton had been appointed Minister of State in West Africa, and on 15th June I spent a couple of hours with him and gave him some idea of the military problems there. I liked him very much. When he took up his post he soon proved himself most helpful to Giffard, the Commander-in-Chief.

During June, we had a good many talks with the American staff about Marshall's plan for transporting an enormous army to the United Kingdom. I met Chaney on 11th June, and we discussed a number of points with regard to American co-operation in 'Round-up', in order to clear the ground for conversations with Donovan who had been sent over to London by the President. On the 16th, I dined again with Chaney to meet Donovan. As I left the War Office to go to the dinner-party, I was handed a message from Washington to the effect that Chaney was to be relieved by Eisenhower as Commander of the U.S. Forces in the United Kingdom, but Chaney did not yet know this, and, of course, I did not mention it.

A great deal of discussion was going on, at this time, about the role of the Air Force. Both Brooke and Pound were profoundly dissatisfied with the arrangements for air co-operation with the Army and the Navy, and for the handling of the Bomber Command. This is a note I made at the time:

'Both C.N.S. and C.I.G.S. want to get it settled that the Chiefs of Staff advise on the allocation of aircraft as between the Services and on the bombing operations in Germany. All sorts of people seem to be trying to run the latter. The P.M. and Harris[1] and Anthony Eden seem to have been having a shot at it lately. Brooke keeps in good form in spite of this welter of con-

[1] Marshal of the Royal Air Force Sir Arthur Harris, at that time Commander-in-Chief, Bomber Command.

fusion, and unco-ordinated and wrong advice from the wrong people.'

I had suggested to Brooke that a possible line of approach to the problem would be for the Admiralty and the War Office to produce a joint paper setting out their views, and for the Air Ministry to produce another setting out theirs; then, since there was no prospect of an agreed solution, that the Prime Minister should decide between us. Brooke did not think well of this suggestion, and it came to nothing.

The Naval and General Staffs would have agreed completely, at that time, on the following order of priority of tasks for the Air Force:

First. Fighter Defence of the British Isles.
Second. The essential needs of the Navy.
Third. The essential needs of the Army.
Fourth. Long-range bombing with what was left.

At this particular moment, Churchill's obsession for bombing Germany resulted in the Navy being very short of long-range air-craft at sea, and in the Army not having the support of bomber aircraft in Egypt to hamper the use by the Germans of the North African seaports, which now included Tobruk.

This is another note I wrote at the time on this subject:

'In my view the only well-founded ground of criticism of our central war direction now lies in the use we are making of our Air Force. . . . If we had diverted, say, 20 per cent of our long-range bomber aircraft to the Middle East, it is doubtful whether Rommel could ever have started his offensive, and more than doubtful whether he could have sustained it at its recent tempo. I should like to take 50 per cent of the bomber effort off Germany even at this late hour, and distribute it in the Atlantic, and in the Middle East and Indian theatres. The price we pay at sea and on land for our present bombing policy is high indeed.'

26

ALEXANDER RELIEVES AUCHINLECK

1942

On 21st June, Auchinleck telegraphed that he had decided not to stand at Sollum because he had no armoured reserve, and that he proposed to fight delaying actions back to Mersa Matruh. On this, a meeting of the Defence Committee was arranged for 9.30 p.m. Eden telephoned to me from the country, but when I told him the Defence Committee was to meet, he said he would wait to discuss the situation till he came up to London. A full meeting of the Cabinet was arranged for 10.30 p.m., to follow the Defence Committee meeting.

I wrote in my diary on that day:

'I expect Winston will put Alex in to take charge. I don't think there is any sign of a concerted German attack on the Middle East from the North (with parachutes, etc.). Rommel will probably do his best to exploit the pursuit, but there must be a pause now. We have lots of tanks in the Delta, and the 8th Armoured Division arrives in the course of the next two weeks—in fact, 100 of its tanks are already there.'

We all felt immensely frustrated and disappointed and, indeed, rather ashamed that the Army was not doing better. We had hoped so much that these operations would go well. I avoided going into the Club, where I knew everybody, and went for meals to another unfrequented little club of which I was an honorary member.

On the 28th June, Rommel had advanced more than half-way from Tobruk to Mersa Matruh, and was pressing on hard. Auchinleck sent a private telegram to say that he had decided to go out and take over from Ritchie himself. He also sent a private message to Brooke in which he offered to resign his command.

We worked hard to arrange the diversion of all possible ships to the Middle East.

On 29th June, Brooke returned to the War Office from America, and I had an hour with him. He told me about the business that had been done in Washington, which was considerable. The Americans were showing a fine spirit and great eagerness to get into the war and, particularly, to increase the flow of American equipment to the Middle East. They were resolved to go ahead, at the greatest possible speed, with the movement of their forces to Britain. The North African and Second Front projects had been thoroughly discussed.

By 1st July, Rommel was only 60 miles from Alexandria. We hoped that, greatly extended as he was, he might be checked at Alamein, but, after so many disappointments, we could not be very confident. Churchill sent a cable to Casey to say that, if Rommel reached the Delta, there must be such a fight as would be put up in Kent if England were invaded.

We began to think of what should be done if we lost the Delta, and we examined the capacity of Basra and the Red Sea ports, and of the inland communications of Palestine, Syria and Iraq. Malta was now in an isolated and precarious position. We tried to console ourselves with the thought that, if we were driven out of Egypt, our strained resources might prove adequate to the defence of a more restricted area in the Middle East. However, by 3rd July, it looked as if Auchinleck would be able to hold Rommel, and even to deliver a counterstroke.

The Prime Minister's speech in the Commons on 2nd July was a great success, and provided a powerful counterblast to the distrust and criticism of his régime. Such criticism had naturally sprung up afresh as the operations in the Desert went from bad to worse. It was clear that our defeat in Libya had been due to a combination of shortcomings in the quality of our equipment and of our leadership, in face of a more efficient and better-equipped German Army, apparently led by a better general than ours. Churchill still had many inveterate enemies who would have liked to see him removed from his post. I see that, on 3rd July, I made a note: 'In spite of what one may feel about Winston's methods and his judgment, I do believe that, on balance, it is best that he should continue as Prime Minister—there is no one else with the personality needed for the job.' Obviously we still thought even then that Churchill had not yet achieved security of tenure.

On 3rd July, General Isaiev, who was in London on a visit from Moscow, and Admiral Kharmalov, the Russian Naval Attaché at the Embassy, came to see me in the War Office, and I explained the general situation to them. Isaiev was an officer of the operations section of the General Staff, and his duties seemed to correspond to those of one of my deputy directors. He was intelligent and agreeable but he was so eager to talk that he would not wait either to have his remarks translated or to hear the answers to his questions. I told the Russians that we were now fairly confident that Rommel was held, and that he would soon be driven back. Isaiev asked what we thought of the possibilities of a German attack on the Middle East from the North through the Caucasus. I said there were no signs of an attack, and that, in any case, the difficulties for the Germans were so great, that they could not develop such a manoeuvre in strength. Isaiev asked, of course, about the Second Front, and, to my surprise, he seemed to understand that the rate of American concentration in Britain and the lack of landing-craft ruled it out for 1942.

By 8th July, it seemed more and more likely that Rommel had shot his bolt for the time being. The armies were facing each other at Alamein, but Auchinleck was not yet strong enough to counter-attack.

Brooke told me that, at a Cabinet meeting on the 8th, Ministers showed signs of impatience that Auchinleck was not resuming the offensive more quickly. He described the meeting as a thoroughly bad one. The Prime Minister was in one of his worst moods. He abused the Army, criticized our generalship, and dwelt on our failure to use the masses of soldiers accumulated in the Middle East. Bevin asked Brooke whether it would not be right to urge Auchinleck to attack. Brooke replied that a false move would be fatal, and that Auchinleck might lose Egypt in five minutes if he made a mistake. In the end, Brooke thought the Cabinet had been induced to leave the battle to Auchinleck, but only after he had spoken very sharply. When the Cabinet broke up, Churchill apologized to Brooke for his offensive remarks, and Brooke invited Bevin to dine with him.

Bevin had a reputation for speaking of military operations in a very direct and often provocative manner, but, as he explained more than once, he wanted to get the background so that he could talk to his workers with knowledge, and he seemed to suspect the Prime Minister of keeping him deliberately in the dark.

Churchill now asked for yet another detailed statement of what every man in the Middle East was doing—it was a habit of his to call for such statements whenever things went wrong, and he was never satisfied, till the end of the war, that the generals could be trusted to keep down the numbers of men behind the lines to the right proportions.

Eisenhower came to see Brooke on 8th July, and Brooke said something to him of his difficulties with the politicians. Eisenhower said that he himself had been plagued by a certain American politician; and after a particularly trying interview with him, had remarked to a young Staff Officer that the said politician would probably drive him off his head. The Staff Officer had replied, 'Well, you know, sir, there are two things that, from the beginning of time, amateurs have always thought themselves experts at—one is strategy and the other is prostitution.'

I heard him repeat this story that night at dinner, to the American General Clark, and follow it up by a dissertation about 'damned politicians'. His neighbour at the table was Arthur Henderson, the Parliamentary Under-Secretary of State for War, of whose identity Eisenhower was unaware. I was amused to see Henderson listen attentively, with a very self-conscious air.

I made a note after this party: 'Eisenhower is very much liked, and is a very pleasant person, with plenty of commonsense and good humour.' This was an opinion that we did not change as the war went on.

We had, by this time, completed a study of what might be possible in the Middle East in the 'Worst Possible Case'—if the Germans occupied the Nile Delta. In that unhappy but, as we thought unlikely, event, we believed we could carry on the war in Syria, Palestine and the valley of the Upper Nile. It seemed to us, all the same, that the Germans had missed their chance by not making Rommel a little stronger, and that any attempt to reinforce him would now be too late. Our chief anxiety arose from the poor quality of our tanks, which was a considerable handicap to our army in the Desert.

The Russian front was still shaky. The Germans were on the Don about Voronesh, and were pressing forward on a front of some 300 miles from Orel southward. In the North, we thought it quite possible (wrongly, as it turned out) that they might get Archangel and Murmansk, or cut off these ports of entry for our supplies, before the winter. We had no sure information of the extent to which the Russian armies had been cut off or withdrawn, and this made it hard to forecast the likely depth of the German advances, and the chances of a Russian front being in existence for the winter. In July, we lost 20 out of 30 ships in the convoy to Archangel. All this resulted in more pressure from Churchill to send an expedition to eject the Germans from the North of Norway, an operation we believed to be quite impracticable. This was not a cheerful phase of the war for us.

On 14th July, Brooke asked me to represent him at a meeting of the Pacific War Council, which met in the evening in the Cabinet Room at No. 10 Downing Street. There were present, Eden, Amery, Attlee, Bruce for Australia, Jordan for New Zealand, Waterson for South Africa, Wellington Koo for China and a Dutchman whom I did not know. The Prime Minister was in the chair, dressed in a blue romper suit under which he wore a white shirt with an open soft collar, but no tie.

Two papers were on the agenda, both put in by the Chinese Ambassador. In the first, it was alleged that Japan was indulging in bacteriological warfare, and details were given of instances of fleas, infected with bubonic plague, being dropped from aircraft. The second paper purported to contain evidence that the Japanese were also using gas.

Churchill looked well and serene. He lit a cigar, and proceeded to give the assembly a general survey of the state of the war, speaking slowly and easily. Jordan began to take notes, but Churchill asked him not to do so because, he said, it distracted his attention. He referred first to our shipping losses and to our efforts to sustain the Russians. Speaking of the situation on the Russian front, he pointed out that the Germans had only $2\frac{1}{2}$ months—75 days—left before the winter began. He gave it as his opinion that the Japs would attack Russia when they judged the moment had come—they would stab her in the back, but it would not be easy. He explained that the Japs had moved four more divisions to Manchukuo, and referred to me for confirmation of this. But he thought that, for the time being, they were gorged with their prey. They had suffered heavy losses at sea, including half their aircraft carriers, which improved the situation of Australia and India. Our forecast that the Japs would turn North and continue their operations in China had been justified.

He said that we were studying plans for offensives against the Japanese across the Bay of Bengal and through the islands from the South. But certain conditions would have to be present before we could move—if Auchinleck beat Rommel, and if the Russians stood fast, those conditions might come about. If Auchinleck did not beat Rommel, and the Germans were able to penetrate the Caucasus, then we should have to devote all efforts to meeting that onslaught.

The whole statement was very well done, although nothing was said that was new or that gave away any secrets. It took about an hour.

'Well, gentlemen,' said Churchill at last, 'that is as far as we can take it today,' and he rose from his chair. A Secretary said, 'But what about the agenda, Prime Minister?' 'Oh,' he exclaimed. 'Is there an agenda?' and, sitting down again, 'Ah, yes, Mr. Wellington Koo, do you wish to raise these matters, or are we to take note of them?'

Wellington Koo said that he wanted a declaration to the effect that we would retaliate in the use of gas if the Japanese persisted. He would like a declaration similar to that given by President Roosevelt and by Mr. Churchill in respect of Germany.

Churchill replied that nothing would be gained by making a fresh declaration, and, indeed, such a declaration would have awkward repercussions for us in India, where we were not prepared for gas warfare.

The meeting then broke up, and the Prime Minister shook hands with everybody, smiling and bowing as he did so.

This Pacific War Council had been set up to meet the demands from Australia, New Zealand and other powers interested in the Pacific, that they should be admitted to discussion of strategy and policy in the conduct of the Japanese war. The meetings were always of the character I have described on this occasion, and no business was ever done, so far as I am aware. Bruce told me, some time later, that he had given up attending, because it was such a waste of time.

The Americans were extremely anxious to undertake a landing in France before the summer of 1942 was over. It was necessary that we should discuss this question with the American Chiefs of Staff, since their appreciation of the situation was obviously quite different from ours; and we were very glad to learn that General Marshall intended to come to London on 17th July to thrash out an agreed policy.

The Americans had been deeply disappointed that we had ruled out a landing in Europe in 1942; they felt that there had not been enough drive behind our strategical planning. They still maintained that something could and should be done in France. We were equally sure that it could not. We had examined every conceivable offensive project in Europe, and we were convinced that, even if we could land in France, we could not possibly hang on there. The German forces in Western and Central Europe could kick us out without calling on a single division from the Russian front. This conclusion was no more pleasing to us than it was to the Americans. And there was a real danger that they might decide, as a result, to switch their main effort to the Pacific, and leave us to stew in our own European juice.

In a telegram which Dill sent us just before Marshall's arrival, he mentioned that Marshall had been studying Sir William Robertson's[1] *Soldiers and Statesmen,* and that he had sent him a copy of Volume I of this work, in which he had marked Chapter 3. We looked it up, and found that this is the chapter in which Robertson emphasizes the importance of concentration upon the decisive point, and in which he states his view that the Dardanelles attack was an un-justifiable diversion of effort from the Western Front. The Americans had evidently drawn the deduction that, in July 1942, France was the decisive front, and that new operations elsewhere must, therefore, be wrong. In this same chapter, Robertson also lays stress on the duty of Service advisers to state their opinions whether asked for them or not. The Dardanelles Commission had supported this view when they pointed out that Mr. Churchill had obtained the support of the Service Chiefs to a lesser extent than he himself had imagined, because they had not spoken out.

Brooke told me, on 18th July, that he had discussed this telegram with Churchill, whose hackles were up over the reference to the Dardanelles. He had said to Brooke that he would make short work of Marshall if he tried to lay down the law on the lines advocated by Robertson. One of my officers told me he had been unable to get a copy of *Soldiers and Statesmen* from any of the libraries—there had been a run on it by Ministers, who were said to be walking about with copies under their arms.

When Marshall arrived, the Prime Minister proposed to take him and the Chiefs of Staff to Chequers for the week-end. But Marshall said he wanted first to have talks with his own people and the Chiefs of Staff, and the Chequers party was postponed for a week. Brooke felt the same as Marshall, and was relieved when Churchill's proposal fell through.

On 17th July, the Prime Minister sent for me and Davidson, the Director of Military Intelligence. It was a cold, wet day, and he was sitting in the Cabinet Room at No. 10 with his back to a big fire, wearing his blue romper suit, and smoking a fat cigar. He was in a genial mood, and he motioned to us to sit beside him on his side of the table (we usually sat opposite). 'Well,' he said, indicating the

[1] C.I.G.S. in the First World War.

sketch map of dispositions in the Desert which lay before him, 'much hangs on this battle. Hours seem like days.' Eden came in a few minutes after we had arrived, and sat down at the table beside us.

Churchill took from a despatch box a sheaf of reports on recent movements of the German forces, and discussed them with us. He then turned to our plans for the reinforcement of the Middle East, and went over the dates by which we might expect fresh divisions to be in action. He hoped the 8th Armoured Division would soon be engaged, and said that he did not see why it should not be, because the roads from the Delta to Alamein were very good. I pointed out that it was not so much a question of the roads, but of reconditioning and overhauling the tanks after the voyage, and of giving the troops time to learn the conditions of the desert.

He then read aloud, with his cigar in his mouth, some of the telegrams that had come in during the day. One contained an account of the war situation which had been given by some neutral foreigner. It said that 1942 was an Axis year, but that 1943 would be an Allies' year, and that Germany was bound to be defeated in the end. When he had read this, he remarked, 'Well, this is all very good stuff from a foreigner.' Then there was something about the war being run by politicians on the Allied side—at which Churchill cocked a comic grimace, and looked sideways at me.

Then he went back to the Desert, and said, 'Well, D.M.O., give us your appreciation of the situation.' There was not much to be said, but I gave my opinion that Auchinleck's strength was now such that he should be able to undertake a successful attack fairly soon.

He agreed. The Italians were obviously useless, and would collapse whenever they were attacked. Then he added, 'If Rommel's army were all Germans, they would beat us.'

He rang for one of his secretaries to ask if there was anything on the tape about the fighting in the Desert; but there was nothing of interest, and he bade us good-bye. As we went out, he said, 'Ring me up at any time if you have any news or would like to give me a fresh appreciation—I am on the scrambler all night.'

After this interview, I wrote in my diary:

'Winston certainly inspires confidence. I do admire the un-hurried way in which he gets through such a colossal amount of work, and yet never seems otherwise than at leisure. He was particularly genial and good-humoured today. I can well under-stand how those around him become devoted to him—and dominated by him. I remember Dudley Pound once saying,

"You cannot help loving that man," and I can quite see the truth of this sentiment. There is one thing that Winston's enemies and critics must admit—he has only one interest in life at this moment, and that is to win the war. Every waking moment is devoted to that. He lives his peculiar life, indoors, and rarely going out. Yet this seems to suit him well, and he shows little sign of wear and tear, and he looks in better health than some of the other politicians who work less than he does. Of course he has not the worry of departmental life, with its constant interruptions and distractions, and he can arrange his routine as he wishes. It is an extraordinary *tour de force* all the same.'

I had a talk with Brooke when I got back to the War Office. He fully agreed with what I had said to the Prime Minister about the situation at Alamein; if Auchinleck did not make a big attack within ten days, he would feel there was something seriously wrong. He said he intended to tackle Churchill about his constant attacks on the Army, and on individual soldiers. He was all too apt to indulge in this practice when other Ministers were present, and they to follow his lead. Brooke thought it was a case of giving a dog a bad name, and that the Prime Minister would never make allowances for the fact that ours was a citizen army, and still badly equipped. Only a few days before, a Minister had deplored this habit of Churchill's, contrasting him with Lloyd George: he said that whereas L.G. had had the gift of making his colleagues feel big, Churchill made them feel small.

Brooke and I went on to discuss the difficulty we were having in fitting the production of weapons and equipment to our strategy. Quantities of unsuitable material were being turned out, and we had to make the best of it, irrespective of our real needs. Oliver Lyttelton had put this problem rather aptly, saying, 'Production is like an elephant with a long period of gestation; but strategy is like a rabbit which goes on producing litters at short intervals, and nothing can alter that.'

We discussed the general situation in the Middle East. As Churchill had said at the Pacific War Council, we could not foresee the outcome of the German thrust against the Russians in the Caucasus, nor of Auchinleck's current operations in the Western Desert. We were by no means despondent; but so long as these issues remained in doubt we felt it only prudent to make various calculations. We worked out the time-table for a possible German advance into Persia; a plan for reinforcing Persia from India, Egypt and the United Kingdom; plans to cover a defeat of Auchinleck by Rommel; plans to defend the Persian oil at all events, even if Auchinleck had to evacuate the Delta. These projects may well sound pessimistic today; but at least they serve to shew how narrow we considered the margin to be between defeat and victory in the Middle East.

The talks with Marshall and Admiral King, who had come over with him, occupied a good deal of our attention in the last days of July. I did not attend them, but I had to provide constant briefs for Brooke. Marshall had come over fully convinced that the summer of 1942, although it was already far advanced, would provide the best opportunity for landing in France.

He opened the proceedings by putting in a paper. In it he advocated the invasion of France on two grounds: it would provide relief for the Russians, and it would satisfy the ardent wish of the Americans to get more troops, both British and American, into action against the Germans. We were fully agreed that it was desirable to open a new front in France; but we were flatly opposed to the American view that it was practicable at this moment.

The Chiefs of Staff argued with Marshall for a week. At the end of the week, on 22nd July, he put in another paper. In this he made it clear that he was quite unconvinced by all that he had heard, and demanded afresh that a landing in France should be undertaken before the summer was over.

Brooke and I had a good many discussions as the conversations proceeded. He said one day that, after he had expounded our case very fully, Marshall had turned to him and had asked, 'Well, how are you going to win the war? You cannot win it by defensive action.' We naturally did not like opposing proposals to take the offensive. But a landing in France seemed to us to be absolutely impossible at that time. We felt we were still in a phase of the war when the chief consideration must be to avoid losing it by making mistakes. We believed most firmly that we would suffer a disaster if we invaded France prematurely. Our information was that the Germans were in a position to concentrate 30 divisions against us there, without taking a single man from the Russian front. They had 47 divisions in Central Europe, and 27 in France. We were sure that even if they did not stop us landing, they would be strong enough to drive us out as soon as it became convenient for them to do so. We believed we would be completely outclassed in the air, and that any aerodromes or ports we might acquire in France would be paralysed by the German Air Force. As Churchill had put it, we should be eating up our seed corn. He had backed our view when he was brought into the discussions, saying that he would have to get the approval of the War Cabinet for any decision reached in the military discussions; and he had asked Brooke whether the General Staff was solidly behind him in his opposition to Marshall's proposals. There must have been about a thousand officers on the General Staff in the War Office at that time, ranging from Subaltern up to Lieutenant-General. Brooke said, 'I think we may assume that, for this purpose, the General Staff means you and me. Tell me whether there is any doubt in your mind.' I laughed, and said, 'None whatever.' And we turned to something else.

This was a cheerless phase of the war, and it was both tantalizing and disappointing to have to turn down Marshall's scheme for striking a blow at the enemy. The Germans had reached the Don on a wide front about Rostov, and we had no idea whether the Russians had managed to save enough reserves to check an advance through the Caucasus. We hoped, though without any solid grounds, that the Russians would still be holding some kind of front when the winter came. But, even if they were routed in the South, we calculated that the Germans could not develop a serious threat to us in Persia before the late autumn. The only good news was that Auchinleck had started his offensive at Alamein on 22nd July. If this failed, we feared the Germans might have forces to spare for the occupation of French North Africa and the West African ports, which would enable them to intensify their attacks on our sea communications.

By 31st July, it was clear that Auchinleck's attack had failed. The Germans in Russia were pushing on over the Don. The Commanders-in-Chief in the Middle East now asked us for a ruling on the policy to be adopted by them should it prove impossible to defend the whole of the Middle East. Should they hold the Delta or, alternatively, the Persian Gulf? They were told that the Persian Gulf would be the more important. If the Germans could free themselves sufficiently from Russia, and concentrate on the Middle East from the North as well as the West, we would probably be unable to hold Egypt in addition to the vital Persian oilfields. On the other hand, we were well aware that the Germans were not in a happy situation, but in one vastly different from what they must have hoped for when they started the war.

Looking back on all our endeavours, we could not but be disappointed. By strenuous efforts, we had piled up resources at the key points, only to suffer repeated failure from bad generalship and inadequate equipment. There was nothing for it but to continue the process, and hope for the best.

In this sombre atmosphere, the conversations with Marshall and King entered their second phase, and, by the beginning of August, to our immense relief, agreement was achieved. The Americans accepted 'Torch', the occupation of North West Africa, as a substitute for the landing in France. We were well satisfied. No other offensive project seemed to us then to be within the realm of practicability. Eisenhower was to be Supreme Commander, and Alexander to command the troops.

On the 2nd August the Prime Minister flew to Cairo; the C.I.G.S. was already on his way there. On the 3rd, Alexander came to London, to hear from me, in Brooke's absence, what his job was to be. Next day, I took him to see Eisenhower, and we spent an hour or so discussing the outline plan. Eisenhower talked a great deal in his downright way. Alexander, on the other hand, was very silent, and listened to all we said imperturbably, without comment. I felt there was little doubt but that he and Eisenhower would get on well together. But, two days later, Churchill cabled from Cairo, to say that he had decided to appoint Alexander to relieve Auchinleck.

Montgomery was appointed in Alexander's place, to command 'Torch', and Eisenhower accepted the change with good grace. But when, a little later, Montgomery was also whisked off to Egypt, to command the 8th Army in place of Gott, who had been killed in an aeroplane accident, Eisenhower showed signs of impatience. I took great pains to explain the reasons to him, and to assure him that Anderson, our third nominee, was a very good man, too.

I thought the decision to split the Middle East Command, taken by Churchill while in Cairo, was a mistake. He had persuaded the War Cabinet, by signal, to accept the hiving off of Iraq and Persia into an independent command. One reason against separating Iraq from Egypt was that the military resources and air forces could be more conveniently allotted to, and moved between, the two countries if they were under the control of one Commander-in-Chief, rather than two, who would have to refer to Whitehall for decisions. But this reason, it had to be admitted, was not very weighty so long as the Germans had not broken through the Caucasus. A second reason against the separation was that Alexander, with only Egypt and Palestine to look after, might be a nuisance to Montgomery in the conduct of the operations in the desert. But in the end the new arrangement worked very well.

27

PREPARATIONS FOR 'TORCH'

1942

I HAD a most welcome break for the second week of August. With my eldest boy, who was on his holidays from school, I went to Port Patrick, the little fishing village on the Galloway coast, where I had spent my boyhood. We fished for trout and sea-trout in the Dunskey lochs and the River Luce, and visited other haunts of my youth.

One day we walked along the cliffs to Knockinaam, and had tea with Lord and Lady Caldecote, formerly Sir Thomas and Lady Augusta Inskip. He was now Lord Chief Justice of England, but it was very obvious that he did not find it so interesting as being a Cabinet Minister.

He reminisced about his time as Minister for the Co-ordination of Defence. He had had no powers save those of persuasion, and no precedents to which he could point. He said it had taken him six months to learn what the job was, nor could he get any guidance out of Chamberlain. He recalled how Chamberlain, as Chancellor, had given a stern warning to the Cabinet because defence expenditure had reached £78 million a year—just about a week's spending at this stage of the war.

Caldecote was a man of sterling qualities, upright and talented; but it was unthinkable that Churchill could have had him in his Cabinet after all that had passed.

War-time holidays were all too short, and after a week I was back at the grindstone. Dill came over from Washington to see us in August, and I dined with him on the 21st. The other guests were Eisenhower, Anderson, Nye, Clark and Handy, my American opposite number. Dill looked well and happy, and ten years younger than when I had last seen him.

As we waited for the party to assemble, he told me that he had been much struck by the contrast between Marshall's routine and that of the British C.I.G.S. Marshall saw the President only occasionally, and, unlike our C.I.G.S., was a very free and powerful agent. His normal hours of work were from 8 a.m. to 4 p.m., and, when he left his office, he would very often go out on the river with his wife, and take a picnic supper. It all sounded idyllic.

After dinner we settled down to a discussion of 'Torch' (the plan for the North African landings), and Dill asked me what I thought of the prospects. I said I was firmly convinced that the plan had got into a shape which would lead to a fiasco. The original plan had been for an attack in overwhelming force, all along the coast from Casablanca to Tunisia. Now the weight of the assault had been whittled down on the grounds that there were good chances of our being welcomed by the French. I thought this most dangerous, and that the forces now proposed should be multiplied by three. Anderson agreed; Dill was non-committal; Nye neither supported my opinion nor argued against it; Eisenhower merely remarked that no one had yet said anything cheerful to him about the plan. The reaction to my *démarche* was hardly enthusiastic.

The Americans went off at half past ten, and Nye and I stayed on for half an hour. I continued with my harangue, and said that it seemed incredible that the Americans, now that they had been in the war for nearly a year, should be proposing to take such a small share in the operation. I felt very strongly that we should take no unnecessary chances in North Africa, because we needed a success so badly; and, further, there was no good reason why we should take chances, because we now had ample resources to make a certainty of it. It seemed obvious that the hearts of the Americans were not yet really in this business, or, at least, that Admiral King's was not; for he was allowing the Pacific war to eat up resources that should be allotted to the German war.[1]

Dill asked why we had not had an outline plan for 'Torch' ready when Marshall arrived. I explained that, before his visit, we had not

---

[1] I was not speaking entirely without evidence, for I had received a letter, dated 18th August, from General Macready of the British Mission in Washington from which the following is an extract:

'We must also remember that the American Navy is not keen on European war; they are all out for "island hopping" in the Pacific and for running a war on their own. There are also other quite powerful sections of the community, who, while prepared to agree with the underlying policy that Germany is the principal enemy, would qualify this by saying that they do not want to fight on a mixed front and want to have an American theatre of war.

'"Torch". Although everyone here is at least paying lip service to "Torch", my impression is that they are not in it heart and soul and at the moment there is quite a tendency to say how difficult various parts of the business are.'

meant to press him to adopt the 'Torch' plan. We had merely intended to urge him to continue and accelerate the movement of American forces to Britain, on the understanding that we could decide later how to use them. In the course of the talks the North African project had come up for decision rather unexpectedly, and the present plan had been proposed and adopted without proper examination. Since his visit we had had it examined by the staffs, and we had come to the conclusion that the forces to be employed were not nearly big enough.

Three days later, I wrote a note on 'Torch' for Brooke.

'The most striking feature of this outline plan is its divergence from the original conception, which was essentially an attack in overwhelming force from Casablanca to Tunisia. Tunisia itself was to be occupied in three to four weeks.

According to this plan, the attack is not to be made in overwhelming force. The occupation of Tunisia within the time laid down would be quite impossible, unless we were welcomed by the French, and had help from them rather than resistance.

No matter what political or other arrangements may be made, in the end the attitude of the French, as well as of the Spaniards, will be determined by the degree of force we display, and by the degree of quick success which we can achieve.

We must face the fact that strategic surprise in this operation is most unlikely. We must also face the fact that, owing to the lateness of the date on which it can be launched, the Germans may be in a position to move into Tunisia before, or very soon after, we begin operations. If the operation sticks in Algeria, we stand to suffer a tremendous disaster. Even if we could maintain ourselves there, the last thing we desire is to open another front, facing the Germans in Tunisia. In this event, it is quite possible we should be unable to maintain the forces, and that eventually they might be completely cut off and lost.

It is proposed to seize Casablanca by a force moving overland from Oran, a distance of 600 miles. If the operations from Oran stick at all, there is grave danger of the Spaniards coming in against us, or at least, acquiescing to a German occupation of Spain, with its grave threat to our communications through the Straits of Gibraltar. Moreover, the chances of landing at Casablanca later would disappear.

The only solution is the use of overwhelming force and quick success throughout the whole of French North Africa.

The whole operation at best is extremely hazardous. The only hope of success is if both we and the Americans put our whole effort into it. It is almost incredible that the American share of the operations should be so weak and half-hearted. In my opinion, we should tell the Americans that we regard the plan as fundamentally unsound in its present shape, but that the project holds good prospects of success if the principle of concentration be applied in our combined strategy. In my view, the plan should be multiplied by about three, and the Casablanca end of it should take place simultaneously with the remainder. The implications must be accepted both in the Pacific and in our aid to Russia.'

Simultaneously, Eisenhower sent his comments in writing to the Chiefs of Staff. These, I was delighted to observe, were an almost exact reproduction of what I had said at Dill's dinner-party. He maintained that the plan was unsound in the shape it had assumed.

On 23rd August, Mason-Macfarlane, the Governor of Gibraltar, came to see me, and we went through the plan together. He agreed with my misgivings, and said that the only way to bring round the French and the Spaniards would be by a quick success, which meant the use of overwhelming force.

I felt we were bound to have some difficulty with the Prime Minister when he returned, for, if these ideas were accepted, it would mean delay in launching the operation, which he most certainly would not like.

There had been a good deal of talk in Fleet Street about North Africa, and I was concerned about the secrecy of the plan. I made this note on 23rd August.

'This plan has had a very bad start. It is known to too many people. It has been explained to the Cabinet. I told Ismay that I thought all this most dangerous. He said that we must be constitutional, but I felt that it could hardly be true that a constitutional defeat would be preferred to an unconstitutional victory.'

The Prime Minister got back from the Middle East and Moscow on the night of the 25th August. At 11 a.m. on the 26th, he sent for me and the D.M.I. to see him in the Annexe. He was not quite ready when we arrived, and I spent a few minutes studying some of his oil paintings which were hanging in the passage outside his bedroom.

One would never have guessed that they were all by the same hand; they varied as much as the many facets of his character.

Churchill was sitting in bed, wearing The Dressing Gown; a half-smoked cigar was in his mouth, and a glass of water and some papers on a table beside him. I expected him to be sunburnt after his travels, but he was his usual baby pink.

He said he wanted to check up. He spoke first of Egypt. 'With the change of commanders, a new wind is blowing in the Desert,' he said. 'The Army was all in bits and pieces, but all that will be put right now. That poor Army has suffered terrible wastage. I have given Wilson a mandate to take command in the Delta, with plenary powers if Rommel attacks while he is there—the Army must have a secure base to allow it to manoeuvre.' He believed Rommel was going to attack quite soon (although our information in London did not lead us to think that he would, for his supplies were believed to be short and his divisions not yet complete).

He took up some papers from his table which showed the strength of the Army in the Desert in men, guns, tanks and other details, and said that he would like them checked; and that he would like a report, that day or the next, on any discrepancies between our figures and Auchinleck's.

Next he turned to the subject of what were called the 'Lower Establishment Divisions' in the United Kingdom, and said he did not want them broken up. I told him we were already preparing a report on these divisions, which had been milked to provide drafts for overseas, and that we should need more men if they were to be kept up to full strength. 'Yes,' he said, 'the Army needs another quarter of a million men.' This surprised me: he had consistently opposed our proposals to increase the Army's manpower.

He spoke of his visit to Moscow. He said that Stalin might have been expected to make out that his situation was bad, when he pressed for a second front, but he had not done this. When they discussed the Dieppe raid, Stalin had remarked, 'Dieppe will be explained by Torch,' which, he said, showed Stalin's quickness of mind in that he connected the two things. 'My general impression,' Churchill continued, 'is that, on the whole, things are all right in Russia. I have bet the C.I.G.S. half-a-crown, even money, that the Russians will hold the Caucasus.' He described Stalin's plans for counter-attack, which sounded very good if only he had the necessary reserves to carry them out. He told us of his dinner with Stalin and said: 'I drank as much or more than Stalin and Molotov together. They only sip their liquor, you know, and I was in quite good order.'

When he asked me what I had to tell him, I said 'Torch' was the big thing at the moment, but I thought the plan was no good in its present form. The forces needed multiplying by three, and the proposed American share was quite inadequate. The American reluctance to do more was a sign that our strategical policies were diverging.

I was glad to have this chance of giving him my views, although I realized he would not be pleased: if they were accepted (as they subsequently were), it would mean postponing 'Torch'. I was therefore not surprised when he at once looked ruffled. His eyes flashed, and he began to declaim. 'Anyone can make a plan for the use of overwhelming strength,' he said. 'There is no time to wait for the Americans to bring forces from the Pacific. I intend to *advance* the date, if it is humanly possible. This is a soft job—not like fighting the Germans. I would be prepared to go ahead *without* the Americans, so long as we have plenty of American flags. What we want is a big show in the shop window. We should do this like the Germans did Norway. Remember how easy Madagascar proved to be.' He had me there; for there is no doubt that he had been right about Madagascar, and we had been unduly apprehensive.

I said that, all the same, I did not think the plan was likely to succeed unless it was strengthened. There was not enough in the shop window, and Madagascar was not a good analogy. The planned 'build-up' of the forces was too slow—3 divisions in 3 weeks, and 13 in 3 or 4 months. We had plenty of soldiers, but we needed more shipping, more naval escorts, more aircraft carriers. I realized very well that we could not wait indefinitely, and that we should not allow the best to be the enemy of the good. But I was absolutely certain that a far bigger force should be used, and on a wider front, including Casablanca at the outset. Moreover, it was of great importance that the Americans should be in the thing wholeheartedly, not only at the beginning, but afterwards.

Our talk lasted nearly two hours.

When, after all these years, I read the notes I made of these discussions, memories are revived of the strong and passionate views we held at the time on matters that now seem of little importance. I am also reminded that Churchill was inclined to be a great gambler in his strategical notions, while I was not. And it is only fair to remember that the greatest military successes, all through the history of war, have resulted from plans that might well have been regarded as gambles before they were attempted. All the same, in this particular case, I think we were right to 'ca' canny'. The 'Torch' plan, as it was at the moment, ominously resembled the kind of gamble that had failed at Gallipoli.

On the afternoon of 26th August, I had a long talk with Brooke, who was in good spirits. I told him that we had been doubtful as to the wisdom of dividing the Middle East Command. He replied that, after he had studied the problem on the spot, he had come to the conclusion that the split was essential. Otherwise nothing adequate would be done to organize our defence in Persia in case the Germans got through the Caucasus. If Persia had been left under the Middle East Command or put under India, it would have been a Cinderella. He also believed that the new arrangement was better fitted to the personality of Alexander, who would be happier with a more restricted responsibility than he would have had under the old arrangement.

Brooke said that Montgomery had been well settled in the saddle before their departure, and had taken complete charge. He described Montgomery's plan of attack, and said it had inspired confidence in everybody, including the Prime Minister. Apparently when Churchill had first planned his trip, he had had no definite idea of moving Auchinleck. But Brooke was sure the change was needed, and he referred especially to the mistakes Auchinleck had made in choosing his subordinates.

He described his flight up the western side of the Caspian. They had flown low, and he had formed the impression that the Russian troops were very thin on the ground, and that the defence works in the Caucasus were backward in preparation.

I told Brooke of my talk with the Prime Minister in the morning, about 'Torch'. He said we must now tackle the problem of striking the balance between waiting and collecting sufficient strength, and I said I would soon let him have full details.

During the next few days, Churchill gave tremendous impetus to the 'Torch' preparations, seeing commanders himself and giving orders direct to the shipping authorities and other government departments concerned with staging the operation. But it soon became evident that it would not be launched until the plan had been fundamentally reshaped. Many telegrams passed between London and Washington during the next few weeks; major changes were made in the political approach to the French, in the composition of the forces, in the landing places; and the date was postponed until November.

On 3rd September, Dill came in to say that he would be leaving for Washington within twenty-four hours. He asked: 'What shall I say about the "Torch" plan? I am expected to advocate it, yet I don't believe in it. If it fails, as I am sure it will, I will be of no more use to you in Washington.'

I told him I was as worried as he was at the way the plan had been whittled down, but that we should be in a better position to judge the prospects when November came along. Dill asked whether I was not anxious about the security of the United Kingdom, and I said, 'No. If "Torch" fails, it will fail in the early stages, and we shall not have committed more than two divisions at most by then.'

On 9th September, Paget, Commander-in-Chief Home Forces, came to complain that the forces in the United Kingdom would be too weak after 'Torch' to repel invasion in the spring. I explained that, if 'Torch' succeeded, it would bring him relief in various ways: our commitments for Egypt would be reduced by the opening of the shorter sea route through the Middle East; there would be some diversion of German forces; as time went on, the strength of the Americans in England would increase. Paget was not quite satisfied by this, and he went off to prepare a new review of his needs.

It seems from my diary that it was not until 24th September that I began to feel confident of the 'Torch' plan. On this day, I wrote: 'I think that, in its present shape, with the big American element, "Torch" has good chances of success.'

Meanwhile, Rommel had attacked in the Desert. He was taking a very big chance in doing so, although we could see his point: the 8th Army stood to gain more than he did, in the course of the following month, in the way of reorganization and reinforcement, unless he could anticipate them.

On 2nd September, three days after the attack had started, I was summoned to see the Prime Minister before dinner. When I arrived at No. 10, he was seated, as usual, at the table, in his blue rompers. He did not seem to be in very good form. He lit a fresh cigar before we began to fight the first stage of the Battle of Alamein on the map.

At that moment it appeared to us that Rommel might wish to develop the battle as he had at Gazala. He had got inside our lines, and his most probable course of action seemed to be to attack northward, in an attempt to destroy our forces piecemeal. It would have been too risky to advance eastward, because he would then have left undefeated troops on his seaward flank.

Churchill asked me what I thought of the battle. I said supplies would be the key to it. Rommel's supply position was shaky, because of his long communications, and because his panzer divisions on the battlefield would have to be supplied through a narrow gap, limited in the South by the Qattara Depression, which might be closed at any moment. Our supply base, on the other hand, was excellently placed right behind the Army. He made no comment beyond remarking that we were fighting Rommel on our own ground.

I went on to say that Rommel would be so weakened by his attack that we might be able to push forward towards Daba, and so cut off his supplies altogether. He looked at the map, and sweeping his hand over the German positions, said that he hoped our whole line might eventually swing round, pivoting on our left, and so close Rommel in against the Depression. 'Anyhow,' he asked, 'you take a favourable view of the battle?' to which I answered 'Yes'; and he proceeded to describe the lie of the ground at Alamein as he had seen it while he was in Egypt. Then we went over the usual points, such as the number of tanks on both sides; the dates reinforcements might arrive in the line; and the situation on the Russian front, where the Germans were attacking but apparently making no progress.

The Prime Minister was obviously on tenterhooks, and no wonder. It was a critical moment in the war, and I suspected he was having difficulties with some of his colleagues. I went off after an hour or so, leaving him with P. J. Grigg, who had been present throughout our talk.

By 24th September, it was clear that Rommel's attack had failed, and we all breathed a sigh of relief.

All through that month, Churchill had been particularly active in suggesting a variety of fresh operations, for which we had no resources, and which would have involved us in a great dispersion of effort. One of Churchill's secretaries once said to me, 'The mistake you people make is that you think what the P.M. wants is a logical, reasoned argument. There is nothing he dislikes more.' The truth of this opinion was particularly driven in on us during the months before 'Torch'.

I think it was at this time that Brooke told me that Churchill had said to him, 'I have got a sore throat and the doctors have knocked me off cigars. That is the worst of having a high-class job—you have to go in for high-class cures. I should have said that a wet stocking round my neck would cure me in a night'.

The war would certainly have been much duller without him.

On 9th October, I returned to London, after being laid up for a week with influenza. I went to see Eisenhower at his Head-quarters, and found him rather harassed. He still held his post as American Commander in the European theatre in addition to being Commander of the 'Torch' forces, and he complained that he was being bombarded with too many political and administrative problems. I was very glad I had gone to see him, because I found that some quite unnecessary misunderstandings had arisen; and as they were smoothed away one by one, he cheered up considerably.

One of these arose from a draft directive which the British Government proposed to issue to Anderson as commander of the British troops. It has been cast in the same form as the instructions given to Haig in 1918, and to Gort in 1939. The usual paragraph had been included, providing for the British Commander's right of appeal to his Government if, in his opinion, his troops were imperilled in consequence of orders given by the Supreme Commander. The Dominion contingent commanders in the Middle East under Wavell had had much the same document; it was almost a time-honoured source of friction. Eisenhower said that he felt instructions of this kind did not breathe the spirit of full and loyal co-operation which he would like to see, and which, to do him justice, he always exemplified himself. He went on to say that he personally had always considered the 'Torch' operation to be unsound strategically, but that as he, for a variety of reasons, had been chosen to head it, he would drive it through in a spirit of loyalty and co-operation, and he wanted the same spirit to be shown by us. He then showed me a long letter of protest which he was about to send to Ismay on the subject.

I explained to him that no British Commander had ever been allowed to take the field without being given a definition of his relations with an Allied Commander-in-Chief and with his own Government; that the draft of the directive to Anderson was almost identical with that under which Foch and Haig had won the war in 1918; and that the right of appeal was only intended for exceptional emergencies such as that which arose in March 1918, when the British Army might have been ordered to retire on Paris and abandon the Channel Ports. But Eisenhower stuck to his opinion that an over-meticulous interpretation of his instructions by the British General might lead to an impossible relationship between him and the Supreme Commander. There was certainly a lot in Eisenhower's point of view, and I felt that the directive might well be modified without any harm being done. In North Africa, it was possible, even probable, that the British forces would not remain concentrated in one particular area, but be distributed among the American troops. I told Eisenhower that I was sure the Chiefs of Staff would meet his wishes without any difficulty. I advised him to modify his letter to Ismay, and he duly recast it in the light of our discussion. I showed his new draft to Brooke, and explained his point of view. The Chiefs of Staff at once agreed.

On 9th October, I made this note:

'The general situation is now moving much in our favour. The Germans are in an awful mess, and they know it. I don't think invasion of the U.K. is likely to become a live issue again, and that the turn of the tide is near. The Boche may try two things—Spain and, in the spring, the Persian Gulf. But we should be able to deal with these. Impending operations have, in my view, very good chances of success, and the Boche can do very little to counter them.'

Our work for 'Torch' was now, to all intents and purposes, finished; and the remainder of October was taken up chiefly with intensive planning for subsequent developments. The old problem cropped up again of striking a proper balance between bombing and providing adequately for the air requirements of the Navy and the Army.

A story was told to me at this time of a dialogue between Churchill and Smuts during their meeting in Egypt:

S.: 'You should take a lesson from Gandhi, and mix more religion with your politics.'

C.: 'Why, I have made more Bishops than any other Prime Minister.'

S.: 'But do you think that has done you any good?'

C.: 'I don't know. But do not forget that you are responsible for all our troubles in India. You had Gandhi in South Africa for years and you did not do away with him.'

S.: 'Well, I put him in prison three times. The only thing that came of it was that he made me a pair of bedroom slippers.'

On 15th October, I attended a meeting of the Night Air Defence Committee, which was held at No. 10. The Prime Minister was in the chair, and the party consisted of Attlee, Anderson, Morrison, Sinclair, Henderson, Sholto-Douglas, Cherwell, Tizard, Llewellin, Pile and various other experts from the War Office and the Air

Ministry. Churchill came in after we had assembled, wearing a new romper suit. He glowered all round when he sat down, and everybody watched him attentively to see if he was in a good humour. He pressed the bell on the table before him and, when a secretary appeared, he said to him that he had come without a handkerchief. After a short delay, his detective came in with one, and handed it to him in an O.H.M.S. envelope. Churchill extracted it, blew his nose, and looked all round again while we sat in silence. Then he got up and spent a moment or two adjusting the electric fire behind his chair, sat down once more, and glowered round again. Next he lit a cigar, and took a sip from his glass of iced water. Then he noticed me, bowed across the table, and said, 'Glad to see you are better.'

The proceedings were opened with statements by Sholto-Douglas and Pile. Churchill asked a few questions and made some little jokes at which everybody laughed—rather like schoolboys with their headmaster. It was now evident—and we noted it with relief—that he was in good form, so we all relaxed and got down to the work in hand. I never ceased to be fascinated by Churchill's demeanour at such meetings, and on this particular occasion I recorded it all in detail.

He remarked that the Press had outrun the tenor of a speech he had delivered in Edinburgh the day before. He had meant to give a balanced statement about the prospects of air raids during the winter, and had intended to convey that there would be raids, probably sharp and heavy, but not sustained as before. This had been interpreted by the Press as an indication that there would be practically no raids at all, and he would have to restate it. All he had wanted to do was to correct an impression that had been given in a rather panicky speech by someone else a few days earlier. Morrison interjected that he was going to make a speech on the following Sunday, and he would put it right. Winston looked at him suspiciously, and said, 'No, no, I can't have you appearing to correct *me*. I will give you a message from me to put in your speech. We must always remember, however, that a balanced statement is of no use to the Press. Yet what we want to do is "to envisage the situation as a whole", as the saying goes.'

28

ALAMEIN AND FRENCH NORTH AFRICA

1942

THE victory of Alamein was a real sunrise at last, the more joyfully welcome for all the false dawns which had preceded it. Montgomery struck on the evening of 23rd October; by early November it was clear that not only had a battle been won: the whole campaign had taken a new and vigorous turn. Good news came from Montgomery every day, and we congratulated ourselves that Rommel (who had hitherto hardly ever put a foot wrong) had not had the good sense to withdraw to the frontier a month earlier. If he had done so, he would have dislocated all our preparations for the offensive.

There was little wonder that, on 4th November, the Prime Minister sent for the C.I.G.S., and said that he was going to ring the church bells. The C.I.G.S. advised waiting a day or two to be quite sure; and in the end they were not rung until after the fall of Tunis.

Meanwhile, the prospects for 'Torch' were growing brighter and brighter, although it was not to succeed without set-backs. There was ample precedent, among our various enterprises in the war, for some mishap to befall the Force Commander; and 'Torch' was no exception. The operation was due to start on 8th November, but General Anderson was still in London on the 4th, having been prevented from flying by bad weather. I tried to cheer him up by giving him luncheon at the United Service Club; and this effort at hospitality must have brought him luck, for he got away later that afternoon.

The 9th November was a good day. Eisenhower reported that resistance had been slight, and his landings successful. Rommel was in full rout, fifteen hundred miles farther East. Altogether there had been a glorious change of climate; and it was almost intoxicating to see our plans working out properly at last, after so many wintry months of frustration and disappointment. We all of us reacted in our several ways to this unaccustomed beverage of success. I had luncheon on the 8th November with a close associate of the Prime Minister, who said that Winston was 'all over the place. He is difficult enough when things are going badly, more difficult when nothing is happening, and quite unmanageable when all is going well.'

But even in this moment of triumph we had to look ahead; and I had several long talks with Brooke during the next few days. We had at last gained the initiative: now we must plan to maintain the momentum. There were two aspects of our Mediterranean problems: we must speed up the movement of our forces into North Africa; and we must examine the possibilities of further action in the Mediterranean. If the Italians dropped out of the war, as seemed possible, the Germans would have to shorten their line. They would certainly have to give up any ideas they might still have of going into Spain; they might even have to clear out of Italy, Sardinia and the Balkans. They would be very strongly tempted to hurry into Unoccupied France (and in those days 'Unoccupied France' was pretty well a country in its own right in the context of strategical thinking); in fact they did so within a very few days of these speculations. Whichever way things went, the important point at this moment was to concentrate our attack on Rommel's sea communications with Tripoli and Benghazi.

Our first foothold on Continental Europe must be sure and permanent. A landing in Italy might not be feasible unless the Germans shewed signs of demoralization. Hitherto we had been thinking entirely in terms of France being the scene of our next big operation. The opening of the Mediterranean was about to result in an enormous windfall of shipping. How should we exploit it? One of the more obvious uses was in the ferrying of more American troops across the Atlantic to the United Kingdom, against the final assault across the Channel; and even so there would be a good deal left for operations in the Mediterranean. It seemed that at last we had something in hand.

Montgomery had now crossed the Egyptian frontier and entered Libya. In French North Africa, we had gained all our first objectives. Darlan had ordered a cessation of hostilities, and we hoped as a result to occupy Tunisia quickly. But it soon appeared that the French ban on hostilities included action by us against the Germans; and the Germans continued to reinforce Tunisia unopposed through the aerodrome of El Aouina, and our hopes of an easy occupation faded quickly.

Churchill was now full of impatience for fresh projects. His view was that, unless we could get to grips with the Germans on the mainland of Europe early in the New Year, the Russians might not be able to hold out for another summer. He summoned the Chiefs of Staff to Chequers one Sunday in the middle of November, and pressed them hard, accusing them of lack of aggressiveness. Brooke told me that Smuts, who had been present, had tried to calm Winston by saying that he thought there was no difference of opinion about the long-term policy between him and the Chiefs of Staff. This was true up to a point, but Churchill wanted things to be done much more quickly than the Chiefs of Staff thought possible.

He had also urged Brooke, at this meeting, to make a heavy reduction in the 'administrative tail' of the Armies in North Africa. He had said, 'The Army is like a peacock—nearly all tail,' to which Brooke had replied, 'The peacock would be a very badly balanced bird without its tail.' This business of a 'tail' was one which the Prime Minister was always raising.

Curiously enough, at this stage of the war, not only was it impossible to reduce our tail: we had to add to it. We were converting static Divisions from a defensive to an offensive basis and 'tails' had to be added to make them mobile.

However much the Prime Minister might press for an acceleration of our operations, the pace was regulated by the number of ships that could be spared for them; and we never had enough. He wrote a note in which he asked for full particulars of the way the ships were being used, saying, 'I intended North Africa to be a springboard, not a sofa.'

He held a number of late meetings of the Defence Committee to discuss future plans, but these were largely a waste of time. On 24th November, Brooke told me about a meeting which had been held on the previous night. The Committee had assembled at ten o'clock, and Churchill had held forth at great length. At ten-fifteen, someone had written a note which he passed to the Secretary of State, sitting beside him—'15 minutes gone and no work done'. At ten-twenty he had taken it back and altered the '15' to '20', then successively, every five minutes, to '25', '30', '35', '40', and finally to '45'. Another night, Smuts sent the Prime Minister to bed, like a small boy, and he went off obediently, as though despatched by his mother.

On the evening of the 24th, I dined with Brooke at his flat. Dudley Pound was there too. The conversation at dinner was all about shooting and fishing and poaching, and we were enjoying ourselves. At ten o'clock, a message came from the Prime Minister asking Brooke to go and see him, but Brooke managed to excuse himself on account of his dinner-party. 'It would only be paddling about the Mediterranean anyhow,' he remarked as he came back from the telephone.

On 2nd December, Brooke dined with my wife and me at our house in Cheyne Walk. He told us various stories of Churchill, Roosevelt and Stalin, most of which have been included in *The Turn of the Tide*. Talking of Stalin, Brooke said:

'He gave me the creeps. He looked pale and even grey, with the flesh hanging from the bones of his face. He didn't register when Winston came into the room—it might have been a footman coming in. All the same, nobody could say that Winston was dwarfed by him. Winston did not like the interpreter, and said he was sure he was toning his statements down as he put them into Russian, and that he was like a hairdresser.'

Brooke gave us an amusing description of his own dealings with Churchill. 'He is extraordinarily obstinate. He is like a child that has set its mind on some forbidden toy. It is no good explaining that it will cut his fingers or burn him. The more you explain, the more fixed he becomes in his idea. Very often he seems to be quite immovable on some impossible project, but often that only means that he will not give way at that particular moment. Then, suddenly after some days, he will come round, and he will say something to show that it is all right, and that all the personal abuse has been forgotten. Another of his habits is suddenly to start using arguments, himself, that you have been putting to him against his own ideas, and he uses these arguments as his own, even to the people who originally produced them, and as if they were something quite new. For instance, I once warned him not to engage in some new commitment too early, and I said, "You cannot tell, six weeks ahead, what may happen." A few days later, at a Chiefs of Staff meeting, he said to us very seriously, "You must never forget that, in war, you cannot tell, six weeks ahead, what may happen."

'Winston has a very lovable and human side, too,' he continued. 'I remember, when we were flying back from America, he came up, in his dressing-gown and yachting cap, and smoking a cigar, to get a first sight of land. And, as we peered down through the clouds, he said, "Do you know, I feel so thrilled! I can imagine the feelings of those men who first flew the Atlantic."

'What I don't like is being sent for to come to Downing Street when I have just got undressed and am getting into my bath about midnight, and then to find that there is nothing definite to answer, and that I only have to listen to an indefinite discussion. And these late sittings are not a good idea—it is very hard to stick to important principles late at night. You often feel you must give way on something sometimes. Then, in the morning, you wake up and think: "Now what *did* I do last night? Was I too weak?" '

I saw Churchill again on 17th December when I attended a meeting of his Air Defence Committee at No. 10. He was still in bed when we assembled; Attlee took the chair until he arrived at 12.45 p.m. and then the meeting livened up at once. The only note I have made of the meeting was of a brush between him and Archibald Sinclair. Sinclair made a protest against a proposed cut in the strength of the Fighter Force. To this Winston retorted, sharply, 'It is not a cut in your assets, but in your ambitions.'

By the first week of December, it was clear that a fairly considerable effort would still be required to clear the Germans out of Tunisia and Tripolitania. But we had little doubt that this would soon be accomplished, and it was becoming urgent to reach decisions as to what our next steps should be.

By this time Brooke was quite determined to continue operations in the Mediterranean during 1943 and not to attempt a landing in France unless, of course, the Germans showed signs of breaking up. Our staff were all of the same opinion. But Churchill now sent a directive to the Chiefs of Staff, the gist of which was that a halt should be called in the Mediterranean about June, in order that we might concentrate in England for the invasion of France. On the same day he summoned the Chiefs of Staff to discuss this directive with him.

Brooke opened fire by telling him that he would ruin everything by a premature attack in France. He explained again that the Germans had 40 divisions in France; that they could bring more in very quickly; that we had not the ships to bring the American Army over in six months; and that, even if this had been possible, there would not be enough landing craft, in 1943, to put the British and American forces ashore in France. Churchill was not satisfied, and during the next two weeks, the staffs worked hard to produce figures to support our case.

The main points of our argument were these. We were not yet in a position to develop two big offensive campaigns simultaneously. We believed that the time would not have come, by the autumn of

1943, when we would be able to tackle the Germans on equal terms in France. To have concentrated our forces in England would have meant calling a halt to operations in the Mediterranean for five or six months, which would give the Germans a dangerous respite. Therefore, we argued, the right course would be to continue to engage the Germans in the Mediterranean, and to knock Italy out of the war. There was no other way of lessening the weight of the German attack on the Russians. If this policy were adopted, our resources would be fully absorbed, and a landing in France would not be possible in 1943.

There were many other arguments in favour of taking advantage of the situation in the Mediterranean. The position in the Balkans, in Turkey and elsewhere would turn in our favour if we continued to press Italy. But the over-riding point was that we could not be ready in sufficient strength to tackle the Germans in France in 1943; and, therefore, it seemed to us to be quite clear that there was no sound alternative but to carry on the fight in the Mediterranean.

On 16th December, the Prime Minister met the Chiefs of Staff. Brooke went off to the meeting rather apprehensively. He took with him masses of statistics, the most telling of which were those which showed our capacity to move troops by sea, as compared with the Germans' power to move them by land. When he came back, he told me that, to his great surprise, Churchill had accepted our case. I could not help wondering whether he had been arguing against the Chiefs of Staff partly to be sure that our calculations had been thoroughly worked out, and partly so that he might be well primed with all the points of the controversy for his discussions with the President. The Americans had meanwhile prepared what they evidently considered to be an equally convincing case for the invasion of France in 1943, and for abandoning the exploitation of our Mediterranean successes, apart from air raids.

It was at least a big step forward that our respective ideas on either side of the Atlantic were now crystallized. The next thing was to convince the Americans that ours were right and theirs were wrong. The fact that Marshall was opposed to our policy did not carry much weight with us, for we were absolutely convinced that we were right, and that Marshall's policy would lead to disaster.

The Americans did not keep us fully informed of their operations against Japan. But we suspected that the scale on which plans were being laid for the Pacific did not quite conform to the agreed policy of defeating Germany first and Japan afterwards. Dill wrote on 16th December:

'Life is not easy here. The American Chiefs of Staff are busy at all levels in framing strategical ideas, and we are not in a very strong position to guide them. At least Marshall is prepared to discuss anything, and at all times to let me know how their minds are working. I have had many discussions with him about major strategy and about policy in Burma and the Pacific. I encourage all these discussions, including Burma. By reason of the fact that we have encouraged Burma planning in a very general way, we have at least got King interested. He now realizes that by helping Burma with ships at his disposal he is actually helping S.W. Pacific. King may be Pacific-minded, but he maintains that no one else is Pacific-minded at all, and that, in fact, he only asks enough to keep the Japanese fully occupied. He said that 1/3 of our forces ought to be directed towards keeping the Japanese in check and 2/3 towards defeating Germany. He might make it 1/4 : 3/4 if pressed!'

All these points of difference which had arisen could be cleared up only by personal discussion. A conference was therefore arranged to take place at Casablanca in the following month.

29

CASABLANCA

1943

On New Year's Day, 1943, I went to Scotland for a few days' holiday with my family. When I returned to London, arrangements had been completed for the Casablanca Conference. Brooke asked me to accompany him, and I was very glad to go, although there was no specific place for me in our delegation.

The weather was bad on 11th January, and we could not fly by Clipper, as had been arranged. It was still bad on the 12th, and the Air Ministry therefore decreed that we should travel by Liberator. After an early dinner in London, we motored for three hours in the dark to the aerodrome, and, since we had to drive without head-lights, we were glad the moon came out as we passed through Maidenhead. When we arrived, we were given a little lecture about how to use our parachutes in case of need, and how to get into the dinghies.

The party in my aeroplane included Lord Leathers,[1] Ismay and half a dozen others. We took off at 1.40 a.m. and flew up into a clear, starry sky; but we soon ran into cloud, and we had to fly blind, nearly all the way, at about 8,000 feet. Our bunks were not very comfortable, but I slept well. I awoke about 7.30 a.m. and was told that we were about to make the landfall. I climbed up to a window near the tail of the aircraft and looked out. We had just emerged from a bank of fleecy white clouds; and there in front of us was a long stretch of sandy beach with a heavy surf breaking on it. The white houses of Casablanca shone in the sun, and the flat cultivated country around the town looked green and fertile.

As we drew near the landing ground, we saw another aeroplane circling—this was the Prime Minister's, and we flew about for ten minutes until he had landed. When we stepped out, Churchill

[1] Minister of War Transport.

walked up, wearing an Air Commodore's uniform, and said, 'Now tumble out, you young fellows, and get on parade.' The Security officers were horrified by this. They had been trying to keep his arrival a secret, and had arranged for a closed van to be driven up to his aeroplane to take him away before he could be seen, but he refused to use it. He shook hands with us all, and then we drove to a little suburb of Casablanca, which had been evacuated and fenced off for us to live in.

The Casablanca Conference has been described so often that there would be no point in going over it again in detail. But I made a few notes, and for the sake of continuity I reproduce some of them.

On the afternoon of the first day, the British Chiefs of Staff held a short meeting to enable Dill to bring us up to date about the Americans' point of view. They were still opposed to operations across the Mediterranean, because they felt the results of these would be to weaken or even to postpone the invasion of France, to reduce the weight of our bombing in Germany, and to use up naval craft and shipping, all for an inadequate return. They also feared that an attack on Italy might precipitate a German descent on Spain to close the Straits of Gibraltar; they thought the Germans could find enough forces for Spain by shortening their line in Russia. Another objection which Dill thought they would raise was that activity in the Mediterranean would be at the expense of the reconquest of Burma. This they regarded as vital in order to keep China in the war, and so continue to absorb Japanese forces. The Americans believed we did not take Japan seriously enough, and did not comprehend how important it was to prevent Japan from strengthening her position so much that she would be difficult to defeat later.

This estimate of the American attitude was what we had expected. We were still convinced that they were wrong and we were right. Now our problem was to get them to accept our strategy, without causing them to lose interest in the priority of operations against Germany. We all felt, I think, that they had bigger ideas than ours, and more drive. But we had as yet no great respect for the quality of their staff work, and did not regard their strategical conceptions as being based on realities.

We found the American officers, behind their hearty and friendly manner, extremely difficult to know; but, from the beginning, we all felt that Roosevelt and Marshall, in particular, were true friends of ours. When I went to bed that night, I picked up a copy of Oscar Wilde's *The Canterville Ghost*, and in it I came across his well-known remark, 'We have really everything in common with America nowadays except, of course, language.' I wished very much that that had been true. Some months later I heard the story of a Polish officer who was sent to the U.S.A. for duty, and who was told that he must learn the language before beginning his military work. After a few days, he came to his Chief in a state of frenzy and said, 'I cannot learn this language. My muscles are not right for it. My jaws are made to work up and down, but the Americans work their jaws sideways.'

The meetings between the American and British Chiefs of Staff, and between the two planning staffs, began on the 14th, and continued daily until the 23rd. Between them, I had a good many talks with Brooke and Dill. I also took a hand in drafting some of the conclusions in which we tried to consolidate common ground. Every morning early, and again in the afternoon, Brooke and I sneaked away with our field-glasses to watch birds on the shore or in the fields, and we were delighted to see a good many migrants from Europe. Harold Macmillan, who was attending the conference as Minister Resident in North Africa, chaffed us one day as we came back with our glasses round our necks, saying: '*Now* I understand why we are taking so long to get any plans made: the birds leave no time for them.'

For the first week or so, we seemed to be making no headway whatever, and Brooke became rather gloomy. Both sides stuck to their guns, and the opposing arguments were repeated *ad nauseam*. Admiral King was the strongest exponent of the Pacific strategy. He believed that merely to hold Japan was not enough and that pressure would have to be kept up if she was not to be allowed to get into such a position that it would take years to defeat her. He urged that our line should be advanced beyond the Solomons; and he declared outright that he feared the British might not be wholehearted in bearing their share of the Japanese war if it were to be left until after the defeat of Germany.

On the afternoon of the 14th, I was walking on the beach during an interval between meetings, when six big aeroplanes flew up from the south, escorted by fighters. This was the President arriving.

Next day, Churchill announced that he would join us at a meeting of the British Chiefs of Staff before luncheon. He appeared, a quarter of an hour later, carrying in his hand an unlit cigar with a match stuck in the end. I remember being surprised that he was wearing a perfectly normal light-grey tropical suit and not his zip rompers. I had become so used to seeing him in these that I had almost come to think of him as possessing no other clothes. He was in a most genial mood. He asked how we were getting on, and Brooke gave him a short account of the impasse which we had reached. Churchill advised the Chiefs of Staff not to be led into assessing the requirements for the Pacific war and then seeing what was left. If we did that, he said, it would be like carrying water from a well in a sieve—there would be nothing left when we got home. He advised them to look at all the possibilities. He said he had produced a short note on the state of the war. The situation in Tunisia was very favourable—in fact better than if we had cleared it up quickly. We had to wear the Germans down somewhere, and it was easier if they came to us and did not wait for us to go to them. This they had done in Tunisia; we should have more of them in the bag eventually than if they had not.

Dill asked if it would be possible for him to do anything to reassure the Americans about Spain, and he said he would. He added that he would not regard a German occupation of Spain as closing the door behind us in the Mediterranean. It would be a great and difficult undertaking for the Germans. And we should remember that we could protect our shipping more easily in narrow waters, like the Straits of Gibraltar, than in the open sea. His view was that we had to fight the Germans somewhere, and he did not mind whether it was in France, or Spain, or anywhere else.

He finally remarked that we should not be impatient, for in his experience negotiations like these took time. He thought that we should probably be at Casablanca another ten days.

On the morning of the 16th, I attended a meeting between Brooke, Marshall, Eisenhower and Alexander, at which we did some useful business. We arranged to change Eisenhower's plans for the coming offensive in Tunisia in such a way as to co-ordinate them with the operations of the 8th Army. At this meeting, Eisenhower remarked, 'Giraud knows no more about logistics than a dog about religion.' And, when he referred to his political difficulties with the French, Marshall said, 'I know how you feel. In my discussions with our politicians, I have found that there are more brass heads among them than brass hats among the soldiers.'

We were well primed in the political problems of North Africa—indeed the despatches sent home by Macmillan were so brilliant and so witty that there was always a competition for the files containing them as they circulated in the War Office.

When our meeting was over, I took Alexander for a walk along the shore. He was very full of his methods for training troops, and said there was nothing like repeated rehearsals for ensuring success in attacks. I had given him a copy of the plan we had drawn up in London for the invasion of Sicily, but I could not extract from him any expression of opinion as to the feasibility of the operation.

Brooke spoke well and convincingly at the Chiefs of Staff meeting that day; we felt we were making some headway and that the Americans were beginning to see the situation more clearly. We were impressed by Marshall's friendliness and honesty of purpose. We could see he required time to consider all the arguments which were being put to him, and that he would need to be thoroughly convinced before changing his mind. It was a relief to find that he was not obstinate or rigid in his strategic views.

On the 17th, however, to our great surprise, we found ourselves back where we had started. Marshall and King took up most of the day in expounding, once more, all their first ideas of the Pacific strategy, and Brooke repeated our arguments against them.

Next morning, King returned to his advocacy of a stronger strategy in the Pacific. He introduced a new argument to the effect that, if we were to suffer a disaster there, this would, in the end, draw more of our resources from the German war than he was asking for. Brooke replied effectively, maintaining that we should limit operations in the Pacific to such an extent as not to prejudice our agreed policy of defeating Germany first. The discussion went round in circles, and there was much repetition. Admiral Andrew Cunningham attended the afternoon session, and expounded the naval situation in a clear and decisive manner, which impressed the Americans favourably.

There was now a general feeling that enough steam had been blown off, and that the time had come to produce a draft statement of strategical policy to guide the course of discussion. Slessor, the Assistant Chief of the Air Staff, volunteered to have a shot at writing the draft, and completed it the same afternoon. He wrote it in sufficiently general terms to command agreement, on the assumption that we had made out our case to invade Sicily as our next major operation, and to postpone the invasion of France until the means were available. In the evening, the British and American Planning Staffs translated his note into a definite programme of items for consideration during the remaining days of the Conference.

Rather to our surprise the Chiefs of Staff, at their meeting on the following day, accepted the draft and the programme, with only a few trifling amendments. The stage was now set for some practical work on the measures to be taken in the next few months.

This sudden *volte-face* on the part of the Americans was perhaps due to a talk they had had with the President and the Prime Minister on the previous evening. We did not conceal from ourselves that the agreement which had been achieved was a short-term one only, but it was enough for the moment. No doubt Dill's quiet influence had also had a good effect. A profound friendship had grown up between him and Marshall; and, although Dill took no part in the formal discussions, the two were constantly to be seen between the meetings, walking in the grounds in deep and earnest conversation.

Long afterwards, Winn,[1] Dill's Personal Assistant, told me two things worth mentioning here. On returning from Casablanca Dill said that very soon the United States would be providing nearly two-thirds of all the material needed for the war. It would therefore be increasingly difficult for the British to claim an equal voice in our joint decisions, a situation not unlike that between us and the French at the beginning of the war. The fact that our point of view got across so often was largely due to Dill, and the immense respect and affection which he inspired in Washington.

When Winn left the United States three months after Dill's death in November 1944, he took leave of Marshall in an interview which lasted half an hour. Marshall said that now Dill was dead, he felt completely lost without him; he had never met a man of such character, integrity, breadth of vision and selflessness. 'Your Alan Brooke,' he said, 'is very good, but no one will ever take the place of Sir John; as far as I am concerned, he is irreplaceable.'

On the 19th, Giraud was invited to meet the Chiefs of Staff after tea, and I saw him for the first time—a tall, fine figure of a man with a regal manner. Speaking in French, he gave us a very clear statement of the part which he intended the French forces in Africa to play, and of his plans for reorganizing and equipping them. Marshall replied, and said that it was the intention of the Allies to supply equipment for the French as soon as ships could be found to transport it. The other Chiefs of Staff spoke in the same sense.

Up till that moment, Giraud had spoken gravely and formally, replying to each Chief of Staff in turn. Now Marshall asked Dill if he would like to say something. Dill struck the right note at once. He spoke only two sentences, saying that he was inspired by Giraud's presence, for he realized how much he had suffered for France, and that he was immensely pleased to see him back and in command of the French forces. Giraud lit up at once.

[1] Major the Hon. Reginald Winn.

'I remember Sir John Dill,' he said, 'as the distinguished Commander of the British 1st Army Corps. In the fighting in France, in 1940, he and I lived in true military brotherhood. When I was taken prisoner, I told the Germans that they had already lost the war, just as they had already lost the First War in September 1914. I told them they would never invade Britain.

'They asked me to sign a paper giving my parole. I said: "I will never sign a paper while I am in Germany. You are my jailors, I am your prisoner. It is your duty to guard me, mine to escape. Let us see which of us performs his duty best."

'It took me a year to escape.[1]

'But here I am today, among you, and head of the French armies.'

At the conclusion of this little speech, we all spontaneously clapped our hands. Then Giraud got up and with great courtesy took his leave.

I went for a walk with Dill, and we sat on a bank near the shore and discussed old times. He said that, looking back on the beginning of the war, he had been C.I.G.S. at an unlucky time. Our fortunes had been at a low ebb and he had had to fight Winston constantly. But he thought we had not made many mistakes. He did not want to stay much longer in America.

On the 20th, the Chiefs of Staff began to discuss the plans for the invasion of Sicily, and the details of other measures which had been decided in principle on the previous day. We were all becoming heartily sick of Casablanca, and we were anxious to get back to our work.

We spent the 21st in a re-examination of the plans to see if we could put them into effect more quickly. This was at Churchill's desire. But nothing came of it. I got to bed at 1.30 a.m.

On the 22nd, the Chiefs of Staff finally approved the plans for the invasion of Sicily, and resolved to press on with the preparations for opening a front in France at the earliest possible moment. Marshall spoke with great earnestness about the importance of sticking to the decisions which had been reached. He said that, when he had come to London to advocate the invasion of France, he had been put off with North Africa. If the plan for Sicily fell through, and he had to accept some lesser operation instead, he felt that someone else would have to be found to sit in his chair.

After this meeting, we all went over to the President's villa to be photographed. This was the first time I had seen Roosevelt, and

[1] Marshal Bazaine escaped from prison after the 1870 war in a somewhat similar manner to Giraud, and at the same age—sixty-three.

I was greatly taken with him. One was struck at once by his fine head and face, and his friendly and charming manner. He was sitting in a wheeled chair in a big room with french windows opening on the garden. Two attendants pushed his chair to the top of the steps leading to the lawn. Then he held up his arms and they picked him up and carried him to another chair outside. Presently Churchill arrived, smoking a cigar as usual, and the photographs were taken, after which the President pinned on General Wilbur's Congressional Medal which had been given to him in recognition of his services in the landing at Fedala.

Business was formally wound up the following day, the 23rd. During the final meeting, the news came of the fall of Tripoli. We were all glad that the conference was over. It was certainly a considerable achievement to have reached such complete agreement after two weeks of discussion, and it was, I believe, to Brooke's personality and drive that this happy result was very largely due.

In the afternoon, I motored to Fedala with Brooke, Dill and Portal, and we saw the beaches where the Americans had landed. An American officer, who had accompanied us, told us that they had had phenomenal luck with the weather, and that there had not been a day since when it could have been done.

Churchill had decided to go on to the Middle East, and, as Brooke was to accompany him, I had to go back to London to push on preparations for the plans that had been adopted. Before we left Casablanca, I destroyed a good many of the notes I had made in the course of the conference because I did not want to have anything with me in writing that would be of use to the Germans in case of a crash or a forced landing on the way home.

I motored with Leathers to the Medouina aerodrome, and we took off for Gibraltar at 2.30 p.m. in our Liberator. We flew low up the coast. It was a lovely day, with blue sky and sea. We passed over Port Lyautey, lying up a river with a nasty-looking bar, and surrounded by green cultivation dotted with little white houses. Presently we left the sandy beaches behind and passed over rocky hills. We wheeled past Tangier into the Straits, then over Ceuta lying round its little bay. For a few minutes there was some difficulty in lowering one of the wheels of our undercarriage, but presently it was got out. We circled round the Rock, and touched down on the new landing strip, where a car was waiting to take us to Government House in time for tea. Before dinner, I walked and crawled with Mason-Macfarlane, the Governor, through miles of tunnels which had been bored through the Rock since the beginning of the war.

We got out of bed at 1.30 a.m., and went down to the aerodrome, only to find that we could not take off because the weather over England was reported to be bad. On this day, I saw more tunnels, but there was also time to sit in the garden for an hour or two, and we went for a pleasant trip round the Rock in Mason-Macfarlane's launch.

De Gaulle and Catroux[1] arrived from Casablanca in the course of the day. I sat beside De Gaulle at dinner, and found him in rather low spirits. He told me that he could not go all the way to an agreement with Giraud, because he believed him to be too much compromised by his past relations with Pétain and the Vichy Government. He also said that there was no hope of setting up a French Government in North Africa—French Africa was not France. He was afraid that there was serious danger, later on, of civil war in France.

After two hours in bed, we took off at 2.15 a.m. Our course was laid a long way out to the West, and we came in to the English coast at Land's End. After a low and rather bumpy flight over Cornwall, Devon and Somerset, we were put down at Lyneham in Wiltshire.

The aircraft bringing home our Joint Planning Staff arrived a day or two later, but, while it was crossing the Bristol Channel, one of its engines caught fire; and two of our best officers, Brigadier Dykes and Brigadier Stewart, were killed in a forced landing.

[1] General Georges Catroux, Member of the French Committee of National Liberation.

30

TUNISIA ENDS; SICILY BEGINS

1943

W E had now settled down to a more or less fixed programme of offensive operations. The initiative had definitely passed from the Germans and Japanese, and our strength grew daily by leaps and bounds. The pressure of work continued to be heavy and incessant, but the interest of the strategy now lay less in London and more in the headquarters in the field. Our labours in the War Office had become more of a dull, heavy grind, and I often longed for relief from their exacting routine.

I met the Prime Minister at Paddington, when he returned a week or two later. He emerged from the train wearing his Air Commodore's uniform and smoking a cigar. I was struck by his fresh appearance—he looked quite untired.

At 5.30 p.m. on the same day—a Sunday—I attended the Cabinet in Brooke's place, as he had gone to his house in the country. The Prime Minister came into the room sucking a cigar and a toothpick. The first item on the agenda was a recommendation from the Viceroy to release Gandhi, who was then in confinement. Churchill denounced the course proposed by the Viceroy as being much too weak—Gandhi, he said, should not be released on account of a mere threat of fasting. If he were to die, we should be rid of a bad man and an enemy of the Empire. Ministers would feel much better if they made up their minds to take a strong line and face the consequences, which, he was sure, would not be serious. P. J. Grigg remarked that he had been given to understand that, when Gandhi fasted, he lived on orange juice with a good deal of glucose in it. Another Minister said that Gandhi was also rubbed with some kind of oil which was quite nutritious. 'Then,' said Churchill, 'it is apparently not a fast, but merely a change of diet. We should not be stampeded.' So Gandhi was not released, and he completed his three weeks' fast in very good order.

The Prime Minister then gave the Cabinet an account of his trip. This he did in a most amusing way. He said little or nothing about the war plans which had been settled, but he discussed the political situation in French North Africa at some length. He deprecated criticism of Peyrouton,[1] saying, 'His chief offence is that he was Home Secretary in the Vichy Government. But, after all, although it may be a misfortune to be a Home Secretary, it is not a crime.'

He spoke of Eisenhower and said: 'I do not know yet whether he is a good general or not. But I am bound to say that I have noticed that good generals do not usually have such good powers of expression as he has. I do not know what good generalship consists of—it must be some sort of sleight of hand.' It passed through my mind that Montgomery was at least one exception to Churchill's rule about powers of expression.

He told the Cabinet of the message he had received from Alexander, to the effect that he had carried out the orders given him, before Alamein, to clear the enemy out of Libya, and that he awaited further instructions.

Finally, he spoke of his visit to Marrakesh with the President, and described how he had had him carried up to the top of a tower to see the sunset over the Atlas Mountains, 'one of the most lovely sights I know in Africa'.

On 30th March, I had the experience of seeing the Prime Minister prepare a speech. At about 11 a.m., he asked me to come and see him in his room in the House of Commons. He wanted to make a statement in the House on the battle at Mareth, and he asked me to sit down and help him compose it. He walked rapidly up and down the room while he dictated, mouthing and whispering each phrase, until he was satisfied with it, before he spoke it aloud for typing. When he had finished, I suggested some alterations and additions, and he asked the typist to take a fresh sheet of paper and dictated a few extra sentences. All this had taken twenty minutes or so.

Next, he sat down, and, with his red ink stylo pen, indicated where the additional sentences were to be inserted. Then, asking the typist to retype the whole thing, he said he would like it sent after him, and went off to answer a question in the House.

Towards the end of April, Wavell came to London to discuss plans for Burma. The recent operations there had been unsatis-

[1] M. Marcel Peyrouton, Governor-General of Algeria.

factory, and, as usual, Wavell accepted full responsibility, saying that he had committed troops to battle which had been badly and insufficiently trained. I had a good many talks with him, and I attended a conference at which Churchill criticized his plans. He said they made him think of munching a porcupine quill by quill. Then, referring to the general strategy of the Japanese war, he said, 'The way to tackle an octopus is to strike at the centre, not to cut off the tentacles one by one. Have you ever read the account of the fight with the octopus in Victor Hugo's *Toilers of the Sea*? When we start bombing Japan from Russia, I will sing:

> "*Ladybird, ladybird, fly away home,*
> *Your house is on fire and your children are gone.*" '

At the beginning of May, Churchill went to Washington for another strategical conference with the Americans, whose plans and ideas were again diverging from ours. I gave Brooke a copy of Alexander's *Birds of the Ocean* to take with him, and, before he went off, he wrote me a note to thank me in which he said: 'Hope to have some birds to tell you about even if I don't succeed in defeating King and Marshall. When we get back we must have a bird film evening.'

These were delightful occasions. We dined at Brooke's flat, or at our house in Cheyne Walk, and Brooke would show us some of his films of wagtails, wrynecks, hawks or sea birds, the last taken by him in the Farne Islands. The war was completely forgotten and Brooke's enthusiasm was as delightful as his pictures were excellent. He generally brought out for our inspection some of his latest acquisitions in the way of old bird books and coloured plates. One evening, David Bannerman brought with him a bundle of George Lodge's lovely paintings for the still unpublished *Birds of Britain*, for which he was writing the letter-press.

These interludes did much to lighten our labours. And there is no doubt that Brooke's interest in ornithology played a great part in maintaining his freshness and energy, and enabling him to carry out his duties so successfully for so long. Even when things were at their most difficult and critical, he could always throw off his official cares and, at a moment's notice, and with the greatest zest, enter into a discussion of some ornithological point. I remember how once, at the end of a long and difficult conference in the War Office, he asked me to stay behind when the meeting was breaking up. When everybody had gone, he shut the door, opened a drawer in his desk, and took out a book. He handed it to me, and asked, 'Have you read this? It is most remarkable.' I looked at it. Its title was: *The Truth About the Cuckoo.*

At the end of the fighting in Tunisia, Montgomery cabled to say he would like to come home for a holiday. He arrived on the 17th May, and I met him at Northolt. His Fortress aircraft flew in, escorted by two squadrons of Polish Spitfires which were stationed at Northolt at the time.

When he stepped out of his aeroplane he chatted with the members of the American crew for a few minutes. He looked well but fine-drawn, and he told me he was a little tired. No wonder! His official photographer took some photographs, and then we drove off, to the accompaniment of cheers from the men at the R.A.F. station, who were assembled to greet him.

On the way up to London, he told me that the Fortress in which he had flown home was the one he had got from the Americans as the result of a bet he had made with Eisenhower about the date of the arrival of the 8th Army in Sfax. He was quite sure the Americans would never try to make a bargain like that with him again. He also discussed his plans for the next operations, speaking, as usual, with the greatest clarity and self-confidence. I deposited him at Claridge's, where his rooms had been booked in the name of 'Colonel Lennox', since we did not want the Germans to know he was coming before he had arrived.

Next day, at his request, we assembled the senior officers of the Canadian division, which was to be sent by sea direct to Sicily, and he gave them an exposition of the 'Husky'[1] plan. This he did in a most impressive way, explaining it all most clearly and with tremendous confidence. He repeated the important points many times—repetition had become a pronounced mannerism of his. His statement was immensely effective, and when it was completed, there could have been no doubt in anybody's mind about what was to be done. 'Of course I shall work up the soldiers,' he added at the end, 'I will give them as their battle-cry "Kill the Italians". Every man must be shouting that as he steps ashore.' I got the impression that any officer who might have come to the conference with misgivings in his mind must have left it feeling that the operation could not possibly fail.

Montgomery had arrived in his desert kit, and he continued to wear it in London—that is to say, his battle dress with a sweater

[1] The code name for the invasion of Sicily.

291

sticking out a foot below his jacket, and, of course, his usual beret bearing the Tank Corps as well as the General's badge. He was to see the King on the 18th May, and he asked me whether his dress would be all right for that. The Military Secretary made enquiries and wrote to me to say, 'He may appear in any clothes that are convenient to him.'

When Montgomery had gone, Alexander came home in turn for a few days' leave. He arrived unexpectedly, very early in the morning, and when he went to his father-in-law's house and rang the bell there was no answer—so, not wanting to disturb them, he went for a walk in the Park. His wife was told he had arrived, and presently she telephoned to the War Office to ask if anyone knew his whereabouts. Nobody did—he was still walking somewhere in the Park. He did not appear again in London except to attend a meeting of the Cabinet. There were no crowds in the street to see him as there had been for Montgomery. He would have preferred it that way.

On 5th June, the Prime Minister and Brooke returned from a trip to America and North Africa. Brooke gave me an amusing description of the talks with the Americans. They had slipped right back to the conceptions with which they had started the Casablanca Conference; they had pressed afresh for an early invasion of France, and were most unwilling to be drawn into large and unknown commitments in the Mediterranean. Marshall had said, during Brooke's visit to Algiers, that he still felt the occupation of North Africa had been a mistake, in that it had diverted our effort from Europe. A *modus operandi* had, however, been achieved and, what was more, Brooke had seen both Crossbills and Little Bustards near Algiers.

In the middle of June Wavell was appointed Viceroy. A few days before he was told about the coming change in his duties, I went with him to the India Office to discuss some points about the military set-up in India. We had a look at a draft of the instructions to be issued to a certain war organization which fell partly under the authority of the Viceroy for political direction. When we had settled our business, Wavell remarked, 'I am satisfied that the instructions will work with the present Viceroy, but I am not so sure they will be all right with his successor, whoever that may be.' A few days later, when he had been told he was to be Viceroy, we had another talk on the same subject, and also about the draft directive for the new Supreme Commander. He now took little interest in the military aspects, but was concerned only to safeguard the Viceroy's authority.

General Stilwell, who went more commonly by the name of 'Vinegar Joe', turned up in London at the end of May, on his way back from Washington to Chungking. I presided over an inter-service conference in the Cabinet Offices at which we heard his views and worked out ways and means of helping him, especially in the organization of the air route through Assam. He was a wizened, shrewd, ascetic man, with the reputation of being a difficult colleague; but we found him reasonable and easy to deal with. He told me that he was looking forward with pleasure to 'getting back to the woods', and that he did not know how we could stand the sort of life of which he had seen something at the Washington conferences. We sometimes wondered too.

I went to Scotland for a week's holiday at the beginning of July. Nothing of interest seemed to happen while I was away, except that there was some toying with the idea of starting another Peninsular War. Brooke had dealt firmly with this, and felt that we would hear no more of it. There were many reasons against it. Our hands were full enough already, and a war in Spain would have been too far away from Germany to offer quick or decisive results. There was little chance of co-operation from the Spaniards, and without it, the campaign would have been politically, and indeed militarily, impossible.

On the evening of 6th July, a day or two before the invasion of Sicily was due to take place, the Prime Minister sent for me and the Director of Military Intelligence, and we spent an hour with him at No. 10. He was in bed when we arrived at 6 p.m., but he soon appeared, in his siren suit, smoking a cigar, and looking well and fat and pink.

I had brought a map to illustrate the plan of attack on Sicily. We were to land a quarter of a million men, and the Americans a similar number. We felt the enemy would be quickly outclassed once we had got a footing on the island. When we had talked about the plan for some time, Churchill got up, and walked up and down the room. 'Well,' he said, 'even if I had the power, I would not call it off.' We did, in fact, feel considerable confidence in the 'Husky' plan; and it was reinforced by our knowledge that the Germans had swallowed our schemes for their deception. We knew they were expecting landings and attacks at a number of other points in the Mediterranean, and the two indifferent divisions stationed in Sicily had not been reinforced.

After a time, Churchill sat down between us again, and said, 'I see that, on this map of yours, Syracuse is printed "Syracusa". I do not like it. You should change it, or the B.B.C. will be getting hold of it.'

By 13th July, three days after the first landings, our forces were well established in Sicily. Brooke was immensely relieved that the operation had started successfully. 'Of course,' he said, 'the thing is not over yet, but the prospects are good.' For the last month, Sicily, had been weighing rather heavily upon him; he had felt the responsibility particularly because Sicily was, to a great extent, his idea. He had stuck to it in spite of doubts on the part of the Prime Minister, and in face of considerable opposition from the other two Chiefs of Staff and, of course, from the Americans. It is fair to say that the decision to occupy Sicily would never have been taken but for Brooke's consistent advocacy. Even Cunningham had opposed it, and had said to me at Casablanca that the operation would be impossible from the naval point of view; his instinct was to take Sardinia instead. Brooke had over-ruled the Planning Staff twice, once before leaving London and once at Casablanca itself.

We discussed the possibilities of exploitation. We came to the conclusion that the Germans would be likely to regard the Balkans as more important to hold, from their point of view, than Italy, and that they had not enough forces to defend both.

The success in Sicily inflamed Churchill, and he immediately began to press for bold action to follow it up and bring about the fall of Italy. He sent a note to the Chiefs of Staff in which he gave his view that we should not 'crawl up the leg of Italy like a harvest bug, but strike boldly at the knee', the knee being Rome. He added as a postscript, 'There is a tide in the affairs of men, etc.'

These sentiments were admirable, but to translate them into action was not easy, or indeed possible. The provision of shipping and of air cover for distant landings were the main difficulties. We spent a great deal of time examining the possibilities of getting ashore about Naples and Rome, but nothing much came of it. We thought, in the end, that a landing near Naples would be too much of a gamble with the Navy and with our limited stocks of landing craft. If the gamble had failed, our operations in the Mediterranean would have been brought to a standstill for months. We judged it better strategy to stick to our plans for crossing from Sicily to the toe and heel of Italy.

Landings on the west coast of Italy could only be done with the full support of the Americans. This entailed persuading them to let us use resources earmarked for France and Burma; and these resources were due to leave the Mediterranean now, if the operations in France and Burma were to be mounted up to schedule.

This aspect of the situation was discussed at a meeting of the Chiefs of Staff in the middle of July, and Churchill was reported to have said, 'It is true, I suppose, that the Americans consider we have led them up the garden path in the Mediterranean—but what a beautiful path it has proved to be. They have picked peaches here, nectarines there. How grateful they should be!'

On the 23rd July, Churchill telephoned to me for details of our casualties in Sicily. I got these from the Adjutant-General's statisticians and read them to him over the telephone. When I came to the total, which I had not bothered to check, he said at once, 'No, that is not right—it is a thousand out.' I added up the figures and, sure enough, the statisticians were wrong and he was right.

31

PLANNING FOR ITALY

1943

On the 25th July, Mussolini resigned, and all our appreciations and plans had to be considered afresh. The most immediate needs were to draw up the military conditions for an armistice and to assess the strength of the forces we would need in Italy. It looked as if the Germans would attempt to maintain a line about Ravenna and Pisa after the Italians had dropped out of the war. We calculated that they might be able to spare for Italy some 13 divisions at least, and 18 at most. If 4 or 5 of these were stationed on their lines of communication, there would still be left about a dozen for active operations. It therefore seemed that we and the Americans should be prepared to provide 16 divisions.

When I discussed this with Brooke, he said he would like me to add 6 more to my estimate, making 22 in all. He did not want to take any chances, and he reminded me that 22 divisions had been found necessary in Tunisia where the front had been about the same length, namely 100 miles. Moreover, we had to allow for the fact that Italy was closer to Germany than Tunisia and could therefore be more quickly reinforced by the enemy. This full complement of 22 divisions could only be found if we could persuade the Americans to let us retain in Italy 7 which were earmarked for Britain in the autumn; these were intended to form part of the invasion forces for France.

We also discussed the advisability of advancing our line to the Italian frontier along the Alps if the Germans elected to evacuate Italy altogether. It was doubtful whether such an advance would be to our advantage. The frontier line would be a much longer one to man than the line across the neck of the peninsula, and would absorb greater forces than the Americans would be willing to provide. The distance our aircraft would have to fly to reach Germany would certainly be less, but this would be offset by the steep climb which would be necessary if they flew from air bases close under the Alps.

Our conclusion was that it would be best not to go north of the Apennines. In fact, we were counting our chickens before they were hatched, and the situation never materialized.

As we proceeded with our calculations and plans after Mussolini's fall, there was a good deal of speculation as to the effect that Italy's collapse might have on the Germans. Many people felt it was legitimate at least to hope that the war might end before the winter was over. This hope might indeed have been fulfilled if the plot against Hitler, of which we knew nothing at the time, had succeeded. Brooke did not share the optimism. He remarked to me that his dates were: Italy 1943, Germany 1944, and Japan 1945.

I made a note on 1st August about Churchill:

'He is far better than before, from our point of view. He towers above all others in vigour, drive and in his grasp of the situation. Brooke is very good with him. He has had some late sittings with the Chiefs of Staff, the usual hour for meetings to assemble now being 10.30 p.m.

Last week, he held a meeting, a sort of indignation meeting, to discuss telegrams from India which pointed out, quite rightly, the impossibility of extensive operations in Burma till after the monsoon. The fact of the matter is that nothing big can be done from India till Germany is finished. But he urged that we should try an operation against Sumatra and Malaya.'

Brooke told me that he was very angry when Winston accused the Chiefs of Staff of having opposed his wishes in the matter of Madagascar and again in Sicily. Brooke replied that, on the contrary, the Chiefs of Staff had advised in favour of both enterprises, and now, having considered the problem in precisely the same way, they were advising against a premature attempt in the Far East.

At the beginning of August, some films of the Sicily landings were shown to us in the War Office. Montgomery's appearances were rather theatrical, for which he came in for a good deal of criticism in London. One day in my Club I listened to a broadcast speech in which he said that some operation or other would be successfully accomplished 'with the help of God'. A member sitting near me interjected, 'Well, Monty has at last mentioned the Almighty in despatches.' Some of his more old-fashioned critics in London tended to overlook the salient point about Montgomery: that he could win battles.

Our occupation of Sicily was completed by the third week of August, and Eisenhower had already sent us his plans for crossing the Straits of Messina. It was now quite clear that the Germans did not intend to carry out a strategic withdrawal in Italy, where according to our reckoning they had about 13 divisions.

In Washington, plans were taking shape for operations in the Mediterranean and from the United Kingdom. We thought them too ambitious and unrelated to the means available. We agreed with the Americans as to what was desirable, but not as to what was practicable. We hoped that our differences of opinion would be resolved at the Quebec Conference, which took place in the second week of August.

On 29th August, I went to Victoria station to meet Brooke, who had returned with Portal a week before the Prime Minister. Brooke said he had had a very difficult time, especially with Churchill, who had been in one of his worst moods for the greater part of the trip. Portal stepped out of the train with a fishing rod under his arm, and we waited for a few minutes on the platform to see that some boxes containing salmon were put in the cars.

Next day Brooke came to the War Office. I spent a couple of hours with him to tell him what had happened while he had been away and to obtain his decisions on some outstanding points. We went through Eisenhower's plans for the landing in the toe of Italy and for the proposed landing near Naples. These plans had been sent to us in an extremely sketchy form. But, under the system of command from Washington which had now been adopted, there was little we could do to criticize or change them. No proper appreciation of the situation had been communicated to us, and we were unable to form any opinion of the prospects of success. The landing in the toe of Italy was to be on 2nd or 3rd September, and that at Naples between 7th and 12th September.

We discussed the conclusions reached in the Quebec Conference. I said I thought they were satisfactory, in that they left most of the bigger issues to be settled in the light of future developments. Brooke said his greatest difficulty in his talks with the Americans had been their strong desire to stick to the letter of agreements made months before, in spite of the fact that the basis on which they rested had completely disappeared owing to the course the war had taken. For example, they had insisted on bringing 7 divisions from the Mediterranean to the United Kingdom in the autumn. When he had argued in Quebec that these might be required for Italy, the Americans had obviously suspected that we did not intend to invade

France in the spring of 1944. In the end, he had accused the American Chiefs of Staff of distrusting the British Chiefs of Staff. Then it had come out that the reason for their distrust was something that Churchill had said to Stimson in London, which had made things very difficult for Brooke. In the end, Brooke had had to agree, against his will, that the 7 divisions should duly come to England— 3 British and 4 American.

I said I felt the Italian problem would solve itself, and that, if the 7 Divisions were found to be necessary in Italy, they would stay in the Mediterranean. I reminded him that, when Foch was asked, in 1914, how many British soldiers would be required in France, he had answered, 'One—and I will see that he is killed.'

Churchill had been extremely trying when possible operations against the Japanese from India had been discussed, and he had also embarrassed the Chiefs of Staff considerably by independent talks with Mountbatten and Wingate. Brooke added, with a laugh, that, after all these irritations, the crowning episode had been when he had been warned off his beat, while fishing for trout, in order to make way for the Prime Minister, who had then proceeded to lose a good fish through his line being too slack.

He did not mention the subject, but I felt pretty sure that he was disappointed in not being given the command of 'Overlord'. He was obviously very tired, and rather depressed. I was glad when he decided to go off for a week's leave in the country.

It was now quite clear that we were not to have our way in the Mediterranean. Brooke had attributed his difficulties in Quebec to the desire of the Americans to stick to the letter of agreement; but there was a more fundamental reason for our differences. American opinion on the landing in France in 1944 was, without a shadow of doubt, 'harder' than ours, and nothing that Churchill or Brooke had said could shake them on this point. The decisions taken at Quebec meant that the forthcoming campaign in Italy would be starved, and that our plans for action in the Aegean and the Balkans would come to nothing. There would also be little support for Turkey if she decided to enter the war. Less was to be done in the Mediterranean and in Italy than we in London had wished to do. On the other hand, what remained of the Mediterranean (and Italian) programme was more than the Americans would have undertaken had we not brought pressure to bear on them.

We now settled down to make a success of the compromise which had been reached. We in London felt that we had made a strategical error in the relaxation of our effort in the Mediterranean;

and we occasionally indulged in regretful speculation when operations stuck in Italy for lack of strength. But this did not affect the
strict observance of the decisions reached at Quebec.

Although the Quebec decisions satisfied no one entirely at the
time, they were probably the best possible for the successful prose-
cution of the war at that stage. It would have been a mistake not to
continue the Italian campaign, for there was no other way open to
us, in the coming winter of 1943–1944, of engaging the Germans on
land in any appreciable strength and of drawing reserves from the
Russian front. We could almost certainly have occupied the whole
of Italy quite quickly had we devoted more of our resources to the
effort. It would have been comparatively simple to land forces from
the sea behind the Germans at successive points on the west coast. But
this could hardly have been done without either postponing the
landing in France, or reducing the scale of operations in the Pacific
against the Japanese. It will always be a question for argument
whether the course adopted in August 1943 was the best for
finishing the war quickly. But the conflicting opinions of the Allies
had been resolved, by friendly discussion at Quebec, into a vigorous
and successful policy, which did not suffer from the weaknesses
which so often characterize warfare waged by coalitions.

On 1st September, Eisenhower sent us details of his plan for
the advance on Naples. We felt that the proposed 'build-up' of the
forces after the initial landings was painfully and, perhaps, dangerously slow; we would have liked to see the operation mounted in
greater strength. But time was too short to criticize or alter the
arrangements, particularly so now that the channel of control was
through Washington. It could also be argued with some force that
the taking of risks was justified at that moment, when Badoglio's
Government was about to sign an armistice.

In the end the operations succeeded by a narrow margin, and
Naples was occupied a month later, on 1st October. The limitation
of the resources allotted to Italy was not felt in this opening stage of
the campaign, but only because the German command decided not
to fight seriously in the extreme south. Montgomery, not realizing
this, had disembarked under a heavy barrage although his landing
was unopposed. We believed the difficulties at Salerno were due
merely to bad planning at Eisenhower's headquarters.

We were now turning our attention, more and more, to preparing for the invasion of France. Our forecast in September was
that 40 British and American divisions would be concentrated in
Great Britain by May 1944, of which 28 would be ready for operations

and 12 in process of equipping and training. This meant that the number of operational divisions in England would be doubled in the next six months. There was a great deal of leeway to be made up in the provision of landing craft and other special equipment. But all the arrangements now moved forward smoothly.

Brooke came back to the War Office on 13th September, still rather tired and depressed. But a fortnight later he had regained his usual spirits, and on 26th September he confided to me the nature of his most difficult problem: he was unable to identify some of the birds in the volumes of Levaillant he had acquired, for lack of a proper French dictionary of archaic bird names.

On 15th September, Churchill was on his way back from America fulminating over the setbacks at Salerno, and sending us broadsides of questions by wireless about the general situation, which took a great deal of time to answer. Soon after his return, in accordance with the usual routine, he sent to the War Office a draft of the speech he had prepared for delivery in the House of Commons on the following day. It was the practice for the draft to be passed round the various sections of my staff for comments, and I used to strike out most of them as being too trivial for the Prime Minister. This time I happened to be out of London, and all the comments went un-winnowed to the C.I.G.S.'s Secretary, who conscientiously tele-phoned the lot to No. 10. When Churchill saw them, he sent a message to Brooke that he would like to see *all* the officers who had criticized his speech, at No. 10, after dinner. Brooke explained to him that it would be impossible to collect them all, as many of them would have gone home for the night, but he said he would come to No. 10 himself after dinner. This he did, and Churchill kept him up till 2 a.m. going over the whole text of his speech.

Carton de Wiart had turned up in London, and he came to see me several times in the War Office. Having been taken prisoner in 1941, when his aircraft made a forced landing in Sicily, he had now been sent out through Lisbon with the Italian emissaries, to help negotiate an armistice. The Italians told him he must travel in plain clothes. He said he hadn't any. So they produced a tailor, who made him a very good suit and a silk shirt, within 24 hours, and charged him nothing, which pleased him very much. He told me he had found it very boring to be shut up for so long with nobody but generals and air marshals for company; the only periods of his imprisonment he had really enjoyed were those spent in solitary confinement, to which he had been condemned more than once.

Wingate lunched with my wife and me one day while he was in London. He was certainly a man of great character, and an entrancing talker. He told us about his experiences in Burma. He had taught his men to eat pythons, which, he said, tasted like boiled chicken. He thought his men kept fit chiefly because they knew they would fall into the hands of the Japanese if they failed to do so. He allowed no such 'nonsense' as refusing to eat meat out of tins, which had been damaged; if a man caught typhoid in such a way, it was really a psychological failure. Soon after his return to India however, he himself was seriously ill with typhoid. Churchill ordered that details of his condition should be cabled to London in order that Lord Moran might telegraph back instructions about his medical treatment.

I never had to do any serious business with Wingate, because his technique was to deal with Churchill direct. We appreciated his courage and his enterprising spirit, but we never felt that his operations behind the Japanese lines had or could have any real effect on the course of the campaign in Burma. His activities seemed to us to be similar to Lawrence's in Arabia in the First War— picturesque but not very important. But it must at least be admitted that his exploits added a touch of colour and romance to a very drab war in Burma.

32

STRATEGY FOR EUROPE, AND THE
WISDOM OF SMUTS

1943

We carried out a rather odd exercise called 'Starkey' in the latter part of August and the beginning of September. It was in some measure a rehearsal of the arrangements for moving troops to embarkation points for crossing the Channel, but its main object was to deceive the Germans into thinking that a serious operation was intended and so to prevent them from moving troops out of France to Russia or Italy, and to bring about an air battle over the Channel. The Germans did not, however, take the demonstration seriously; they continued to move troops out of France while it was in progress, and there was no reaction in the air.

On the evening of 8th September, I motored down to Folkestone, with two friends from the War Office, to see the final phase of 'Starkey'. We dined at the Queen's Hotel, and then walked to the end of the pier. It was a lovely moonlight night, and calm. We could see the flash of bombs being dropped by our aircraft on the French coast, and leaflets which showed up like fireworks in the beams of the German searchlights. The German anti-aircraft guns were shooting, and shells were bursting high in the distance. When we went to bed we were disturbed for an hour or so by air-raid alarms and by the firing of our guns but, after midnight, all became quiet and we slept well.

Next morning (9th September), we got up at 6 o'clock and went up to the top of a hill near the town. It was calm and rather hazy. Some 450 ships and landing craft were taking part in the final demonstration, with orders to sail to within 10 miles of the French coast, and we could see some of them. But there was no reaction whatever from the Germans. It is true that we had jammed their

radio-location apparatus and that they did little or no air reconnaissance. But it seemed clear that they had recognized the whole
business as a bluff.

After breakfast we motored to Dungeness, but all was still quiet.
At Dover Castle we watched some of the troops carrying out
embarkation drill, and saw something of the excellent staff
work. Then, after lunching off Dover soles, we motored back to
London.

In the general business of the war, it now seemed almost too
good to be true that the initiative had passed so completely into our
hands, and that nothing ever went wrong with our operations. The
only thing needed to make us quite happy was an improvement in
our relations with the Russians. Everybody was in good spirits.
Work was as hard as ever, and a good deal of it was now beginning
to be concerned with commitments which were likely to arise after
the Germans had collapsed.

Among the plans we had on the stocks was one for the occupation of Germany. We had to make some sort of estimate of the
forces needed for this purpose after the fighting stopped. An
argument was advanced that it would be more economical to use
air forces rather than soldiers for the occupation of Germany. But
this idea was soon abandoned: it was obvious that the quelling of
disorders by indiscriminate bombing would be too inhuman to be
permitted, in peace conditions, by either the British or the American
Government. Bombing would, moreover, have been ineffective.
The theory of occupation by air forces had been demonstrated to be
false before the war when the British Government had given it a
trial in Palestine. But memories were short, and the failure there had
already been forgotten by many people in authority.

Apart from the occupation of Germany, we should have two
other main commitments after the end of the war in Europe. The
first obviously would be the reinforcement of the Japanese theatre;
the second, the satisfaction, to whatever extent the Government
might decide, of the numerous requests from the Foreign Office for
keeping order, supervising elections, preventing civil war, and so
on, in a great many foreign states. Tentative plans began to take
shape as we worked away at these problems with the Americans.

Another matter which we began to turn over in our minds was
the strength of the forces which we should retain in peace-time. To
us there seemed to be only one great power who could be regarded
as the possible enemy: Russia. From this arose the question of what
side Germany might take in a future war if the Russians were to

cling to their half of Germany after the war was over. These ideas were not communicated to the Cabinet at this time, but when it became known, a few months later, that we were thinking along these lines, we received a stern rebuke, and were told to desist from mentioning possible tension with Russia, or from taking Russia into our calculations as a potential enemy.

The rest of 1943 was marked by growing differences of opinion between the Americans and ourselves as to future policy in the Mediterranean. Had we had our way, I think there can be little doubt that the invasion of France would not have been done in 1944. There has been some dispute since the war as to the conflict of opinion between us and the Americans on this major point of strategy. I have not kept copies of the official correspondence which passed on the subject; but perhaps the whole atmosphere of those last two or three months of 1943 is best recalled by reproducing notes made at the time.

'13*th October*, 1943. Returned from leave 8 October. All the week I was away Winston was agitating for an attack on Rhodes. C.I.G.S. argued in vain that we had resources sufficient only for Italy, and that we must not divert forces to the Aegean. The Germans have 19 divisions in Italy, and show signs of fighting harder than we expected in central Italy. They could maintain bigger forces in Italy if they could spare them, and we cannot be sure they will not scrape up further divisions, in which case we might well be forced to send more troops out from home, or stop the movement home of the 7 divisions (3 British, 4 American) during the coming winter.

On Saturday 9th October the P.M. had actually decided to go to Tunis with C.I.G.S. to discuss with Commanders-in-Chief ways and means of mounting an attack on Rhodes, provided Marshall could come across from the United States. Luckily, Eisenhower, after a conference with Andrew Cunningham, Alexander and Jumbo Wilson, cabled to say that it would be impossible to find the forces, and the project has now fallen through. It does seem amazing that the P.M. should spend practically a whole week on forcing forward his ideas about taking an island in the face of all military advice.

Jumbo Wilson chanced his arm in occupying Cos and other Aegean Islands. But this was a justifiable risk. The Germans suffered heavy losses in shipping, etc. It now remains to be seen whether we can hang on to the other islands. Jumbo is being given a free hand as to whether he should withdraw or not.

C.I.G.S. is in very good form in spite of many wearing and useless debates with Winston.

The occupation of the Azores was announced yesterday and seems to have gone off quietly.

14th October. Very peaceful today—a lull in the strategical centre at No. 10.

It has now been settled that I should become Assistant C.I.G.S. (Operations) with the duty of co-ordinating and controlling the directorates of Operations, Intelligence, Plans, Post-Hostilities Plans, and Survey (Maps). This, in fact, is practically what has been done by me as D.M.O. for the past three years—a slightly smarter name, no extra pay, though!

21st October. The war goes very well. The Russians seem to be breaking through on the Dnieper, where they have established a substantial bridgehead. If their advance continues, the Germans will have difficulty in getting out in the south, and will probably have to give up the Crimea and go back to the Bug.

In Italy the momentum of our advance has slowed down, and, although the Germans are falling back from the Volturno to their next position, they show signs of fighting toughly in the difficult hill country to the North. However, they are having much trouble in the Balkans and show no signs of being able to increase their concentration or effort in Italy in the near future. If they could spare more forces, they would undoubtedly wish to launch a counter-offensive.

Alexander cabled to the C.I.G.S. last Sunday asking that I should go out and discuss his difficulties with him. He wants more landing craft so as to be able to land a force behind the Germans. We cabled back that his situation did not take us by surprise, that we had never been under any illusions as to the problem before him, and that our difficulty all along had been to persuade the Americans that our commitment in Italy would be a heavy one. C.I.G.S. said he would gladly send me or, indeed, go himself if he thought it would help, but he feared that any opinion from our side would be suspected by the Americans who seemed to have an ineradicable impression that our hearts were not in Overlord and that we took any opportunity of diverting to the Mediterranean, resources which they considered should be concentrated in Great Britain. C.I.G.S. added, as the most effective line of action, the suggestion that Alexander should send a plain and outspoken appeciation to Eisenhower and ask him to send it on to the Combined Chiefs of Staff.

Today my personal assistant handed me a note as follows:

"D.M.O.

With reference to this morning's C.I.G.S. Summary, the Private Secretary to the Prime Minister telephoned this afternoon to point out two little discrepancies upon which the P.M. had commented:—

(1) 'CALVI' was spelt wrong.
(2) The word 'further' was used; the P.M. says that when it is a question of distance the correct word is 'farther'.

(Sgd). W. R. V. ISAAC
Lieut.-Colonel,
P.A. to D.M.O."

There is still a very distinct cleavage of opinion between us and the Americans as to the correct strategy in Europe. C.I.G.S. feels very strongly that we should exploit the openings in the Mediterranean and extend the range of our offensive operations to the Aegean and the Balkans. The Germans are sitting on a volcano in the Balkans, and we could start an eruption if we had the forces to spare.

The P.M. has come round to this point of view too, and has just said he would like to tackle the Americans again upon it, but I must say I see no chance of converting them—especially in view of Marshall's impending appointment for Overlord. [Note: We thought at this time that he was to be Supreme Commander.] I think, however, it does not matter very much because the chances of the Boche being still on his legs next spring are becoming more and more remote.

We have concluded our exhaustive staff studies of possibilities in the S.E. Asian command. The big over-riding fact there is that nothing considerable can be done till the German war is over. We are telling the Americans what we propose to do in the next campaigning season, with the limited forces available.

Dudley Pound died today, and is universally mourned. I have had much to do with him and have never known him other than kind, imperturbable, humorous, and extremely sound on all naval problems. He never looked much beyond the naval aspect of things.

Brooke is pursuing his studies of African birds. He told me the other day that he had found an unknown Roller in Levaillant —he thinks it must have been painted from a composite skin made up from several different birds. Levaillant, apparently, often renamed birds according to his own whim. I have arranged with Colonel Kreft, the South African military representative in London, to get Brooke a copy of Roberts' *Birds of South Africa*.

We have had small air raids every night for the last week or so—not much damage but a good deal of noise. A flat in Kensington quite near us was hit the night before last and seventeen people killed.

28th October. I had a talk with C.I.G.S. about Leros and Samos. I said I considered the price we were paying was too great (it included half a dozen cruisers and destroyers sunk or damaged). The Germans have air command and there is no immediate prospect of our being able to release further air forces to support the garrisons, nor of our being able to extend our occupation of the islands, owing to the demands of the Italian theatre. On the other side of the balance sheet is the damage we have done the Germans in sinking ships, drowning their men, and shooting down their aircraft, and in containing these German forces in the Aegean and alarming the enemy and inducing him to believe further operations are pending, which, of course, ties up considerable forces farther afield in the Aegean and in the Balkans. But, on balance, I thought we should come out, if it was not already too late. C.I.G.S. agreed, but, in the discussion at the Chiefs of Staff meeting, sentiment moved the other way, and it was decided to hang on. I think the Middle East Command has made an error of judgment in hanging on so long—they had a free hand given them a fortnight ago.

The P.M. has taken a strong line with the Americans on the Mediterranean versus Overlord strategy. As he says, it is no use planning for defeat in the field (i.e. in Italy) in order to give temporary political satisfaction. All this will mean a meeting in the near future with the American Chiefs of Staff and, if we carry our point, a postponement of Overlord.

31st October. During the past week matters have moved steadily to a head with regard to the divergence of view on future strategy between us and the Americans. Alexander has sent in his appreciation of developments in Italy from which it is clear that:

(a) his immediate advance on Rome is being slowed up for lack of landing craft to mount amphibious attacks round the German flanks, and

(b) his later operations may well demand, not only more shipping and landing craft, but more troops.

This we foresaw months ago, but the Americans would not see it. The trouble is that, if we give Alexander what he wants, and if we allot further resources for operations in the Aegean and the Balkans, as we should do to take full advantage of the situation, Overlord must perforce be postponed. The Americans take the view that this is a breach of contract and almost dishonourable.

The impasse arises from the fundamental difference in the British and American points of view as to what is possible in a combined operation. A study of history shows that, when combined operations have failed, they have failed generally from slowness in "build-up" on the part of the attacker. Otherwise, when well planned and well executed, they have generally succeeded.

We have examined the possible build-up in France most carefully, and we have now arrived at a fairly sound estimate of what the Germans should be able to do in certain conditions of pressure from Russia and from the Mediterranean. Unless these conditions are satisfied, the attack on France cannot be launched.

But another point is that we have never yet carried out a successful combined operation in face of strong opposition *on the beaches*. (In Sicily and at Salerno we were not strongly opposed.) In France we may expect such opposition. A demonstration of a landing, which was carried out last week at Studland, shows that we have a very long way to go in development and use of means of effecting a landing in such conditions.

All this is not realized by the Americans. It is true, I think, to say that we have a far more realistic idea of the operational problem with which a commander is faced than they have. [Note added in 1951: The truth is, of course, that, at this time, neither we nor the Americans could possibly know the perfect solution to these problems. Between us, we eventually hammered out a solution that worked. But, looking back on it now, I think it is only fair to say that the Americans were probably more nearly right than we were in this particular matter.]

For instance, Eisenhower, when he was here, was full of confidence about taking on the French operation. When he was faced with North Africa, he became far less confident. When faced with Sicily on the spot, with complete command of the air and the sea, he reported that he could not take it on if there were more than two German divisions in the island.

The Americans rely far more than we do on the effect of overwhelming air power. They think that it can prevent the enemy from concentrating fast, and that it will enable us to subdue strong coast defences. These ideas are illusory, in the light of experience up to date. Air power has never yet in this war interfered seriously with the Germans' power to move their armies. In Sicily, overwhelming air power did not prevent the Germans from withdrawing practically their whole force from the island.

This is the difficulty. In Washington, I believe, ideas are too theoretical, and there is a lack of operational experience and a sense of reality.

In the end, I suppose we shall probably go into France, with little opposition, and then the historians will say that we missed glorious opportunities a year earlier.

That the Germans are resisting so strongly in Italy shows what importance they attach to keeping us off the Rome airfields. If we get our long-range bombers there soon, it will be a devastating blow, and may well bring about a complete collapse.

Winston has been very good on some things. He is handling the change of view in our strategy, as set out above, with supreme skill in putting it to the President and Stalin. Telegrams and minutes flutter out from No. 10 to the Chiefs of Staff and Commanders-in-Chief. Nothing is too small for him.

3rd November. Many rumours of internal unrest in Germany. Continued Russian successes, and the Crimea now cut off. It looks more and more likely that the Germans may crack up within a fairly short time.

In the meantime, we have to reckon with the situation that might arise if the Germans shortened their line in Russia and withdrew troops from Western Europe during the winter (when invasion by us is unlikely), and then made a heavy counter-attack upon us in Italy. We have been working on an appreciation of this, and it seems clear that we should at least have more landing craft in the Mediterranean. We cannot have these without postponing the always problematical Overlord. This we want to do, and the Americans don't. All this must be thrashed out at another conference quite soon.

The Aegean business still drags on. If we cannot get airfields from the Turks, we should come out of Leros and Samos, but the state of the moon prevents an evacuation till the last week of November. In the meantime, the problem may be solved by a successful German attack on the islands. It started as a legitimate gamble, but now there is a great danger of throwing good money after bad. The P.M. has had the bit between his teeth in all this, and it is probably true to say that it is due to him that the island occupation has been pushed so far, and that we have hung on so long.

Yesterday, Laycock[1] gave my meeting of Dominion officers a talk on the Salerno operation at which he was present. He had fallen into the rather common error of attributing our success to our air superiority and our naval bombardment. I reminded the meeting that there were two other important factors, viz., the tenacity of our own troops and the blunders of the Germans. If the Germans had employed all the forces within reach, instead of dispersing to watch the coast and to oppose Montgomery, we should have been back in the sea, in spite of the efforts of the air force and the navy.

One night in November, we dined with the Walter Elliots, and the conversation turned to the blessings and evils of a prolonged period of peace. A day or two later, someone drew my attention to Ruskin's dictum upon this subject as recorded in *The Crown of Wild Olive*—

"We talk of peace and learning, and of peace and plenty, and of peace and civilization; but I found that those were not the words which the Muse of History coupled together: That on her lips, the words were—peace and sensuality, peace and selfishness, peace and corruption, peace and death. I found in brief, that all great nations learned their truth of word, and strength of thought, in war, that they were nourished in war, and wasted by peace; taught by war, and deceived by peace; trained by war, and betrayed by peace; in a word, that they were born in war, and expired in peace."

7th November. Lunched today at White's with Stuart Menzies. When he went to see the P.M., in bed one morning recently,

---

[1] Major-General R. E. (later Sir Robert) Laycock became Chief of Combined Operations in succession to Mountbatten, when the latter went as Supreme Commander to S.E. Asia in the autumn of 1943.

Winston said, "Now I do not wish you to talk this morning—you will understand the reason presently. There has been a serious leakage of information from the Cabinet." At this moment the P.M.'s big Persian cat leapt up to the windowsill. "Now," said Winston, "you see it is as I thought—my cat is signalling with his tail to the pelicans in the Park."

About the middle of November. We had an interesting discussion the other day, on a suggestion of Leahy's[1] that the new Supreme Commander (who it is thought will be Marshall) should control the whole land and air war against Germany in Europe, on the grounds that co-ordination could be exercised efficiently only by one man commanding both the Mediterranean and Western fronts, that the air offensive had as its main object to lead up to the attack by land through France, etc.

I gave this note on the subject to C.I.G.S.:

> The issue raised in this telegram and the telegram on control of the air forces is a fundamental one which can be settled only by the Prime Minister and President. What the Americans are asking for is in fact almost complete control of war against Germany on land and in the air. It would be impossible for the Government of this country to surrender its responsibilities to this extent. The system proposed by the Americans would set the Commander-in-Chief for Europe over the Chiefs of Staff, which is an impossible situation.
>
> It seems useless to go further with the discussion of the directive on the Chiefs of Staff level until the big issue has been cleared up.

Brooke agreed that this must be our line. Winston cabled to Dill to say that there would be an explosion if he were to propose such a thing, but this he would not do while he held his present office. Dill cabled back immediately that Leahy had dropped the idea. This is rather an interesting illustration of the place where the line must be drawn between the authority of the Commander-in-Chief and that of his Government.

We have now crystallized our ideas as to the strategy to be advocated in the coming conference. The main points are—to continue the offensive in Italy, to increase the flow of supplies to partisans in the Balkans, to bring about an upheaval by inducing the Balkan powers to break away from Germany, to induce Turkey to enter the war, and to accept a postponement of Over-

[1] Fleet Admiral W. D. Leahy, Chairman of U.S. Chiefs of Staff.

lord. All these proposals have been worked out in a fair amount of detail here, and the stage is now set for the discussions.

17th November. Leros was lost today after four days of stiff fighting, in which our men conducted themselves with determination and gallantry. The whole business was a gamble, at first legitimate. . . . When it became apparent the gamble was not going to come off it was wrong to throw good money after bad. . . . Wilson said the moon made evacuation difficult till after 26th November, but, as it was possible to send in so many reinforcements, it should have been possible to evacuate. The P.M. pressed the whole scheme most ardently. . . . This is a good example of the price we have to pay occasionally for Winston's confidence in his own military judgment.

Brooke got off last night (for Cairo and Teheran) after being delayed by weather for 48 hours. The conference will be a difficult one. The Americans seem to think we have acted in an almost underhand way over the Mediterranean. . . . This is curious because we have felt almost the same about them. Brooke feels that the war may have been lengthened by as much as six months by the American failure to realize the value of exploiting the whole Mediterranean situation. . . . The time has come for plain speaking on both sides.

22nd November. Lunched at the Ritz with a French party. . . . De Lattre de Tassigny[1] held forth in impassioned terms about the power of Germany. . . . He believed that the Germans would not be overcome till the troops of the Allies had trodden them underfoot *in* Germany, that Hitler would continue his Wagnerian career and finally go up like a volcano, perhaps in self-immolation, at Berchtesgaden. He did not believe that the war could be finished by next spring. . . . I still believe that the Germans will crack before they are finally hemmed in, within Germany, because I do not believe that Hitler will be able to control them, in their vast numbers, to the extent that D. L. de T. thinks.

Mathenet[2] quoted Joffre's maxim for the great leader, "*De ne rien faire, de faire tout faire, de ne rien laisser faire.*"

29th November. We expected a good deal of criticism of the Kos and Leros operations in the debate on the Address. So we gave Attlee a carefully prepared statement, making the best of it, and provided Grigg with a full dossier as he expected that he would have to wind up the debate. Grigg asked me to go down

[1] The French General who later commanded the French Forces in 'Anvil.'
[2] General Mathenet was Head of the Free French Mission in London.

to the House to hear the debate and advise him on his reply. So I went down after lunch and sat behind the Speaker's chair. Attlee's statement was accepted quietly, and, in spite of a few criticisms, it was soon obvious that little interest was taken in the operations and that the attention of the House was concentrated upon other subjects. After an hour, Grigg said it was not worth while waiting and I went off.

10th December. We have now identified over a hundred possible sites in North France for the German secret weapon which is being propaganded by the Nazis. The evidence seems to point fairly definitely to pilotless aircraft, and we are actively working out ways and means of countering them.

The minutes of the Teheran Conference reached us yesterday. . . . The Russians and Americans have had their way. Time will show whether this is justified. . . . The conclusions can hardly be accepted without reservations, and rightly so, for it is impossible to predict, months ahead, whether the circumstances will justify an operation which depends for its success on the strength and disposition of the enemy when the time comes. Even so, the conclusions have hardened our strategical policy and have committed us, more deeply than before, to courses of action which, it is true to say, we should not have adopted had the conduct of the war been entirely in our hands. It is not at all impossible that these courses will prove to be right. . . . We will certainly put our whole effort into making a success of them. For this, present plans will require much strengthening.'

Of course, we soon heard a good deal of gossip about the Teheran Conference, which I will not attempt to set down, except only for this story told to me later on by Martel, who attended in his capacity as head of our Moscow Military Mission. In the course of his speech at an official banquet, Stalin referred to his 'good friend, Mr. Churchill', and added, 'I hope I may call him my good friend.' At this, Churchill was heard to mutter, 'Yes, you may call me "Winston" if you like—I always call you "Joe" when you aren't there.' Then, when Churchill made his speech, he referred to the great decisions that had been taken, how these decisions would now be translated into action, and that, in the meantime, the Germans would have to be misled and mystified as to our intentions. Thereupon, according to Martel, Stalin remarked audibly, 'That's all right, so long as one of your mysteries is not the Second Front.'

.   .   .   .   .

To end my narrative of the events of 1943, I include this account of a luncheon-party given by P. J. Grigg, on 19th November, at the Dorchester Hotel, for General Smuts. Half-a-dozen of us came from the War Office, and Smuts brought his son, who was acting as his A.D.C.

Smuts was in his Field Marshal's uniform, and looked well and alert for all his 73 years. I was much impressed by his sincere manner. Whenever a question was addressed to him, he knitted his brows, appeared to concentrate on the subject, and answered readily in eloquent terms. In fact, his gift of simplifying issues was perhaps the most marked feature of his conversation. His philosophical outlook was apparent in everything he said. His keen sense of humour constantly broke out. There was no general conversation, for we all wanted to sit and listen to him; his talk was fascinating.

Someone asked him what technique he thought a Commander-in-Chief should adopt in dealing with Churchill; the question arose out of a discussion of Churchill's ardent support of the Leros operation.

Smuts: 'Well, I think he would have to have a command of rhetoric. But even then he would always be talked down—I have seen it myself.'

When asked whether he thought Leros had been worth while, he said, 'I believe it was worth trying. After all, the place is a fortress, and I imagine we had an obligation not to leave the Italians in the lurch.'

Somebody remarked that Churchill would be much better if some of those around him were removed—the men who dealt in details which he should leave alone, and who thus exercised a malign influence upon him.

Smuts: 'Winston is his own malign influence. But in great things he is very great, in small things not great.'

Speaking of Russia he said, 'Stalin is the new Russian Tsar. He is not out for Communism, but for power politics.'

Someone asked what line he thought we should take with Russia.

Smuts: 'Oh, you will deal with that problem in your usual way. You will find a compromise. I am not laughing at that. It is your great gift.'

Then he spoke at some length about the British Empire.

'Members of exiled Governments,' he said, 'all except France, have spoken to me of possible inclusion in the British Empire. They have seen how South Africa has been preserved and yet is independent. That is a thought that is worth pursuing.

'Let me tell you the story of my first meeting with Winston. He had been captured, as you know. I was then on General Botha's staff as the attorney-general of the Republic, and so I had to deal with his case. Winston was a scrubby, squat figure of a man, unshaved. He was furious, venomous, just like a viper. Of course, South Africa had never heard of him before. Winston said it was an outrage that he was being held prisoner. He said he was a war correspondent. I shook my head and said, "I know nothing of war correspondents. You have been taken armed and in command of troops." He had assumed command of the armoured train, in which he was travelling, when the Commanding Officer was killed. I sent him to Pretoria as a prisoner. Afterwards I described the case to Botha. I said there was something in Winston's point of view, and, besides, we had allowed Amery to go free, and he was also a war correspondent. Botha said, "Well, if you think there is something in Winston's view, we had better let him go." So I signed an order for his release. But, by the time it reached Pretoria, he had escaped. I told Winston the last part of this story some years later. It was the first he had heard of it. All that shows that the South African war was a gentlemanly war, perhaps the last.

'Winston has told his part of the story in his book, *My Early Life*. I told him that, in my opinion, that is the best of his books. It is a simple story, told in plain Anglo-Saxon, without frills.

'I met him next when I came to London in 1905. I was sent to try to get some form of self-government for South Africa. The first man I had to see about it was Winston—he was Under-Secretary of State for the Colonies. Of course, I was down and out. I found it very hard to deal with my new masters. I stated my case. Winston said he had never heard anything so preposterous. He said England had conquered South Africa only three years before, and here was I asking for my country back. He declared he would never stand for breaking up the British Empire, and so on and so forth, with all the embroiderations[1] we know so well. I saw all the other Ministers, too. I made no headway. Morley was sympathetic. He said he agreed with most of what I had said, but that British public opinion would never stand for it. Then I saw Campbell-Bannerman, the Prime Minister. I spent an evening with him. Of course I had some good ammunition. I reminded him of his own speeches during the South African war. I put it to him that he had to make a choice between having another Ireland or a friendly country within the Empire. At last he said, "General, you have convinced me." The rest of the story is told

[1] This was Smuts' actual word.

316

in Lloyd George's book. Next day, Campbell-Bannerman summoned the Cabinet. He spoke for ten minutes on South Africa. Some
of the Ministers were almost in tears. They all supported the grant of
home rule. That I regard as the greatest achievement for the Empire.
It opened a new chapter.'

Speaking of America, he said, 'We must remember America is a
new country—not like England. You are like old wine. They are still
fermenting. But they will be a great power, and not only commer-
cially. We are inclined to forget the President's difficulties. There is
a very strong undercurrent against him. The things the Americans
do are based partly on ignorance, partly on their determination to
get power. We have learned hard lessons in the four years of the war.
They have had no hard lessons. Yet we do not want to wait another
four years while they learn them.'

Of Brooke he said, 'I have the greatest respect for him. I believe
him to be a really great man. I first realized his greatness before
Alamein. Winston and I were discussing the situation. We had a
better army than the Germans. Yet there was Rommel sitting on
top of us, and threatening Egypt. I said to Winston, "What we need
is a good general." Winston said, "Yes, but whom do you suggest?"
I said, "Why not Brooke?" Winston replied, "A good idea. Speak to
him about it." Well, I did, and Brooke said, "This is a very tempting
thing. . . . But my place is by the Prime Minister." He slept on it, and
next morning, he repeated, "My place is beside the Prime Minister.'
That was a great thing to do. That is why we brought out Alexander.'

Of India he said, 'The last two years have shown that the difficulty in India is not political, but religious—the conflict between the
Hindu and the Moslem. But the light is beginning to shine. The
more enlightened men of both religions are beginning to realize that
India can avoid breaking into pieces, in chaos and civil war, only
under the British umbrella. As that becomes more widely realized,
India will, I think, accept inclusion in the Empire as the lesser of
two evils. But we will never see a settlement while Gandhi is alive.
Gandhi looks on Western civilization as the evil spirit which
seduces the Asiatic soul. Nothing will ever change his belief.'

Of our Cabinet he said, 'Your Cabinet meetings are good stuff,
but they are monologues.'

Grigg made a little speech after the luncheon, and read a letter
which Brooke had sent him for the occasion (he was away). In this
letter Brooke had said something about our high appreciation of
Smuts' wisdom and counsel, and that he had been supported and
sustained by Smuts in critical decisions.

Smuts replied, 'I wish to keep this letter. I like collecting testi-monials.' (Here he put the letter in his pocket.) 'I believe that we shall win such a victory in this war as has been unknown in the history of the world. Our prestige will be higher than that of any country ever before. We have stood fast and endured when all the other nations that were attacked by Germany have gone down, and while America looked on as a neutral. We will emerge with our reputation higher than ever. But we shall be badly damaged and impoverished. It is important that we should rise to the occasion. I believe that the British Empire will rise to the occasion. There is a spirit, a soul, in the Empire, that will enable it to endure. We shall have to take the lead. After the last war we sank back into ease. We followed false ideals—the whole world did so. The lead was taken by others who were less worthy, with the result we see. In my opinion, there will be two colossi after the war. In Europe, Russia. No other country will recover in our time. France will not be a great power again, at least not for a generation. The other colossus will be North America. Between these two I would like to see built up another colossus—the British Empire. It will be the only one of the three with a world-wide Empire.

'We are now about to enter upon a new chapter in the history of mankind. We should thank God for Hitler. He has done a great service to the world. He has brought us back to a realization of brute facts. He has got us away from ideas and ideals and rhetoric. Facts are the only things that matter. Hitler has shown that Hell is still here on Earth. He has, in fact, taken the lid off Hell, and we have all looked into it. That is his service to the human race.

'The fact that I am here today, feeling myself among old friends —I should say new friends, for I feel rather like Methuselah now— that is a thing that illustrates the greatness of the Empire. Nothing like this could have happened under any other power. In the Boer war I fought against you. It was a war that tried Africa sorely—and you, too. In the last war I found myself a general fighting for you, and commanding an army of almost every colour under the sun, from black to white. In this war, to my astonishment, I found myself promoted Field-Marshal. I thought, at first, this might mean being put on the shelf. But it has not turned out that way.

'We are fortunate to have the wonderful, high-spirited, and wise leadership of the Prime Minister. I trust he will still be here to lead us after the war.'

33

STRATEGY FOR 'OVERLORD'

1944

W_E felt that Brooke could not have done more than he did to advocate the full development of the Mediterranean strategy. But there were no longer any thoughts of attempting a return to it, and we loyally accepted the new policy which entailed giving 'Overlord' first priority, since it had at last been given a definite date. This was a relief, and, of course, it made our work much easier. We now pushed ahead with the measures that were required to strengthen 'Overlord' and to achieve the concentration of forces it demanded.

It was obvious, but at the same time disturbing, that it would be impossible to keep the decision about 'Overlord' secret. The first plain indication that the new plan was afoot was when Eisenhower and Montgomery were ordered to England. Then speeches began to be made about it, and soon the newspapers were full of it. One morning in the first week of January, Brooke remarked to me that all this, and the political influences which came into play, made him shiver and reminded him of the prelude to the disastrous Nivelle offensive in 1917.

Montgomery arrived in London on 2nd January, and came to see me next day. He was calm and cheerful as usual, and he looked very fit. He told me of his visit to the Prime Minister at Marrakesh on his way home. Churchill had given him a copy of the 'Overlord' plan in the state to which it had been brought by Morgan[1] and his combined staff at Norfolk House, and had asked for a preliminary opinion of it. This Montgomery had set down in a note of three typewritten pages, dated 1st January, of which he now handed me a copy.

---

[1] Lieutenant-General Sir F. E. Morgan, Chief of Staff, Supreme Allied Commander (COSSAC). He had been responsible for preparing the 'Overlord' plan, pending the appointment of a Commander.

With the obvious proviso that he must reserve his considered opinion until he had discussed the plan with the naval and air authorities, Montgomery had put forward two suggestions: first, the front of the landing was too narrow and the forces not big enough; second, if possible, the Caen–Cherbourg area should be reserved for the British effort, and the Americans landed on the front St. Malo–St. Nazaire–Brest.

When I had read his note, I told him that, so far as we in London were concerned, there would be no difficulty in securing agreement to his first point; but that the means of strengthening the plan lay mainly with the Americans, who would have to be convinced, too. As regards his second suggestion, I said I did not think it would be found practicable, but we would have it examined.

Montgomery told me that he had looked in at Norfolk House, where the detailed planning for 'Overlord' was being done, and that his thoughts had moved farther. He now wanted to cancel the proposed landing in the South of France and to use the landing craft and other shipping, thus freed, to swell the main force for Normandy. This was a proposal with which we agreed in the General Staff, but we knew it would not appeal to Churchill or the Americans.

He came in again after luncheon for half an hour, and later had tea with me and Bedell Smith,[1] who had come in, too. Bedell Smith was also in favour of cancelling the landing in the South of France, and he told us that he had obtained Brooke's consent to broaching the subject to the Prime Minister when he got back to North Africa. Montgomery said that we had all we needed in Italy, and that we should attempt no more there. The airfields already in our possession were near enough to Germany and the Balkans for all we wanted to do, and we would save unnecessary casualties if we gave up the idea of an advance to the Pisa–Rimini line. I certainly felt that every possible ounce of our energy should now be concentrated on the main enterprise. But, as was soon to be seen, this was one of those ideal conceptions of strategy that are very hard to realize in practice.

During the following month, Montgomery often came in to discuss with me the progress of the plans for France, and to hear news of the Italian campaign. He was very critical of the operations in Italy, and especially of the landing at Anzio. He said again and again that this operation had not been planned far enough ahead: 'It is not so much the landing, but what is to happen afterwards, that should be thoroughly thought out.' Churchill, too, was much upset by the setback and stalemate at Anzio.

[1] General Walter Bedell Smith was Chief of Staff to General Eisenhower.

January had been a particularly busy month for us. A note in my diary reads: 'We have been hammering away at the European and Pacific strategies in a strenuous endeavour to get decisions which are badly wanted. The P.M. is taking a most active interest in all details and on some points is not at all in agreement with what is recommended. Much time and energy have gone to debating issues with him, and more will be necessary.'

For some time I had been feeling very run down, and, at the beginning of February, I had myself overhauled by a doctor, who found that my blood pressure was abnormally low. He recommended me to get away from the War Office, and suggested that I should go to Scotland and catch salmon. He said he was quite sure that the more salmon I caught the better I would feel. I told Brooke that I thought I must either have a change of job or a good long holiday. He chose the latter, and my wife and I went north on 7th February, to the Borders of Scotland.

The Border country was like another world. There was even plenty to eat. We made many expeditions, mostly on bicycles, into the Cheviots, Lord Dunglass[1] let me fish the Tweed at Birgham. We had lovely days of warm winter sunshine and I remember fishing more than once in my shirt-sleeves. They were halcyon days indeed, and when I got my first spring salmon of the year on the 17th February, it was the real turning point of my cure. The doctor had been perfectly right.

I returned to work on 13th March. In the month I had been away, very little had been done to advance the arrangements for the war, and the effort to get that little done had been immense. The system of control had now become very complicated. So many people had to agree, in London and in Washington, before a new step could be taken, that it was hard to make any progress.

I gathered that Churchill had been particularly exacting. I wrote in my diary on 24th March, 'The effort left for the war, after dealing with him, is really almost negligible.' I saw him on 16th March at a meeting of the Night Air Defence Committee and noted, 'He did not look too well, but he ran the meeting with humour and with his usual skill.'

In Italy, we were accomplishing more than we could have hoped for earlier, in that we were containing such a big German force. The Germans had made a bad mistake in leaving there so many divisions which might have given us more trouble elsewhere.

The hold-up at Anzio had a marked effect upon our other plans.

[1] Now Earl of Home.

On 24th March, I made a note:

'Anzio has made it easier for us to get a bigger concentration of force for "Overlord"—it has brought home the sort of situation that may well arise in France, and the need for great strength. It has also made it easier for us to make a case to get the South of France operation cancelled and the resources transferred to "Overlord".'

I saw Montgomery frequently in March. He was full of confidence. And so apparently were we, for I made a note in the last week of the month that I thought the prospects were good.

On 5th April, I wrote a summary of the main problems on which we were engaged. The three big issues were:
(a) In the Far East: whether the British forces should be used in the Pacific or in the Indian Ocean,
(b) In the Mediterranean: whether to land in the South of France at the expense of the offensive in Italy, and
(c) In Western Europe: how the air forces could best be used to prepare the way for 'Overlord'.
When put on paper, my thoughts took the following form:

'The strategy against Japan remains in a state of deadlock. The P.M. issued a directive to the Chiefs of Staff in favour of the Indian Ocean. The Chiefs of Staff have asked him to reconsider this on the grounds that they have not yet completed their examination of the alternative strategies, and that there are still comparatively unknown factors to be taken into account, e.g. the capacity of Australia as a base, the capacity of India, the shipping possibilities, etc., etc. They have pointed out, however, that the examination, so far as it has been taken up to date, leads them to believe that the Pacific strategy, should it prove to be militarily practicable and politically acceptable, would lead to a substantial shortening of the war against Japan; it would enable us to use the forces and resources of the Empire in a more closely related and concentrated effort than would the Indian Ocean strategy; and, further, it would not delay the recapture, by our own forces, of our own territories in Malaya and the East Indies.

The P.M., up till now, has been obsessed with the Indian Ocean strategy and he believes that, politically, it is inevitable for us. The Americans have been lukewarm, to say the least of it, in asking our help in the Pacific. . . . It is therefore not at all a straightforward subject. But it would be a thousand times easier to make some headway in arriving at a decision if the P.M. would accept military advice and back his own advisers. . . . I do not suppose we shall get a decision on this before "Overlord". In the meantime, vast energy has been expended fruitlessly here, and tempers frayed without any result which helps the war. The Chiefs of Staff have been in a state of desperation time after time. If we could only get on in a rational manner here, we could at least arrive at some basis of discussion with the Americans.

As regards (b) (i.e. the question whether to land in the South of France), we hold the view here that the over-riding consideration in the Mediterranean at the moment is to contain the maximum number of German forces there during "Overlord". The British Chiefs of Staff feel that to mount an expedition against Southern France will inevitably mean going over to the defensive in Italy and a long period of quiet in the Mediterranean (six to eight weeks) at the very time "Overlord" is being prepared and launched. We have not enough infantry for both an Italian offensive and a large-scale operation against Southern France. Despite all possible efforts, we have failed to convince the Americans of this, and they are obsessed with the idea of the French landing and even suggest it should take place a month after "Overlord", by which time they could send more landing craft to the Mediterranean. After weeks of correspondence we have arrived back at the point where we started. . . . The machinery for running this war is truly the most exasperating that could be devised.

Alexander has now told us that he cannot mount an offensive till the middle of May—the P.M. describes this as "desolating delay". Alexander is coming home within the next few days to discuss his plans. Naturally we should have liked the date to be earlier, but I hope that Alexander will not give way to pressure on this.

As regards (c) (i.e. the use of the air force before "Overlord"), the plan made by Leigh-Mallory and Tedder[1] is to continue the

---

[1] Air Chief Marshal Sir Trafford Leigh-Mallory was Allied Air Commander-in-Chief; Sir Arthur (afterwards Lord) Tedder was Deputy Supreme Commander.

attack upon the German Air Force as a top priority, and, from now onwards, to use the surplus air force against railways leading to the "Overlord" area. A meeting was held at the Air Ministry on 25th March to discuss this policy, and I attended it to represent the C.I.G.S. The General Staff in the War Office had never seen the plan. . . . It seems incredible that a problem of this kind, which is so much a military problem, should not have been based on a proper appreciation by the General Staff, and that our military transportation people should not have been consulted. But such is the case.

The discussion went in circles. Eisenhower was quite unaware (until I told him) that we had not been consulted. He also seemed unaware how vast the task would be of damaging railway communications to such an extent that *military* movement would be hampered. The capacity of the highly developed railway system in Western Europe is such that only 20 per cent or less of it would be required for purely military purposes. I pointed out that in spite of frequent and heavy attacks on railway targets in Italy where the communications were more restricted and more vulnerable, there had been no significant interference with strategical movement there, and that I was doubtful whether we should be any more successful in France.

Eisenhower's comments at the meeting showed at once his weakness and his strength—his weakness in lack of real knowledge of his plans and over-delegation to subordinates, and his strength in avoidance of friction. He repeated several times that all he wanted was the best support he could get and that the United States and the British Empire could not afford a failure in this operation.

In the end he and Portal accepted the plan, subject to its amendment on advice from the War Office. There is still a bad gap in our organization for integrating air and general staff work on such projects.'

(Our advice was subsequently given in favour of thickening up the attack on the German Air Force and concentrating upon other military targets such as transport and tank depots, leaving the attack upon lines of communication until the eve of the battle and later. Another point which we pressed was that every care should be taken to reduce to a minimum the slaughter of French and Belgian civilians.)

Reading these notes again now, after the lapse of years, I feel more than ever convinced that we were never able to harness our air power to the war effort in the most effective way. One of our great difficulties in planning the use of the air forces in 'Overlord' arose from the fact that, owing to the long-standing divergence of view between the Air and General Staffs, we found ourselves in 1944 saddled with a force which was sadly deficient of types of aircraft suitable for close co-operation with the Army, and of airmen trained for that role. We had to do the best with what we had, but the waste was colossal in many directions.

As it turned out, it would not have mattered if we had not dropped a single bomb before 'Overlord' with the object of checking military movement. For six weeks or so, the Germans did not attempt or even desire to move their divisions in the Pas de Calais, or elsewhere, towards the scene of action in Normandy; they could not bring themselves to believe that the indications collected by their Intelligence Staff of our intention to make further landings were bogus, and designed by us to deceive. I would be quite wrong to claim that we foresaw this at the time; but the much-vaunted 'interdiction' programme did not contribute as much as was hoped from it, or claimed on its behalf.

Montgomery came to see me on 5th April, and discussed Italy, Alexander and his plans. He suggested a main attack from the Anzio bridgehead and taking away the American forces on the main front from Clark's command, since he could not control both them and the bridgehead. The battle on the main front was a single operation which should be under a single commander, namely Leese. When I saw Brooke that evening, I told him about Montgomery's suggestions. Brooke agreed in principle, but felt that he could not put them to the Americans.

I had talks from time to time with M. Hubert Pierlot, the Prime Minister of the Free Belgian Government in London, about problems affecting the Belgian contingent in England which was training hard. One night when I dined with him at Boodle's he told me that he believed it would be a help to him in establishing his Government in Belgium if we could arrange for this contingent to take an active part in the landing in Normandy and in the subsequent operations. I spoke to Montgomery about this and he very kindly arranged to attach the Belgians to the Guards Armoured Division. They arrived in Brussels in due course on 3rd September at the very head of our advance.

I wrote a note on 6th April which shows how we felt about 'Overlord' as the critical time drew near:

'There is a good deal of anxiety, although it is not much talked about. There is a very general feeling that we may get ashore and establish a base and a front, but that things may not move quickly so far as advance is concerned. Developments in Russia will govern the situation very largely. . . . No one can tell what is intended by the Russians in the next few months.'

On 7th April (Good Friday), I spent the whole day at Montgomery's headquarters in St. Paul's School, listening to an exposition of the 'Overlord' plan. I reproduce my notes as they were written at the time:

'Monty led off with a talk of an hour and a half, broken by a ten-minute interval in the middle; he went over the Army plan with great lucidity. The most striking feature of his conception is the deliberate nature of his proposed operations. He means to expand the bridgehead gradually, get ports, and eventually arrive, in about three months, on the line of the Seine–Paris (exclusive)–Brittany ports. Of course, if an opportunity offered for a quick advance towards Germany, he would take it. But the main idea is to get established in great strength. All this is quite sound.

Ramsay[1] followed with a description of the naval plan. His problem is certainly formidable. The number of craft to be marshalled and conducted to the coast of France, through the mine-fields, and in face of sea and air attack, is enormous. The weather will be hard to judge and is all-important.

Leigh-Mallory ended the general description with the air plan. In this sphere we have overwhelming superiority.

After luncheon we had Bradley[2] and his two Corps Commanders, who described their proposed operations in more detail. Then Dempsey[3] and his two Corps Commanders, Bucknall and Crocker.

All this constituted a heavy dose for absorption in one day. But it was well worth while to hear it in this way.

When the conference started in the morning, Montgomery had asked us not to smoke on account of the bad ventilation of the room. Later on he announced that he had had a message from Winston to say that he would join us after tea. Monty added that,

---

[1] Admiral Sir B. H. Ramsay, Allied Naval Commander-in-Chief.
[2] General Omar Bradley, the American Army Commander.
[3] Lieutenant-General Sir Miles Dempsey, the British Army Commander.

as the Prime Minister would undoubtedly arrive with a large cigar, smoking would be allowed after tea. He made the announcement in such a puckish way that there was a great roar of laughter.

Winston duly arrived. He looked puffy and dejected and his eyes were red. When he had taken his seat, Montgomery spoke again for ten minutes, as he said, to emphasize three main points. The first was that he himself had the most complete confidence in the plan. This confidence must be imparted all the way down the chain of command—he had no room for any doubters. He said that, in effect, the assault was by two Armies against two German battalions, which was all they had on the coastal sector at that moment, and we were backed by tremendous Allied air forces and by the Navy. His second point was to emphasize the need for boldness and enterprise in pushing forward mobile forces—even a few armoured cars 20 miles inside the German lines would create confusion and delay. His third point was the need to get aerodromes quickly in France for our own air force, so as to cut out the cross-channel flight and get close co-operation. Monty did it extremely well. He is a highly skilled speaker, and he shows great sense in selecting and emphasizing points, and not too many of them.

Winston then mounted the platform. He was in a short black jacket and had a big cigar as usual. He said he had not been convinced in 1942, or in 1943, that this operation was feasible. He was not expressing an opinion on its feasibility now. But, if he were qualified to do so, and if he were one of us, he would have the greatest confidence from all he had heard of the plans. But he had hardened very much on *this*: that the time was now *ripe*. We had experienced commanders, a great allied army, a great air force. Our equipment had improved. All the preparations, strategical and tactical, had been made with the greatest skill and care. We were now going to write a glorious page in the history, not of one country or of two, but of the world. He felt very strongly that this should not be an operation designed to dig in on a bridgehead. At Anzio we had lost a great opportunity—*there* was a lesson for all to study. The object must be to fight a battle. We needed a battle to break the will of the Germans to fight. Therefore he was glad to hear what had been said about pushing forward armoured spearheads, and *unarmoured* spearheads. He ended by wishing good luck to all engaged in the operation.

Winston spoke without vigour. He did not look up much while he spoke. There was the usual wonderful flow of fine phrases, but no fire in the delivery. I thought he was going to burst into tears as he stepped down to sit beside Eisenhower and Monty and the Chiefs of Staff while the officers filed out of the room. But I heard afterwards that members of the audience who saw him on that day for the first time were tremendously impressed and inspired.'

On 15th May, Eisenhower arranged another conference at St. Paul's School for a final presentation of plans. My account of it, written a few days later, was as follows:

'The P.M. and Smuts sat through the whole thing from 10 a.m. till 5 p.m., and The King came for the morning session. The King made a very good short speech before he went off; it was perfect for the occasion, and created an excellent impression on the Americans, as well as on us. I met Alan Lascelles[1] at dinner that same evening; and he told me that he had no idea The King would speak until he got on to the platform.

It was very cold. Winston and Smuts came in overcoats, and kept them on for luncheon (in the officers' mess). I got hold of a blanket, which I shared with an Admiral and an Air Marshal; and we were glad to have it on our knees.

Monty went through his plan with his usual clarity and confidence, and Ramsay, Leigh-Mallory, Bradley and the others repeated their statements of 7th April. The plan had not been much changed since we heard it before—except in detail.

Monty said he expected Rommel to attack at once on the beaches, and then, after a few days, to mass for a more serious counter-attack.

Smuts spoke for a few minutes, very seriously, and said how much he had been impressed, in the course of the day, with the gravity of the operation, and the danger of things going wrong in the complicated arrangements.

Winston wound up by speaking for about half an hour in a robust and even humorous style, and concluded with a moving expression of his hopes and good wishes. He looked much better than at the last conference, and spoke with great vigour, urging offensive leadership and stressing the ardour for battle which he believed the men felt.'

[1] Sir Alan Lascelles was the King's Private Secretary.

In May, I made notes of talks and meals with Curtin, Blamey, Pownall, Koenig, Noiret, Spaak, and Huggins of Southern Rhodesia. Little did I realize how long and enjoyable an association I was to have with the last-named, a few years later.

One evening we dined with Brooke, and saw some of his new acquisitions, including a fine copy of Madame Knipe's *Monograph of the Pigeons*. A few days later, while we were discussing some Cabinet papers, Brooke broke off to tell me that he was trying to get photographs of a Marsh Tit, but that he had been defeated at first by the speed with which the tit entered its nest. He had then hit on the idea of putting a stick across the entrance to the nest. As a result he secured an excellent film of the bird as it first examined the obstacle, and then removed it. It had been a nice piece of ingenuity; and on 31st May, I saw the end-product of another and still more ingenious idea: I spent an interesting day in a launch looking at the artificial piers and breakwaters assembled for 'Overlord' off Bognor. I also saw a mass of shipping at Spithead.

I am not going to tell afresh the great story of D-Day, the culminating moment of so many weary years of planning; but here are a few vignettes from my diary:

'On the 4th June, the wind was blowing half a gale; and Eisenhower sent a message to postpone the landing by 24 hours. Provision for this had been made in the plan. In the evening, as I walked home along the Chelsea Embankment, the wind was stronger than ever.

On the 5th Eisenhower told us that he had decided to go ahead with the assault on the next day. Montgomery telephoned to me from Portsmouth to say that it was quite calm there, and that the weather forecast indicated that the sky would be clear and therefore good for aircraft on the 6th.' [As is now well known, it would have been extremely awkward if 'Overlord' could not have been launched on the 6th: that was the last day, for a fortnight or so, when tide and light conditions would be right.]

On 6th June:

'A good day. I was awakened at 5 a.m. by the roar of aircraft over London. When I went to the War Office the first reports were coming in, which showed that the assault had succeeded beyond expectations. Very little opposition on shore, and practically no interference with our shipping. At mid-day Montgomery telephoned to me to report that the British Army had landed and gained a line three miles inland. Later in the afternoon we learned that the left American Division was still held up on the beaches, but the right American Division had landed almost unopposed. The airborne troops were all put down successfully with very few casualties. Monty said to me on the telephone that he intended to go over tonight. If things were not going well, he said, he would put them right; if they were going well, he would make them go better. A German panzer battalion is reported near Caen. There will undoubtedly be some fighting tomorrow, and we shall see a battle in a few days. But we have got over the first hurdle successfully, which is a great relief.'

34

TWO CONTROVERSIES

1944

During the next two months, in addition to the routine work of carrying on the direction of the war, we were heavily engaged in two strategical controversies, and in both of them we were eventually overruled. We felt very strongly about the subjects in dispute. On reflection, I have not modified the terms in which these notes were written, but have reproduced them in their original form. It must be remembered that we believed passionately that we were right. In this chapter I reproduce first the notes which refer to France and Italy, and then those on the Pacific and the Indian Ocean. To make it easier to follow the course of the arguments I have departed from chronological sequence.

The points at issue had already been debated for some time, but it had now become urgently necessary to reach decisions. The first question was whether we should make a further landing in France, at the expense of operations in Italy, and the second whether British forces should be used in the Pacific rather than the Indian Ocean. The first meant a battle with the Americans, the second with the Prime Minister.

'*9th June*. The news from Italy continues to be excellent. I have drafted telegrams to Wilson and Alexander to ensure that nothing is done to check exploitation. We shall be able to decide by the end of the month what resources can be allotted to Alexander for further operations North of the Pisa–Rimini line, and what, if any, should be diverted to another landing in France. We may have to draw on the Mediterranean to reinforce "Overlord", which is going to be a stiff, long and hard-fought business. The advance inland is behind schedule, and what we want most is plenty of room to pour in reinforcements.

13th June. Sent another telegram to Alexander suggesting he should turn East before Ravenna lest the Germans escape to the North, and also to avoid having to break through the prepared Pisa–Rimini line.

19th June. We cut off the Cotentin Peninsula last night. This should soon give us a better line to hold and should put 20,000–30,000 Germans in the bag. As we increase our pressure here the Germans will be in a dilemma. They can hardly bring in their forces from the South of France and the Bay of Biscay without losing too much politically, and there is for them no good solution of the difficulty. When the Russians start up, as they say they will soon, I believe the pressure on the Germans will become too great and they will crack—perhaps in two or three months.

It has been settled provisionally with the American Chiefs of Staff that Alexander should not go beyond the Pisa line unless the Germans are very weak, and that we will do another amphibious operation instead. The difficulties of military movement in North Italy are so great that this has been forced upon us.

22nd June. We should get Cherbourg at any moment. The Germans have made a mess of it by putting in their forces piecemeal, but their fears in other directions have compelled them to do this.

There are still hopes that Alexander may break up the German Army in Italy completely by a good hard punch on the Pisa line, or South of it. We are now examining his next move intensively.

Alexander wants to go on into Austria via Ljubljana. The objection to this is that he would arrive before the Julian Alps in September or October, with winter coming on, and only two roads for an advance. A big force would thus be immobilized unless the Germans were disintegrating—in which case Alexander would not need a big force. Therefore, the right course seems to be to give Alexander a free hand *South* of the Alps, then he can threaten the Julian front with small forces. His surplus forces should be used for two purposes:

(a) an amphibious operation against France (we have examined three possibilities, viz. Biscay, Sète, and Toulon; of these the last seems best in every way), and
(b) reinforcing Normandy.

The relative importance of (a) and (b) to be determined

before the earliest date for launching (a), which is probably 15th August.

Had a talk with Brooke about our past strategy, and we discussed some of the big decisions. There is no doubt that Brooke has been uncannily right on all the big things. He has borne the brunt of these decisions almost alone, and the brunt of the fearful struggles to convert the P.M.

23rd June. Eisenhower has given his opinion that he cannot spare shipping to help Wilson in "Anvil".[1] . . . He says he would like "Anvil" to be done on a reduced scale by 30th August at latest, or by 15th August if possible. He has not, I think, appreciated fully the assistance to "Overlord" which is given by Alexander's operations in Italy. [The Germans had reinforced Italy with 4 divisions, making a total of 20] . . . If "Anvil" is to be mounted by 15th August, resources will have to be withdrawn from Alexander progressively from 7th July. This would give him a free run for another month. If we can put in "Anvil" then with fair hopes of success, we shall gain the support of the French *maquis*, and the Germans will either have to detach forces to deal with them or clear out of the whole of the South of France. If we cannot mount "Anvil" with good prospects, we can bring divisions round from the Mediterranean to reinforce Eisenhower. Had an hour with Brooke on all this, and this is the line he has agreed to take. But we shall have to be careful not to base our case on Alexander being allowed to destroy the Germans in Italy, because the Americans, for some curious reason, cannot see the force of that, and would regard it as a breach of contract not to carry out "Anvil".

Winston is, meantime, very keen to push on to Vienna by the Julian Alps and "thrust in a dagger under the armpit". The Julian operations are impossible unless the Germans are finished.

26th June. Cherbourg fell today. Alexander is still stuck at Trasimene.

Jumbo Wilson now says he cannot mount "Anvil" by 15th August without starting to hamstring Alexander on 28th June. Also that he cannot do it after 20th August, on account of weather.

The American Chiefs of Staff, as we expected, are saying that we should stick to our contract, and do "Anvil" on 1st August, regardless of the effect on Alexander.

I saw Brooke this morning and suggested we should try to get

[1] Landing in Southern France.

"Anvil" ruled out, which would mean that Alexander could finish his battle (i.e. destroy Kesselring's forces South of the Alps), and the surplus forces brought round, after that, to join Eisenhower. Winston has produced a long printed memorandum which favours this course, but which goes too far in advocating an advance by the Julian Alps to Vienna. This last, I think, should be kept to ourselves for the moment.

Brooke had arrived at much the same conclusion as mine. He said we had led the Americans by the nose from Casablanca to Florence, and it would not be easy to put this policy over on top of all that. They are so inclined to regard fresh ideas, to match new situations, as breaches of contract.

Eisenhower has now offered to release shipping for "Anvil" after all, which does not make our task easier.

After lunching with Winston, the Chiefs of Staff gave instructions to draft a telegram shooting down "Anvil", and, in the evening, I went through the draft with Brooke before he took it to Winston.

28th June. The U.S. Chiefs of Staff have reacted by saying our arguments are illogical and unacceptable. . . . I don't think we shall convince them.

30th June. Deadlock over "Anvil" worse than ever. Roosevelt has cabled advocating "Anvil". Both his and his Chiefs of Staff's views obviously coloured by antagonism to an American campaign in Balkans and towards Vienna, at expense of heavier reinforcement of France. The red herring was started by Jumbo in his original project for the advance through the Julian Alps. . . . C.I.G.S. felt this morning we might be forced into this wrong strategy by American intransigence.

At their meeting this morning, our Chiefs of Staff decided there was no prospect of shaking the Americans, and that, as time is getting short, we must give way. . . . A report to the P.M. was drafted in this sense. . . . We are trying to save something by asking the Americans to send some further divisions and shipping to the Mediterranean, to avoid taking too many of the former from Alexander and too much of the latter from Eisenhower. Brooke remarked that he felt the Germans were about finished anyhow, and that they were not fighting as they used to do, in France, Italy or Russia.

14th July. We have told the Americans that we think it ("Anvil") wrong strategy. I am sure it is. If there is any doubt, the thing is to concentrate overwhelming force in the right place, and the right place now is Italy, where we have good evidence that the Germans are willing to fight hard and send in further reinforcements, thus relieving pressure on Montgomery. But the Americans, including Roosevelt, are obsessed with the idea of getting Marseilles so that they can pour their divisions into France quickly. . . . We will put our best effort into it, now that it is agreed.'

'Anvil' was eventually carried out on the 15th August. But before the landing took place there was a last-minute attempt to cancel it.

'On Friday, 4th August, I heard that Eisenhower was thinking of asking for a cancellation of the landing in the south of France, due for 15th August, and the switching round of the ten divisions involved to N.W. France, in view of the successful advance into Brittany and the prospect of getting more ports soon. Eisenhower had a talk with the P.M., as a result of which the P.M. summoned a meeting of the Chiefs of Staff and dashed off a telegram to the President advocating the idea strongly. This he did against the advice of the C.I.G.S. A telegram of this kind immediately arrays against us all the forces of opposition in the United States Chiefs of Staff, etc., but Winston is delightfully unconscious of this. They have a deep suspicion that Winston dominates the British Chiefs of Staff and they distrust his strategical ideas. The propositions did seem attractive at first, but, after a little examination and a furious exchange of telegrams over the weekend, it became clear that it was much too late to make the change with advantage. The expedition has already begun loading and there are not enough ships on the spot in the Mediterranean to bring the divisions round quickly— it would be October or November before they could arrive. Besides, it is clear that the ports in N.W. France will not absorb any more than can be brought from the U.S.—there are about 40 divisions there awaiting shipment. So, in the end, the proposition was finally dropped on 10th August.'

Two days before the landing, on 13th August, my last note on 'Anvil' reads:

'The landing is due on Tuesday. The Germans are weak in the area chosen. . . . An unfortunate operation, I fear, and not the best application of forces available, which would have been better divided between Italy and North-West France originally. ... The whole conception of the landing in Southern France has changed imperceptibly. It was originally meant to go in about the same time as the Normandy landing when it might at least have attracted some of the German forces otherwise available for Normandy.'

The strategy to be adopted in the Japanese war produced a long wrangle between the Prime Minister and the Chiefs of Staff. The discussions dragged on over the three months preceding the Quebec Conference in September, where the final decisions were taken.

Broadly speaking, the plan favoured in the General Staff was to join forces with the Americans in the Pacific and to leave the Indian Ocean and Burma in *statu quo*. We felt this course would shorten the war against Japan, and would, in the end, result in the recovery of British and Dutch possessions more quickly than if we assaulted them directly.

'*14th July*. The indications are that Winston is going to overrule the Chiefs of Staff on the Japanese strategy and insist on our effort being across the Bay of Bengal towards Malaya, etc., instead of from Australia in conjunction with the Americans. ... I don't think his increasing insistence on carrying out his own ideas matters very much now, because the war is past its crisis, and we are bound to win even if we make mistakes.

19th July. The P.M. has not given a decision on the Japanese strategy, and does not look like doing it. He has now summoned Mountbatten home for consultation. He said to Ismay, the other day, that he feared he (Churchill) was not now "combative enough", and he accused him of being "a bromide" in trying to get settlements and agreements. He told Ismay that his job was to prod him and help him to make rows and oppose his advisers, or words to that effect. Very good in a way, but I do wish Winston would give up strategy as his special fun, and inter-ference in small military matters. However, he certainly won't, and we must make the best of him with all his defects, as well as his great qualities. Brooke and others who work with him certainly have affection for him as well as great loyalty.

24th July. Winston is still postponing the decision on Pacific strategy, and he seems as obstinate as ever in his desire to have a separate theatre, free from American control, in spite of the fact that he has been strongly and continuously advised against it on military grounds.

4th August. Mountbatten has sent two plans by cable—one for the conquest of Burma after an airborne and seaborne invasion of the South seizing Rangoon, and the other for an advance to Mandalay from the North. . . . But I am still convinced that it would be more effective, and best in every way, to combine forces with the Americans in the Pacific. If we do the Indian Ocean plan, we can still provide a good fleet detachment and some air force for the Pacific, which the Americans may think enough. But we should, from every point of view, take as big a share as possible in the main drive on Japan if we are to keep our proper place in Far Eastern affairs after the war.

There are so many difficulties of personalities and politics in the problem that the result is unpredictable. We still hope for an early decision, however, and the P.M. is being pressed for one by the Chiefs of Staff.

10th August. During the last few days a policy has been formulated for the Japanese war. This involved two days (7 hours on each day) of exhausting arguments between the P.M., Chiefs of Staff, Mountbatten, and various ministers. The C.I.G.S. was told by Winston at one point that it was no good losing his temper. He replied that he was not losing his temper, but was in despair that the P.M. would not give the decision he had been pressed to give for over six months. The P.M. retorted that it had now been proved wise not to have given a decision before, and he repudiated any idea that harm had been done by the delay. Throughout it was obvious that he was still strongly wedded to the Sumatra operation, but, fortunately, the resources are not available for this. It would be a pointless operation. He was in favour of taking Rangoon and stopping at that point and allowing the Japs in Burma to rot, so obviating the clearing up of the country "swamp by swamp". Taking Burma from the North was like "eating the porcupine quill by quill", he said, reverting to his old simile.[1] C.I.G.S. pressed the case for completing the conquest of Burma, so freeing troops from the Assam front which is a festering sore. . . . In the end it has

[1] In London we were all wrong about the conquest of Burma from the North which we thought impracticable on account of the lack of communications. We had underestimated the efficacy of air supply, and the weakening of the Japanese forces in Burma, owing to their supplies and reinforcements being cut off by the American operations in the Pacific.

been decided to propose to the Americans that we should send a strong fleet to the Pacific at once, to operate if possible under MacArthur with the Australian divisions and air force, to recapture Burma from the South if we can assemble the forces in time before the March monsoon begins (this depends upon the date of the defeat of Germany), and prepare both India and Australia for the operation of our forces. This is good so far as it goes. The great achievements have been to get the P.M. off Sumatra, and to get the Fleet to the Pacific. It is questionable whether it would have been much better to send the divisions we can free from Europe (probably six) to the Pacific if we have time to get Burma back before the monsoon.

13th *August*. I often wonder what historians will make of the strategic planning in this war. When they read the minutes of the discussions they will not get a true idea of what took place, because they do not reproduce the arguments.

Winston remarked the other day that the operations of June bear the stamp of a great design to anyone not acquainted with their inner history. The Anzio landing came in as a great aid to the capture of Rome, and the capture of Rome (on 4th June) fitted beautifully, in the end, into the June operations in Normandy, although it was meant to take place much earlier.

15th *August*. Winston now wants to keep open the choice whether to clear up Burma after the capture of Rangoon or to attempt something else. He has cabled this from Italy, where he is touring as Colonel Kent. We think this is a pity as it removes the best reason for the operation in American eyes, namely, opening up the road to China. I said to the C.I.G.S. that anyhow we had moved one step forward, to which he replied ruefully that for every step forward we are driven four back. I said that we had, in the end, kept Winston from going to all the queer places he had been set upon, for example, Trondheim, or the North of Norway.

Now Winston is set upon the tip of Sumatra. I think we shall keep him off it, but he has been more obstinate over this than anything since Pantellaria in 1940.

19th *September*. We have got the Quebec decisions. On the whole they are good. And perhaps, in view of the American feeling for a monopoly in the Japanese war, they could hardly have been better. The P.M.'s view has prevailed. I am not sure that this is wrong, in the light of all the conflicting interests involved, although I should have preferred personally to see our main

Army effort made in close collaboration with the Australians and New Zealanders. The advantage is that we shall have the credit of having cleared the Japanese out of British territory by force of arms, which counts for a good deal. The Navy and the Air Force will provide our share of the Pacific operations.

The difficult problem of staging early operations against the Japanese is still with us. . . . This is one of the most difficult and intricate problems we have had yet.

In the light of later developments I believe the C.I.G.S. has steered the best possible course. What we are now to embark upon is, in my view, the second-best course, but not a bad second-best. We really do not know whether the Americans would have agreed to our original suggestion, because it was never put to them seriously.'

35

A VISIT TO MONTGOMERY

1944

I HAVE been running ahead of the order of other events; and I now return to the middle of June.

On the night of the 12th/13th the Germans started their bombardment of London with flying bombs. The first few nights were very noisy owing to the ineffective shooting of our anti-aircraft guns. Much to everybody's relief, the guns were stopped firing within London on the 18th, and we were then able to sleep well in spite of periodical explosions. By 19th July, between 3,000 and 4,000 people had been killed by flying bombs, half a million houses damaged and 14,000 destroyed. A great many people left London, or were evacuated. Our house in Cheyne Walk was very old and rickety. The front door was blown in one night, and most of our windows, in course of time, were smashed by bombs. But, although the house was sometimes badly shaken, we suffered no further damage beyond the loss of plaster from some of the ceilings. The restaurants were very empty, and, one night in July, when I dined with a friend at Prunier's, there were only about twenty people there. Nevertheless, life went on very much as usual, and we often dined out with friends, or had them to dine with us.

One day in July I lunched alone with S. M. Bruce[1]—at his house in Princes Gate. On the way there, near Hyde Park Corner, I was just missed by a flying bomb, by a few yards, which killed two people and injured nine. We discussed Australian politics and personalities, and he gave me his views on Imperial relations as he would like to see them after the war. He said he believed that there should be a central Imperial organization in London, not a new idea, but one that has always been rejected in the past

[1] Now Viscount Bruce of Melbourne.

by the Dominion Governments as liable to derogate from their complete independence of Westminster. We also talked about strategy in the Pacific, on which he was endeavouring to formulate the advice he should give to his Government. The Australians, as I knew, were inclined to favour the view of the Chiefs of Staff that we should co-operate with them in the Pacific rather than act separately in Malaya and elsewhere.

Towards the end of July we considered whether we should ask Eisenhower to take the bombing of London into special account in his plans for the advance to Germany. I advised against it, feeling that it would be wrong to allow his conduct of the campaign to be influenced by a consideration of this kind. We felt that, in any case, the development of the operations would soon clear the Channel coast. We had no definite information about when the attack by rockets might begin; but we estimated that the Germans then had available over a thousand rockets, each carrying seven to eight tons of explosive, as against the one ton of the flying bomb.

On 14th August, Gort came to see me on his return from Malta. He was very pleased to be going to Palestine and said that, now MacMichael[1] had been shot at, he really thought it looked like being fun.

In August Montgomery invited me to pay him a visit at his headquarters in France, which I was delighted to do. The account which follows was written at the time.

'On Thursday, 17th August, motored to Heston with Warren, Monty's Canadian A.D.C., and found his Dakota awaiting us. Busy scene at the aerodrome, planes coming and going, and crowds of military passengers, mostly American. We took off punctually at 5 p.m.

I asked the pilot (a young American) to fly round the beaches, so that I could see the mulberry harbours, etc. Entered Cherbourg harbour which was full of shipping. I think I saw the old Chateau near Sottevast where we had our 52nd Divisional Headquarters in 1940. The country looked peaceful and unspoilt even when we got farther round the bay, but, on the next day, I saw on the ground how much destruction had taken place.

We had passed a number of convoys in the Channel, but I was surprised to see the vast amount of shipping lying at anchor off

---

[1] Sir Harold MacMichael, Gort's predecessor as High Commissioner.

the Normandy coast. It is extraordinary that we should have such command of the sea and air as to be able to anchor ships in safety in such numbers, and, further, that the tremendous army and air effort can be sustained from such a base, consisting largely of open beaches. The British mulberry harbour seemed wonderfully perfect and well organized, and we had a good view of break-waters of sunk ships, etc. All ships were flying balloons, which gleamed in the sun, and lorries were crawling up the beaches and away along the roads.

Recognized Bayeux Cathedral and some other landmarks. Swung away South after flying round the coast almost to Caen, and, in another twenty minutes, we saw the red smoke signal from the landing field near Monty's headquarters, a few miles North of Vire. The landing strip, which had been created by merely bulldozing the hedges between three stubble fields, seemed remarkably small for our big aircraft, but the pilot landed with great skill and pulled up with twenty yards to spare—no more. Two or three smaller aeroplanes of Monty's lay about the edges. A car drove up, and in five minutes I was in his headquarters—a scattered camp of caravans and marquees on a hillock, and occupying a few pleasant fields in which were grazing cows.

An A.D.C. conducted me through a gap in the hedge to Monty's particular field, in which no trespassers were allowed. Monty, in shirt and corduroy trousers, looked fit and cheerful. He took me into his map caravan to see the latest situation. He was hoping to close the gap about Falaise and so to cut off the large German force still in the pocket.

Presently we went into the caravan again to have another look at the map. I asked Monty if Patton had been out of control, because it had seemed to us that he should have turned North, and not gone to Orleans, or so far towards Paris. Monty replied that Orleans was Patton's own idea, but that he was quite happy that the long "touch line" had been created along the Southern flank of the German line of retreat through Paris. He intended Patton to swing North now.

Monty took his usual line that all had been done according to plan, and that he was very satisfied. It is true that this is all according to plan, but what is not so clear is whether Patton's initiative has not speeded up the whole business enormously. My impression is that it has.

Monty was serene and cheerful and pleasant. I must say

I like him enormously. He is certainly enjoying himself immensely, and no wonder.

He called for his batman and said he would have his bath and that dinner would be at eight, and I retired to the caravan that had been allotted to me.

At dinner, in an open marquee, there were Monty (in the only comfortable chair) and his personal staff, namely, Kit Dawnay and three A.D.C.s.

We talked about my trip to France with Hore-Belisha in 1939, when we had visited Monty's division, and we speculated about how things might have turned out under a different plan. If another man, as British Commander-in-Chief, had protested, and protested successfully, against the advance into Belgium (which Monty regarded as a mistake), we might have been unable to extricate our Army from its entrenched positions on the French frontier, past which the German advance would undoubtedly have swept on both sides.

Leigh-Mallory came in late, to stay for the night, and joined us at the dinner table. We talked about the railway bombing plan before the landing, which I still believe did not interfere seriously with the German strategic dispositions. Leigh-Mallory rose at once to this, and asked if I had not read his statement in *The Times*. I said I did not regard that as evidence, and that I should like much to see the real evidence.

At this point Monty called to the waiter, "Bring the betting book." The waiter at once brought it, with a pen. The betting book is a leather-covered visitors' book in which many amusing bets have been entered—all in Monty's handwriting. There was one on whether the Pope would still be in Rome when the Allies entered the City; others concerning the dates by which we would take Rome, finish the war, etc., etc. Some of the bets were marked "Settled".

"Now," said Monty, "let us get this clear," and he wrote the terms of our bet in his book, with promptings from us both. When Leigh-Mallory was at a loss to describe his opinion of the bombing, Monty suggested that he believed it to have been "the cat's whiskers", and wrote that down.

He asked us to sign the entry, and we did so. It read as follows:

Air Chief Marshal LEIGH-MALLORY bets General KENNEDY £5 that the long-term bombing policy against railway communications was the cat's whiskers and without it the Allies might well have been driven back into the sea.

T. LEIGH-MALLORY

JOHN KENNEDY

The Speaker of the House of Commons to be the referee.

B. L. MONTGOMERY

General

The dinner-party was great fun. Monty drank water, but produced a bottle of good claret for me. He said, "I had a spoonful of white wine the other night, but I did not like it." We all dined in our shirt-sleeves—it was a lovely summer evening. Monty hardly referred to the battle, which was now at its crisis.

After dinner we listened to the wireless news for a few minutes. Then Monty asked me to come with him to hear the reports of the liaison officers.

We climbed into his office caravan, in which were some cages of canaries, covered up for the night, but squeaking and scuffling occasionally. Monty lounged in a chair before the map while his young liaison officers (four or five of them) came in, one after the other, and described the situation on the sectors of the front they had visited during the day. The Canadians had had heavy fighting, but had got on in spite of that, and the gap was closing considerably. On the left the Germans were pulling out to the North. Reports had come in from the air that the Germans were moving barges over to the South bank of the Seine in daylight.

The whole situation indicated that the Germans had at last realized they could no longer win the battle South of the Seine, and were endeavouring to get away. But, in the pocket, there was still a surprisingly large number of divisions.

Monty listened attentively to all the details. Then Crerar[1] telephoned to say that the Poles had got Chambois (this turned out to be a mistake—it was Champeaux they had got, which meant the gap was still open). Monty told Crerar he must push on, regardless of casualties, and close the gap, and that he must shoot *everything*, during the night, that was moving East, and that it could not be helped if we shot friends or refugees by mistake.

After this conversation, Monty remarked that the fate of the

[1] General H. D. G. Crerar, commanding 1st Canadian Army.

Germans was sealed: the turning point had been when they decided to counter-attack at Avranches. "I knew they were doomed when they decided to do this," he said.

He then called in Dawnay, and dictated his evening message to the C.I.G.S.

This done, Monty gave me an outline of his future plans, and I suggested he should cable them to Brooke who was due to leave London for Italy next day. He said he would send me a draft in the morning. It was now 10 p.m. and we went to bed.

18*th August.* Next morning, at about 7.30 a.m., Dawnay brought me a message, in Monty's own handwriting, and asked me to discuss it with him at breakfast.

We amended his draft a little and the gist of it was as follows:

After crossing the Seine, 12th and 21st Army Groups should keep together as a solid mass of some forty divisions which would be so strong that it need fear nothing. The force should move northwards. 21st Army Group should be on the Western flank and should clear the Channel coast and the Pas de Calais and West Flanders to secure Antwerp. The American Armies should move with their right flank on the Ardennes directed on Brussels, Aachen and Cologne. The movement of the American Armies would cut the communications of enemy forces on the Channel coast and thus facilitate the task of the British Army Group. The initial objects of the movement would be to destroy the German forces on the coast and to establish a powerful air force in Belgium. A further object would be to get the enemy out of V.1 or V.2 range of England.

He said he had discussed all this with Bradley who had agreed, but that he wanted to get the C.I.G.S.'s views before discussing it with Eisenhower. I told him this plan was exactly what the C.I.G.S. would want. The message was sent off to Brooke, and he replied, in a few hours, that he entirely agreed.

It was a lovely morning, with thick mist at first in the hollows. Later, it turned hot and sunny.

At breakfast, after we had got the cable away to the C.I.G.S., Monty told me that a telephone message had been sent to the German Major who was holding out in the citadel of St. Malo, to tell him that, if he wished it, he would be given a motor drive to Orleans and Chartres, to show him how wrong his information was that he could soon be relieved, and that he would then be returned to his fortress. Moreover, Monty said, he had been offered a visit to his mistress, who lived in a neighbouring village. But he had refused. Monty was very much amused.

He said that some of the Germans had got out of the pocket, but that, whether they had or not, it was "a very great victory". He added that any of the German forces which crossed the Seine from the South would be useless for months to come, and that those to the North were second-rate and few in number.

After breakfast he sent me off in a jeep with Warren. We drove to Bretteville, and on to the Falaise road, and up to Caen. Visited 2nd Canadian Corps Headquarters where orders were being given for a concentration of guns to shoot up the trapped Germans, and we heard some grumbling at Air Force bombing of our own troops. . . . The Canadians were still trying to close the gap about Chambois with their own armoured division and the Poles.

Much damage had been done to the towns, villages and farm-houses in the area of the British fighting—mostly by bombing. Caen was a scene of utter destruction, caused by our bombing on D-Day to cut the bridges, except for the part of the town round the cathedral and the cathedral itself. Looked into the cathedral to see William the Conqueror's tomb.

The dust on the roads was trying. Saw great convoys of lorries moving up to the front, and heard the guns and saw a few shells, but the back areas were rapidly becoming empty of soldiers. I felt so sorry for the French civilians who have suffered so much in this part of the battlefield—their feelings about "liberation" must be somewhat mixed.

We returned through Bayeux, which was comparatively undamaged, and I looked in at the main headquarters. Monty's system of command is most impressive. He keeps his main headquarters twenty or thirty miles away and, as a rule, sees only the two chiefs, De Guingand and Graham,[1] and them only once a day or so. They can telephone to him. This results in Monty being left in comparative peace, with plenty of time to think, and no fuss or worry about details. This is the more surprising to me because, in my opinion, Monty, when he was a Brigadier, went in for detail too much. His control is perfect now. His relations with his staff and his commanders are "matey", but it is clear that they have the most terrific respect for him, and there is not the least doubt that he is in absolute control. I think he is

[1] Major-General Sir Miles Graham, in charge of Administration.

also good in his relations with Eisenhower, although mischief-makers say there is friction.

Back in time for tea, and had an hour's talk with Monty in his caravan before dinner. Talking of the battle, he repeated, "It is a great victory, whatever is in the bag." He had been out during the day to see the Guards Division.

He took a copy of his last order of the day out of a drawer and said, "I wonder if that nice boy of yours would like to have this. I expect he'll sell it. But he might like it." Then he wrote my son's name on it, and signed it, and handed it to me.

We discussed The King's coming visit, which Brooke had asked me to do. (Next morning, before breakfast, Dawnay brought me a charming letter which Monty had written to Lascelles, in which he suggested that the King should come "and share our life", whenever he liked, for a couple of days. Dawnay asked me for suggestions, but I had none to offer.)

Dick O'Connor[1] came to dinner, looking well, but quiet and silent as usual.

Monty spoke about the Prime Minister's late habits and said that, if he were C.I.G.S., he would refuse to attend late meetings and would send his Chief of Staff to represent him. He asked me what I thought Winston would do. I said, "He would probably say, 'I understand quite well, General, that you must always go to bed at 10 p.m., and I will be content if you will send someone to represent you.' Then, when you read the minutes next day, you would be horrified to find what had been done." "I would not read the minutes," Monty replied. "Then," I said, "things would happen. Disasters would take place. Winston would rub his hands and say, 'A few more disasters and I think we shall soon see General Montgomery at our evening meetings.'"

Monty continued that, when there was a difference of opinion, he would resign if his advice was not taken. I said that was a weapon that could be used only on big issues, and that the technique used by a C.I.G.S. had to be different from a Commander-in-Chief's.

After dinner Monty took me again to his caravan to hear the evening reports, and to hear him dictate his evening message to the C.I.G.S.

A peaceful night again, except for a few bombs dropped in the far distance by German aeroplanes.

[1] Lieutenant General Sir Richard O'Connor, commanding 8th Corps. He had been captured in the Desert in April 1941, but had escaped from Italy in December 1943.

In the morning Monty's camp was being broken up for a move, and, as soon as we had finished breakfast, the last marquees were to be dismantled.

He then asked me to sign his visitors' book, and I said good-bye, and motored to the airfield. Took off in the Dakota—again a narrow shave with such a short run. As we neared the Isle of Wight we circled to look at some wreckage in the sea with boats and a destroyer standing by, evidently picking up survivors. Low cloud and rain over England. We landed at 10.15 a.m.'

I duly sent Monty's letter to the Speaker, and a few days later I received the following in an envelope marked, 'Personal and Private—Re Wagers'.

	RUFFSIDE HALL,
24.VIII.44	SHOTLEY BRIDGE,
	Co. DURHAM

My dear General Kennedy,

I enclose my reply to General Montgomery. If you think that I should not address the 'All Highest' in such a frivolous manner, please tear it up: I have tried to enter into the fun of the bet.

I can easily send a more formal acknowledgement!

I am sorry to have been so long in answering your letter but at the moment I am on holiday trying to pursue the grouse bird which this year unfortunately is only conspicuous by its absence.

When the evidence is available, I shall hold myself at your service.

Yours sincerely,
D. CLIFTON BROWN

I read his letter to Monty and then despatched it. It was as follows:

SPEAKER'S HOUSE,
S.W.1.

24.VIII.44.

My dear General,

I have received your letter of August 19. Naturally I am

348

flattered by the faith that you display in Mr. Speaker's impartiality but at the same time I think that this is the first time since the days of Cromwell that the Speaker has been detailed off for a job by the G.O.C.! However, I will do my best to consider the evidence impartially when it becomes available.

I thank you for your advice as to securing legal advice about the exact meaning of 'the Cat's Whiskers'. I am therefore consulting one of our legal lights in the House of Commons. Irresponsible persons may think that M.P.s might just as well discuss the meaning of 'Cat's Whiskers' as some of the other things they talk about. I would never suggest for one moment that such a thought has ever crossed your mind.

Secondly, I propose to consult one of His Majesty's Judges. Sometimes they have to sentence people to be hanged and as, in certain quarters, high-ranking officers who have backed a loser have been made to suffer the same penalty, I want to ensure that there will be no fatal results of any verdict that I may give.

I tell you this in order that you may see that I am taking up most seriously the duty for which you have nominated me. Should I fail to secure satisfactory replies to my enquiry, as a last resort I shall try the Church. The Archbishop of Canterbury is a person who appears to know a lot about all sorts of things and maybe he will be able to interpret the exact meaning of 'Cat's Whiskers'!

Yrs. sincerely,
D. CLIFTON BROWN
Speaker.

36

STRATEGY FOR GERMANY

1944

THE campaigns in France and Italy progressed with varying fortunes, and my notes on the operations, which had, for me, great interest at the time, would now have none for the reader of this narrative. But two controversies which occupied much of our attention in the autumn of 1944 are worth recalling.

The first centred on the plan of campaign and system of command to be adopted under Eisenhower. The first news we had that Montgomery was to be deprived of command of the land forces, and his strategy to be rejected, was contained in a letter to me from him dated 21st August.

In this letter he told me that on 20th August Eisenhower had held a staff meeting at S.H.A.E.F. to draw up plans for the future conduct of operations. At this meeting it had been decided to change the system of command on 1st September, and to send a portion of the force eastwards to the Saar. De Guingand, who was present, had suggested that Montgomery should be consulted before any action was taken, and this was agreed to. Next day Montgomery had sent a note to Eisenhower of which he enclosed a copy in his letter to me. In this note he had stated emphatically that the quickest way to win the war was for 'the great mass of the Allied Armies to advance northwards, clear the coast as far as Antwerp, establish a powerful air force in Belgium, and advance into the Ruhr'. This, he added, was a whole-time job for one man, and that 'to change the system of command now, after having won a great victory, would be to prolong the war'.

Montgomery had a long discussion with Eisenhower on 23rd August, and argued his point of view with great force. But he was overruled. He kept us in touch with all this. In the War Office I had appreciations prepared, on which the C.I.G.S. might form an opinion. But in the face of American sentiment and determination it would have been impracticable to make an issue of the matter on the Chiefs of Staff or Government level. The system of command was duly changed on 1st September, and Montgomery's plan of campaign finally rejected. It will always be an interesting subject for discussion by students of warfare whether or not the war was, in fact, prolonged for another six months or so by these decisions.

Although we disliked the new method of conducting the campaign, we remained, for some time, over-optimistic about the probable date of victory against the Germans. This is borne out by my contemporary notes. On 28th August, for instance:

'The whole fabric of Germany is toppling. Rumania out and Bulgaria coming out. The Germans will hardly be able to withdraw their forces to Germany from the Balkans or the French coast, even if they begin now. In France, it looks as if there would be a stand on the Somme, in which case we shall round them up the sooner.'

On 6th September:

'If we go at the same pace as of late, we should be in Berlin by the 28th. The Germans have only ten to twenty divisions to man their frontier, as against a requirement of seventy to eighty. We should, therefore, go into Germany quickly. Then we may be faced with guerilla fighting.'

But soon there were signs that operations were slowing down, and that the Germans were making a remarkable recovery.
On 11th September:

'Letters and telegrams from Monty show that he is dissatisfied with the conduct of operations. He feels that Eisenhower is attempting too much in endeavouring to support two thrusts simultaneously into the Saar and into the Ruhr. He has had a talk with Eisenhower and impressed his views on him. We can do nothing. Any intervention on the Chiefs of Staff level could do no good, and probably would do harm. . . . Monty takes a gloomy view of the whole situation and thinks his operations are now bound to be slowed up and the war prolonged.'

One result of the checks we were now beginning to suffer was irritating enough, although not of vital consequence. We now had to face the prospect of a longer bombardment by long-range rockets than had previously seemed probable. My wife and I had gone down to Much Hadham in Hertfordshire on 8th September and, on that evening, we heard an explosion rather like the distant discharge of a heavy gun. This was one of the first pair of rockets to be fired, probably from Holland, and it fell at Epping; the other came down in Chiswick.

The second of the two controversies was among ourselves. The point at issue was whether or not to mount an expedition ('Dracula') against Rangoon before the monsoon. We did a great deal of work on the plans, in which we never had much confidence. The project depended upon success in the attack on Germany, failing which the necessary troops could not be released for transfer to the Far East. So great were our doubts of the soundness of the Rangoon operation that on 11th September, when commenting on the setbacks in France and Belgium, I wrote:

> 'One good result, however, of all this, is that it now appears quite impossible to withdraw the divisions and administrative units from Monty in time for the Rangoon operation to be mounted by mid-March. The situation in Italy also precludes early withdrawal of the Indian divisions and other administrative units.'

On 2nd October the Rangoon operation was finally cancelled, much to the relief of us all. The Prime Minister agreed 'without further argument, but with regret'.

On 12th October, I wrote:

> 'We cannot get going properly now till we have Antwerp. This, we believe, will not be before December. . . . Then a further period is required to pile up proper resources for a drive across the Rhine. Monty's immediate tasks are to clear the country west of the Rhine. These operations are now in hand. It may be Christmas before we can tackle the Rhine crossing in strength.
>
> In the meantime Eisenhower is concentrating the 9th U.S. Army on Monty's left. With its preoccupation in Holland, 21st Army Group can now take a smaller part only in the advance across the Rhine, and will probably be directed on the Munster

area, while the main attack is done by Bradley farther South. On the right (Saar, etc.), nothing much will be possible, owing to the need for concentration on the left.

In Italy, Alexander's offensive is fizzling out owing to the exhaustion of the troops, whom Alexander has described as "whacked", and to the weather. There are no reliefs available, owing to the withdrawals to Southern France. However, a larger number of German divisions are being contained in Italy than would have been the case if the Germans had withdrawn to the Piave. We have lost the chance of smashing them up.

. . . The Germans will be punished heavily in the remaining stage of the war. It is impossible to say how long they will last. The war might be over any day. On the other hand, the reign of terror instituted by Himmler may prolong it for six months.'

On 22nd October, Brooke returned from his trip to Moscow with Churchill, and, on the 25th, he dined with us in Cheyne Walk and brought with him a bottle of vodka and some caviare. I had a number of bird pictures to show him, which I had bought from George Lodge.

On 26th October, I made a note that I had read Arthur Bryant's *Years of Endurance* and had been especially impressed by two points. The first was that Pitt and his Ministers were immensely more ignorant of strategy than Churchill and his War Cabinet, and that Churchill appeared a paragon in strategical matters as compared with Pitt; the second, that the military mistakes made by the British, in the early stages of the war with the French, were remarkably numerous and serious.

Another note I made on this day was:

'We are all beginning to feel that the German war may drag on till the spring or early summer of 1945.'

At the end of the year, I collapsed with acute sinus; and, exhausted as I was, I took a long time to recover. I was sent off to Scotland on sick leave. Brooke kept my place open for some months, but I had done the job longer than anyone had ever done it before, and felt it was time for new blood. For me the war was over.

EPILOGUE

During the spring and summer of 1945 I gradually recovered. When the war ended in August, the idea of returning to the Army in any capacity whatever seemed to me like the prospect of flogging a dead horse; so I sent in my papers, and settled down to lead a country life on the Borders of Scotland. No sooner had I done so than I was asked to go out to Southern Rhodesia as Governor in succession to Admiral Sir Campbell Tait, who had just died.

I was seven and a half years in Southern Rhodesia; and in odd half-hours, and on occasional holidays at the Cape, I drew this narrative together. As I did so I could not help contrasting the world it describes with the new world in which I found myself. Our plans had been all for destruction; every aspect of our lives had been shot with austerity; hardship and suffering surrounded us; exhaustion and frustration had come near to overwhelming us all. I shall never forget the impact of arriving in Southern Rhodesia. Here was a new world indeed, expanding, growing, buoyant, stimulating, refreshing; inhabited by the kindest people imaginable; full of vitality, resilience and a robust faith in the future. I had the luck to have, as my Prime Minister, Sir Godfrey Huggins, now Lord Malvern, for virtually the whole of my term of office. With his light-hearted wisdom, haphazard genius and stout commonsense, he had led his young country for almost a quarter of a century; and I enjoyed every hour of our association.

It is now nearly twenty years since I began my long spell at the War Office on the eve of the war, and thirteen since I finished it. We began with an army which was trying—through no fault of its own—to expand too late, and with a nation which was rousing itself from a deep sleep as the lava began to flow. All through the war we were still paying the price for the belatedness of our preparations. It was like trying to spread new and untried canvas in a full gale; sail after sail blew into tatters as soon as it was set. The miracle was that, despite all our buffetings, we were able to keep on course.

This narrative, apart from being cut by nearly half, is much as I left it in Southern Rhodesia six or seven years ago. I have tried to apply to it those Johnsonian maxims which my editor has quoted in his preface. I have tried also to preserve the contemporary atmosphere, and I have sought to keep everything which might be useful for the future. I want, before I finish, to make two points clear.

First, despite our tussles with the Americans, our relations with them remained surprisingly good. This was largely due to Dill, who was wonderfully cast in the role of intermediary in Washington. (One shudders to think how nearly he went instead to be Governor of Bombay.) I shall always count myself privileged to have served him. The Second World War was the greatest in history; the British-American coalition the most successful, so far as winning the war was concerned. The provisions for winning the peace were another matter, and mercifully outside my province.

Secondly, I realize I may be judged unduly critical of some of the personages who pass across the pages—of Hore-Belisha, Ironside, Gort, Wavell, Auchinleck, and especially of the titanic Churchill himself. I could have left my story lying in its tin box; I could even have destroyed it; but having once decided to publish, it seemed to me wrong to purge it of all criticism. The result would have been utterly false. For good or for ill, this is the war as I saw it from the niche in which I served. Any distortions or wrong perspectives there may be are genuine tricks of the light, deriving from my environment.

No soldier ever had more generous and forbearing masters than I. The massive figure of the great Prime Minister towers above them all. Neither his stature nor his place in our annals can be diminished by glimpses of his petulance, or revelations of how difficult it was to chase all the butterflies conjured up and released by his limitless fancy. His glory remains.

INDEX

INDEX

Germany—*contd.*
fighting spirit of troops, 198
French co-operation with, 131
moral effect of bombing on, 131–2
moves troops from France, 303
over-optimism over defeat of, 351
partitions Poland, 28
plans of attack (1942), 216
plans for occupation of, 304
Poland attacked, 15
recovery against allied forces, 351
resistance in Italy, 305
retreat in France, 344
rumours of internal unrest in, 310
Russian pressure on, 187
secret weapon against Britain, 314
strategy for, 350–3
threat to Low Countries, 1
vulnerability to air bombing, 132
Gezira, xviii
Giarabub, 243
Gibraltar, 65, 75, 131, 160, 214, 223, 230, 238, 263, 280, 282, 286
Giffard, General Sir George, 119, 178, 217, 246
Gillard, General, 37
Giraud, General, 282, 285, 287
tribute to Dill, 284
Golikov, General, 149
Gordon, Major, 10
Gort, Lord, 5 *et seq.*, 64, 149, 150, 230, 269, 341, 343, 356
and memorandum on re-equipment, 6
anger at Hore-Belisha criticisms, 40
appointed C.I.G.S., 4
appointed to Malta, 231
C.-in-C. of Field Force, 18
friction with Hore-Belisha, 13, 18–19, 22
in Palestine, 65
love of flying, 11–12
with the B.E.F., 35, 36, 37
Gott, General, death of, 259
Graham, Major-General Sir Miles, 346
Grand Strategy, xii, 30, 46, 87, 101, 116, 134
Grant tanks, 233
Graziani, General, 74
Great Britain (*see* Britain)
Greece, 73, 75, 76, 80, 82, 83, 91, 92, 96, 97, 100, 102, 123, 125, 130, 133, 145
a major error, 139
Australian forces in, 190
decision to support, 85

Greece—*contd.*
evacuation advised, 98–9
German threat to, 72, 82
intervention in, xv
invaded by Italy, 61
judgments on campaign, 86–7
opening of operations in, 87
withdrawal from, 114
Grigg, Sir P. J., 204, 268, 288, 313, 315, 317
Guingand, General de, xiii, 33, 34, 37, 101, 346, 350
'Gymnast', 178

HABBANIYAH, 114, 117, 126
Haig, Field Marshal Earl, 11, 107, 119, 125, 133, 135, 138, 269
Haile Selassie, Emperor, 72
Hailsham, Lord, 14
Halifax, Lord, 14, 20, 49, 50
Hamilton, Admiral Sir Louis, 238
Hamsteen, General, 246
Handy, Brig.-General T. T., 260
Hankey, Sir Maurice (Lord), 5, 25, 27, 49, 115, 228, 229, 231
memoranda to Churchill, 232
Harcourt, Admiral Sir Cecil, 44, 45, 46
Harriman, Averill, 104
Harris, Marshal of the R.A.F. Sir Arthur, 246
Hart, Captain Liddell, 14
Harwood, Rear-Admiral Sir Henry, 164
appointed naval C.-in-C., Middle East, 224
Hassan, xvi
Havre, 54
Heligoland Bight, 17
Hemingway, Ernest, 65
Henderson, Rt. Hon. Arthur, 251, 270
Himmler, 353
Hitler, Adolf, 2, 12, 13, 23, 28, 29, 66, 81, 87, 88, 112, 113, 114, 128, 142, 147, 313, 317, 318
plot against, 297
Hoare, Sir Samuel (Lord Templewood), 14
Holland, 17, 29
Home, Earl of (Lord Dunglass), 321
Hong Kong, 182, 184, 185, 186, 187, 191, 192
Hopkins, Harry, 153, 155, 156, 157, 160

INDEX

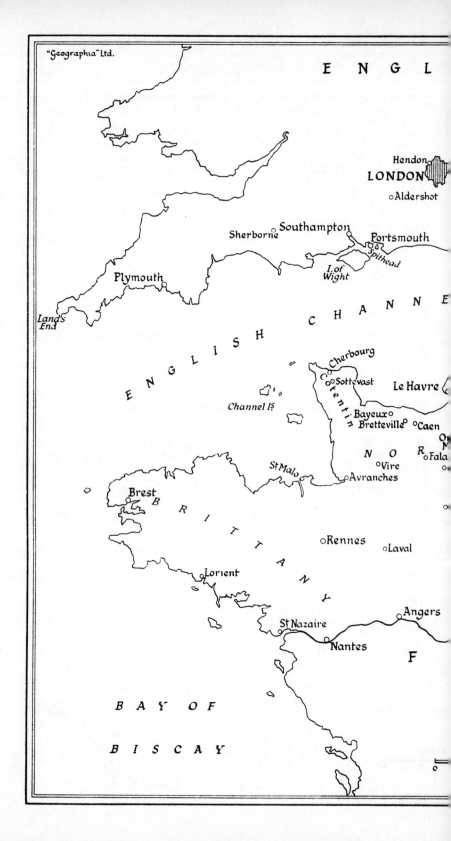

"Geographia" Ltd.

E N G L

Hendon
LONDON
oAldershot

Southampton
Sherborne   Portsmouth
Spithead
I. of
Wight

Plymouth

Land's
End

E N G L I S H   C H A N N E

Cherbourg
oSottevast
Le Havre
Cotentin
Channel Is
Bayeux o
Bretteville o   oCaen

N O R
oVire   Fala
St Malo
Avranches

Brest   B
R I T T A N Y

Rennes   oLaval

Lorient

Angers
St Nazaire
Nantes   F

B A Y   O F

B I S C A Y

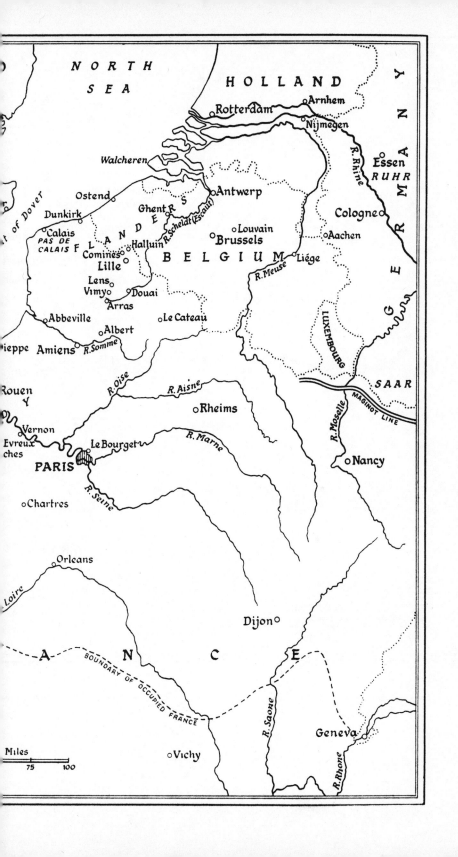

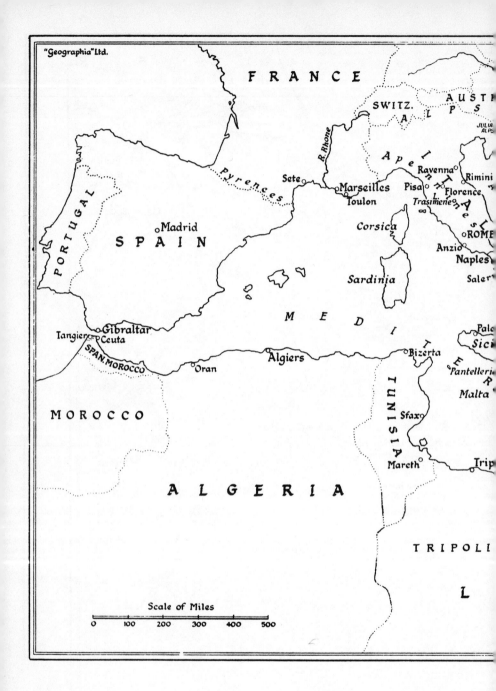

"Geographia"Ltd.

FRANCE

SWITZ.

AUSTRA S

JULIA ALPS

PORTUGAL

R.Rhone

A p e

ITALY

Pyrenees

Sete

Marseilles

Toulon

Pisa

Ravenna

Florence

Rimini

L.

Trasimene

Madrid

SPAIN

ROME

Corsica

Anzio

Naples

Saler

Sardinia

M E D

I

T

Gibraltar

Ceuta

Tangier

SPAN. MOROCCO

Oran

Algiers

Bizerta

E

R

Pale

Sici

Pantellerie

Malta

MOROCCO

T
U
N
I
S
I
A

Sfax

Mareth

Trip

A L G E R I A

TRIPOLI

L

Scale of Miles

0   100   200   300   400   500